The Diaries of Maria Gyte
of Sheldon, Derbyshire
1913 – 1920

TONY GYTE

The Diaries of Maria Gyte
of Sheldon, Derbyshire
1913 – 1920

Edited and Introduced by
Gerald Phizackerley
Archdeacon of Chesterfield 1978-1996
Priest in charge of Ashford and Sheldon 1978-1990

with a Foreword by
His Grace the Duke of Devonshire

Scarthin Books
Cromford
1999

Published 1999 by Scarthin Books of Cromford, Derbyshire
©1999 Gerald Phizackerley

http://www.scarthinbooks.demon.co.uk
e-mail: clare@scarthinbooks.demon.co.uk

Cover Elisabeth Stoppard and Mike Susko
Set in Monotype Scala by Masson Multimedia, Bonsall, Derbyshire
Maps drawn by Ivan Sendall
Extracts from *The Church of England and the First World War*
by Alan Wilkinson are printed by permission of the publishers,
SCM Press Ltd, London.

ISBN 0-907758-96-7

Printed by Bell & Bain Ltd, Glasgow

Contents

"He was only a stolid young farmer...; only; but such men, I think were England, in those dreadful years of war."

Siegfried Sassoon *Sherston's Progress*

Foreword

Chatsworth
Bakewell
Derbyshire

I regard it as a privilege and honour to write a few words about Gerald Phizackerley's edited version of Maria Gyte's First World War Diaries.

Having heard the Archdeacon once quote from these diaries during a sermon at a service I attended in Chesterfield, I know these Diaries will be of the greatest interest and, indeed, importance. The Diaries show the impact of the horrors of the Great War on an ordinary family living in the heart of rural England. The Diaries are an evocative and powerful record of life at that time.

Andrew Devonshire

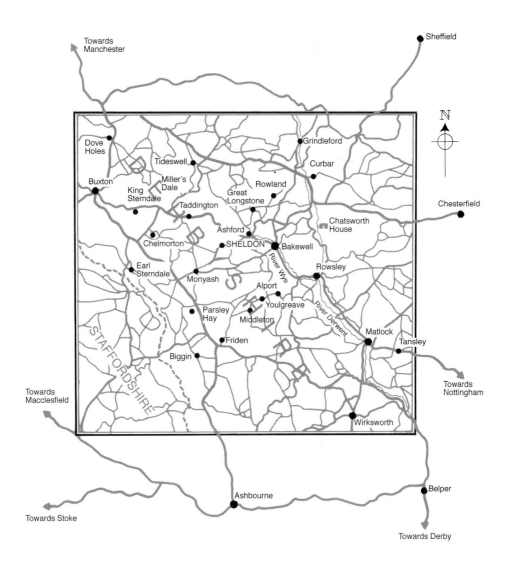

Map of the Area
Showing towns and villages mentioned in the Diaries

List of illustrations

Frontispiece

Tony Gyte in uniform

Maps

Photographs

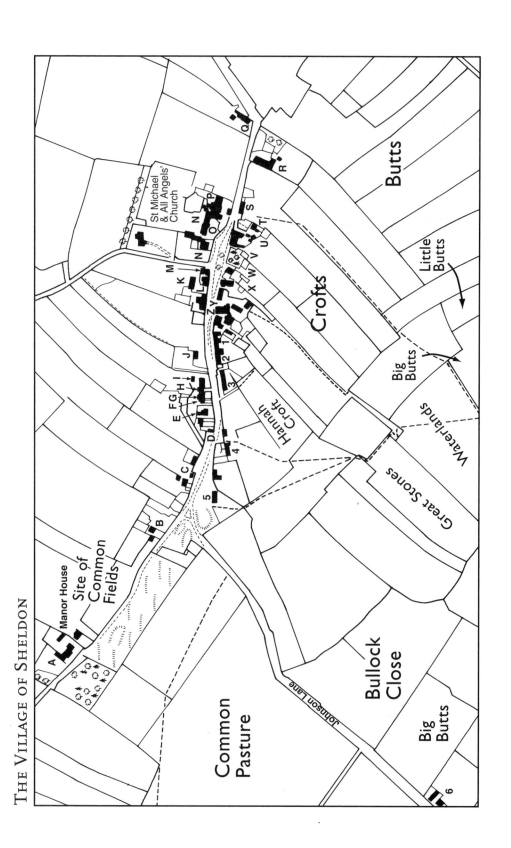

The Village of Sheldon

Manor House
Site of Common Fields
St Michael & All Angels' Church
Butts
Little Butts
Big Butts
Crofts
Waterlands
Great Stones
Hannah Croft
Common Pasture
Johnson Lane
Bullock Close
Big Butts

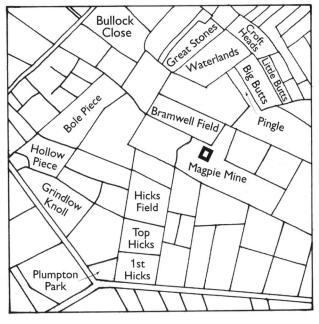

Fields mentioned in the diaries

Code	Property	Tenant
A	Manor House Farm	Herbert Frost
B	Rose Cottage	Alf Manderfield
C	Rose Farm	Fred Carson
D	Smithy	
E	School	Closed 1933
F	Cottage	J. Carson
G	Cottage	S. Wilton
H	Barn with G	
I	Town End Cottage	David Frost
J	Ivy Cottage	Ivy Morton
K	Devonshire View Farm + outbuildings	Alf Brocklehurst
L	Cottage	Wm Brocklehurst
M	Cottage	Sam Bramwell
N	Home Farm + buildings	John Frost
O	Woodmans Cottage	Ben Sheldon
P	Yew Tree House	Geo. Brocklehurst
Q	Lower Farm + buildings	Wm Naylor
R	Woodbine Farm + buildings	F.W. Brocklehurst
S	Barn with N	
T	2 cottages	Fred Buxton
U	ditto	Hy Simpson
V	3 cottages	G. Eaton, Edwin Smith, Mrs Simpson
W	Probably a barn	
X	South View	J. Brocklehurst
Y	Devonshire Arms	Anthony Gyte
Z	Cottage Joiner's shop above	E. Brocklehurst
1	Duck Tree Cottage	Tom Gyte
2	Cottage	
3	School House	
4	Nursery Cottage & buildings	Wm Brocklehurst
5	Ivy Cottage	Geo. Bramwell
6	Johnson Lane Farm & buildings	R. Bonsall

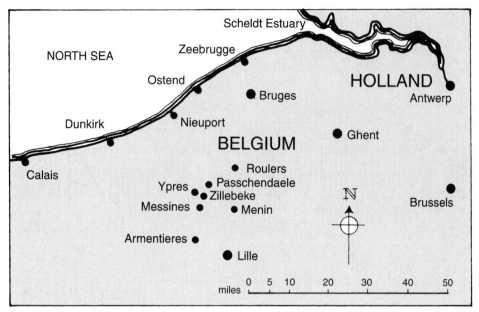

Zillebeke in Flanders

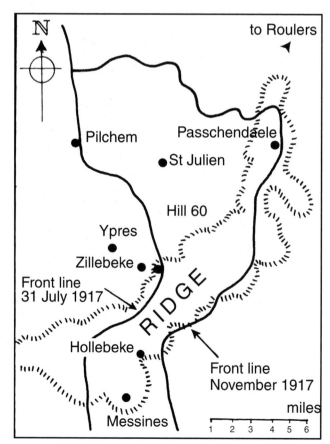

The Battle of Passchendaele showing the front lines during Tony's time in Belgium

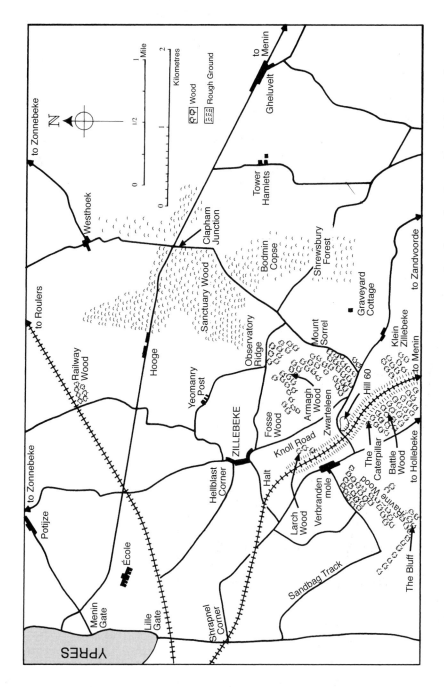

Battle Areas near Zillebeke showing Bodmin Copse where Tony was first buried and Larch Wood where he was finally interred. Hill 60 and the Caterpillar are eminences produced by the spoil when the railway cutting was first dug

Introduction

The local and national background to the Diaries

The Diaries of Maria Gyte of Sheldon are not only an everyday story of country folk but also a powerful indictment of war. They reveal the effect which the Great War had on the small Derbyshire village of Sheldon, near Bakewell, in the Peak District. Almost like a Greek tragedy, they show the reluctant but inevitable steps by which young Tony, the youngest of the Gyte family, was called up, briefly trained and sent to France. This young farm lad arrived in Flanders in the autumn of 1917, just in time for one of the most awful conflicts in the whole war, the Third Battle of Ypres, known as Passchendaele. Tony was soon killed. His mother, Maria Gyte, a woman of great fortitude, confided to her Diaries her grief and sense of desolation. Her daily record, her recalling of events and their anniversaries, must have been a kind of therapy for her as she expressed her shock, anger, bewilderment and sadness. Perhaps she found it easier to write, than to speak, those deep things of her heart.

Sheldon

Sheldon, in the quaintly picturesque terms of Kelly's Directory of Derbyshire 1916, "is situated on an eminence and commands varied and extensive views of the surrounding country". At an altitude of 1000 feet above sea level, it is exposed to rigorous weather conditions which do not make for easy farming. The population in 1911 was 128 and most of the inhabitants were involved in farming: cattle, sheep, pigs and hens; wheat, hay, turnips and potatoes. Some also worked at the Magpie Lead Mine but this was not as active as it had been in the 1850s when the population was as high as 197 and included 14 Cornishmen who had brought their leadmining skills to Derbyshire. Today, the total population is about 80. The Magpie Mine has closed, but farming still continues.

At the time when the Diaries were being written, there were three focal points in the village: the Devonshire Arms, the School and the Church (St. Michael and All Angels). The Gyte family were involved in all of them. Today, only the Church continues its original function. (A new public house has been opened on the site of the old Devonshire Arms which contained the upstairs Dancing Room.)

Devonshire Arms

The Devonshire Arms was both a public house (with a dancing room in a barn) and a farm house, and was situated half way up the village street on the left hand side. It is still possible to discern from the different shades of the stones above the door where the inn sign used to be. The Gyte family had been innkeepers there for over a century, and they continued to run it until it closed in the 1960s. Even then it had no beer pumps; the ale was fetched from the barrels in pint and quart jugs just as it always had been.

In 1913 when the Diaries begin, the Gyte family consisted of Anthony aged 50, farmer and publican, and Maria aged 56, and their six children: Mary (26), Tom (24), Emily (22), Ethel (20), Evelyn (18) and Tony (16). There was also Maria's sister, Hannah (64). Maria Gyte suffered from rheumatoid arthritis which rendered her virtually immobile and she had to be carried everywhere she went. Indoors this was done by means of a wooden chair with shaft handles which she called her "rickshaw" (23.3.18). Out of doors she had a bath chair (she describes the purchase of a new one from Chesterfield), or else she was taken for occasional trips in a horse-drawn float round the scattered fields of the farm which she surveyed with a professional eye. Despite her immobility, Maria Gyte was aware of all that was going on in the village, and, through her newspaper, of much that was going on in the world. Village events and world events were recorded day by day and side by side: decisions in Parliament, and reverses in France were indiscriminately mingled with a cow calving, or the amount of the collection in Church on Sunday, or "stopping the tap" on someone who had had too much to drink. Sitting in the "parlour" or the "house place" of the Devonshire Arms, Maria listened, observed, and shrewdly commented. Take, for example, this cameo of an encounter at the bar: "Jim Goodwin was greatly offended at our Ethel. He said that she had served him with such a little gin for twopence. He got up and went out of the house. Perhaps our serving of gin is like his greengrocery. He will not give much away." (28.6.15)

There is often a sense of immediacy about her writing. The Diary, and her pen and ink, must always have been readily available. On New Year's Day 1919, the Lay Reader Mr. Stephenson arranged a tea for the village in the schoolroom: "Rough, snowstorms. The girls are getting ready for the tea Mr. Stephenson is giving tonight. Mr. and Miss Stephenson have just arrived and are sitting warming themselves just before going up to school". You can almost smell the wet clothing and hear the rubbing of hands before the fire.

Nearly every entry is prefaced by a reference to the weather. This is understandable when one realises the influence of the weather upon the daily pattern of the hill-farmer's life. Farm workers were directly exposed to all the rigours of wind, rain, snow and, more rarely, sun. They had to be ready to terminate one task and start another according to the prevailing conditions. The range of their skills was extensive. When Anthony Gyte had to fill in a form to claim exemption from military service for his son Tom, he listed the "exact occupation of our Tom" as follows: "Milking, ploughing, sowing, stacking, thatching, sheep shearing, attention to sheep at lambing time" (17.12.15).

The daily care of the animals was a heavy responsibility. Not only was there the relentless programme of milking, and transporting the churns along difficult roads in time to catch the morning train at Longstone station two and a half miles away, but there was also the particular care which had to be exercised at times of lambing or calving. There were many occasions when one or several of the men were with an animal during the night, supervising a difficult birth, and not going to bed until it was almost time to get up again.

It was not only the men who had to be tough. The women too lived a vigorous and rigorous life. Ethel and Evelyn, during the early part of the War, worked as VAD (Voluntary Aid Detachment) nurses at the old Bakewell workhouse which had become a hospital for wounded Belgian and English soldiers (14.11.14). Vera Brittain has graphically described in her *Testament of Youth* the heavy duties which she was performing as a VAD nurse at this period just a few miles away at Buxton. She lived quite near to the Buxton hospital. But Ethel and Evelyn Gyte had to walk more than three miles before they began their duties at Bakewell. They used to set off in all weathers. On November 15th 1914 Maria Gyte recorded: "Very winterly this morning. A good deal of snow has fallen during the night. Our Ethel and Ruth Brocklehurst started from Sheldon at half past eleven ready to be on duty at one o'clock in Bakewell.

It really was not fit for them to walk. They have to remain until 9 o'clock tonight and then to walk home. They will not arrive until after 10 o'clock".

The domestic duties at the Devonshire Arms must also have been considerable. There were the meals to prepare for a large household which would also include workers in the fields, and hospitality for both the regular and the casual visitors to the inn. Fires had to be laid, lamps had to be trimmed, washing had to be done, the dairy had to be whitewashed, rooms had to be papered and decorated - all these were tasks which Ethel and Evelyn regularly performed. Their sister Emily did not enjoy good health, so they would look after her as well.

One of the regular duties mentioned in the Diaries was the making of cheese. This was always a good way of disposing of surplus milk. In an article in the 1961 Winter edition of *The Countryman*, F. W. Brocklehurst, a son of Thomas William Brocklehurst who lived in the farmhouse at the bottom of Sheldon, recalled the cheesemaking of his childhood: "Two farmers would join to make the larger cheeses in big pans, each holding about forty gallons. The milk was carried from the fields on yokes, perhaps with another can held in front, for distances of up to a mile. Some was heated on the fire to bring it to a certain temperature, and rennet or part of a calf's stomach would be added before the pan was covered and left to turn. When the milk had curdled, Mother would use first her arms and then a wooden bowl to break it down and divide the whey from the curd, which she pressed to the bottom of the pan, while taking off the whey. Next she cut up the curd and put it in a cloth under a small press to extract more whey. After dinner it was taken out, put in a pancheon and crommed, or worked with the hands, salt being added and thoroughly mixed in. It was then put into a cheese vat, fitted inside with a tin garth that could go down as weight was added. After a day or two in a large press, consisting of a big square stone fitted on to a screw and fixed in a frame, it was put in a drying room."

Another activity in which the Gyte family was regularly involved was the killing of a pig and the disposal of the meat. Maria Gyte made frequent references to this aspect of life on the farm. F.W. Brocklehurst in the article already mentioned recalled the process: "We usually kept a sow or two and fattened one, after perhaps two litters, to kill in the autumn. As they were fed on maize meal and bran, the back fat was about five inches thick, going down a long way before there was any sign of lean. It was quite an event when the pig was killed. There was a pig killer in the village, and he would come down about two o'clock and, with extra help to hold it, stick the pig, some of the blood being caught to make black puddings. Meanwhile water had been boiled to scald off the bristles. Afterwards the pig was hung up, and the liver, kidneys, heart and so on were removed, to be divided among relations, who would in turn send us a share when they killed a pig. The pork also was cut out and divided up in the same way. The following day the rest of the carcass would be put in salt, with brown sugar and saltpetre added; it was usually rubbed till moist, so that the salt would penetrate better. The charge for killing and cutting up was half a crown - quite a nice sideline at that time." The custom of sharing the meat with relatives is referred to by Maria Gyte in this entry: "Alf Brocklehurst brought us some pork with the understanding that we send him some when we kill a pig" (29.11.16). The bargain was fulfilled a fortnight or so later: "Matthew Hodgkinson killed one of our pigs and cut it up the same day. We estimate its weight at about 20 stones" (12.12.16). "We have sent pork out to Alf Brockley, John Brockley and Billy Naylor in return for what they sent to us. Our girls have been rendering fat" (13.12.16).

In addition to the members of the Gyte family, there were others who were engaged in the work of the farm either on a permanent or temporary basis. William Gould was part of the Gyte household and had his own room at the Devonshire Arms. He died in 1929 aged 73. On his gravestone in Sheldon Churchyard he is described as "a faithful servant of the Gyte's family for over 50 years". It was customary for wages to be paid once a year, with one week's holiday from Christmas Day until New Year's day. About £20 a year was the average wage for a man living in. In 1919 the Wages Board gave a permit for William Gould to be paid ten shillings per week with board and lodging; William was obviously a valued member of the farming team. He was illiterate as is evident from the occasion when Maria answered a letter written to him by the Bakewell Postmaster enquiring about some damage which had been done to the Sheldon letter box: "Dr. Sir, As Wm Gould cannot write himself I am writing for him. Your letter was read to him and he says that he did not see anything of the occurrence you name. I am sir, Yrs trly M. Gyte" (22.1.16). Holidays for farm workers were few and brief. On Christmas Day 1916 "William Gould was paid and off he went somewhere" - but only two days later "Gould came back tonight. He had spent two nights away, I think at Monyash" (25 and 27. 12.16). Summer holidays were equally brief. Billy Naylor was another regular worker on the farm. On August 27th 1917 "Billy Naylor went from Bakewell on his holidays". On August 29th "Billy Naylor came back from his holidays. He went to Manchester and stayed all night and then went to North Road to his sister Mary's". Vincent Hallows was also a regular worker - eventually he was to marry Ethel Gyte. There were in addition casual workers like Big Jim and Watercress Jack who appeared regularly at harvest time, and about whom one would like to know a little more. But Maria kept her eye on all of them and knew what each was doing: "Tom sowed the small seeds on Grindlow Knoll and Vincent sowed hay seeds. Anthony was rolling in Bramwell Field, Wm was harrowing on moor and Sam Bramwell was gapping" (9.5.19). Casual workers were paid at the rate of six pence per hour "with tea and beer and other meals at times" (8.8.16).

The Devonshire Arms was a centre of activity involving many people whether as workers on the farm, villagers seeking relaxation or travellers looking for refreshment.

The School

Maria Gyte, before her marriage, had been the village schoolmistress. The school was situated towards the top of the village and is now the Hartington Hall. It had been erected in 1878 and was intended for 40 children. In 1908, the average attendance was 36. Conditions must have been very cramped and the single teacher must have been greatly exercised to give an adequate education to all these pupils of various ages. Perhaps it was the difficulty, if not the impossibility, of this task which caused the breakdown in health of Miss Ann Hallam in 1916. "Our Tom went on his bicycle for Dr. Fentem to attend Miss Hallam who is in a very low nervous state. He came and said that she must be kept quiet and not be left as he was afraid of Brain fever setting in" (9.7.16). Dr. Fentem, and his son Tom who was also a doctor in Bakewell, called upon the Vicar in nearby Ashford, the Revd. H.E. Sherlock, the Chairman of the Managers, and advised that Miss Hallam should be given immediate leave of absence. The Lay Reader was sent up from Ashford "to see about Miss Hallam", and Maria's sister Hannah, and another woman from the village, stayed all night with her because "she is in a poor way". The next day a meeting of the School Managers was held at the Devonshire Arms and one of them, Anthony Gyte, sent a telegram to Miss Hallam's parents who lived near Chesterfield. Mrs. Hallam came over but apparently went away again. However, the following day Miss Hallam "seemed worse excited this morning". Tom Gyte "went to the Dr. but he sent word for her to be taken away". A telegram was despatched and Mr. and Mrs. Hallam came to collect their suffering daughter. "Mr. Hallam paid for telegram which Anthony sent" (11.7.16). After the summer holiday, Miss Hallam was back, but not for long. There was trouble over the Sunday School with Miss Hallam acting "very high handed". On August 28th she "had to come out of school owing to illness and there is a holiday this afternoon. Mr. Sherlock called here and said that he was going to telegraph to the Education Authority that she is unable to go on teaching owing to her nervous breakdown." So that was the end of poor Miss Hallam's time at Sheldon School.

There was some stopgap teaching help from Miss Stubbs, the sister of Ashford's schoolmaster, until Miss Polly Bramwell arrived. The manner of her arriving was not at all to Maria's liking. "I hear Miss Polly Bramwell commenced teaching in Sheldon School. Neither Anthony nor Thos. Wm. B. knew anything of this and I do not believe any of the managers knew except Mr. Sherlock. This is a nice state of affairs to go over the heads of managers like that." (1.5.17). A couple of months later she informed the Vicar of her displeasure. "Mr. Sherlock called here and he seemed annoyed when I spoke about Polly Bramwell being appointed teacher. She has been put on the paysheet for this month and not a word has been said about it to the other managers" (6.7.17). However, Polly Bramwell's appointment was only for a short time. In October she married John Gregory and went to live at Dove Holes near Chapel-en-le-Frith.

Her successor was Miss Broadhurst whose career in Sheldon was not without its difficulties. One of these was resolved by the diplomacy of Maria Gyte. In 1918 the Lay Reader was Mr. Stephenson and he wanted the Sheldon children to learn a new hymn and the practice was to take place in the school, as it was holiday time. He intended to be present while Evelyn Gyte played and the children sang. But "Miss Broadhurst did not want the children to meet in school as she said the measles might be caught. The children are all running together in the street so I do not quite see how practising a hymn in school would affect them. She asked Evelyn yesterday what Mr. Stephenson wanted to teach them hymns for as she could do that (the jealousy of her!). I suggested to Mr. Stephenson that he should wait until Miss Broadhurst re-opened school after the holidays and the same night he should have the children to practise the hymns he wants. This was agreed to by him" (25.7.18).

Miss Broadhurst blotted her copy book on another occasion. This was when funds were being collected to pay for the marble war memorial which was to be erected in the Church. "Miss Broadhurst sent 10/- towards war memorial regretting she could not give more as she was going to give to Ambergate (mean old thing). She is getting about £175 a year teaching Sheldon children" (7.5.19). Further evidence of unsatisfactory relationships appears two months later. "Mr. Stephenson went to Ashford and brought Miss Broadhurst's salary. She happened to be coming down the street opposite our house and when he offered it to her she would not accept it and told him he must take it up to her house as she had a train to catch. She was most insulting to him. He left salary at our house and she fetched it tonight." (26.7.19). It does not come as much of a surprise to read that two months later: "Miss Broadhurst's furniture was taken by tractor. She is leaving Sheldon I understand in October" (12.9.19).

The school building was used for many purposes other than simply as the school. Parties for birthdays and weddings were held there. Confirmation classes and evening classes also took place, the latter covering such subjects as fretwork, cheesemaking (6.5.16) and French. Consideration was given to the school's possible use, along with the Church and Chapel, as a place of safety for refugees from the east coast which was under threat from bombardment and from Zeppelins. Anthony Gyte was the chairman of the Sheldon committee looking into the matter. On March 22nd 1916 "Mr. Sherlock called here today and has gone to measure the church, chapel and school dimensions in anticipation of refugees"; but none in fact were to come. The school was also the venue for money raising events such as the sale to produce funds for the Red Cross, or the St. Valentine's Fancy Dress Ball in 1919 to provide new lamps for the church. Both these events illustrate the widespread involvement of a large proportion of the village population in such social occasions. No less than 30 people took the trouble to dress up for the Ball in costumes such as Daffodil (Miss Leah Brocklehurst), Queen of Hearts (Miss Ethel Gyte), Chef (Mr. Stephenson) and Highlander (Mr. T. Gyte). Entertainment was essentially homemade. Village people played the piano, sang, did recitations and took part in sketches. The enjoyment was in the planning and the preparing as well as in the performing and the watching. Although Maria Gyte hardly ever went to the school for any of the events, she was aware of all that happened there.

The Church

The Church of St. Michael and All Angels was built in 1865 on land just to the north of the village street which had been given by the Duke of Devonshire and consecrated as a burial ground in 1853. This church replaced a smaller building which had stood in the village street since the fifteenth century and was reputed to be the smallest chapel in the county. That church had been dedicated to All Saints - the reason for the subsequent change of dedication is not known.

At the time of the Diaries the Vicar was the Revd. Harry Ernest Sherlock, a bachelor who lived at Ashford and was the incumbent of both Ashford and Sheldon. He was a graduate of Cambridge and had been ordained in the Peterborough Diocese in 1889. After two curacies, he was appointed Vicar of St. George's, Leicester, from 1895-1906. There is then a gap in his history until he became a curate again, at Buxton, in 1909. Three years later he moved to Ashford with Sheldon where he remained as Vicar until his retirement in 1940.

There was also in Sheldon a Primitive Methodist Chapel which had been built in 1848. Until 1876 there were two Chapel Services each Sunday, but then they were reduced to one. However, by 1912 they were back to two even though the membership in that year was only three. The Society steward at that time was David Frost. The Chapel does not figure much in the Diaries. There was a Shrove Tuesday tea there in 1915, Ethel played the harmonium there in January 1916 (16.1.16) and the following month "Mr. David Frost preached at Sheldon tonight" (13.2.16). From 1919 to 1928 no Services were shown for Sheldon on the Circuit plan. There is now no trace of the building which formerly stood at the bottom of the lane leading to the Church.

One of the Churchwardens of the parish church was Anthony Gyte. The other was another farmer, Thomas William Brocklehurst, who lived in the farm at the bottom of the village street - he is usually referred to in the Diaries as 'Thos. Wm.' and his surname was sometimes shortened to 'Brockley'. The Church Treasurer was Maria Gyte and she was meticulous in her financial duties. In preparing for the 1915 Vestry Meeting she reported: "I have balanced up the Church accounts and am right to the half penny. £2.16.3 in hand" (6.4.15). One can imagine the frustration, and then the relief, which lay behind the entry for the following year: "I was busy with the church accounts and could not make them balance right. However, later on I found out that the pound we were short of was in an envelope in the green box where we keep all church money etc" (4.4.16).

All the Sunday services are mentioned week by week, usually with an indication of the numbers present, and the amount and destination of the collection. Although Maria herself did not often attend, no doubt because of the physical difficulty of getting there, she made sure that she knew who had conducted the service, what the sermon was about, and how long the service took.

Sunday must have been a busy day for the Vicar with three services at Ashford and two (and sometimes three) at Sheldon. He was assisted by a series of Lay Readers. This is an ancient lay office in the church which had been revived in 1866. There appears to have been a good supply of Readers as one followed another at Sheldon with little gap in between. There were five over a period of six years. One of them, Captain Collier, was an officer of the Church Army. Another, Mr. Stephenson, was a gardener at a nearby large house, Churchdale Hall. All of them exercised a pastoral ministry in the village as well as a liturgical one in the Church.

It is clear from the Diaries that a devoted ministry of pastoral care was exercised by the Vicar and his Readers. It was a rare week when no visit to the village was recorded of one or the other. Sometimes the Vicar walked, sometimes he came on horseback, on one occasion he attempted to come by car and got stuck in a snowdrift. When he called at the Devonshire Arms, which was frequently, he had to be prepared to discuss, and sometimes to defend, his sermons. On September 19th 1914 Maria recorded: "Mr. Sherlock called and had tea and we had a long conversation about his sermon last Sunday. I told him he had spoken rather strongly about the young men of Sheldon not being patriotic" (19.9.14). The following January she took him to task for not giving credit where it was due: "Mr. Sherlock took the service in Sheldon Church this afternoon. All ours went to the service except Tony and myself. The Vicar made no allusion to the men who had enlisted" (24.1.15).

But she would defend the Vicar when others criticised him! "Alf Brocklehurst used some abusive language about Mr. Sherlock, cursed and swore about him because of something Mr. Sherlock was reported to have said to Bertha Bramwell about the bell-ringing at Sheldon Church. I spoke up for the Vicar but told AB that I should not tell Mr. Sherlock what he had said. He must tell him himself" (10.6.16).

The subject of the war, the Church's attitude to it and the fact that the clergy were classified as non-combatants, were matters of hot debate. In 1915, the Lay Reader, Mr. Weadon, had been outspoken at a public meeting at the school on the first anniversary of the outbreak of the war. A resolution was passed that the war should go on until Germany was vanquished. Mr. Weadon, who was in the Chair, said "there were more men who ought to go out of Sheldon" (4.8.15). This whole matter was much in Maria's mind because of her own sons and their possible liability under the recruiting scheme which was being proposed by Lord Derby. On November 17th 1915 "Mr. Weadon called here tonight and we had quite a huffy conversation over Lord Derby's recruiting scheme. Sam Rowland asked him a few questions and I asked how it was that clergymen would be exempt from serving. Mr. Weadon said a few things that I did not like."

There was another matter over which Maria disagreed with Mr. Weadon and that was the length of his sermons. There are many references to the lateness of the hour when people got out of church. "People get tired of his long addresses" (21.4.16) she said, and although she did not usually herself suffer, because she was not there, she had every sympathy with those who did. There was one occasion when the congregation did not leave until ten past four from a service which began at 2.30 p.m. It was much better with the Vicar: "Mr. Sherlock took the service in church this afternoon. The congregation was out at 25 minutes past three o'clock, some difference between this and Mr. Weadon's time" (16.5.15). Perhaps, however, Mr. Weadon redeemed himself in Maria's eyes - he left the parish in 1916 and joined the Army. In 1918 he was working as a nursing orderly in Egypt and he wrote then to offer his sympathy concerning the death of Tony.

It was in her bereavement that Maria particularly appreciated the ministry of the Church. On the first Sunday after the official notification of Tony's death, a memorial service was held in which special hymns were sung: "Mr. Sherlock preached a very good sermon and referred to 'Tony Gyte'. A very sympathetic sermon" (18.11.17). After the service, the Vicar called on Maria who was at home and prayed with her. "He left me his sermon to peruse." That is evidence of Mr. Sherlock's sensitive bereavement ministry. The public worship in which Tony was named and honoured, the choosing of special hymns, an appropriate sermon which he left for Maria to study, his praying with her in her home, are all aspects of a caring ministry.

Maria also drew comfort from the ministry of a Lay Reader who came to Ashford and Sheldon in 1918. He was Mr. Stephenson, (already mentioned) a gardener at Churchdale Hall. He appears, in fact, to have been a Reader in training at that time for he did not pass his exams until the end of 1919 when he received his licence and was admitted as Lay Reader in Derby. He offered much personal support to the Gytes with his frequent visits, and through his efforts on their behalf to discover more about the details of Tony's death in action, and also the whereabouts of his grave. On February 16th 1918 Maria wrote: "Mr. Stephenson has been most kind in getting a friend of his to make enquiries about my poor Tony. This friend is a vicar. Mr. Stephenson brought a letter which he has received from his friend." She then quotes the letter which had been written by the Chaplain to Tony's regiment, the 17th Sherwood Foresters. It was the sort of letter which Army Chaplains must have written on numerous occasions, offering whatever comfort was possible in terrible tragedy. It deeply affected Maria: "I felt awful when Mr. Stephenson gave me this letter. I gave way to my grief." (16.2.18). Thus it was that a Lay Reader in training helped her in the sad process of coming to terms with her grief.

It was Mr. Stephenson also who organised Sheldon's celebration in July 1919 for the ending of the war. He arranged the house to house collection for the sports ("those who had been talking most gave the least" Maria observed tartly 22.7.19) which were to include a cricket match between ladies and gentlemen. The proceedings began with "a very impressive service, held in Church by Mr. Stephenson. The people and children of Sheldon walked in procession and G. Ward carried a laurel wreath which was made by Mr. Stephenson and deposited on the altar. The service was in remembrance of the fallen lads" (24.7.19). The procession of the village population and the laying of the wreath, with a flag flying from a hastily erected pole, must indeed have been impressive. After the service, the Vicar and others called on Maria and "tea was sent from the school as well as to other invalids".

Later in 1918, "Mr. Stephenson brought a picture here which he has given in memory of the fallen lads of Sheldon. He wants it hanging in the church" (2.10.18). That was probably the picture which still hangs in Sheldon Church. It is called *The Great Sacrifice* by the artist James Clark. It was published in the Christmas 1914 number of the *Graphic* which offered further copies for sale in the following year, calling it "the most inspired Picture of the War". It shows a young soldier lying dead with a small wound in his forehead; his rifle with fixed bayonet is lying to his left, and his lifeless right hand is resting upon the feet of a crucified Christ with the smoke of battle in the background. In *The Church of England and the First World War*, Alan Wilkinson says that this picture "was soon hanging in many churches, homes and hospitals" (page 147).

On the first anniversary of Tony's death, which fell on a Sunday, it was Mr. Stephenson who "took the service this afternoon and mentioned all the dear lads that had to give up their lives in the awful war" (2.11.19).

All the evidence points to the Church playing an important role in the whole life of the village. The regular Sunday worship, the continuing ministry of baptisms, weddings and funerals, the diligent pastoral visiting, the organisation of village events, the signing of official forms for sugar permits and such like, the provision of Christian education through Sunday School, Confirmation class and sermon, all bear witness to an unspectacular but faithful Christian presence.

Local and National Events

One of the intriguing aspects of the Maria Gyte Diaries is the reporting of national events and local incidents side by side. Although physically Sheldon was a small, isolated peakland village easily cut off from the rest of Derbyshire when the snow came (and in Sheldon the snow comes horizontally more often than vertically!), it was, however, never insulated from the wider world. In some ways, communications were better then than they are now. Letters by messenger from Bakewell arrived at 8 a.m. The Wall Letter Box was cleared at 8.25 a.m. and 6.15 p.m. each weekday, and there is evidence in the Diaries of letters arriving even on Sundays. At least one of Tony's many letters from the Front arrived in Sheldon within four days. The telegraph service was in frequent use and telegrams were sent with some of the kinds of message which go by telephone today e.g. the time of a visitor's expected arrival or even a cricket score. The railway was a vital element in the system of transport and communication. Longstone station on the Ambergate and Manchester section of the Midland railway was the nearest access point, two and a half miles from Sheldon. Bakewell was the next at three miles, from where passengers and goods could go to Chesterfield, Derby and London. Getting the churns to the station in time to catch the 8.40 a.m. milk train at Longstone, or in times of hot weather to catch the night train at Bakewell so that the milk did not go sour before being sold, were key points in the daily farming timetable.

Conversation with visitors to the Devonshire Arms provided Maria Gyte with many contacts which linked the village with the wider world. On May 29th 1917 "A lady and gentleman who are staying at Ashford (from Nottingham) called here. They lived quite close to young Ball the airman and knew him quite well. The Germans have now got young Ball a prisoner. He is only 20 years old and has brought about 42 German aeroplanes down". Captain Albert Ball, a pupil of Trent College, won the VC, the DSO and two bars, and the MC, destroying 43 aircraft before he himself was shot down on May 7th 1917 and killed. A memorial stone, erected after the war by his father Sir Albert Ball (a Mayor of Nottingham), still marks the spot in an open field in Northern France where he crashed. No doubt when the conversation in Sheldon took place just three weeks after the crash there was still hope that the young hero might have survived.

Newspapers from Sheffield were the means by which most national and world events were communicated to, and studied and evaluated, in Sheldon. It is interesting to compare such war time records as Vera Brittain's *Testament of Youth*, and the Reverend Andrew Clark's Diary *Echoes of the Great War*, with the Gyte Diaries and see how the same events were being interpreted in Buxton, Great Leigh in Essex, and Sheldon.

Two issues of national importance made a particular impact on Sheldon. They were Conscription and the National Mission of Repentance and Hope.

Conscription

In the early months of the War it was hoped that there would be sufficient volunteers to make conscription unnecessary. Asquith, the Prime Minister, believed that there was so much opposition to conscription that it could not be introduced until it was quite clear that the voluntary system of recruitment had failed. In May 1915 Maria Gyte read her newspaper and commented: "A coalition ministry is to be formed and I am afraid Conscription is coming soon" (20.5.15). Lord Derby, the Secretary of State for War, was appointed director-general of recruiting and he was responsible for the system known as the Derby Scheme. This was an attempt to increase voluntary enlistment and avoid conscription. It involved a personal canvass of all men up to the age of 40 who were invited to attest their willingness to serve. Men in certain 'starred' occupations such as munitions work or mining were excluded from the canvass. Tribunals were set up to hear appeals for exemption on personal or occupational grounds. On May 21st 1915 when the men of Sheldon were manuring the land in preparation for the 10,000 cabbage plants which Anthony Gyte with William and Alf Brocklehurst were purchasing that day in Derby, "All the young men in Sheldon from 17 to 40 had their names put down at a meeting in Sheldon School for military purposes" (21.5.15). The names of such men throughout the country were to form the Parliamentary Recruiting Committee's National Register.

In June, churchwardens Anthony Gyte and Thomas William Brocklehurst attended a recruitment meeting at Bakewell as official representatives of Sheldon. Two days later recruiting posters arrived in the village, and Anthony received a letter from the Vicar expressing the hope that more young men would offer themselves at the recruiting meeting at Sheldon the following Saturday when Captain Seymour, the Recruiting Officer, was to speak.

Similar activity was, of course, going on all over the country. In his diary the Revd. Andrew Clark, Rector of Great Leigh, reported in his Essex village a "profusion of recruiting posters which ... the squire's daughters have put up on all tree trunks, gate posts, barn walls" (1.5.15. page 58 *Echoes of the Great War*). The farm foreman at Great Leigh did not approve: "Enticing more men away from the land, when too many have gone already. If the government want more men let them take idlers, not workmen. Unless the war is over before August, and some of the men come back, there will not be enough men to get in the harvest" (page 58). The Rector reported much indignation among farm hands at being badgered by a recruiting sergeant to enlist. This was shown by the fact that "every recruiting poster ... has been torn down; torn into shreds; and cast away" (page 61). The view of the Essex farm hands was: "We will go, when we like, or when we are ordered". The Rector concluded "Conscription, being just, would be welcome" (page 58).

At that stage, five men had joined the Army from Sheldon: William Hallows, Fred Brocklehurst, Anthony Brocklehurst and Sam Wilton who were in the Grenadier

Guards, and Alf Wildgoose in the Sherwood Foresters. They had joined up in January 1915. But the pressure was clearly on for more to go. After the Recruiting Officer's visit, "some leaflets were distributed to the men who had not recruited". (27.6.15) In her newspaper Maria noticed the progress of the 'National Register Bill' (8.7.15) through the House of Commons, and also the Kaiser's threat to get to Calais at any cost. She also read a report of Lord Kitchener's speech at the Guildhall calling for "Men, Money and Munitions" (9.7.15). Tom and Tony both received a book "telling them to enlist either for munitions or military work" (14.7.15). Maria believed that all the young men of Sheldon had received one.

Recruiting pressure built up again in November. "Our Tom received Lord Derby's letter" (2.11.15). and "Mr. John Frost called with papers over recruiting" (11.11.15). In the House of Commons, Mr. Asquith "said that if the single men did not come up as they ought there would be some form of conscription" (12.11.15). It was at this time that the "huffy" conversation with Mr. Weadon took place, which has already been noted, on the subject of clergy exemption (17.11.15). Debate continued in Sheldon about Lord Derby's Scheme and Maria did "not know what the country will be brought to over this cruel war" (23.11.15). All this must have fuelled the fire which burst out when the Vicar paid one of his usual visits to the Devonshire Arms: "Mr. Sherlock called and had tea and a very heated argument I had with him over the war" (26.11.15).

Under the Derby Scheme men had to attest by 4 p.m. Sunday December 12th. This led to a flurry of activity at Bakewell Recruiting Office. Eleven Sheldon men attested but only three were passed as medically fit: "George Goodwin and our Tom went to attest. Our Tom passed for active service on the field but George Goodwin did not pass, he has varicose veins. Our Tom drew 2s. 9d" (3.12.15). This left "four young men in Sheldon who have not attested yet ... Our Tony has not but he is only just 18" (7.12.15). Maria's son-in-law Clement Wager, who had married Mary Gyte and lived at Rowland near Longstone, also attested at this time. "Dr. Jackson said that Clem was as good as they made them and so of course was passed" (14.12.15).

There was a similar rush to attest at Great Leigh. The farm workers there were advised to do so on the grounds that if they were called up, their master would say whether they could be spared or not. If they did not put their names down, it was doubtful whether, if they were called up, there would be any possibility of appeal. The consequence of that advice, said the Revd. Andrew Clark, "has been a great rush of men to the recruiting officer. This is not voluntary recruiting, but compulsion in a dishonest form". He also mentioned that "the officer who attended at the council school on Wedn. evening this week said that, if men hung back, they would be hauled out with a rope round their neck". He added the comment: "This is voluntary enlistment!" (page 100 *Echoes of the Great War*). Maria Gyte does not record anything so blatant at Sheldon, but the psychological pressure to comply must have been considerable.

Efforts were now being made to secure exemption for Tom. Anthony filled up forms detailing the nature of Tom's work on the farm (17.12.15). Maria noted the debates in Parliament about compulsory service. "I could understand it better if it was for all, but parsons are exempt and those who have conscientious objections". Anthony appeared before the Tribunal in Bakewell to appeal for Tom. He was asked detailed questions about the farm and was told that he would hear the outcome in a few days. After all that ordeal, Anthony "had to go to bed with a sick headache" (15.1.16).

But his efforts were successful. Tom received a postcard from the Recruiting Officer saying that he "was to fetch his armlet on Tuesday next (between 2 and 8 o'clock)"

(22.1.16). The Rector of Great Leigh had seen the first such armlet in his parish a month earlier. "The 'Derby Armlet' was in evidence today. It is a band of dark khaki cloth about four inches wide, with a red crown on it. Arthur Thos. Stoddart had it on in Church. I passed, on my way back from morning service, a lad, bicycling with it. It is for men who have been 'attested' for service." (op cit page 102) Tom duly collected his armlet on January 25th 1916 but "the recruiting officer did not say anything to him about being starred or whether he had been put in a later group" (25.1.16). But a month later "Our Tom received a paper from the Central Tribunals to say that he would be treated as being 'starred'"(24.2.16).

Despite this concession, Maria disliked the whole system. She noted that after the passing of the Conscription Act in January 1916, "the local Tribunal for the Military Service Act was chosen and consisted of the same gentlemen acting as Tribunal under Lord Derby's scheme" (7.2.16). She read in the paper that married men had to take the place of single men in reserved occupations. She concluded that "the Derby scheme is nothing but a farce and the tribunals no better" (1.3.16), because they were allowing very few exemptions, and she claimed that "farmers are shown no favour" (1.3.16). She did not feel that Tom's star was any real security: "The single men are being well badgered to suit the married men under the detestable Derby scheme. They are about to unstar men who have been starred. It is abominable how they pester the poor single men" (25.3.16). In June, Anthony went to the Bakewell tribunal over Tom's 'Star'. "Tom was put back four months" (3.6.16).

But not all Sheldon young men were so fortunate. Several had had their appeals dismissed. Maria suspected that "there are a few in Sheldon who are very bitter about our Tom getting put back four months among whom are Sam Rowland and Alf Brocklehurst and I do not care about Sam Wilton's talk. Sam Rowland was very sleering tonight saying that Jack Armit would not get off because he was not a milk seller and other things" (5.6.16). The next day "Our Tom had a postcard this morning with a man on, and one in khaki, and a few words 'This little pig stayed at home'. On the address side was written 'Do not be the pig who stayed at home'. We have our suspicion that it is S. Rowland, Alf Brockley and Sam Wilton as they were looking at something and laughing the other night" (6.6.16).

As it turned out, Maria's fears about Tom were not realised. But on the day that she was describing the bitterness and jealousy about Tom's deferment, she also recorded: "Anthony took Tony to Bakewell. Tony attested and drew 2s. 7d.". That was June 5th 1916.

Tony's future was to be different from his brother's.

The National Mission of Repentance and Hope

On the same day that Tom received the offensive postcard, Mr. Weadon, the Lay Reader, called at the Devonshire Arms "with an invitation to attend a mission in the schoolroom 'To Make England Better'" (6.6.16). This was the first step in Sheldon's participation in the National Mission of Repentance and Hope. The planning for this nationally had begun in 1915 when the Archbishop of Canterbury, Dr. Davidson, invited twelve priests to report to him on "The Spiritual Call to the Nation and the Church". This group, which included William Temple who himself was later to be Archbishop of Canterbury, recommended "a National Mission ... through all the cities and towns and villages of the land" (*The Church of England and the First World War* page 72).

In a speech to Convocation, Archbishop Lang explained the title of the Mission: "We have called it a national Mission of Repentance and Hope; Repentance because we are called to bid men and women everywhere to repent of the sins which have stained our civilisation and brought upon it the manifest judgment of God, and Hope because, during the closing period of this terrific ordeal in the midst of increasing strain and sacrifice and sorrow, our people will need the strength of Hope, and in those difficult days that are coming, when the old order will have gone and the duty will be laid upon the nation of seeking a new order in a new world, we must present before the minds of the nation the one hope, Christ, His Mind, His Spirit, for the rebuilding of a new world" (*The Church of England and the First World War* page 76).

The news of the Mission was not greeted with any enthusiasm by the Rector of Great Leigh who did not have much confidence in the leadership of the bishops. He wrote in March 1916: "The Bench of bishops seem lost to any sense of manly or true feeling and enslaved to the whine and insincerity of cant". (*Echoes of the Great War* p. 150)

He returned to the attack in August. "The old women on the Episcopal bench are devising old-womanish national Missions, and relays of women preachers ... but will not move a finger to lighten the Church service of dreary incrustations of a by-gone age, or allow reasonable liberty of substituting reasonable alternatives for intolerably long and weary psalms and lessons for the day. The consequence of this Episcopal stick-in-the-mud policy is that the English people are being driven away from the Anglican Church. (*Echoes of the Great War* page 150). As a parish priest, the Revd. Andrew Clark was being critical there of the limitations of the Book of Common Prayer in meeting the needs of the time, a limitation which was also being experienced by Chaplains at the Front. But the Essex Rector reserved his most humorous scorn for a National Mission Service at Braintree Church. He did not attend himself (nor it seems did he have any Mission Service in his own parish) but he received a detailed report of the sermon preached by the Bishop of Sodor and Man: "He frowned, he smiled, he wept, he wrung his hands, he waved his hands; he thumped the pulpit; he whispered, he roared; and all through he babbled, for over forty minutes. For the most part he said, with great emphasis, things that had no meaning" (*op cit* page 160). But there were two joyful moments. One was when the Bishop in one of his hand wavings sent his gold watch, "which he had laid on the side of the pulpit spinning, smash into the aisle and said: 'Oh my brethren, dearly beloved, don't think of my watch. There are things more important than my watch. There is the mission. There is the mission'". The second joyful moment for the weary congregation was when the Vicar of Braintree, after the forty minutes, " went to the altar to say the concluding prayers, but had to wait while old lawn sleeves picked up the shattered watch". (*Echoes of the GreatWar* page 161).

How was the Mission received in Sheldon? Cautiously, at first, but then with increasing interest. Two days after Mr. Weadon's visit to the Devonshire Arms, "Mr. Sherlock came to see us and he had dinner about a quarter to 7 (stew, mashed potato and sago pudding and cheese, butter etc.)". He then went to school when a meeting was held (about the Mission of Repentance and Hope) in the schoolroom. About 12 persons were present. Anthony did not go as he was busy with farm matters. It appears that plans were made to prepare for the Mission by a series of midweek prayer meetings and Church services. On Wednesday June 21st Maria records: "A Prayer meeting was held at our house tonight just before 9 o'clock. Mrs. Ed, Ruth and Doris, Mrs. Craven, Aunt H and our girls and I were there". Prayer was obviously women's work, as no man was present! That evening the men were more interested in a visitor to the Devonshire Arms who had called a year or two earlier and was now suspected of stealing ferrets and dogs: "some men followed and watched where he went to"

(21.6.16). The next night there was the first of what appear to have been regular Thursday services in the Church: "Mr. Sherlock held a service in church tonight. There were 10 or 11 present" (22.6.16). Mr. Weadon conducted such services in July. The Mission itself took place in October and was conducted by the Revd. J.R. Towers who was a curate in Buxton. Information about it was in some leaflets brought from Ashford on October 20th by Miss Grover. (The Grover sisters were good friends to the village and regularly brought up the parish magazines; they were generous in providing flowers for the Church at the Festivals and treats for the children of the school.)

On Monday October 23rd "Mr. Towers and Mr. Sherlock took part in the National Mission tonight. A pretty good congregation". It did not, however, include Tom Gyte - he went to a whist drive and dance at Ashford! On Tuesday, "there was Holy Communion in Sheldon Church at 9 o'clock this morning. The missioner celebrating, 11 present. There was another service at 12 o'clock midday and another tonight". "Mrs. Tinsley" (who lived at the Rookery, Ashford) "called in to see me, also Mr. Towers the missioner who is lodging at Bramwells (Polly)". The evening meeting took place in the School: "A good attendance at school. The missioner seems to be very well liked. Anthony, Tom, Tony, Emily and Evelyn were there" (24.10.16). On Wednesday, "Holy Communion at 9 o'clock, service at 12 (noon) and a service for women at 3 o'clock. Practice for choir at 7.30 and a service for all at 8 o'clock. A good number present in school tonight" (25.10.16). On Thursday: "Service (Holy Communion) in Sheldon Church, service at 12 (noon) and Mr. Towers came and celebrated Holy Communion for Mrs. Ed and myself in our parlour at 2.45. He afterwards called and had a nice chat with me". Mr. Towers conducted another service in the evening in the school, along with the Vicar and the new Lay Reader, Mr. Hayward, and then was conveyed by motor to Ashford.

The Mission concluded on Sunday October 29th: "Holy Communion this morning in Sheldon Church 20 present. Mr. Sherlock and Mr. Towers celebrated. Service this afternoon by Mr. Sherlock and Mr. Towers. All went to Church from our house except myself and William (Gould). Collection for church mission £1.1s.7d.". (29.10.16). Nationally, the Mission was not felt to have been very successful. It had not, for example, touched the William Goulds of England. Hensley Henson, the Bishop of Durham, could not "observe or discover any lasting improvement in the religious situation. The churches are still confronted with the perturbing problem of popular indifference" (*Church of England and the First World War* page 78).

But the fact that William Gould, the farm worker, is actually mentioned as not having attended church is some indication of the mission's modest success in at least bringing such a person into the evangelistic scope, even if it did not actually succeed in getting him to church! There are other indications in the Diaries that the Mission did continue to have an effect in Sheldon. For example, in the following year, on June 7th 1917, "A mission for children was started at 7 o'clock tonight. A procession marched from the school to Church, singing hymns. A cross was carried in front. Our Ethel and Evelyn and other choir girls joined in procession. Mr. Sherlock and Mr. Hayward were in attendance. Mrs. Tinsley and the Misses Grover were there as well". The presence of people from Ashford at that event is another example of modest progress in interparochial relationships. After all, it was only a few months before the Mission that there had been an estrangement between Sheldon and Ashford over a supper for the two church choirs. This had been smouldering for some time ever since a previous choir supper when mugs had been "put on the supper table at Ashford, and the Sheldon choir drank out of them whilst glasses were on the Ashford choir table" (20.1.16). Even the fact that the Vicar had drunk from a mug, and not a glass, had not been enough to assuage Sheldon's sense of grievance! So the accepted presence of some Ashford parishioners at Sheldon children's mission was not without significance.

Of such stuff of human relationships is village life composed and it is not inappropriate for the success of a National Mission of Repentance and Hope to be measured in such a humble context.

Tony Gyte

Over sixty years after his death, Tony Gyte was still clearly remembered by at least one person in Sheldon. This was George Brocklehurst, an octogenarian, who had been contemporary with Tony Gyte. He described Tony as being "a gentle sort of lad"; when he was little, "he used to play with dolls, like". *The Derbyshire Times* said that Tony "was of a quiet, retiring disposition, but well liked". There is evidence in the Diaries that he was thoughtful, conscientious and affectionate. Working as he did on a peakland farm, he must also have had qualities of considerable strength and endurance. Tony was 15 when Maria, at the age of 56, began her Diaries. Just after his sixteenth birthday Tony had his first long trousers. Also at that time he was confirmed, along with George Brocklehurst and seven girls from the village. Mr. Sherlock had given weekly instruction, and it was after one of these confirmation classes that Tony discovered that the Vicar had left his watch behind at the School. Tony took it home. It was decided to send the watch to Ashford Vicarage the next morning by way of Uncle Will Brockley who would be taking the milk float to Longstone station and passing the Vicarage on the way. Unfortunately, Uncle Will was not as careful as he might have been, and the pressure of a milk churn broke the watch glass (29.11.13). Tony was similarly observant a year or so later when he found a silver flask out in the fields (9.2.15). This was handed over to the policeman at Ashford. It was later claimed by a Miss Whitehead, and Tony's virtue received a reward - five shillings.

As he was the youngest child, it was natural that Tony should have had a special place in his mother's affections. It is significant that during one period when Maria was too ill to complete the entries in the Diary herself, it was Tony who did this for her. For four days in October 1916 when "mother came to bed very poorly," Tony kept the record going. His entries are written in a careful copper plate hand and signed 'Tony' after the last one. The quality of the handwriting is a testimony to the instruction received in the village school. Tony used his mother's style of recording the day's events, in fact he may have written at her dictation; but he was careful to use the first person when he described his own success in finding some sheep which his brother Tom had failed to do (4.10.16).

As Tony's call-up drew inexorably nearer, although no indication is given of his feelings, he must have been aware of the fears and anxieties of his parents. Both Anthony and Maria strove energetically for the deferral of his conscription. One wonders at the forbearance of the Army authorities in responding so patiently and courteously to Maria's persistent letters. Her efforts resulted in delaying Tony's departure for training. But eventually he had to go.

He went first of all to a training camp at Cleadon near Sunderland (10.5.17). He wrote home almost every day. In one letter he said that he was trying to settle, and in another he enclosed a few violets which he had picked when he had been on coastguard duty on the cliffs near the sea. He sent his sisters some silver and enamel brooches of his Notts and Derby regiment (25.5.17). He was finding Army food inadequate - one round of bread and marmalade was not enough for breakfast, especially when he had to go on route marches of nearly twenty miles (11.6.17). Food parcels from home were a welcome supplement.

On July 1st Tony returned to Sheldon for his second - and last - leave. He arrived in Derby at 2 a.m. and slept in an easy chair at the YMCA until it was time to catch the milk train to Bakewell. As soon as he got home, he went upstairs to see his mother and put his arms round her. July 1st was a Sunday, and being the first Sunday of the month, there was a celebration of Holy Communion in Sheldon Church at 9.30 a.m. Tony went to that, and then on to the moor, no doubt to see the state of the fields. Maria had already written to the CO in Sunderland asking for an extension of Tony's leave so that he could help with the hay harvest. She was referred elsewhere but, after writing, she received no reply. So she wrote to the CO again and was then told that the leave could not be extended (4.7.17).

On July 5th, just after 9 a.m. Tony set off back to camp. That was to be the last time that Maria would see him. A year later, the details of his departure were still vivid in her mind. "It was awful for me his mother. He had got to the staircase after saying 'Goodbye' and I called him back. He put his arms round me and I blessed him and he said he would be a good lad" (4.7.18). He was several hours late arriving back in camp. For this offence he lost a day's pay, and was confined to barracks for three days. His letters revealed his homesickness, and his expectation of being sent to France within the following few days. He arrived in France on July 12th - just in time for the Battle of Passchendaele.

The Battle of Passchendaele

David Lloyd George described the Battle of Passchendaele as "one of the blackest horrors of history". Of the million British soldiers who died in the Great War, a quarter of them lie within the few square miles around Ypres. It is estimated that more than 40,000 bodies of those who died by bullet, shell or mine, or else by drowning in the Flanders mud, were never recovered. Their bones are still being unearthed each year by the farmers' ploughs, along with tons of rusting munitions.

On June 7th 1917, "a lovely growing day" at Sheldon and the first day of the village Children's Mission, the British detonated a million pounds of high explosive which had been set in a series of nineteen mines dug deep beneath the German lines on the Messines Ridge, which was an arc of gently rising ground overlooking Ypres. The shock wave was felt in London. Vera Brittain recalled it as "a strange early morning shock like an earthquake" (*First World War* Martin Gilbert page 337). The success of this operation encouraged General Haig to launch another offensive towards Passchendaele. If this too were to be successful there was a good chance of driving the Germans out of Belgium and recovering the ports of Ostende and Zeebrugge. But the conditions were not right. That part of Belgium was a natural bog. Shelling and bombardment had destroyed the system of ditches with the consequence that the land quickly flooded. Despite this, General Haig was confident of success, even though others, including Lloyd George, judged otherwise and tried to dissuade him. Haig even arranged for cavalry to be in reserve so that they could charge forward and defeat the enemy, after the preparatory shelling and the infantry attack. But when the battle started, and continuous rain fell, the land became a sea of liquid mud into which guns disappeared, and men and horses sank and drowned. Progress was only possible over lines of duckboards floating on the mud. One eyewitness described the area in these terms: "As far as the eye could see was a mass of black mud with shell holes filled with water. Here and there broken duckboards, partly submerged in the quagmire; here and there a horse's carcase sticking out of the water; here and there a corpse. The only sign of life was a rat or two swimming about to find food and a patch of ground. At night a yellow mist hung over the mud; the stench was almost unbearable. When gas shells came over the mist turned to brown. It smelt like violets. The smell of violets was the sign of danger". (Private H. Jeary, 1st Battalion, Queen's Royal West Surrey Regiment *Voices and Images of the Great War*, page 255).

It must have been a terrible situation for youngsters like Tony Gyte to cope with. In Lyn Macdonald's book *They Called It Passchendaele*, there is this account by an officer of the Royal Fusiliers describing his platoon crouching in the dank in shell holes among the mangled remains of the dead: "Most of my boys were young Londoners, just eighteen or nineteen, and a lot of them were going into a fight for the first time. Regularly during the night I crawled round to check on my scattered sections, having a word here and there and trying to keep their spirits up. The stench was horrible, for the bodies were not corpses in the normal sense. With all the shell-fire and bombardments they'd been continually disturbed, and the whole place was a mess of slime and bones and decomposing bits of flesh. Everyone was on edge and as I crawled up to one shell-hole I could hear a boy sobbing and crying. He was crying for his mother. It was pathetic really, he just kept saying over and over again, 'Oh Mum! Oh Mum!' Nothing would make him shut up, and while it wasn't likely that the Germans could hear, it was quite obvious that when there were lulls in the shell fire the men in shell-holes on either side would hear this lad and possibly be affected. Depression, even panic, can spread quite easily in a situation like that. So I crawled into the shell-hole and asked Corporal Merton what was going on. He said, 'It's his first time in the line, sir. I can't keep him quiet, and he's making the other lads jittery'. Well, the other boys in the shell-hole obviously were jittery and, as one of them put it more succinctly, 'fed up with his bleedin' noise'. Then they all joined in, 'Send him down the line and home to Mum' - 'Give him a clout and knock him out' - 'Tell him to put a sock in it, sir'. I tried to reason with the boy, but the more I talked to him the more distraught he became, until he was almost screaming. 'I can't stay here! Let me go! I want my Mum!' So I switched my tactics, called him a coward, threatened him with court-martial, and when that didn't work I simply pulled him towards me and slapped his face as hard as I could, several times. It had an extraordinary effect. There was absolute silence in the shell-hole and then the corporal, who was a much older man, said, 'I think I can manage him now, sir'. Well, he took that boy in his arms just as if he was a small child, and when I crawled back a little later to see if all was well, they were both lying there asleep and the corporal still had his arms around the boy - mud, accoutrements and all. At zero hour they went over together." *They Called It Passchendaele*, pages 171, 172).

It is doubtful whether those who were in high command at the rear, from where they were directing the operations at the front, were fully aware of the terrible conditions. There is the celebrated story of Haig's Chief of Staff, Lieutenant-General Sir Launcelot Kiggell, paying his first visit to the front after the Battle of Passchendaele was over. He is said to have been reduced to tears as his car lurched and slithered over the battleground. "Good God", he muttered, "did we really send men to fight in that?" He was then told that conditions were much worse further up.

Tony's Death

In the quiet churchyard at Sheldon, there is a tombstone to the west of the Church which bears this inscription:

IN LOVING MEMORY OF

ANTHONY

THE BELOVED SON OF

ANTHONY AND MARIA GYTE

WHO DIED FROM WOUNDS NOV 2ND 1917

AND WAS INTERRED AT THE LARCHWOOD

RAILWAY CUTTING ZILLEBEKE BELGIUM

AGED 19 YEARS

Today, the Larch Wood Railway Cutting Cemetery is another haven of peace. It is near Zillebeke which is 4 kilometres south east of Ypres. The ordered rows of white Hopton (Derbyshire) stone, commemorating 856 soldiers, are set in a walled area within agricultural farmland with several farms nearby and bounded on one side by the single railway line between Ypres and Commines. The towers of the churches and Cloth Hall of Ypres can be seen in one direction and the low cratered prominence of Hill 60 in another. Hill 60 (60 metres in height) was composed of the spoil from the construction of the railway cutting, and was the site of one of the mines detonated on June 7th. The memorial to Tony is not far from the entrance to the cemetery. It has the words "Known to be buried in this cemetery" above the regimental badge and then the inscription:

70156 PRIVATE

A. GYTE

NOTTS AND DERBY REGIMENT

2ND NOVEMBER 1917 AGE 19

At the base of the memorial, relatives were allowed up to four lines for a personal inscription, with a maximum of 28 letters and spaces in each line. Maria chose just two lines from a familiar hymn which Tony would have played on the harmonium at home:

ANGELS TO BECKON ME

NEARER MY GOD TO THEE.

We do not know the precise circumstances of Tony's death. But we do know what the weather was like in Flanders at that time. Haig's Diary reads:

"*1 November* Glass rising slightly. Dull day but no rain. Observation bad.

2 November Glass rising slightly. Dull misty day. Bad observation."

(*The Road to Passchendaele* John Terraine page 320).

In Sheldon, November 1st was "A most miserable misty day. Does not clear at all" and November 2nd was "very misty".

Tony belonged to the 17th (Service) Battalion of the Sherwood Foresters known as the Welbeck Rangers. On October 19th 1917, this Battalion relieved the 14th Hants. Regiment in the trenches at Tower Hamlets and Bodmin Copse which were to the east of Zillebeke. For the next few days, 200 men at a time were burying cables and carrying equipment to dumps at the front line. On October 22nd the Battalion War

Diary records: "Minor operation by No. 7 Platoon. Lr 'B' Coy. under 2/Lt Pettigrew against Dugouts at J.21.d.7.9. Owing to the bad going and strong resistance of the enemy the objective was not gained. A considerable amount of valuable information was obtained."

On October 24th, the Battalion left the trenches and embussed at Shrapnel Corner just outside Ypres, arriving at Vyverbeek Camp at 2.30 a.m. on October 25th. The next few days were spent in cleaning up. This lull gave Tony the opportunity to write home. His letter arrived on October 29th: "We received a letter from our Tony. He had been in the trenches for four days" (29.10.17). There was "Battalion bathing" on the 26th. On the 28th, the Battalion "moved by Route March to No. 2 Camp Vierstraat Wood." The next three days are noted as "Routine" with musketry classes and box respirator drill at night. Enemy activity is recorded on November 1st (when Tony wrote a birthday letter to his father). It is likely that this was the date when Tony received his fatal wounds. "Routine during morning. Bn. parade at 2.30 p.m. (300 strong) under Major Cassy and proceed to Larch Wood Tunnels. Three parties of 100 each work till 9 p.m. on digging, throwing up breastwork, draining and carrying under very bad conditions owing to mud and gas shelling." But there is no mention of any casualties.

On November 2nd, the day Tony died, no further shelling was reported: "Baths allotted to two companies in morning. Remainder of Bn. on P.T. and Yukon Pack drill under Company commanders." (Yukon Packs, a Canadian invention, were frames of wood and canvas designed to enable mules to carry loads of over 100lbs, but their weight tended to drag the animals down into the mud.)

Major Creamer, the Regimental Secretary of The Worcestershire and Sherwood Foresters Regiment, to whom I am indebted for these extracts from the Battalion War Diary, writes: "It is interesting to note that the battalion was not in direct contact with the enemy on the day that Pte Gyte died. It is likely that he had been wounded earlier and died of wounds on that day, although when this is the case the Regimental Roll of Honour will usually record 'Died of Wounds'. In Pte. Gyte's case the entry is quite clearly 'Killed in Action'. We have a mystery I'm afraid..." However, it is clear from Maria Gyte's Diary that she understood that Tony "died of wounds". (22.11.17).

The superscription on Tony's memorial, "Known to be buried in this cemetery", indicates some confusion. In the Register at the entrance to the Larch Wood Cemetery, there is this information: "The unnamed graves number 321, and special memorials are erected to 81 soldiers from the United Kingdom ... known or believed to be buried among them." This is an indication of the chaos and confusion which must have reigned despite the apparent orderliness of the Battalion War Diary. On December 9th 1917 Maria received a letter "from the Register of Soldiers graves saying that Tony's grave had not yet been located." On February 13th 1918 "A letter came from Register of Graves enquiry office saying that our Tony was reported buried South East of Ypres, North of Hollebeke." Three days later the letter from the Chaplain, the Revd. J.A.A. Baker, (dated February 5th) arrived: "I have this day seen his company officer and the stretcher bearer who took Gyte to Clearing Station. The boy did not live long after he was wounded. He was hit in stomach, leg and arm. He was taken to the Casualty Clearing Station but I think did not live long nor was able to speak much. Gyte is buried in Bodmin Copse near Ypres. This is all that can be said." This letter was written three months after Tony was killed. On April 13th 1918 Maria wrote: "I received a letter saying that my poor Tony's grave had been registered and a wooden cross was put over it. We are very pleased his grave has been located", but the exact location is not mentioned.

Bodmin Copse, at the edge of Sanctuary Wood, fits the description of "South East of Ypres, North of Hollebeke." Edmund Blunden in *Undertones of War* describes Bodmin Copse at that time as "a small and wiry wood ... with tumult and bullets and sometimes shells in the air around" (op.cit. page 218). But one wonders why Tony was initially buried there and not near the Larch Wood Tunnels, which were about 2.5 kilometres to the south west, where presumably he had been wounded and where there had been a cemetery since April 1915. But ...this is to raise a calm query some 80 years after the event. Contemporary experience was more horrific as is demonstrated in the following statement from a Rifleman: "Sooner or later the stretcher-bearers would get to you on the Somme, but at Passchendaele the wounded didn't stand an earthly chance. At one aid post a doctor said to the stretcher-bearers 'Only bring back men we've got a hope of curing. If you get a seriously injured man, leave him to die quietly. Too often you bring men back here and before we can help them they're gone. You're wasting your time and ours.' I thought that was a terrible thing to say. But that was Passchendaele!" (*1914-1918 Voices and Images of the Great War* Lyn Macdonald page 247). Tony was fortunate to have been picked up and carried to the Casualty Clearing Station.

Tony's first burial in Bodmin Copse may have been like those described by Lieutenant King of the East Lancashire Regiment: "We were each told to take a section of men and one NCO, draw rubber gloves, sandbags, and an extra ration for the men, and take our section out to the battlefield area to bury the dead ... We did that job for two days running. And we didn't just dump them into a hole. We committed each one properly to his grave. Said a little prayer out of a book issued to us. 'Ashes to ashes, dust to dust'. The men all stood around and took their hats off for a moment, standing to attention. 'God rest his soul'. A dead soldier can't hurt you. He's a comrade. That's how we looked at it. He was some poor mother's son and that was the end of it." (*They Called It Passchendaele* page 211). That was a sentiment with which Maria Gyte would certainly have sympathised. In July 1918, as she thought back each day to the year before, she wrote: "I think many times a day of my poor Tony. He was so young to have to sacrifice his life and oh! how many thousands more dear lads have gone under in this awful war" (30.7.18).

The Battalion War Diary gives some restrained indication of the terrible conditions at that time. On November 7th, the Battalion moved to the front line at Tower Hamlets, just east of Bodmin Copse.

> "*November 9th* Quiet day in line. Lewis Gun team of 'A' Coy. hit by shell 3 killed and 3 wounded.

> "*November 10th* Gas projectiles fired on LEWIS HOUSES. Front line cleared before the operation. Very wet all day. Trenches all water logged and sides falling. Relieved by 16th Bn. SHERWOOD FORESTERS. Relief complete 3 a.m. Battalion in support in CANADA ST. TUNNELS.

> "*November 11th* Battalion on working parties. The tunnels are very wet and the men are in danger of contracting Trench Foot.

> "*November 12th* All battalion out on Working Parties. The sick are much in evidence, there being over 70 on sick parade mostly with foot trouble.

"November 13th Relieved by 14th Bn. HAMPS. REGT. Relief complete by 5 p.m. On relief proceeded by March Route to RIDGE WOOD "D" CAMP.

"November 14th Routine. Day spent in cleaning up. The Camp is very muddy making it impossible for the men to keep clean.

"November 15th Battalion bathed at BRASSERIE BATHS.

"November 18th TRENCHES. Battn. relieved by 16th BN. SHERWOOD FORESTERS and on relief proceeded to support line in BODMIN COPSE."

On the same day that the Battalion moved to Bodmin Copse where Tony Gyte lay buried, a memorial service in his honour was held in Sheldon Church. "Hymns *On the resurrection morning, Jesu lover of my soul,* and *Abide with me* were sung"

All that Maria and Anthony could do was to try and manage their grief. Perhaps the Diary made that a little easier for Maria than for Anthony: "Anthony is not well at all. He is fretting so much for our poor lad, how he used to get up in a morning to go working on the farm. It is awful to think we shall never see his dear face again in this world but we have to keep living somehow" (19.11.17).

In February 1918 the War Office wrote to say that Tony's affairs had been settled and sent a form which had to be completed in the presence of a minister or magistrate (22.2.18). In March, "Anthony received P.Office order for 6 guineas which belonged to our poor dear Tony. Fancy a life for that sum. Oh dear! my poor lad to think of it. We have not received a thing which belonged to him. He had a watch, money belt, Photos etc., but none comes to us." (15.3.18). However, on March 23rd "We received our poor Tony's things. Letters and Photos, Wallet, belt, scarf, 3 religious books, 11 stamps. His watch did not come and there was no money in belt." The watch did eventually arrive - it came by registered post on September 4th. One can only admire the efficiency of the system which, despite the chaos of the time, delivered the possessions of a dead soldier to his grieving parents. But it took Maria some time before she could bear to look at Tony's things (9.4.18).

In all her troubles, Maria demonstrated a patient and brave endurance. She was no doubt assisted in this by her Christian faith and the pastoral ministry of her Vicar and a succession of Lay Readers. Her belief in the spiritual ministry of angels was revealed in the quotation chosen for Tony's memorial in the Larchwood Cemetery:

"Angels to beckon me

Nearer my God to thee".

The same belief prompted her to choose some sentimental verses which she copied out (14.10.18) in order to have some beribboned cards printed for the first anniversary of Tony's death:

"Gone from our home, oh! how we miss him,

Loving him dearly, his memory we keep;

Never while life lasts shall we forget him,

Dear to our hearts is the place where he sleeps.

In a land of strangers our dear lad does lie,

> *Not one of us there to bid him 'Good-bye!'*
>
> *But the Angels of GOD keep guard o'er his soul*
>
> *Till we meet him again at the call of the roll."*

Perhaps the dedication of Sheldon's Parish Church, St. Michael and All Angels, to which she gave such faithful service as Treasurer, had some influence in her thinking. Perhaps also the fact that Tony died at All Saints' (November 1st) and All Souls' tide (November 2nd) was of some further Christian comfort to her.

The pencilled entries in the diary for November 21st and 22nd 1920, which record the accident when Maria was being carried upstairs in her "rickshaw", are the last in her own hand. Emily took over the Diary for a week, and then Evelyn continued until May 28th 1921. But these entries are brief and increasingly perfunctory. However, we do learn that after the accident, "Father and Tom sleep together in the big room," and also that Mr. Stephenson came every night to read to Maria. On December 18th, the entry records: "Very cold yet. Mother got up for first time since her fall; upstairs." After that, there is no further reference to Maria; it appears that she never resumed her own writing of the Diary. After Evelyn's final entry, the remaining pages of this book are blank.

But we do know that Maria survived until November 1934 when she died at the age of 77 and was laid to rest in Sheldon churchyard by the Revd. H.E. Sherlock. Anthony died in 1945 aged 81. Their names are inscribed below Tony's on the gravestone in Sheldon churchyard. At the top of the stone are two clasped hands, and there is an angel on either side.

Gerald Phizackerley

One of the cricket balls presented by the Chatsworth Cricket Club to Tom Gyte – on this occasion, June 12th 1912, he took all 10 wickets for 34 runs. See page 234

The Diaries

1913

Oct. 7th   Very wet all day. Anthony, Thos. Wm. and John Brocklehurst went to Over Haddon and bought two shire rams. Ours cost 6 pounds and half a crown returned. Thos. Wm.'s and John Brocklehurst's cost £5. 10s. od. with one shilling returned. I went into the dancingroom[1]. A nice number there. Mr. Thacker called and I had a conversation with him over the meat bills. He returned 1s. 7d. that had been paid twice over. Ethel paid 9s. 7d. for a cheese.

Oct. 8th   Very misty and wet at times. Very poor weather for the cows. Anthony took some hens down to Elias Oldfields (42). Mr. Sneap popped in at dinner time but he went back tonight. Anthony took him to the station. A few in today. Miss Grover came and had tea here. She brought 10/6 towards choir fund 2/6 to church box and her sister 2/-. Anthony sold to Mr. Sneap 5 ewe lambs for 28 shillings each.

Oct. 9th   Wm. fetched a hen cote from Bakewell station (Hebden Bridge). Anthony, Tom and Tony went on moor setting up cows and belting sheep[2]. Red cow (far end of five shippon) pecked her calf[3].

Oct. 10th   A good fine corn day. Wm. leading cabbage out. Anthony, Tom and Tony raking. Sold F. Goodwin 2 dozen cauliflower at 1s. 6d. per dozen.

Oct. 11th   Dull and wet. George Ward and Rebecca Carson were married[4] at Sheldon at about half past eight this morning by licence (Mr. Sherlock performed the ceremony). The hunters turned out at Sheldon today. A few in this morning drinking ale. Anthony turned ram to ewes. I have been up in dancing room every night this week. I do not think it has been as throng a Saturday night as usual. Mr. Sneap came again tonight. The wakes ends at 10 o'clock for which I am very thankful. Anthony sent cheque for 9 hen cotes (Somersetshire). Anthony sent cheque to Saunders and Taylor for Heating Apparatus £45.5s. od.

Oct. 12th   We are all rather tired today. Anthony and Mr. Sneap are having a ramble. Mr. Collins took the service in Sheldon church. Clement Wager came tonight.

---

1   The dancing room was the upper part of a nearby barn
2   Belting: tidying up the rear end of ewes
3   Pecked: aborted
4   See entry for 18/1/14

Oct. 15th A better day today but a little drizzly at times. Anthony, Tom and Tony got some potatoes (moor). Prince Arthur and the Duchess of Fife married today.

Oct. 17th A lovely day for the corn. Sun and wind. Getting corn in Bole Piece. Elias Oldfield paid Anthony £3.0.0. towards what he owes for cockerels and other fowls.

Oct. 18th Finished corn on moor. Been for rakings today. Finished Bole Piece. Brought that home about 350 thrave[1]. Had word this morning that the hen cotes are sent off (Somersetshire). Fred Bramwell was paid 16 shillings out of men's club money to buy prizes for the whist drive on Oct 24 next.

Oct. 19th Rather dull but fine. Our Tom and Tony went with their aunt Hannah to Middleton. Mr. Collins preached at Sheldon.

Oct. 20th Anthony went to market. Bought Emily a small dress basket and straps (2/-). Tom was thatching corn stacks on moor.

Oct. 21st Dull but fine. Tom thatching on moor. Anthony and Tony thatching corn stacks in stackyard. The men are working and have been for a week or two at Robinson's farm (where he used to live). They are painting all round and not before it was wanted as there has not been a bit of paint on for years. Luke Gregory and his men are doing the work. Ethel and Evelyn took me out in my chair up and down the village.

Oct. 22nd A very bright day today. Anthony and Tony thatching in stackyard and Tom on moor. John Brocklehurst and J. Naylor fetched hen cotes from station but there were no perches.

Oct. 24th Very frosty and cold. Our men and Jack Naylor are getting potatoes on moor. I have sent receipted bill to end of September 30 to Mr. Archer. I also made out milk bill to and including Oct. 16th and sent it. This bill amounts to £22 2s. 1d. The old hunting men came today and had refreshments. Mr. Sherlock called here and had tea afterwards taking a confirmation class in Sheldon School. There was a whist drive in the school tonight. Our Evelyn won 1st prize for ladies (Ladies companion). Our Mary got the booby and our Tony got the booby for gentlemen. B. Wildgoose, our Mary and Kate Brocklehurst got the refreshments.

Oct. 25th Anthony, Tom and Tony are busy today colouring the tup lambs ready for the fairs next week.

Oct. 26th Mr. Sherlock took the service in church this afternoon. Rather gloomy but mild.

Oct. 27th Anthony took the milk and then went to Bakewell. Bought two new jerseys (for himself and Tony) and a pair of slippers for himself and a

---

1   A thrave consisted of a dozen sheaves

pair of boots for Evelyn. Mr. Collins called here. Mary, Ethel, Evelyn, Kate and Ruth Brocklehurst went to Ashford Hall to attend the nursing lessons. Getting potatoes on moor.

Oct. 28th   Anthony went to Buxton fair with tup lambs. He sold three, two to Ellis Dicken at £3. 10s.od. each and one to J.E. Mycock (Flagg) for £3. 0s. od.

Oct. 29th   Anthony, Thos. Wm. Brocklehurst and Alf Brocklehurst went to Tideswell Fair. Anthony sold three lambs. One sold for £2. 15s. od. and half a crown back. One sold for £2 12s. od. and the other made £2 10s. od.. Eben Brocklehurst (Potteries) came in tonight. He said that he had not been to Sheldon for 13 or 14 years. The men found 5 hens worried with something on moor. Thos. Wm. Brocklehurst has had some worried.

Oct. 31st   The men have been getting potatoes on moor. Our girls and Kate and Ruth went to Castle Hill (Mr. Payne Galway's) to tea. Quite a number of the Red Cross members were there. Mr. Sherlock held a confirmation class and there was a Managers meeting afterwards. Mr. Collins called here. Ethel paid James Goodwin 2. 4d. for Wm. Gould's club money. Polly Roberts stayed with me while our girls were away.

Nov. 1st   A very nice day today. Our men have finished getting potatoes today. We have a fine lot. Thos Wm Brocklehurst has had 11 pullets killed today. Some people think a fox is about. It is getting a very serious matter. Thos. Wm. has had above 20 killed this week or two. Sent for a bag of coke (8d) for church.

Nov. 2nd   Youlgreave Wakes Sunday. Holy Communion at half past nine in Sheldon Church. Mr. Sherlock officiated. Mr. Collins took the service this afternoon. Collection in church (5s. 7d.). A very wet and stormy night. C. Wager stayed here until after ten as it was pouring with rain.

Nov. 3rd   Very windy this morning. Anthony, Mary and Ethel went to Bakewell. Mary and Ethel had two teeth each extracted at MacDonalds. Elias Oldfield paid Anthony £3.0s.od. for fowls he had some time since. He now owes six shillings. Richard Skidmore came up this afternoon and bought a tup lamb off Anthony for £3 0s. od. Tom and Wm. went to Sterndale for lime. Brought 38 cwt which cost £1 7s. 10d. This lime is for repairing meres[1] for us. Tony and Wilf Goodwin began turnip cutting.

Nov. 5th   The late Sarah Shimwell's sale (Rowsley). Our Anthony went. Emily Haywood and our Emily came back from Compstall (from Jack's). A good bonfire was lit at Sheldon and the young ones had roasted potatoes. Our Tom, Tony and Wilf Goodwin on moor. Wm. Gould carting clay from near Birchill.

Nov. 6th   Rather dull today. A meeting of the *Women's Sewing Party* was held in Sheldon schoolroom and it was decided to have a *Social* in a fortnight.

---

1   A mere is a specially constructed shallow pond in a field for watering sheep and cattle.

Nov. 7th A very nice day today. Anthony, Tom, Tony and Wilf Goodwin are pulling and pitting turnips on moor. They have made 18 pits. Mr. Hartopp[1], Mr. Robertson and Mr. Twelves called today and had lunch. The old hunting man came and had bread and cheese. Mr. Sherlock and Mr. Collins came up to school as confirmation class was held.

Nov. 9th Anthony's birthday (50). A very nice day. Mr. Sherlock took the service in church. Anthony, Tom and the girls went to church. Tony and I stayed at home. C. Wager came. Tom, Tony and three of our girls went to Monyash church tonight (Wakes). Ethel and Evelyn took Emily in Mrs. Ed's chair.

Nov. 10th A very misty and wet day. Anthony took the milk and afterwards went to the Board of Guardians. Tony met C. Gould with the two cows that Anthony sold him last week. He gave Tony a cheque for £40. Wm. fetched coal for us and afterwards went for coke for the church. The girls went to Ashford.

Nov. 11th Very stormy at times today. Anthony, Tom, Tony and Wilf Goodwin in turnips on moor. Wm. Gould fetching clay. Took R. Bramwell half a load of potatoes and Edwin Smith half a load. Mary, Ethel, Evelyn, Tony and Kate and Ruth Brocklehurst went to Bakewell. The girls went to Castle Hill (nursing lessons) and Tony was measured at Mr. Hills for a new suit (1st long trousers). Mary took a tray cloth and a loaf of bread and Ethel three tea cakes (plain) to the Town Hall ready for the show. Miss Hallam sent some of the children's work.

Nov. 12th Another wet and windy day. Mr. Ronston[2] came and was paid up for beer and brandy that Anthony had to fetch and the ordinary bill. These three bills amounted to £7 9s. od. when the discount had been taken off. Our men are not able to do anything on the land as it is so very stormy. I began knitting a scarf for soldiers.

Nov. 13th Tony's birthday (16). Wet. Mr. Ronston came and was paid up also Harold Hanley and he was paid. Walter Beswick's wife died (childbirth).

Nov. 14th Rough today. Hail storm etc. Mr. Sherlock called and had tea. Mr. Collins called. A confirmation class was held in the schoolroom. Mary went to the Chrysanthemum show (Bakewell).

Nov. 16th Rough and showery. Mr. Sherlock took the service in church. Wm. Naylor found eleven of his fowls killed. People think it is a fox. It is a pity that it cannot be caught. C. Wager came tonight.

Nov. 17th Bakewell fair. Rough winds. Mary went to Buxton to have her teeth attended to. Anthony bought a young mare coming three for £20. 0. 0.

---

1 Mr. Hartopp was the Chatsworth agent of the Duke of Devonshire
2 Mr. Ronston was the traveller for Ormes, the grocers at Bakewell.

and a crown returned. Mr. Brocklehurst (uncle) taken poorly in our house with diarrhoea.

Nov. 18th A very wet rough day. Mary was to have gone again to Buxton but it was too stormy. Mary and Evelyn were up at school practising for social on Thursday next.

Nov. 19th Not as rough as yesterday. Mary went to Buxton and came back with her teeth. She had three put on at a charge of £1 11s. 6d. All the girls went up to school at night practising for social. Tom went as well.

Nov. 20th Very wet and rough. Wm. Gould and our Tony are leading turnips home from moor. A social was held at the schoolroom. Mr. Skidmore and son brought a Gramophone and a most enjoyable evening was spent. There was singing, dancing, recitations and selections played (Gramophone). Mrs. Ed. Brocklehurst and I stayed until 20 minutes to twelve o'clock (too late). 7s.11d. profit.

Nov. 21st Very wet. Anthony and Wm. Naylor started by 1st train to Belper where Mr. Sneap met them. Naylor took four cheeses to Mr. Sneaps and then went forward to Langley Mill to see Harry Buxton. Evelyn paid 13s. 1d. for cheese (to Aunt Lizzie). Anthony came home tonight. He bought from Mr. Sneap a young filly coming two years for £18.0.0. He did not bring it with him.

Nov. 22nd Brighter day today, rather frosty. Men on moor cutting turnips. Wm. Gould and our Tony are carting them home. Young Thorpe from Ashford (chickens) bought two young pigs from Anthony (£1 6s. 0d. each). Lord Henry[1] spoke at Monyash.

Nov. 23rd A brighter day. Mr. Sherlock took the service in church. Not warm. I do not know whether Edwin Smith understands the new heating apparatus, but people complained of the cold. C. Wager came tonight.

Nov. 24th Rather cold and a bit frosty. Tom went with the milk this morning. Anthony took 6 tup lambs and 2 ewes to market and sold them for £2 11s. 0d. each (the tups) and £1 16s. 6d. each for the old ewes. Tom went to Alport for oatmeal and bought a cockerel. Tony and Wm. Gould carting turnips home from moor.

Nov. 25th Mrs. Fred Wilson (Bakewell) called here and had tea with me also J. Hicks. Wm. Naylor arrived home from his visit to H. Buxton (Langley Mill). Mr. Sherlock and Mr. Collins came up to church as there was a Baptism. Robert Bramwell's baby boy (Robert James). The girls did not go to Castle Hill tonight (nursing lessons).

Nov. 26th A very nice day today. Wm. Gould carting clay. Anthony fetched the young filly from Bakewell station which he had bought from Mr. Sneap. Mr. Knight called here. Tony and Wilf Goodwin finishing pulling swedes on

---

[1]   Lord Henry Cavendish

moor. Now the swedes are finished, there are 50 pits (on moor) and 17 loads have been brought home.

Nov. 27th A nice day today. Anthony, Tony and Wilf Goodwin spreading lime on moor this morning. Tom carting stone and gravel from Magpie[1] for meres. Wm. Gould carting clay. Tony and Wilf Goodwin picking potatoes this afternoon (to sell) some going bad.

Nov. 28th Rather drizzly today. Mr. Sherlock and Mr. Collins came up tonight. Mr. Collins had tea here. A confirmation class was held in the schoolroom. Mr. Sherlock left his watch there and our Tony brought it home. We decided to send it by Uncle Will Brockley.

Nov. 29th Close and warm and rather fine. The hunters turned out at the Rookery, some of them called here. Old Mr. Knight came and had tea. Mr. Collins called here over Mr. Sherlock's watch but we had sent it by uncle Will and he broke the glass by pressing a milk churn against it.

Nov. 30th The last day of the month. Very close and drizzly. Mr. Collins took the service in church. Wm. Bramwell's baby christened by Mr. May (Monyash) (a girl). Mr. Fred Roper and his wife were here. C. Wager came.

Dec. 1st Anthony went to Bakewell market and afterwards called to pay the rent at Ashford. He told Mr. Hartopp how he would like the Hollow Piece mere doing up.

Dec. 3rd Very rough winds. Tom and Gould were carting clay this morning and Tom went to fetch the gelt from Isaac Shimwell's. Anthony lent Andrew Maltby (overlooker at Magpie[1]) an old plan of the mine where the bodies of the men who were smothered years ago were found.[2]

Dec. 5th Very winterly. Thunder and lightning snow etc. Andrew Maltby brought the plan back. The men's club held a dance in schoolroom, about 20 present. The sum of 5s. 3d. was taken at the door. James Goodwin and E. Smith were paid 5 shillings and two half gallon of beer were bought for them so there was not enough money taken for expenses. Our Mary and Emily did not go to the dance but Tom, Tony, Ethel and Evelyn went. A confirmation class was held in schoolroom before the dance. Mr. Sherlock came.

Dec. 6th A very dull day today, rather drizzly. J. Goodwin came for potatoes. Our Mary had a postcard from Mr. P. Galway asking that the members of V.A.D. should go on Tuesday next to Bakewell to parade.

Dec. 7th Dull. Holy Communion in Sheldon church at 9.30. 9 present. Mr. Sherlock celebrated and also took the service in afternoon (collection

---

1 The Magpie lead mine
2 In 1833 the Red Soil murders took place where two rival groups of miners at the adjacent Magpie and Red Soil lead mines disputed territory underground and lit fires of straw and oil to smoke each other out. Three men died. At Derby Assizes in 1834 the Magpie miners were acquitted.

7s. 1d.). The banns of marriage between G. Eaton and Elsie Brocklehurst were published. C. Wager came. He had been shot in the face and shoulder yesterday. Dr. Fentem took pellets out of his shoulder but did not take the ones out of his face. Our Tony had his first long trousers made by Mr. Hill, Bakewell.

Dec. 8th Anthony took milk and afterwards went to Bakewell Board of Guardians. Our girls went to Ashford Hall for lessons. Sister Francis was instructing.

Dec. 9th Rough and wet. Tom took Mary, Ethel, Evelyn and Kate and Ruth Brocklehurst dressed in full uniform (nurses) to Castle Hill. There were 42 members of the Red Cross. Marched from there down to the Square in Bakewell. The Queen stopped her car at the drinking fountain bottom of Station road and the Duchess of Devonshire introduced Mrs. Payne Galway (commandant) to her Majesty. The nurses got very wet and Mrs. Lees (Ashford Hall) advised our girls to take off their dresses which they did.

Dec. 10th Mr. Herbert Frost's youngest son (Isaac) was found dead in bed this morning. This child had suffered with eczema since it was a month or two old (some say since vaccination). Mr. Frost had taken some cocoa for Mrs. Frost who was in bed with the little one and she gave it a drink about half past six and its mother found it dead just after seven after Mr. Herbert had gone to Leek. The Dr. (Tom Fentem) was fetched and he told them to let a policeman know (no inquest).

Dec. 11th Dull and cold this morning. The Queen who is at Chatsworth passed through Ashford this morning on her way to Lyme Hall, Lord Newton's place. Ethel and Evelyn took Emily in Mrs. Ed Brocklehurst's chair to Ashford where they had a good view of her Majesty as she passed in motor. Our Emily says the Queen is the nicest lady she has seen. Some schoolchildren helped Emily back home. Our Tom, Wm. and Uncle John Brocklehurst are fetching clay for our mere. They saw the Queen.

Dec. 12th Dull and cold. Our Tony with other candidates for confirmation went to Ashford Church tonight when Mr. Sherlock informed them how to proceed tomorrow. Dr. Jackson was fetched to Aunt Louisa (pleurisy).

Dec. 13th Mr. Herbert Frost's child was buried today. Confirmation by Bishop of Derby at Ashford Church. Our Tony, George Brocklehurst, Elizabeth Ann Brocklehurst, Gertrude Brocklehurst, Edith Goodwin, Doris Brocklehurst, Alice Brocklehurst, Hilda Carson, Gladys Brocklehurst were the candidates from Sheldon.

Dec. 14th Our Ethel's birthday (21). She has had a few nice presents. Tom Oldfield (Youlgreave) came to Sheldon today and told me that Jim Needham (Matlock) was dead (last Thursday). Mr. Sherlock took the service in church. He walked from Ashford and was quite fatigued. Three men from Sheffield came and had dinner.

Dec. 16th Ethel held her birthday party. There were 18 sat down to tea and they passed the evening in singing, recitations etc. Mr. Collins called here (Pheasants arrived from hunt).

Dec. 17th Superintendent Lakin and Mr. Wood (Rutland) called to ask if we had heard anything of a lost pony (Mr. Tinsley's). Monyash policeman also called for the same purpose. Mr. Sherlock called and had tea. There was a Managers meeting in shoolroom. Our girls and Kate and Ruth Brocklehurst went to Castle Hill (nursing lessons). Mrs. Collins had a baby boy.

Dec. 18th Rather dull. Wm. Gould carting clay. Tom and Tony, Wilf Goodwin spreading lime on moor. An examination for members of Red Cross at Ashford Hall. Dr. Jackson examined. Our girls and Kate and Ruth went. They were difficult questions. Mr. Tinsley's pony was taken to the Rookery last night, dressed up very gay. Mr. Ed. Brocklehurst had his pig killed (Ben Naylor).

Dec. 19th B. Naylor cut up Ed. B's pig and it weighed 16 stones all but 4 lbs. Mr. Sherlock called here. He held a class for those who had been confirmed. Pheasants for dinner today. Finished loading clay. It has taken about 55 loads of clay in both meres, and about 90 loads of gravel for both meres and two loads of lime. The meres done up are the Bullock Close and Hollow Pike.

Dec. 21st A very nice day today. All at our house went to church this afternoon. Mr. Sherlock preached. Elsie Brocklehurst was there and heard her own banns published for the last time. C. Wager came.

Dec. 22nd Rather dull but fine. Anthony went with milk and afterwards to Bakewell to attend the Farmers' Club dinner. Tom and Wm. leading manure (28 loads to 1st Hicks field). Tony and Wilf Goodwin picking potatoes etc.

Dec. 24th Cold and a bit of sleet. Elsie Brocklehurst and George Eaton were married this afternoon at Sheldon. Mr. Sherlock performed the ceremony. Her father gave her away and Anthony, Leah and Alice walked. Mr. Collins was there. All our children went to tea at night. Thos. Wm. Brocklehurst had 18 pullets and a cockerel worried by a fox, and Mr. Sheldon had one killed and two missing this morning. We received a turkey from Mr. Sneap (none from Orme's at present).

Dec. 25th Xmas Day. Holy Communion (collection 7s. 3d.). Mr. Sherlock administered but by some mischance he overlooked Mrs. Ed. Brocklehurst who had gone to receive the Sacrament. There were about 20 communicants. Those who had been confirmed on Dec. 13th last were there (our Tony was one for 1st time). The Xmas singers went round singing.

Dec. 27th Rather fine today. Wm. Gould, Alf Wildgoose and Sam Wilton also two of Carsons girls and Wm. Carson went to see *Cinderella* at Buxton. Goodwins had half a load of potatoes.

Dec. 28th Winterly this morning. A sprinkling of snow. Anthony took the milk but he is not at all well. His hand goes so numb. His cold seems a little better. He traced the fox down the dale, and also down our fields. Some other men were also on the look out but could not catch him. Mr. Sherlock took the service in church.

Dec. 30th Very winterly and sharp. Plenty of snow. Anthony took the milk this morning. Tony has a severe cold. We had the turkey that came from Orme's. A tea and dance up at school. Mrs. Bramwell and our Mary assisted by Kate Brocklehurst had trays.

Dec. 31st Fox caught in Shacklow Wood. The last day of the year. Very winterly with snow and frost, but there was a bit of nice sunshine at intervals. A good party of men went out fox hunting at about half past ten this morning. There were about 30 or 40 including 14 guns. Some from Sheldon, Ashford, Taddington and Clement Wager from Longstone. Anthony, Thos. Wm. Brocklehurst, John Frost, C. Wager, John Flewitt jun, Wm. Twelves, Alf Brocklehurst etc. were some of the guns and it was shot by C. Wager at the end of Shacklow nearest Aubreys. It was a vixen fox and there was another put up but it got away. After hunting in Shacklow they came and had something to drink and afterwards went to Bole Hill and Magshaw where a fox was traced but they did not get that. Mr. Spencer (Haddon Grove) came over to our house to say that one had been traced. Eight or 9 hens had been killed by one of the vermin at Haddon Grove. A merry party in tonight. Wm. Naylor took off to Ashford instead of fox hunting.

The Diaries of Maria Gyte 1913 – 1920

1914

Jan. 1st   Very cold and winterly. Anthony took fox to Wm. Twelves. Our Tom's birthday (25). Ben Naylor killed a hog pig this afternoon for us. Two christenings at Sheldon Church (Mr. Sherlock) Sarah Brocklehurst's baby boy and Bertha Bramwell's baby girl.Our Tom stood godfather to Sarah Brocklehurst's boy Thos. William, and our Mary stood godmother to Bertha Brocklehurst's girl (Clarice Ann). Tom went to Chelmorton social tonight.

Jan. 2nd   Most of the snow has gone and it is still thawing. I was taken in my chair to look at the pigs, the one killed yesterday and others. Ben Naylor came and cut up the pig which weighed 23 stones.

Jan. 3rd   A postcard came this morning (from Miss Cross) to say that all our girls had passed in the recent examination (Red Cross). Kate and Ruth Brocklehurst also had word that they both had passed. Our Tom stoked the fire at church as Mr. Smith had gone to Monyash.

Jan. 4th   Holy Communion in Sheldon Church. Mr. Sherlock administered. Mr. Collins took the service this afternoon. Collection in church 5s. 8d.

Jan. 5th   A very nice morning. Anthony went with the milk and afterwards to the Board of Guardians (the Duke of Devonshire was there). Ethel and Evelyn, and Kate and Ruth Brocklehurst are gone to Matlock to a competition which is being taken part in by members of the Red Cross by different contingents in Derbyshire, at Rock Side Hydro (Dr. Marie Orme). The girls got back just before 10 o'clock tonight having missed one train and almost got too late for the last owing to them going to the picture palace. Evelyn got a prize (invalids feeding cup). 5 prizes for Bakewell contingent.

Jan. 6th   Some fresh snow fallen this morning. Thos. Wm. Brocklehurst traced a fox from his land at Kirkdale to Mr. Sheldon's hencotes. A fox had been on this track before when Thos. Wm. had 18 pullets and a cock killed. Men with guns and beaters went out this afternoon to have a fox hunt. In about two hours they came back with a dog fox having been successful in finding his lair which was under a rock in Shacklow and very near where they shot the vixen last week. When seen the fox was sitting on the rock and John Frost shot at him and wounded him and our Tom and Alf Brocklehurst shot and hit him and John Frost shot again and I think that finished him. Our Tom and Alf Brocklehurst tossed up for his carcase. Our Tom won and he has taken possession.

Jan. 7th   A very keen winter's day. Anthony and Tom have been very busy skinning the fox. I have been very bad this day or two with Rheumatism in my eyes. Mr. Knight the old hunting man came in today.

Jan. 8th   A mild day today. Mr. Fred Hall came for Orme and Co. instead of Mr. Ronston (who is ill with Influenza). Paid him up to date. Harold Hawley came and was paid. Mr. Archer sent cheque. We also received 5 shillings from Smedley and Mellor. Mr. Sherlock came and had tea here.

Jan. 9th   Very mild but drizzly. Anthony and Tom gone ploughing on moor. The members of the Sheldon church choir went to Ashford where a supper was provided for Ashford Church choir and Sheldon Church choir in the school room. The following went from Sheldon: Our Mary, Ethel, Evelyn and Tony, Kate and Ruth Brocklehurst, James Frost, Clarice Brocklehurst and Elsie Goodwin. Sent milk bill to Mr. Archer (£18.17.3.).

Jan. 10th   A very wet drizzly day. Mr. Ed. Brocklehurst put hymn board up in Sheldon Church. This hymn board was presented by Miss Grover (Ashford) for Xmas day (1913). Anthony began giving corn to the sheep.

Jan. 11th   Very cold today. Mr. Sherlock took the service in Sheldon Church. Our Mary went to Longstone after service to tea (Mr. Wager's). Aunt Lizzie's birthday today.

Jan. 12th   Very frosty and cold today. Anthony went to Bakewell and saw Dr. Knox about his arm. He gave him some liniment to rub it with. Clement Wager, Miss Wager and our Mary went to Buxton to a furniture sale. Clem bought a lot of furniture (very reasonable) which cost 30 pounds. They got back by the last train after a very busy day. Tom fetched his Aunt Hannah from Middleton.

Jan. 14th   Cold and dull. Mr. Collins came here with letter from Education authority (over Wm. H. Brocklehurst's letter to them over children) and with money for Gisborne's[1] charity (Flannel). This flannel was distributed amongst those entitled at 8 o'clock tonight by our Anthony (senr.) and T.W. Brocklehurst.

Jan. 16th   Very dull and cold. Mrs. Morton's party tonight. Tom and Wm. gone ploughing on moor. Anthony went on moor this afternoon for hay. All our children went to Mrs. Morton's party and each one had a present. I think everyone enjoyed themselves, and stayed until twelve or one o'clock.

Jan. 18th   Very cold. Evelyn has got a bad cough and has had no sleep for a night or two, so she stayed away from church today. Anthony and the others went. Mr. Sherlock took the service. A baptism, Rebecca Ward's baby (Ida). It ought to have been called Ida Carson but Mr. Sherlock left out *Carson*.

---

1   The Revd. Francis Gisborne, a former Rector of Staveley, left money for the provision of flannel for the poor of a number of Derbyshire villages including Sheldon.

Jan. 19th Bitterly cold. Anthony went with milk and afterwards to Bakewell. Tom and Tony were picking potatoes for sale. Anthony paid Mr. Hill for Tony's clothes (long trousers) and Tom's knickers. He also paid for Trap licence (Mr. Gratton) and filled up papers for dog exemption. Billy Naylor sold his sow to H.J. Nelson for £11.0.0. with half a crown returned.

Jan. 21st Rather warmer. T. Hawley called for Wm.'s Insurance card. Anthony filled Beatrice Wildgoose's card and sent it to London. John Brocklehurst went for coke for Sheldon Church which cost 9/-. C. Wager came and brought rabbits.

Jan. 25th Cold and drizzly and very windy. Mr. Sneap and Anthony went on moor. Quite a gloom was cast over Sheldon this afternoon by the death of Mrs. Goodwin who was confined about 2 o'clock and died about three. This was her 16th child (a boy) and both mother and child died. Dr. Tom Fentem was with her when she died and had been three or four hours but could not save her. Mr. Collins took the service in church which was cold. I do not know whether Wm. Smith attends to the fire very well. C. Wager came.

Jan. 27th Wm. Naylor brought us a cheese (19lbs). I did not pay him. Poor Nelly Goodwin was buried today. A large funeral. A strange clergyman read burial service.

Feb. 1st Rough winds but mild. Holy Communion in Sheldon Church. Mr. Sherlock administered (9.30 time). Collection 1s. 9d. Mr. Collins took service this afternoon collection 7s. 2d. C. Wager came. Anthony went to bed after dinner. He is not at all well, cold, indigestion etc.

Feb. 3rd A lovely day today. Dr. Philip and Dr. Tom Fentem came to Wm. Henry Brocklehurst's little boy (Willie) who is very ill (jaundice). Sam Wilton also went again to the Dr. tonight for him. The little lad had been very sick and vomited such dark coloured stuff.

Feb. 4th A very nice day sunshine but rather cold. Little Willie Brocklehurst died at a quarter to five this morning (aged 2 years). Tom, Wm. Gould and Wilf Goodwin spreading lime on moor.

Feb. 5th Another very nice day. Mr. Ronston came and was paid up. Anthony had called (between his dates of coming) at the shop and bought a box of cigarettes which he paid for. Mr. Knight (the old hunting man) came and had refreshments. He was hurt about a fortnight since by falling from among the shrubs at Castle Hill into the road beneath (at after 11 o'clock at night). His shoulder and hand were injured. Miss Grover called with magazines. Received milk and cheese from Mr. Archer.

Feb. 6th Rather cold today but a nice day. Wm. Naylor is digging little Willie Brocklehurst's grave as Edwin Smith is at Manchester. His sister died and was buried last Tuesday. Mr. Smith has not come back yet.

Feb. 7th   A wet and windy day. Little Wm. Henry Brocklehurst was buried this afternoon. Mr. Sherlock came here. He got B. Wildgoose's Exemption certificate card and Anthony sent the number to the Insurance Commissioners (London). Anthony lit the fire at the Church but it took him a long time as the wind blew the smoke downwards. E. Smith has not returned yet. Mr. Sherlock said that he ought to get someone to perform his duties when he goes away.

Feb. 8th   A nice day today. Mr. Sherlock took service in Church. The banns of marriage between Lewis Edward Elliott and Hannah Ward (Earl Sterndale) were called out for the first time. We heard tonight that Dr. Knox of Bakewell was dead. He died very suddenly this morning. We shall miss him as he has been our Doctor for many years. All the time Anthony and I have been married (27 years) and in Anthony's father's and mother's time as well.

Feb. 10th Very nice weather for the time of year. Re-assembling of Parliament. I should think there will be some heated debates what with Home Rule, Welsh Disestablishment etc.

Feb. 11th After a very rough night comes a very lovely day today. Sunshine and calm. Dr. Knox buried at Bakewell. Mary and Ethel are gone to Rowland today to have a look at Mary's future home (on marriage). Broughton's traveller called. I bought some towelling. Tom finished ploughing the Upper Green Sir (6 ac. 3 roods 9 perches). Alf Brocklehurst had two lambs (1st in Sheldon).

Feb. 12th Very rough today. Cecil Twigg called here. I heard that there were 22 cases of scarlet fever in Ashford.

Feb. 14th Valentine's Day. Very rough and wet. Kate Brocklehurst held her birthday party tonight. She was 21 years old on Feb. 9th last. Willie Needham (Hasland) came. He is very tall and thin. All our children went to the party. Sam Rowland brought his Gramophone in our house tonight. It is the best I have ever seen. A good many came in.

Feb. 15th Rough today. Our Mary is in bed with influenza. She could not go to church so Evelyn took the organ which was her first attempt at playing in Church. She managed very well. Mary came down a bit at night. C. Wager came. Mr. Sherlock took the service.

Feb. 22nd During last night there was a great downfall of rain and the wind was very rough but it is calmer this morning. Evelyn played the organ in Church this afternoon as Mary is in bed. Mr. Sherlock took the service. The third time of asking between Lewis Edward Elliott and Hannah Ward. Our Mary came down a bit tonight. C. Wager came.

Feb. 26th A very fine day, plenty of sunshine in morning. Our Tom came back tonight. He went to the London shire horse show yesterday. Anthony fetched the Church harmonium to our house and put it before the fire as the notes stick. Our Mary is a little better. Mr. Frank Cox-Wilson's men are putting bricks in Mr. B. Morton's grave ready for the monument which is to arrive. Mr. Collins left Ashford.

Feb. 28th The last of February. It has been a very fine month. A full house tonight. Wm. Arthur Haslam came from Bakewell, plenty of singing with one or another. Mr. Potts and Mr. E. Smith are working at Mr. B. Morton's grave. Alfred Fawkes called here. I refused him more drink. C. Wager came.

March 1st A lovely day. Celebration of Holy Communion. Mr. Sherlock came. He also came for the afternoon service. Collection 10 shillings. Anthony went to Church. C. Wager came.

March 3rd Rather wet today. Mr. Collier the new lay reader called here this afternoon. Ethel, Kate and Ruth Brocklehurst and Beatrice Wildgoose went to Longstone Schoolroom to attend a series of nursing lessons given by Dr. Marie Orme. The same four girls went last Tuesday night.

March 4th Hannah is busy cutting out Mary's wedding dress. She has made three, Emily's, Ethel's and Evelyn's. She has to make Clarice's. Wet today. Our Ethel has got influenza. Tony set two hens.

March 5th Very wet today. Ethel seems better. Mr. Ronston came and was paid up by cheque (£6 7s. 0d.). Mr. Collier took the service tonight in Sheldon Church, at seven o'clock. Evelyn played. Sheep brought in tonight.

March 8th Rather misty and wet this morning but turns out better this afternoon. Mr. Sherlock took the service in Church this afternoon. C. Wager came.

March 10th Frosty this morning. Snowing a little at intervals. Mr. Archer sent cheque for milk (to Feb 14). Mr. Hartopp's letter came saying Anthony could have 4 bags of cement. Two more lambs tonight. Men from Manchester finished putting up the late Mr. B. Morton's monument.

March 14th Rather rough and showery. Miss Grover sent patterns of matting. She is going to give matting to go down aisle in Sheldon Church and in vestry etc. A good few in the house tonight. Tom went to be measured for a new suit (Mr. Hills). Mr. Wm. Bramwell (Monyash) paid for some turnips.

March 15th Rather showery today. Mr. Sherlock took the service in Church. Chose matting for Church. A sheep lambed two lambs. E. Naylor gave Mary a piano cover.

March 18th A rough winter's morning, snow etc. Clears up and is quite a fine afternoon. Polly Naylor is helping our girls to colour-wash the kitchen. Captain Collier called this morning before I was up. Mrs. Ed. came in this afternoon. Wm. Gould fetched coal for us (16/6 per ton).

March 20th Very misty this morning. Our Mary has gone to Derby with C. Wager to buy several things for their wedding.

March 22nd Mr. Sherlock took the service in Sheldon Church this afternoon. Very hot in Church.

March 24th Nice bright morning. Anthony went with milk and then round by Bakewell for a paper for parlour. Ethel and Evelyn went to Bakewell. They got two very nice hats and I will write for two more like them.

March 25th Lady Day. Sent a letter to Mrs. Stewart ordering two more hats. Neddy Smith swept parlour chimney after keeping us waiting above half a day.

March 27th Snow showers this morning but turns out a nice day. Our Mary received 12 dinner plates from Alf and Jenny Brocklehurst and 2 basins and a soap dish from Mr. Wm. Brocklehurst (uncle). The sow farrowed tonight (10). Anthony sat up until half-past one.

March 28th Mary and Ethel went to Bakewell and got some more useful household things. They also got two more hats for the wedding. A good many in tonight. We had selections on S. Rowland's gramophone. One pig was found dead this morning.

March 29th Wet. Our Mary's and Clem's banns were published for the 1st time. Mr. Sherlock took the service. Our little pigs are all nearly dead. The old sow has clammed[1] them and still she has milk. Our girls and Tony have tried all they can to get them to suck but the little pigs are too weak.

April 4th Looks rather like rain but none comes. Received egg money from W. Kitson. I went out in my chair to Church gates. A full house tonight, singing etc. Mr. Ed. Brockley went to Youlgreave (club) and Alport. Miss Grover came with magazines and in this magazine it said that the collections taken in Sheldon Church on Easter Sunday would be taken towards paying the lay reader. The Churchwardens were not informed of this and were not so pleased as we do not know whether we shall be able to find the money for our ordinary Church expenses.

April 5th A strange clergyman took the service in Sheldon Church this afternoon. All from our house went to Church besides Tony and myself and I was very bad with pains in my left ear and throat. Tony kept applying hot handkerchiefs to the place.

April 6th Anthony went to Bakewell. Brought his own and Tom's new suits of clothes (Hills) and paid for them (£6.10.0.) £3.10.0. for his own. Very severe storms today. Thunder and lightning and hail. Presents came from Uncle T.W. Brocklehurst and a lamp from Evelyn and Tony. T.W. Brocklehurst received £1.0.0. from the Duke of Devonshire for Sheldon Church (Anthony changed the postal order).

1   Clammed: withheld the milk

April 7th Mary went to Bakewell this afternoon, got caught in hail and rain but sheltered in Balston's hayshed. She brought my hat from Stewarts but Evelyn's shoes were not come in. Anthony, Thos. Wm. and John B. went to the Duke's short horn sale (Chatsworth). Received a letter from Mr. Sherlock in which was a cheque for £5.0.0. which he had received from the Duke of Devonshire for Sheldon School. Mary took this to the bank and Sheldon Church bank book to be balanced up.

April 10th Good Friday Wet and cold. Mr. Collier took the service in church. Mary getting things ready for her wedding. Sarah Brocklehurst and Jenny, Alf's wife, have been very kind in helping Mary with baking etc. A great procession at Ashford (Church people).

April 11th Rather fine and more mild today. Anthony brought matting etc. for the Church (Sheldon) from Miss Grover. Miss Grover and her sister gave our Mary a very nice biscuit barrel. The eldest of them came up and had some tea this afternoon. Boiled ham and tongues, 2 hams and 3 tongues (Aunt Louisa boiled one tongue).

April 12th Rather windy and cold. Mr. Sherlock administered Holy Communion in Sheldon Church at half past nine this morning and published our Mary's banns for third time. Mr. Collier took the service in Church. Collection 18s. 9d. which was taken towards lay reader's stipend.

April 13th A very fine day, rather windy but plenty of sun. Our Mary's and Clement Wager's wedding day. There were a many people in Sheldon and in Church to see the wedding at 2 o'clock. The carriages (two of C. Critchlow's) each with a pair of horses (white ear caps and whips tied up with white) brought Clem and his brothers, sister and sister in law (Albert's wife came) and Harry Trickett. The brothers of Clem who came were Jasper, Wm., Albert, Tom and Jim and Miss Wager. Our Mary and the four bridesmaids carried a lovely bouquet each, Mary's all white. The others with coloured flowers and white ones. They all looked very well indeed and were afterwards photographed by Sam Kitson. The tea was set out in Sheldon Schoolroom and looked grand. 2 hams, 3 tongues, jellies, custards, and tinned fruits, cake etc. A dance was afterwards kept up into after twelve o'clock when the carriages came and took the bride and bridegroom to their own home. (One of the drivers was the worse for drink and Wm. Wager drove one back to Longstone.) Mary had a beautiful lot of presents. Wm. Gould and Tom shifted a cabin for S. Rowland.

April 14th Another lovely day. Steeplechase on Flagg Moor. A many people came through Sheldon. Jasper, Wm. and Albert Wager called and had something to eat, also Wm. Holmes. Tom and Tony went to the races (1st time going).

April 15th Vestry meeting in Church. Only three present. Mr. Sherlock, Anthony and Thos. Wm. Brocklehurst. The old ones were nominated. (Paid J. Goodwin 5s. 0d. for playing at wedding). Sent cheque to T.H. Howard (13s. 3d.) and one to our Mary (£1.19.0) for organ playing in Church. 7

shillings in hand in Church accounts. Finished sowing Bole Piece and harrowed it once.

April 17th Plenty of sun but the cold east winds are very frequent these last few days. Mr. Collier called here and Hannah, Mrs. Ed. and I had quite a long conversation with him. Anthony paid him £18.18s. 9d. taken at the Easter Sunday collection. Sam Rowland's ferret got out and was let out of his box and it killed 8 hens and 77 chickens belonging to Billy Naylor. Monyash policeman called them (Naylors) up between two and three this morning. The policeman's dog killed the ferret. Naylors also had a year old calf hung. Found out afterwards it had speed.[1]

April 19th Lovely weather continues. Five Sheffield people (the old lot) came and had dinner, and a gentleman from Leek had bread and cheese and we had a long conversation. Mr. Sherlock took the service in Church. Our Evelyn played the harmonium. There are a lot more in the choir now. Mary and Clem came over tonight from Rowland.

April 21st Another grand day. Just like summer. Warm and plenty of sunshine. It is 35 years today since I came to live at Sheldon (April 21st, 1879). Finished sowing oats on moor (opposite Red House). Anthony and Emily went with a lot of Mary's things to Rowland tonight. Ethel went as well but she started in afternoon and walked there and afterwards to Longstone (nursing lessons). Ethel and Evelyn cleaned bathroom.

April 26th A lovely day today. Some callers this morning from Bakewell, some looking for lost horses (Critchlows). Mr. Sherlock took the service in Sheldon Church. Ethel and Evelyn took me out in my chair tonight as far as Naylor's. Billy helped me up home again.

April 27th Anthony went with milk and afterwards to market. Tom took two cows to Bakewell. Ben Thompson bought them (£35). Anthony paid the late Dr. Knox's bill to Goodwin and Cockerton (£10.16s.0d.). This bill was for attending our girls for measles last year. Ed. Brocklehurst paid rent (up to March 25th last). J. Goodwin paid for some potatoes (17s. 6d.). Anthony paid Bagshaw a tithe 2s. 8d. (for Mr. Sherlock).

May 2nd Sheldon cricketers went to Biggin and managed to win the game. (Sheldon 54/Biggin 28). Arrived home just before 10 o'clock. Our Tom got 8 runs. Mary and Clem came over tonight.

May 3rd Rather showery today. Holy Communion in Sheldon Church this morning 9.30. A strange clergyman administered (19 present). Capt. Collier took the service this afternoon. Collection (12s. 4d.) for Church expenses. Ethel, Evelyn and Tony went to Rowland tonight. Tom took his Aunt Hannah to Middleton. Six persons came from Sheffield today and had dinner, 4 gentlemen, 2 ladies.

1 Speed: disease affecting young cattle producing fluid in the legs, due to mineral deficiency.

May 7th   Brighter and milder today. Received cheque from Mr. Archer to April 15th 1914. Our Ethel and Kate and Ruth went to Bakewell to Dr. Marie Orme's nursing lessons. Mr. Sherlock came here. There was a Managers' meeting at school. Billy Naylor's mare foaled at about 3 o'clock this morning (colt).

May 8th   Very cold and showery. Thunder at times today. I did not get up until 3 o'clock this afternoon.

May 9th   I think the weather gets colder. A telegram came to Alf Wildgoose saying that the Sheldon cricketers must not go to Chatsworth today as the ground was not fit. A merry party in tonight. J. Goodwin with violin, singing and step dancing with a few of them.

May 10th   Drizzling and cold. Not fit to go to Rowland as I had intended to do. Captain Collier took the service in church.

May 11th   Anthony went with milk and afterwards to Bakewell market. Our Tom also went with a cow of ours. T.W. Brocklehurst took his white bull. Our cow made £16.10.0. Thos. Wm did not sell the bull. Tom had a new pair of Sunday boots and Tony a pair of every day ones.

May 13th   Still cold. Our men are setting potatoes on the moor. Anthony went to Copyhold court (Ashford). Mr. Parton came and was paid by cheque for beer. I also paid him for hop bags (2s. 9d.). Mr. Sherlock came up on horseback, called here.

May 14th   A bright day today. Captain Collier called before I was downstairs. Our men setting potatoes on moor.

May 17th   A lovely day. The sun was very hot. Anthony, Tony and I went to Rowland to see our Mary and Clem. The drive was grand. I have never been to Rowland before. I think it is a pretty little hamlet. It seems very healthy, and very quiet and peaceful. Clem's garden looked very nice. Our girls had visitors for dinner (3 Sheffielders) and for tea 4 strangers! Mr. Collier took the service in Church and the collection was taken for Diocesan purposes. Our milk cows lay out for the 1st time this year at night.

May 21st   A very bright day today. Received photos of our Mary's wedding group. I sent one to Middleton and one to Matilda Brown (Hasland). I also gave one to Sally Brocklehurst, Jenny Brocklehurst and Bertha Bramwell. Also one to Mrs. Ed., Naylors, Clarice B. Some of our men have been gardening and Anthony has been drawing cabbage rows on moor. Unionist Victory for N.E. Derbys here:

Major Harland Bowder	6469 votes
Mr. J.P. Houfton (Liberal)	6155 votes
Mr. J. Martin (Labour)	3669 votes

Polling yesterday.Poll declared (last night) at Markham Hall, Staveley.

Ascension Day   Capt. Collier took service in Sheldon Church. Our Tom took horse and dray and shifted coops for Sam Rowland into Lewis E. Elliott's field. He went with two loads from S. Rowland's place.

May 22nd Rather dull and looks a little like rain. Anthony and Thos. Wm. Brocklehurst went to Derby to buy cabbage plants. They bought 20,000. 8,000 for us. 2,000 for Alf Brocklehurst. Thos. Wm. bought his own, some for his brother John, and some for Carsons. They saw Mr. and Mrs. Sneap at Derby. Got back to Sheldon about 10 o'clock. Wm. Hallows (Sheldon) got hit by a cricket ball and had to go to the Dr. who put three stitches in his face.

May 24th Some rain. All our people went to Church except Tony and I. Captain Collier took the service in Church.

May 25th Billy Naylor's gelt farrowed 9 pigs during the night. Anthony went to the Rural District Councillors meeting at board room. There was voting for a new steam roller but those who voted against won the day. Anthony bought another heifer off George Ardern for £16.0.0. Unionist victory at Ipswich (Polling last Saturday). Our Tom, Tony, Wm. Gould and Wilf Goodwin were on moor setting cabbage plants.

May 26th Quite a frost this morning. Plenty of sun and wind but rather cold. Wm. Gould fetched a drayload of wood from Battery.[1] Anthony and other men on moor setting cabbage plants. Mr. Ronston came today (two days earlier than usual) and was paid up (£5.4s.0d.). A clergyman from Withington came and had lunch. Passed Home Rule in House of Commons (last night). Majority 77. Our Tom went to Hassop Station and brought 8 cwts of stuff for Sam Rowland.

May 28th A nice day today. A bit warmer. I have read in the paper what damage the frost has done to things that are growing, potatoes, kidney beans etc. I had a letter this morning from Miss Grover (Glamorgan). In it she asks me to get some flowers for Sheldon Church for Whitsuntide and saying that she would not be able to be at Ashford owing to the death of her aunt. Our men on moor. They have been breaking in the young horse (Susan) and planting cabbage.

May 29th Wm. fetched two dray loads of old wood from Battery. Mr. Sherlock called and had some conversation about having a night school at Sheldon. He also paid 5d. that Mr. Collins had paid short (for Diocesan collection last year 4s.8d.). T.W. Brocklehurst went for broody hens with Sam Rowland. An awful disaster at sea (River St. Lawrence). *The Empress of Ireland* ship was struck by a collier (ship) and went down in about 10 minutes. There are supposed to be above 1,000 people drowned (about 337 saved).

May 30th Rather dull this morning but turns out a nice day. Sheldon cricketers went to Chatsworth. All the sheep in Sheldon were washed today

---

[1]   D.P. Battery Co., electric accumulator manufacturers, Bakewell

(Ashford). One of ours had the misfortune to break its leg. Anthony, Ethel and Evelyn set the leg. Received a telegram from John Naylor senior who was playing with Sheldon that the score of Sheldon was 159, Chatsworth 42. A good many in tonight.

May 31st Holy Communion in Sheldon Church at 9.30. Mr. Sherlock administered. Ethel placed the flowers in the vases. These flowers (white narcissi) were bought at Bakewell (3 shillings) and Mrs. B. Morton sent some as well. Two gentlemen from Nottingham stayed at our house all night. No collection this Whit Sunday.

June 1st Whitsun-fair. Anthony and John Brocklehurst bought 3 pigs each from S. Robinson (32s. each). Tom and Tony went to the fair. We made a cheese today and plenty of people kept popping in at intervals. A Managers meeting at school. Mr. Sherlock came up and had tea and stayed until 7 o'clock and had supper then and afterwards went to the Entertainment at school. He sang two songs playing his own accompaniments. The entertainment passed off all right. I went. Captain Collier took the money which was received at the door.

June 3rd A very nice day today. Anthony received a letter from Mr. Sherlock saying that Mr. Beaven[1] (Taddington) would take the night school at Sheldon during the winter months. Anthony finished sowing swedes on moor. Captain Collier called to ask who would take charge of the money taken at the Entertainment for organ fund. I said I would but I should have a separate account from church expenses. (Did not bring the money.)

June 6th Cold. Biggin cricketers came to Sheldon. Sheldon won easily. The scores were: Sheldon 65 Biggin 25 (one bye). Our Tom took 5 wickets for 12 and Wm. H. Brocklehurst bowled 5 out for 12. Our Mary came just after dinner and brought the dog Bob with her for a run. She brought us 4 rabbits. She went back as far as Ashford with milkcart and called at Mr. Daybell's for a box of books which he brought from Hassop station. These books had been lying at the station for nearly a week. These were sent by Mr. Harrison (Sheffield).

June 7th Rather cold and drizzly. Ashford Wakes. Captain Collier took the service in Church (Sheldon) collection 11s. 7d. Anthony went to bed after milking (with headache).

June 8th Cold and gloomy, very little rain comes. A gentleman called here and had bread and cheese, coffee etc. In course of talk it came out that he was County Inspector of Schools. We had a very interesting conversation over education matters. A cow calved (bull calf).

June 9th A very wet day and very cold. I could hear it raining very heavily during last night. Anthony and Tom and Tony are busy getting things ready

1 F.W. Beaven, clerk to Tideswell Pension Sub Commitee, and husband to Catherine Beaven, head teacher of Priestcliffe School.

for another building up back yard. Mr. Collier sent £1 6s. 3d. by Fred Brocklehurst (proceeds of the Entertainment Whit Monday). S. Furniss (Ashford) who had been wrecked on the *Empress of Ireland* landed at Ashford. He had been to Canada.

June 10th The weather seems very showery and unsettled with thunder and very cold and rough. The sheep that broke its leg at the last sheepwashing was so bad that Anthony shot it, and then it was shorn and had 13 lbs of wool. Uncle John Brocklehurst is helping Anthony to build a place up back yard. A Managers' meeting at school. Mrs. Ed. and I were put on a committee for continuation classes (night school). Mr. Sherlock called here and Captain Collier.

June 11th A very nice day today. Plenty of sun and wind. Tom and Wm. Gould have gone with corn to be thrashed to Flewitts. Also uncle John Brocklehurst, Anthony and Tony have been on moor fastening gates etc. to keep the cattle out of Fallow field - they got in yesterday.

June 12th Rather gloomy but close at times. Anthony and Gould took dray and horses and fetched 4 railway carriage tops from Bakewell station. They had two journeys.

June 13th The sun is very hot today but there is a very rough wind. Dove Holes cricketers came to Sheldon. They came to Longstone Station. Sheldon won. The score was Sheldon 40, Dove Holes 34. Three of the Dove Holes team were a smart lot. They stayed drinking at Ashford and were late at the cricket field. After the match they came here and were very noisy. Ethel stopped the tap on them and one of them put one of our best little knives in his pocket and went off with it.

June 14th Hot sun and rather windy. We all went to church this afternoon. Mr. Sherlock took the service. I had not been for many a week.

June 16th A very nice day but looks a bit like rain. Tom, Wm. and Uncle John B. took corn to Ashford to be threshed. Anthony sold the oats to Mr. Flewitt. Black oats 22 shillings and white oats 23 shillings per quarter. Tom hurt his thumb. Captain Collier called with a paper to be signed (over night school). Mr. Spencer (Haddon Grove) called with a friend. One of the heifers bought off Ardens calved (cow calf).

June 17th Very hot today. Tom, Tony and Wm. went on moor shearing sheep. Tom clipped 10, Tony 5. Anthony took Emily to Rowland. He also took 11 hens and 11 chickens which were Mary's. He went to Bakewell station for artificial manure and then coming back he slipped in float and hurt his arm and leg. Eliza Naylor came up and let me look at her arm which had been bitten or stung with something. (It looks like blood poisoning.)

June 18th Very hot this morning. Anthony went with milk. Tom, Tony and Wm. went on moor shearing sheep. Anthony took the dinner and among them they clipped 21. A thunderstorm came on and they went into cabin whilst the shower lasted. Awfully close yet. Ethel, Ruth and Kate B are gone in uniform to the Town Hall, Bakewell (Red Cross). They had to be there at 2 o'clock prompt.

June 19th Very hot. Tom finished shearing this morning. All the lambs in Sheldon were dipped today. Ethel is very busy baking tarts etc. ready for cricketers tomorrow.

June 20th Very hot this morning but goes cooler this afternoon. Chatsworth cricketers came and Sheldon won. Sheldon got 51, Chatsworth 37. Our Tom bowled 7 out.

June 21st Very hot this morning, but there was a storm this afternoon. Thunder, lightning, hail and rain. Captain Collier took the service in Church.

June 26th Very hot today. Our Mary's birthday (27 years). Anthony bought some strawberries from Elias and T. Ashton. I was picking all afternoon and now we are making jam. Made out bills for cricket club tea. Captain Collier called and wanted to know who provided for choir trip and school treat. The young mare (Mr. Sneap's) was put in float for the first time (went very well). Sowing rape on moor and artificial. A cricket meeting in the parlour tonight.

June 27th A very lovely day. The sun was very hot but there was a nice breeze. There was a cricket match between Sheldon and Monyash played at Sheldon. The scores were Sheldon 40 Monyash 20. Some say that Sheldon made a score of 41 or 42. Our Tom bowled 5 for 8 runs. Wm. Henry Brocklehurst also bowled 5 for 10 runs. There was a full house tonight. Sheldon have played 6 matches this year and won them all. Anthony has given them half a gallon of beer every match, only tonight he gave 1 gallon. Mr. Sneap came tonight.

June 28th A lovely day today. Anthony and Mr. Sneap went on moor. Brought a cow off moor which is going to peck its calf. Mr. Collier took the service in church. Archduke Franz Ferdinand (heir to Habsburg monarchy) assassinated at Sarajevo by Gavrilo Princip.

June 29th Very hot today. Tom was thatching in stack yard the corn that had been fetched off the moor. Tony and W. Goodwin were striking turnips. Anthony and Mr. Sneap went to Bakewell and afterwards Mr. Sneap went home. Anthony bought two pigs (from young Alsopp) for our Mary at 32 shillings each. Evelyn and Tony went to Rowland this afternoon. Young Alsopp took the pigs to Rowland.

June 30th Awfully hot. Received cheque for two milk bills. Anthony went round by Bakewell and banked them. Captain Collier called and said Mr. Sherlock was ill in bed.

July 2nd Very close and sultry this morning. A storm came on after dinner, not as severe as yesterday. Some nice rain fell which would do good.

Tom, Tony and Wm. are on moor striking and weeding turnips etc. Captain Collier called here.

July 3rd　　Colder today. Some nice rain fell and the men had to leave their work on moor and come home. Ethel went to Bakewell for shirts for her father and Tom, also straw hats for Tom and Tony.

July 5th　　Rather dull and looks a little like rain. Mr. Sherlock came up in a motor and officiated at Holy Communion (9.30). Evelyn and Tony went to Church but Ethel stayed away. The service this afternoon was taken by Capt. Collier. The collection amounted to 7s. 8d. for church expenses. Mr. Sherlock took the service at Taddington after he left Sheldon. The ten Nottingham men went back this afternoon.

July 6th　　Anthony went to Bakewell market. A storm came on about six o'clock. Lightning, rain, thunder. Some nice rain fell but did not long continue. Mr. Joseph Chamberlain was buried at Birmingham. He died in London on the 2nd of July.

July 8th　　Rather dull, showery at times (slight). Anthony, Tom, Tony and Wilf Goodwin and Wm. in turnips horse hoeing and earthing potatoes up.

July 11th　　Our men in turnips on moor and Wm. mowed part of Grindlow Knoll. Ethel went to Bakewell tonight and bought shirts for her father and Tony and a hat each for herself and Evelyn.

July 12th　　There was a thunderstorm about half past five o'clock this morning. The rain came down in torrents. Very gloomy afterwards and more rain fell during the afternoon. Captain Collier (C.A.) took the service in church this afternoon. Irish labourer arrived.

July 19th　　Very gloomy. The rain came in torrents between four and five. Our Tony had started to feed the fowls. Got very wet. Mr. Sherlock took the service in Sheldon church this afternoon. Frank Sheldon and another man and two young women came in the house this afternoon. Frank Sheldon years ago lived with Mr. George Furniss as farm lad in this village.

July 21st　　A very good hay day today. Getting hay in Grindlow Knoll and Hick's field. 11 Grindlow 3 Hicks. Captain Collier called. There were a good many people in the house tonight. Harry Doxey came here and he said he had traced a hen of his at Alf Brocklehurst's. 2 hawkers were in (Finney one) and big Jimmy the Irishman. Jimmy had been on the booze.

July 22nd　　Dull this morning but there is plenty of wind and the sun comes out after dinner. Orme's man brought 3 kils[1] ale (I ordered 4 of ale and 2 barrels of beer). The King yesterday summoned 2 out of each party to a conference over the gravity of Home Rule:

　　Lord Lansdowne and Mr. Bonar Law (Unionist)

1　kil: short for kilderkin, a cask holding 16 to 18 gallons

Sir Edward Carson and Captain Craig (Ulster)
Mr. Asquith and Mr. Lloyd George (Liberal)
Mr. John Redmond and Mr. John Dillon

Our men got three loads of hay (Hicks). Wm. mowed Top Hicks field and Plumpton Park. Alf Brockley and Jack Naylor took H. Doxey's hen back. H. Doxey had threatened to send a policeman.

July 26th Very wet today at times. We had mutton and chickens and our own new potatoes today. All our folks except Tony and I went to church. Captain Collier took the service. A party of Sheffielders came in during the church service but did not stay long. Ethel and Evelyn went to Longstone Church tonight. Anthony Regan (Irishman) was paid up tonight and left (not satisfied with food: he wanted meat. He had been drinking at Bakewell.) Mary played organ at Longstone Church.

July 29th Very dull. Not a very good hay day but the men managed to get 3 loads out of Top Hicks field. 5 loads altogether out of this field as two loads were got last week. Mr. Sherlock called here and had tea. He called at several houses.

July 31st I thought we should have had a very nice day today but it is one of the sort we have had for several days. Very gloomy, no sun or wind to do much drying of hay. Anthony is raking with the young mare we had from Mr. Sneap. There were five loads of hay got out of Bramwell field. Wm. Gould mowed the Waterlands. Austria and Serbia at war.

August 2nd Very wet. Holy Communion this morning at 9.30. Mr. Sherlock administered. The vicar also took the afternoon service. Mr. F.J. Cox-Wilson brought him up in his (Mr. Wilson's) conveyance. Collection in Church (10s. 0d.). Mr. Carson came in to see us. (Hurried Cabinet meetings over War.)

August 3rd Very showery at times. Anthony and Tom took the young horse in milk float through Ashford to Bakewell to get it used to motors etc. I believe it went all right after a while. There was a full house tonight. Mr. Bole and Mr. Craven and a man and woman who are staying at Alf Brocklehurst's and a good many Sheldon people. Singing and Dancing etc. Men on Naval reserve called up.

August 4th Rather gloomy at times. Men working in the hay (Waterlands). Wm. mowed Croft heads. Nothing can be talked about but the *war*. This has come on so suddenly. First Austria and Serbia. Then Russia mobilises. This does not please Germany and she invades France before war is declared. England has fought for peace but it is feared that she will have to fight as Germany is proving very aggressive. Sir Edward Grey's speech in paper this morning. Wm. also mowed Little Butts. England declared war on Germany.

August 5th Rather gloomy and showery. All our folks went to the cattle show except Ethel. Government officials were commandeering horses for

War. The Germans are not having it all their own way according to the papers.

August 6th Wet and Drizzly. No hay day. Our Tom has taken oats to Alport Mill. Men were examining the horses in station (Longstone) yard this morning to get them for the war. Quite a number have been taken away from round about Bakewell. I answered a postcard to Mrs. P. Galway. She had sent asking whether our girls would be willing to serve on a V.A.D. either in the United Kingdom or Abroad. We are fixed in a very awkward position at home. I am helpless and all the work in the house has to be done by Ethel and Evelyn so I answered and said that if there was a great necessity for nurses one of the girls would respond if we could get outside help. Kate Brocklehurst answered that one of them should go either in United Kingdom or abroad.

August 7th Rather finer today but at times very gloomy. Our men and Mr. Ed. in hay. Anthony is taking milk every morning and evening for some time as our horses are old and perhaps would not do for war purposes. The Government officials are buying all horses that are fit. A card from Mrs. Payne Galway calling an urgent meeting of members of Red Cross for 5.30 tomorrow. According to the *Sheffield Daily Telegraph* the Germans are suffering reverses. The brave Belgians are repulsing them finely. Mr. Asquith made a grand speech and the Government have voted £100,000,000 for war expenses.

August 8th A thorough wet day today. According to this morning's paper the Belgians repulsed the Germans. The Germans had 25,000 killed and wounded. The Belgians refused to grant 24 hours armistice. Kate Brocklehurst has gone to a meeting at Bakewell (Red Cross). Government officials were on the lookout for suitable horses for war purposes at Bakewell and other places. Anthony went with milk again and also to Bakewell (Orme's) for gin which was sent up and charged 16s. 6d. per gallon. Kate brought word that the members of the Red Cross must be ready when they hear from War Office.

August 9th A most miserable wet day. Four of our people went to church this afternoon. Ethel, Emily and I stayed at home. Captain Collier took the service. Special hymns were sung on account of the war and the National Anthem at the close.

August 10th A good day. Plenty of sun and wind. Anthony took a cow to Bakewell and sold her for £17.10. Tom took the milk, and then the following went into hayfield: Tom, Tony, Wm., Mr. Ed., and Wilf Goodwin. I wrote to Williams for aprons for the girls.

August 13th Very fine and warm. Busy in hayfield. Horses are being bought for war all around Bakewell. Wm. finished Big Butts, Pingle and one of Hick's fields. I went out and was sitting under Mr. Ed.'s trees this afternoon.

August 14th Anthony's and my wedding day (28 years). A very grand day. Got some hay out of Big Butts (8 loads). Miss Grover called with magazines. A good full house tonight. The men like to hear the war news.

August 15th A very misty morning and showery about dinner time. Afterwards brighter and finer. No fresh war news this morning. The men were working a bit in the hay this afternoon. Harry Roper came to sit with me a bit. A full house tonight. Billy Naylor made a speech to the men about defending their country and also promised (if they were short of money for the war) to give a sovereign. The Vino Sacro wine came.

August 16th A lovely day. Plenty of sun and wind. I was taken on the moor in float this morning. Anthony, Tony and Emily went as well. The corn and roots and stock look grand. We have some fine young stock on moor. Everything seems to be doing very well. Tom went to Rowland (on young mare of Sneap's) to see Mary and Clem. Emily, Ethel, Evelyn and Tony went to church this afternoon. There was a collection for the *Prince of Wales* fund which amounted to £1 4s. 0d. Wm. took the milk with our old white mare. There seems to be a great call for horses yet (for war purposes). Anthony has been bad with indigestion this last day or two. Captain Collier took the service in Sheldon Church this afternoon.

August 17th A very heavy dew this morning but turns out a lovely afternoon. Our men got 11 loads of hay out of Big Butts and Pingle and 1st Hicks field. They did not quite finish. Anthony is bad with indigestion. I went and had tea with Mrs. Craven and Mrs. Ed. (under the tree in front of Ed.'s house). It was Mrs. Craven's little daughter's 1st birthday. A meeting was called (over the war) to be held in the school room, but very few were there.

August 18th Rather gloomy at times. Tom and Wilf Goodwin were cleaning out a mere on the moor. Anthony and Tony fetched a small load of hay out of Hicks field so we finished the hay today. Wm. was carting water on moor.

August 19th Fine, but rather gloomy. I was up early this morning. Ethel and Ruth Brocklehurst went to Holme Hall to practise bedmaking, washing invalids in bed etc. Four strangers came in, a man and woman and afterwards 2 men whom I thought were foreigners. The last two ordered tea and bread and cheese and said they would be back in a quarter of an hour or twenty minutes. Everything was got ready for them but the men did not come.

August 21st Rather gloomy but turns out a nice day. Our Mary sent two cockerels out of her lot and one white leghorn from Harry Trickett by her uncle Will from Longstone Station. The Germans occupy Brussels.

August 22nd A fine day. Our Tony and Wm. Gould went for lime ash etc. The Eyam man came for eggs (9 a shilling). Tom went with Sheldon cricketers to Monyash. Sheldon scored 55. Monyash 28. Our Tom bowled 5 out for twelve runs. This is the 7th match won by Sheldon this season. Rained tonight.

August 23rd Early this morning the rain poured down but afterwards gets fair, but gloomy. All our people go to church besides Tony and I. A party of men and women came in tonight. They had some children outside. The women especially seemed a cheeky lot. I did not approve at all of some of their talk. One (alluding to our house) said *This is the house that Jack built.*

August 24th Tom went to Chatsworth for cement. Wm. Gould was shifting coops for Sam Rowland and then went to Bakewell for beer (Burton Brewery). Tony was digging to find stoptap. It took some time to find. Ed gave him a helping hand. After a deal of trouble they found it so as they could turn the water off. Cox's plumber came and mended the soft water cistern and the tap of the other water.

August 25th A fine day. Anthony and Ed and our men have been hacking up all the pavers in front of our house, and fetching stone and gravel for asphalt. We heard of the British casualties (in fighting the Germans) which was stated in Parliament to be over 2,000. Our Hannah came from Middleton. She rode to Bakewell with Orme's van (driven by Hambleton) and then came to Sheldon with Fred Brocklehurst (with cart). Miss Lees sent bundles of wool and calico for socks and shirts for soldiers.

August 26th Very wet this morning. Fine at intervals and thunder and rain at times. Anthony, Ed, Tom, Tony and Wm. Gould are busy (fetching gravel from Magpie) and laying cement in the front.

August 27th A fine day. Wm. went to Hassop for cake. Anthony went to Bakewell for hen cotes and also brought another bag of cement for the front. Ed, Tom and Tony were laying the front and Anthony and all were working at it this afternoon. A man called in here and was talking about having had ham and eggs here a great many years ago.

August 28th A fine day. The Sheldon schoolchildren were given toys etc. at the school by Miss Grover. Miss Grover thinks it would not be right for them to have their treat as they have been accustomed as the war is so serious. Captain C called here and had tea and we had a long talk.

August 29th A pleasant day. Tom was thatching the stack down the fields and Tony was thatching that on moor. Tom went in the afternoon with Monyash cricketers to play Bakewell. Monyash won. Our Tom did not bowl. He scored one, not out. Anthony has been bad with diarrhoea today. He ate 3 plums and a bit of tomato and onion yesterday and he seems very upset today. Some good war news about the British Fleet. The British Fleet made a surprise attack on the German fleet (which seems to be hid behind Heligoland) and sunk 4 German vessels and disabled another.

August 30th Rather dull but fine. A gentleman called here and had tea, and we had a long chat about the war. Anthony is a little better today. Captain Collier took the service in Sheldon Church. Mr. Sherlock is away on holiday (for a month).

August 31st The last day of the month. A fine day. Anthony went to Bakewell and afterwards fetched the oatmeal from Johnson's mill at Alport. Tom and Tony have been thatching stacks, Tom down the fields and Tony on moor. Tony finished on moor and Tom finished down the fields. Anthony and Ed and John Frost and Sam Bramwell were collecting for war fund.

Sept. 2nd A lovely day. Very bright sunshine. Our men are corn cutting on moor and Wm. Gould is leading water for cattle on moor. Our Evelyn and Kate Brocklehurst are gone to Holme Hall (Hoyle's) this morning to practise for the Red Cross work. Captain Collier came up (service in church). Cow calved - cow calf.

Sept. 3rd Very fine. The sun is awfully hot. The men are on moor in corn. They are Anthony, Tom, Tony, Mr. Ed., Jack Naylor, Wilf Goodwin and Wm. Gould. Disheartening news from the seat of War. Germans are within 30 miles of Paris. The French Government is removed to Bordeaux. A many in the house tonight but they were quiet and subdued. My sister Bessie came to see us today. She came from Manchester (1st train) and Anthony brought her up in milk cart. She had been staying at Jack's (Compstall) since last Saturday. Our Ethel and Ruth Brocklehurst went to Bakewell (Red Cross).

Sept. 4th A great change in the weather. Plenty of wind but no sun. Bessie and Evelyn took the dinner on moor. Same men working in corn as yesterday. No fresh war news this morning. Received £4.0.0. from Wm. Mitson for eggs. Good news tonight from war bureau. Either our navy or the Russian have damaged 7 German ships about the Kiel Canal and others are reported sunk. Mr. Asquith made a grand speech in which he said our army were undefeated and unbroken.

Sept. 5th Very pleasant today. A cooler air and not much sun. Our men have finished cutting corn on moor. Sheldon cricketers are gone to Dove Holes to play. Hick's conveyance took them. Our Tom and J. Naylor and Ed left corncutting at noon to go. Wilf Goodwin and Sam Wilton helped this afternoon in corn. Mr. Knight came and had luncheon. Sheldon cricketers lost, Dove Holes scored 29 Sheldon 20. Our Tom bowled 8 out for 12 runs.

Sept. 6th Fine. Holy Communion. Mr. Sherlock administered at half past nine. George and Arthur Haywood came on motor cycle and trailer from Middleton. They went back after tea. Tom Morton and Clara Brocklehurst's banns published. Our casualties at war are 15,000 killed, wounded and missing. The Germans have sunk 15 fishing vessels in North Sea with mines. Mr. Collier took the service in church this afternoon. A collection for church expenses (10s. 2d.). Our Bessie and Hannah went out walking.

Sept. 8th Better news from war bureau. The French and British are driving the Germans back from Paris towards the German territory.

Sept. 10th Rather misty this morning but clears out and is a lovely afternoon. Evelyn and Kate Brocklehurst are gone to Bakewell (Red Cross).

Our men are in the corn. Finished thatching. The Germans are still retreating.

Sept. 12th Very wet. Tom and Wm. Gould are gone to Chatsworth for poles for haybarn. Anthony and Tony have been on moor and have to go again today as there are some lambs with maggots. The war news seems to be satisfactory for the Allies (England, France, Belgium and Russia). Our Tom and Wm. heard that Fred Wilson's brother (Tom) had committed suicide by cutting his throat.

Sept. 13th Very showery. All went to church except Tony and I. Mr. Sherlock preached a war sermon. Ethel and Evelyn went to Longstone church tonight.

Sept. 14th My birthday (57 years old). Very wet with small drizzling rain this morning. Anthony met C. Gould with a black cow and afterwards went to Bakewell Board of Guardians. C. Gould did not pay for cow.

Sept.15th Rather gloomy. Mr. Craven left Sheldon to go to Liverpool to set sail for West Africa. Mrs. Craven and George went to Longstone station. Anthony took Mr. Craven's luggage. Our Tony fetched 12 lambs from Wallwins (Dirtlow) which his father had bought yesterday for 31 shillings each. Some parts of the day were fine and our people were in corn until a heavy shower came on. Ethel and Tony went to Bakewell tonight and on their way they called and paid Mr. Wallwin for lambs. Tony was measured for cord trousers at Mr. Hills.

Sept. 18th Rather finer, but looks very dull at times. A letter came to Sheldon enquiring about the rifle range and how many times the members practised. There is no rifle range. The practice the Sheldon youths have had is with a little sort of a rifle up at the school during the winter months. Dora Needham (that was) had a daughter born.

Sept. 19th A little finer but showery at times. Our men managed to put two of the railway tops on posts. They used old Naylor to pull. It took them a long time as they are awkward things and very heavy. Mr. Sherlock called and had tea and we had a long conversation about his sermon last Sunday. I told him he had spoken rather strongly about the young men of Sheldon not being patriotic. Our Ethel and Evelyn went to a demonstration (Red Cross) at Ashford. Kate and Ruth B also went. All the nurses had tea at the Rookery. There was a meeting here (cricket).

Sept. 20th Finer but very cold and windy. A good day for drying the corn. Emily and Aunt Hannah and myself stayed at home. All the others went to church. Mr. Sherlock took the service.

Sept. 21st Very fine. A good day for fielding the corn. Anthony went with milk and afterwards to Bakewell. He got back in good time and all our men and Mr. Ed were putting up the hay barn (tops). There was a shooting party today and we prepared luncheon for 8 beaters and tea for 4 gentlemen which amounted to 15 shillings. Mr. Wood left us a hare. A collection was made in our house amongst the men for the Red Cross which amounted to 2/6. Gould paid for cow (had it last Monday).

Sept. 23rd Another grand day. Plenty of sun and wind. Our men are leading corn and Thos. A. Sheldon and Uncle John Brocklehurst are helping as well. Jack Naylor went for 4 more kils of beer this morning. Mr. Barnett (Smedley's traveller) came and was paid for June lots of beer. There is owing now for 8 kils those fetched yesterday and today. Our Evelyn and Kate Brocklehurst are gone to Bakewell (Red Cross). The men got 12 more loads of corn from the moor and 6 more out of Bole Piece.

Sept. 26th Fine but rather dull at times. Anthony and Tony have gone to Mr. Sneaps by 1st train this morning. They have taken him the cheese (bought from Naylors) and a red cap cock and hen. The war is still going on. More men are wanted to fill up the places of those killed and wounded. The casualty list is awful. The three warships which were sunk by Germans last week have lost a many officers and men. 60 officers and 1,400 men. A cow calved (cow calf). Our Tom took old Naylor to help draw a load of furniture up Grindlow Knoll. Anthony Brocklehurst took one of Frost's horses as well. The furniture was going to Harry Ardern.

Sept. 27th A very fine day. Captain Collier took the service in church. Anthony and Tony came back tonight from Mr. Sneaps.

Sept. 28th Very rough and drizzly at times. Anthony and Tom took two of our bulls to market. Tony sold some cock chickens to Needham of Chelmorton. 3 couple at 3s. 9d. per couple. 1 fowl at 1s. 10d. and one at 1s. 6d. Total amount 14s. 7d. The bulls were sold one for £9.0.0. and the other for £12.0.0.

Sept. 29th Very fine. Mr. Knight called here. I was taken in my chair up the back yard to look at the hay barn and the building that has been put up a while since. Our Tom sold some fowls today. Service in church tonight (Capt. Collier).

Sept. 30th Very fine. Our young bull hung itself this morning. Anthony had seen it all right and had just come in for a bit of lunch and in a few minutes he found it. Its throat was cut and it bled well. Tom fetched Joe Johnson's brother (Jess) and it was skinned and dressed. A shoot today. 2 gentlemen and six beaters. We provided lunch and tea. Our Tom and others are mowing the churchyard today. Mr. Wood, Mr. Lowthian and Mr. Sherlock had tea.

Oct. 1st Anthony received telegram from Mr. Deniss. Mr. and Mrs. Deniss came over from Dore Hall. They had tea and afterwards went back. He said he would give £6.0.0. for the young bull. Capt. Collier called here.

Oct. 2nd Rather gloomy and drizzly but turns out a very nice afternoon. Wm. took the carcase of the young bull to Baslow to meet Mr. Deniss. The girls are getting ready for the harvest thanksgiving which is being held tonight as well as next Sunday. Collection at tonight's service was 10s. 9d.

Oct. 3rd   Fine. Clara Brocklehurst was married to Tom Morton (at 2 o'clock). The hay was carted out of the churchyard.

Oct. 4th   Rather gloomy. Mary and Clem came this morning. Our Mary played the harmonium in church (Harvest thanksgiving). Mr. Sherlock administered the sacrament at 9.30 this morning and also took the service this afternoon (Captain Collier was here as well). The collection this afternoon amounted to £2 10s. od. Mr. and Miss K. Grover were at church. The church was full. We had forms placed in aisle.

Oct. 5th   Fine. The night school began.

Oct. 6th   Very fine. All the sheep and lambs in Sheldon were dipped today in our yard. Mr. Joseph Anthony came and weighed the wool (all those that had wool). Ours came to over £22. Our Mary is helping as well. There was a whist drive tonight at the school. The prizes all went out of Sheldon. Gould fetched some cake from Hassop.

Oct. 8th   A lovely day. Our men were getting potatoes on moor. They got 10 rows. (Wm. G. vomited in bed). We had a grand leg of mutton for dinner but the men stayed on moor until milking time. A lot of people in the house place tonight (singing etc.). It does not suit some people in Sheldon that we are not having dancing this wakes. It does not seem a proper thing when so many are laying down their lives in the grim battle with the Germans.

Oct. 9th   Another fine day, although there was a shower or two early this morning. A man dressed in khaki was in our house this morning. Our men are getting potatoes on moor.

Oct. 10th   Very dull today. We prepared 12 luncheons for beaters. There were three guns viz: Mr. Lowthian, Mr. Wood and Dr. Flint (Buxton) who came for tea. The bill came to 18 shillings which was not paid as Mr. G.H. Wood had not the money with him. Mr. George Bramwell died this morning. People were very shocked to hear of the fall of Antwerp (Belgium) and of the occupation of that city by the Germans. Two thousand of our marines retreated into Dutch territory. It is a dreadful blow to poor Belgium who has suffered so much. It is a great blow to the British Empire as well. The wakes end in 1913.Our ram was put with the ewes today. Tony had a new coat and waistcoat.

Oct. 11th   Very fine. Mr. Sherlock took the service in Sheldon church this afternoon. A gentleman called here who lives near Leek and I had a long conversation with him over the war. His name is Miller or Milner.

Oct. 12th   Very fine. Bakewell fair. Anthony went with young horse. Ethel and Kate Brocklehurst are gone to Rowland to see Mary. Mr. Deniss paid £6.0.0. for the carcase of the young bull which was hung.

Oct. 13th Very fine. Our men (except Anthony) were getting potatoes on moor. Jack Naylor was helping us. Mr. George Bramwell was buried today at 3 o'clock. The funeral was a very large one. All his sons and two daughters were there and a many other relatives and friends. Mrs. Bramwell did not follow to the grave.

Oct. 17th Very dull but fine. The men finished getting potatoes on moor (6 rows today). Very grave news in paper this morning. The cruiser *Hawk* was sunk by the Germans and many lives lost (above 400). Anthony and Tom coloured the tup lambs.

Oct. 18th Fine. Read better news in Sunday paper. Four German destroyers were sunk by our vessels off the Dutch coast. Five of ours were engaged. The victorious British flotilla led by the light cruiser *Undaunted* arrived at Harwich amidst tumultuous cheering from the crowds on shore and from the crews of other warships in the Harbour. The ships engaged were *Undaunted* cruiser, (Capt. Cecil Fox), Destroyer *Lance, Lennox, Legion* and *Loyal*. Mr. Collier took the service in church this afternoon.

Oct. 20th Fine but dull. Wm. and Tony are carting lime. Made Mr. G.H. Wood's bill out for luncheons which amounted to 19 shillings. The bill for the last luncheons was not paid so I put that in (18 shillings). Sam Rowland paid Anthony the 18 shillings tonight so I must make the bill for 19 shillings out. The shoot was in Taddington Woods today. We had no gentlemen for tea. 15 luncheons = 15s. One and a half gallons ale 3s. 6 minerals 1s. od.

Oct. 21st Rather showery at times. Wm. and Tony went for lime. They are carting it to the Bole Piece nearest Johnson Lane. Two pullets began laying.

Oct. 25th A very wet and miserable day. Mr. Collier took the service in Sheldon Church this afternoon probably for the last time as I hear that he is leaving Ashford this week.

Oct. 26th Fair, clear and a fine day. The battle is still raging between the Allies and the Germans. Sometimes a bit of good news comes and at other times some that is very disquieting. One of our naval destroyers (*Badger*) chased a German submarine off the Dutch coast and succeeded in ramming and sinking it. The official list of our killed and wounded and missing in this morning's paper is awful reading. There seem so many. Anthony went to Bakewell and paid Mr. Hill for Tony's cord trousers. Mr. Needham (Chelmorton Public House) bought some cockerels from us. Made bill out to Mr. G.H. Wood which came to 19s. 3d. for Oct. 20th 1914. Wm. and Tony went to Earl Sterndale for lime.

Oct. 27th Rather showery at times. Ethel went to Bakewell to buy a dress skirt each for herself and Evelyn. Hers was pretty fair but Evelyn's was too short. The girls are expecting to go to Bakewell next Thursday to get ready for wounded Belgians.

Oct. 28th Rather finer but cold. Evelyn changed her dress skirt (Clarks). Tom went to the gas works (Bakewell) for coke which cost 7s. 6d. (for the church). He bought 10 cwts.

Oct. 29th Cold and dull. We tied up our milk cows tonight. Ethel, Evelyn and Kate and Ruth went to Bakewell (Workhouse Infirmary) to prepare for wounded Belgians. Prince Maurice of Battenberg has died of wounds in battle.

Oct. 30th Haven Fair. Very cold and stormy. The night has been awful for wind and rain. Anthony did not go to the fair. He was working and trapped his finger with a paver. The Russians are making the Germans and Austrians retreat all along the line. The Allies gain a little in Belgium but the driving out of the Germans is very slow. In South Africa the news is a little better. The men joining in rebellion against the Government are Maritz, Christian de Wet (the one so slippery in Boer War) and Beyers. General Botha seems to be very firm and is striving very hard to quell and punish the rebels who do not seem to be making much progress. Prince Louis of Battenburgh has resigned his office as *First Sea Lord* owing to his birth and nationality. The new lay reader Mr. Weadon called and had tea.

Oct. 31st Very misty and wet. Mr. Wood and Mr. Lowthian called here. They were going partridge shooting. Mr. Wood paid for the last luncheon (19s. 3d.). We got 5 luncheons for today and 1s. 3d. worth of bar and 2 minerals and 3 teas = 9s. 9d. (Paid by Mr. G.H. Wood). Read in paper that Sir John Fisher had been promoted to *First Sea Lord* in place of Prince Louis of Battenberg. The Turks have fired on Russian vessels. Read in tonight's paper that Lord Nairne formerly Lord Charles Fitzmaurice (son of Lord Landsdowne) had been killed in action.

Nov. 1st Very misty and dull first thing but clears up a little later in the day. Mr. Sherlock administered Holy Communion in Sheldon Church at 9.30 this morning. Mr. Weadon takes his first service this afternoon (collection 8s. 5d.) for church expenses. Tom went on horseback (young Sneap) and Tony walked to Rowland Wakes.

Nov. 2nd Very misty but clears up later. Very cold. The first Pheasant shoot of the year in Shacklow. Several beaters are gone out of Sheldon. Our Tom is one of them. Mr. Franks is providing for all. Anthony went with milk and then to Bakewell. Tony fetched the milk float as his father was going to a sale at Stoney Close near Bakewell cemetery. Anthony bought in 2 stacks of hay and 2 cows for Fred Hill who has taken Stoney Close Farm.

Nov. 3rd Very misty and wet early this morning but clears up later in the day. The Turks are acting a very deceitful part against the Allies. It is said that some Bedouins are gone over the Egyptian frontier. This is owing to German intrigue.

Nov. 4th Very misty indeed. The Germans are coming out of their nest with some of their ships. On being seen by the British they retreated but managed to sink one of our Submarines. The firing could be heard at Lowestoft. Our casualties are very heavy in Belgium these last few days and there is awful slaughter amongst the Germans. Mr. Robert Smith came and bought a tup lamb from Anthony (50 shillings). Mr. Thacker came to look at one of our heifers. He did not buy. The lay reader called and had tea. Anthony insured our fodder etc for more money with the same company that we have been paying for several years.

Nov. 5th   Very wet this morning. Cleared up a little. The children had a bonfire but did not keep it up so late. The members of the night school attend very well and it seems to be a great success under Mr. Beaven.

Nov. 6th   Misty and dull. Anthony took milk and then went to Bakewell for Brandy. Bought Tony new boots. Tom Wilson paid Anthony (by cheque) for tup lamb he had last Sunday.

Nov. 7th   A brighter day today. Official news (Press Bureau) of a Naval disaster to our Fleet. The ship *Good Hope* is lost and it is feared the *Monmouth* is very seriously damaged and stranded (Chilian coast). Our men have been pulling swedes this week (carted them from Moor). Miss Grover called with magazines. She also paid 3 shillings for flowers I got her for last Whitsuntide. I sent three pairs of gloves for soldiers 1s. 6d. each. Miss Lees took them.

Nov. 8th   Fine. Mr. Sherlock took the service in Sheldon church this afternoon. Monyash Wakes. Our Tom and Evelyn went to the church tonight and heard the new vicar preach.

Nov. 11th   Rough. Very wet. The German ship *Emden* that has done so much damage to our merchant ships has been caught (and took fire) by the Australian Ship *Sydney* Commander Glossop (whose family were from Over Haddon). The *Moenesbergh* another German Ship has been bottled up in shallow water by Drury-Lowe a Derbyshire man. The Russians are advancing on German territory. They have now the Turks to deal with as well as the Austrians. Ben Naylor killed Ed Brocklehurst's pig (18 stone 10 lbs).

Nov. 12th   Another wet and windy day. Mr. Ronston came and was paid up for beer and brandy that Anthony had to fetch and the ordinary bill. These three bills amounted to £7 9s. 0d. when the discount had been taken off. Our men are not able to do anything on the land as it is so very stormy. I began knitting a scarf for soldiers.

Nov. 13th   Our Tony's birthday (17 years). A most miserable wet and windy day.

Nov. 14th   Very cold and frosty. Ethel and Ruth Brocklehurst began duties as Red Cross Nurses (at the Workhouse Infirmary Bakewell) to the wounded soldiers. There are about 14 Belgian and English wounded arrived at Bakewell.

Nov. 15th Very winterly this morning. A good deal of snow has fallen during the night. Our Ethel and Ruth Brocklehurst started from Sheldon at half past eleven ready to be on duty at one o'clock at Bakewell. It really was not fit for them to walk. They have to remain until 9 o'clock tonight and then to walk home. They will not arrive until after 10 o'clock. Mr. Sherlock took the service at Sheldon this afternoon. We had pork to dinner today which we had from Mr. Ed Brocklehurst nine and a half pounds. We shall repay this when we kill a pig. The war is still going on. The other day we learnt that the *Monmouth* was lost as well as the ship *Good Hope*. Heard that Lord Roberts died last night at 8 o'clock in France where he had gone to review the Indian troops. He died of pneumonia.

Nov. 18th Very frosty and cold. Anthony went round by Bakewell after taking the milk this morning and brought some bacon and beef. The beef is to make sandwiches for shoot next Friday. Made Mr. Woods bill out for last shoot. A motor (Lees) brought Ethel and Ruth back tonight. They got here just before half past nine o'clock. Tom Critchlow called to bid *Goodbye* to us as he has re-enlisted in R.F.A. He is going to Newcastle tomorrow. New taxes on beer, income and tea. Halfpenny per half pint. 3d. per lb tea.

Nov. 19th Very cold and frosty. A few from Sheldon went to see Tom Critchlow off. A motor came for him to Monyash. There are several enlisted at Monyash viz. Herbert Prince, Joe Handley, J. Millington and W. Millington (Susan Millington's son). Arthur Millington and W. Bagshaw are going into the Yeomanry (Chatsworth). Ethel and Ruth B. walked back tonight.

Nov. 20th Very cold. Our girls had to get luncheon ready for the shoot in Taddington Woods. 12 luncheons beer 3s. 3d. Mineral 4s. 8d. Ethel and Ruth walked back from nursing at Bakewell Infirmary.

Nov. 21st Very cold and frosty. Evelyn is getting her things ready as she has to go on duty (nursing the soldiers at Bakewell) tonight at 9 o'clock. A good many in tonight and a great deal of arguing over farmers. The chief spokesmen were S. Wilton, Alf Wildgoose, S. Bramwell, Alf. Brocklehurst, Sam Rowland. (A lot of ridiculous talk.)

Nov. 22nd Very frosty and cold. I was in the kitchen all day, but I was very cold indeed as it is such a draughty place. Evelyn and Kate B got home at quarter past nine this morning. Evelyn went to bed before dinner but could not sleep. Mr. Sherlock took the service in Sheldon Church this afternoon. Ruth Brocklehurst took the organ as Evelyn did not attend service (in bed). She and Kate set off to Bakewell to be on duty at 9 o'clock tonight.

Nov. 23rd Bitterly cold. East wind and frost. Evelyn and Kate got back between 9 and 10 this morning. Evelyn had been very sick during the night (at the Infirmary Workhouse) but she seems better and went to bed just before 11 o'clock this morning.

Nov. 24th Very cold. Emily's birthday (24 years). Wm. and Tony went for lime. Kate and Evelyn got back from their duties between 9 and 10 o'clock this morning.

Nov. 25th Very cold, some slight showers during the day. Tony and Wm. went again for lime. Kate B and our Evelyn got back at about the usual time. These two started an hour earlier tonight as there was a meeting at 8 o'clock. A few in the house talking about the beer tax. We have not raised our beer at present. We are thinking of doing so on the 1st of next month.

Nov. 29th Rough and showery at times. Our Ethel and Ruth went on duty to be there at one o'clock. Mr. Sherlock took the service in church. Evelyn played organ. A collection for foreign missions. The money was not brought to our house. Clem came in about tea time. He stayed all night. He and Mary slept in little room over pantry. Ethel and Ruth had to walk home from the infirmary. They arrived here about 10.30. I was in parlour today.

Nov. 30th Awfully rough and very wet. Clem went with milk cart. Anthony bought a heifer off Herbert Frost £17 10s. od. The Duke of Devonshire's rent day. Fred Needham, Ashford (Devonshire Arms) is very ill and we have three in Sheldon whom Dr. Fentem is attending viz Mr. B. Sheldon, Stanley Brocklehurst and little Ida Carson. Received paper to be filled up of those who are willing to enlist for the war. We had a heifer pecked her calf this morning and one a night or two since. We have had a many this year and it makes things very awkward especially when milk is wanted.

Dec. 1st Very rough and wet. We rose the beer today for the first time since taxing. We sold two glasses to Charles Hicks who called. Some in tonight drinking gin, ginger ale and whiskey, but no beer was drunk. Ethel and Ruth got another ride to Ashford (Lees). They got in just after ten o'clock.

Dec. 2nd Very rough and cold. Ben Naylor killed a pig for us and one for Mr. Ed. Sold a glass of beer to a Jew with pack and a glass or two each to Robert Bramwell and G. Goodwin. People do not seem willing to pay the extra.

Dec. 3rd Very rough. We all overslept this morning (except Wm.) seven o'clock. When Anthony went up to the backyard he found the heifer we bought off Herbert Frost (Monday) calving and both cow and calf were nearly hung. B. Naylor cut the pig up. It weighed 16 stones 8 lbs. and Mr. Ed. B's was 16 stones. Ethel and Ruth came back by motor (Mr. Lees) and arrived at quarter past nine. I believe there are a few young men in Sheldon who have been signed on (Householders census). We bought a cheese of Billy Naylor (32$^1/_2$ lbs). I paid him.

Dec. 6th Very rough and cold. Ethel and Ruth B are gone on duty for one o'clock. At 9.30 there was Holy Communion in Sheldon Church. Mr. Sherlock administered, only 8 present. Mr. Weadon took the service this afternoon, collection 6s. 4d. The service was rather long - 4 o'clock when people came out.

Dec. 7th   Very rough and wet. Anthony took six hogs to market and sold them at 47 shillings each. He afterwards went to the rural district councillors meeting. Evelyn and Ruth Brocklehurst went on duty for one o'clock. Evelyn took the soldier McGilvery a photo of our girls and Ed's in nursing costume. He is leaving the Infirmary tomorrow.

Dec. 8th   Very rough and cold. Anthony is not well; his eyes pain him. I daresay it is with being out in the rough winds. Albert Redfern bought the old cow which we think had tubes-in-udder for £3.0.0. Tony went on the road with Albert's son driving the cow.

Dec. 9th   Very cold. A few in tonight. One or two of them had a pint or two of beer, the first since rise. Ethel got home just after half past ten tonight. Two of the soldiers (White and Melville) had been out and came back to hospital quite drunk, and White was so disorderly that the Workhouse master was fetched and both soldiers were put in the cells at the Workhouse. White broke down the cell door and was escaping.

Dec. 10th   Read in paper that there had been a naval fight in the Atlantic. The British squadron under Vice Admiral Sir Frederick Sturdee sank three German cruisers viz *Scharnhorst* flying the flag of Admiral Graf von Spee, the *Gneisenau* and the *Leipzig*. Two other German cruisers were in the action but made off and were pursued by the British. The British casualties were very slight. This happened near the Falkland Islands on December 8th. The Russians are gaining victories and it is reported that the Kaiser is ill.

Dec. 11th   Very rough and cold. Another German cruiser was sunk as well as above. Ruth Brocklehurst and Evelyn went on for duty at one o'clock. They rode back from Bakewell to Ashford in motor, and are expecting to be off duty (Red Cross) for a fortnight.

Dec. 12th   Very rough, cold and wet. John Brocklehurst carted coke for Sheldon church (free) 6s.6d. worth.

Dec. 13th   Very misty and showery afterwards. Mr. Weadon took the service this afternoon. He keeps the congregation rather late.

Dec. 16th   Rather finer but cold. Tom and Wm. have been for clay. Heard that Hartlepool, Whitby and Scarborough had been bombarded by four German cruisers and much damage done and people killed and wounded.

Dec. 17th   Very wet and stormy. Fred Prince called in tonight and was talking of things which happened when he was a soldier.

Dec. 18th   Rather finer this morning, but has been very wet during the night. An awful lot of damage to life and property was done by the Germans on Wednesday last. There are 97 killed and 217 injured in the three towns.

The castle at Whitby was partly demolished. Emily and Evelyn are going to Bakewell shopping with their father who is taking the young horse. The girls and their father got back between five and six o'clock and have bought hats for themselves and Ethel which they leave to be trimmed at Broughtons. Egypt made a British Protectorate.

Dec. 19th A snowstorm today. Our girls' hats came tonight by milk cart. There are more victims of the East coast German naval raid. There are above 100 deaths and many injured. A good many in tonight drinking spirits.

Dec. 20th Frosty, slippery and cold. Mr. Sherlock took the service in Sheldon church this afternoon. Anthony and Tom had to sit up until 2 o'clock this morning with the heifer we had from Mr. H. Frost as it was very bad. Anthony thought it was inflammation but I am glad to say it is improving.

Dec. 24th Frosty and cold. A grand day for the time of year. Miss Grover sent two lovely vases for Sheldon Church. Our Tony and Wm. took three and a half loads of potatoes to Mr. H. Frost's at 9 shillings per load which were paid for on delivery. Billy Naylor raffled a sucking pig in school. Tom one-arm[1] Brocklehurst won it and Sam Wilton bought it for half a sovereign and paid for some beer as well. Tony plucked the turkey ready for tomorrow. The Germans dropped a bomb on Dover which fell in a garden but no damage was done.

Dec. 25th Xmas Day. Frosty and very cold. Holy Communion in Sheldon Church administered by Mr. Sherlock, 10 present. Mr. Weadon took the service this afternoon, collection (7s.4d.) for Church Army. We did not receive the money. The singers went round tonight. They went to Dirtlow first. We had the turkey for dinner.

Dec. 27th Cold and frosty. Afterwards snow and sleet. Mr. Weadon took the service in Sheldon Church and afterwards called here for tea. Ethel and Ruth Brocklehurst went on duty (with wounded Belgians) and got back from Bakewell before 10 o'clock tonight. They rode in Mr. Lee's motor from Bakewell to Ashford.

Dec. 29th Frosty and snow storms at intervals. A tea party and dance was held in the schoolroom. Kate had to go on duty at 9 o'clock tonight and our Ethel and Ruth came off duty at 9 tonight. Charles Hicks called here (the worse for drink).

Dec. 30th Severe frost and snow lies on the ground. Our Ethel and Ruth went to Bakewell Infirmary to be on duty for one o'clock. It is believed that the bombs dropped by British sea planes on Cuxhaven (on Xmas Day) have done considerable damage. Fred Goodwin fetched from our place half a

---

1   He lost an arm through an accident with the winding machinery in the Magpie Mine. He was also known as Wingy-one-arm. As boiler man, he used an extended sleeve to wind round the shovel to enable him to keep the furnace going, literally, single handed. (*The History of Magpie Mine*; Peak District Mines Historical Society)

load of potatoes. Anthony brought 26 stamps (3d. stamps) for Beatrice Wildgoose's card (insurance) and I filled it in for week ending Dec. 28th (1914). I also filled up Wm. Gould's insurance card. Awfully rough tonight. Ethel and Ruth B. got home just before 10 o'clock.

Dec. 31st A lovely day after a night of storm and wind. Ethel and Ruth went on duty at Bakewell for one o'clock. Joe Carson was refused drink and he used some very nasty talk. I told him to go, and come when I sent for him.[1] Old uncle had had enough whiskey and he did not like being stopped from having more.

1   He returned on August 22nd 1915!

Jan. 1st   Awfully rough and snow. Tom's birthday (26). Our Ethel and Ruth went on duty for one o'clock and had to walk back all the way after 9 o'clock and did not arrive until nearly 11. George Olivant (Queens) was fined £5 and costs for serving drink to a drunken man (naval man).

Jan. 2nd   A calm after the stormy one yesterday. Tom Critchlow R.F.A. came here this afternoon. He has to go back to Newcastle tomorrow. He says that there are about 60,000 troops there. Our Evelyn and Ruth B went on duty (Red Cross) for one o'clock. Mr. Sherlock called here and had tea.

Jan. 3rd   Very stormy. Mr. Sherlock administered Holy Communion in Sheldon Church at 9.30 this morning. 8 present. He also took the Intercession service this afternoon. A collection was taken for the Red Cross work. £1 0s. 3d. was taken by Mr. Sherlock for that purpose from Sheldon.

Jan. 4th   Very dull and much of the snow has gone. Anthony went to market and afterwards went to the Board of Guardians. He brought Emily and Evelyn a new pair of Goloshes. Emily's cost 2s. 11d., Evelyn's 2s. 3d. Evelyn and Ruth went to Bakewell. Received a letter from Mr. Luxmoore.[1]

Jan. 5th   Very dull, misty and damp. Evelyn and Ruth B. went to Bakewell Infirmary (Red Cross work) and got back getting on for 11 o'clock tonight. We got 12 luncheons for Mr. Wood's shoot today. 2 gallons of beer and 4 minerals which amounted to 18 shillings, the beer was 5s. 4d. Answered Mr. Luxmoore's letter.

Jan. 6th   Very nice day but cold. Ethel and Ruth Brocklehurst went to Bakewell to be on duty (Red Cross) at one o'clock. The magazines were sent to me by Miss Grover to be given out in Sheldon. A good many in the house tonight keeping up their birthdays. Sam Rowland brought gramophone. Anthony sent a receipt to Mr. Sherlock which that gentleman had sent instead of cheque for Dole Flannel for Sheldon. Evelyn gave receipt to Mr. Weadon (at practice).

Jan. 7th   Wet and dismal. Evelyn and Ruth B went on duty at Bakewell (Red Cross). Got back getting on for 11. A few in tonight. Lord Kitchener's speech in paper made last night in House of Lords. A lot of engineers from Buxton marched through Sheldon.

[1]   The Revd. J. Luxmoore was a former Vicar of Ashford and Sheldon.

Jan. 8th   Very cold and damp. Tom and Wm. went ploughing but the rain came on. Anthony received word from Wm. Kitson to send egg box at 7 per shilling. Evelyn and Ruth went to Bakewell to be on duty for one o'clock. Mr. Sherlock called here this afternoon. Jim Goodwin paid for eggs.

Jan. 9th   Very cold but fair. Mr. G.H. Wood called and had luncheon here. He also paid up to date for beaters' luncheons £2.15s. 0d., and also rent for building used by Sam Rowland due Xmas day 1915. A few in the house tonight. Tom and Tony went to Ashford to a concert.

Jan. 10th   Frosty and very cold and afterwards snow and sleet. Hannah is in bed today with influenza. Posted (in Sheldon letter box) Beatrice Wildgoose's Insurance card. Kate B. owes 6 nights with tonight for milk. Ethel, Evelyn and Ruth are having a fortnight's rest from Red Cross nursing. Mr. Weadon took the service in Sheldon Church. Kate B only paid for tonight's milk leaving 5 owing 1s 0d. this lot and £1.8.0. of old bill.

Jan. 13th   Dull and wet. Anthony had a letter from Mr. Stubbs inviting Sheldon choir to supper on Friday next.

Jan. 14th   Cold. Anthony and Tony took the young horse (Mr. Sneap's) to Bakewell. They bought some cheese and paid for it from Orme's. Tony bought some collars for himself and Tom and some tins for bacon etc.

Jan. 15th   Very rough and wet. Read in papers that the Germans had won a bit over French as the latter had to fall back and owing to the floods could not get on much with the fighting. Anthony went to Parsley Hay for sheep cratches.[1] He did not bring them as they were damaged. Tom, Tony, Ethel and Evelyn went with others to the choir suppering. It poured in torrents. They got back just before 12 o'clock. I was sitting up when they came back.

Jan. 17th   Very frosty and cold. Ethel and Kate B started from home about 7 o'clock to be on duty (Red Cross) at 8 o'clock this morning until 9 tonight. They have an hour or two off in the middle of the day when they take a walk. Mr. Weadon took the service in Sheldon Church. W. Kitson sent egg money up to date, Wm. Gould called at P. Office for it. Ruth Brocklehurst has been in bed two days with sickness and diarrhoea. Ed. B. fetched milk and paid for it.

Jan. 18th   Very frosty and cold. Anthony went to market. Vic has 7 pups. A full house tonight. A collection was made for Wm. Hallows who is expecting to go to Newcastle on Wednesday (RFA). The sum of 2s. 9d. was raised amongst the customers and 2s. 4d. was given to Anthony to buy him (Hallows) half a pound of thin twist. The other 5d. was handed to Hallows to spend as he liked.

Jan. 19th   Dull and rather damp. Anthony went with milk and called for the thin twist for Hallows and gave it to him. Policeman Young who went from Ashford to join his regiment (Grenadier Guards) called here with

[1]   cratch: manger or crib

Mellon who used to be a policeman at Bakewell and left to join his regiment after war was declared. Mellon had been to the front and got wounded and had been in hospital and had come to Bakewell on furlough. He expects to go back tomorrow. Thos Skidmore came with a conveyance to fetch our Hannah to Rowland as our Mary was confined of a son about twelve o'clock today.

Jan. 20th Rather showery but mild. A motor came for the following who had signed on for the war. Wm. Hallows, Alf. Wildgoose, Sam Wilton, Fred Brocklehurst and Anthony Brocklehurst. Tom and Wm. Gould carting clay (from Birchell) for meres. The above young men who signed on all passed the doctor.

Jan. 22nd Very dull. Thawing. Had a letter from our Hannah. She says that Mary and the child are pretty well but the child is awkward to suckle and cries a lot. Our Tony has had to go to Bakewell (Thackers) for beef for luncheon tomorrow.

Jan. 23rd Dull. Fred Brocklehurst, Anthony Brocklehurst and Sam Wilton were fetched by motor car to Buxton to enlist (Grenadier Guards) and then be drafted to Caterham (Surrey) where they will join Wm. Hallows who went there last Wednesday. Anthony's sister Fanny is no better. Mr. Weadon called here and had tea.

Jan. 24th Fine and mild. Our Hannah's birthday (65). All the girls are off duty (Red Cross) for a time. Mr. Sherlock took the service in Sheldon Church this afternoon. All ours went to the service except Tony and myself. The vicar made no allusion to the men who had enlisted.

Jan. 25th Frosty and cold. Evelyn is not very well (sick). Read in paper that a naval battle took place in the North Sea (yesterday, Sunday) between the British and German Fleet. The British ships engaged were *The Lion and Tiger, Princess Royal, New Zealand* and *Indomitable*. The German ships were *Derfflinger, Seydlitz, Moltke* and *Blucher* and other cruisers. The *Blucher* was capsized and sank just after one o'clock and two other battle cruisers were seriously damaged.

Jan. 26th Fine. Mr. Sherlock called here. There was a managers' meeting at the school. The minute book (Sheldon School) cannot be found. Two doctors at Fanny's. There are some poorly people in Sheldon. Old Wm. Brocklehurst and Alf, the last named has pleurisy. Fanny B, Mrs. Bramwell, Mr. James Frost and others.

Jan. 27th Very winterly and cold. A sprinkling of snow. Our Evelyn is sick at intervals. Anthony and Emily are not well. Jim Goodwin and Alf Wildgoose have been here this afternoon. Ben Naylor killed our pig. Tom has just gone on his bicycle to Bakewell for a few things for our poorly folk. A collection was made in our house for Alf Wildgoose and the sum of 5s. 9d. was raised. Others who were not in the house gave him something afterwards.

Jan. 28th Frosty and cold. The recruiting officer brought a motor for Alf Wildgoose and I hear they called for George Briddon at Monyash who has enlisted in the Life Guards for twelve years. Alf Wildgoose enlisted in the Sherwood Foresters. Our Tom and Jack Naylor went to a Whist drive and dance at Ashford. G. Briddon came back as he was too old for Life Guards.

Jan. 30th Frosty and cold. Anthony's sister Fanny is very low. The Russian Jew called for eggs but we had none for him. They are eight for a shilling now. Corn is very dear being £1.1s. per bag. Heard that Alf Wildgoose is gone to Derby. He did not know where he would be drafted to next. We owe Mr. Thacker for 3lbs of shin beef. Fred Brockley came from Caterham (Surrey) tonight. His father had sent a telegram for him as his mother is so bad. His father went with milk to Bakewell station and then went to Millers Dale thinking Fred was getting off there and he got off at Bakewell.

Jan. 31st Snow. Very cold. Mr. Weadon took the service in Sheldon Church. Anthony is not so well yet. The indigestion is very bad. Mr. Wm. Brockley (old uncle) is very ill, and Mrs. Bramwell.

Feb. 2nd A very cold and windy day. Drizzling rain at times. Fanny (Anthony's sister) passed away. Will and Fred were at Bakewell when she died. There are a very many people ill with influenza.

Feb. 3rd Very rough winds and cold. Anthony and Ethel went to Bakewell (young Sneap) and bought costumes and blouses (Broughtons). Anthony was measured at Mr. Hills for a new suit of black clothes. Ethel and Evelyn's costumes fit pretty well but Emily's is too big. They bought a wreath (artificial) 7 shillings.

Feb. 5th Very windy and cold. Fanny (Anthony's sister) was buried at 3 o'clock this afternoon. Mr. Sherlock read burial service. Fred did not attend funeral as he is ill with influenza.

Feb. 6th Dull and very wet in the morning part but clears up after dinner. Clem Wager came to see us. He says that Mary and the baby are going on all right. Frank Bramwell and Matthew Gregory were in our house tonight. Clem Wager sang one song and Billy Naylor was (as usual) merry. He gave Clem a bit of cheese to take with him.

Feb. 7th Very misty and afterwards very wet. Holy Communion (9.30) 12 females and 2 males were present. Mr. Sherlock administered. The service this afternoon was taken by Mr. Weadon. Collection for Church expenses 13s. 3d. Ethel went with Ruth Brocklehurst to be on duty at 1 o'clock as Evelyn had to play organ in Church.

Feb. 9th Very cold and windy. There has been a great amount of rain between last night and this morning. Our Tony found a small silver flask in the New Closes. Alf Brockley is collecting eggs for the wounded soldiers in the Front. We gave him 6 today. The box holds 29. They are taken to Creswells (Bakewell) which is the depot. We still send milk to Belgians (Rangemoor) and have been doing so for weeks (free). Evelyn and Ruth arrived at home late (after 11 o'clock). There had been a concert and dance at the Workhouse and the Red Cross nurses (on duty) were invited. Our Evelyn and Ruth had a dance with the Belgian soldiers.

Feb. 12th   A nice day but rather cold. Evelyn and Ruth B went on duty for one o'clock. They finished tonight for a term of a few weeks. Mr. Weadon called here tonight.

Feb. 14th   Very cold and severe (frosty). Mr. Weadon took the service in Church this afternoon. He keeps them in so long (10 minutes to 4). Ethel gave Ashford policeman the silver flask that our Tony found down the fields (New Close) and I also told Miss Lees and she said she would make enquiries amongst the hunt.

Feb. 16th   Shrove Tuesday. A very bright Winters day (frosty). A tea at the chapel this afternoon.

Feb. 17th   Very wet this morning and all through previous night but clears up a little this afternoon. Our children are very busy preparing for an exam of the evening scholars. Emily has been sick after every meal this last day or two.

Feb. 20th   A bright day, rather cold. The hunters turned out at Sheldon. I should not be disappointed if they never came again. I think some of the so called ladies think they can do anything in our house. Three ladies came in and had the use of my bedroom and one gave the girls one penny. The other two gave nothing. None of them had a drink of anything. I wonder how many it would take to pay our licence of these kind. Two of Dickens men brought their own food and coffee and sat here eating it etc. These two spent fourpence between them, a glass of beer and a ginger beer. Tom and Wm. went for clay.

Feb. 21st   Another fine day. Our Tony went to Rowland. Mr. Sherlock took the service in Sheldon Church this afternoon.

Feb. 23rd   Frosty and cold. The recruiting sergeant (Buxton) called here and enquired if there were a Wilson lived at Sheldon. He meant Sam Wilton. Fred Brocklehurst has gone back to Caterham (Surrey). He went by the 1.57 train to London with P.C. Young (Ashford).

Feb. 25th   Very frosty but the sun shines and the day turns out very bright. Ben Naylor kills us a pig. The Germans are very busy sinking our ships and one or two of the Americans. Tom and Wm. are leading manure on to moor.

Feb. 27th   Cold. Beatrice Wildgoose sent in her resignation as school cleaner. The 1st lamb was born today.

Feb. 28th   Cold. Mr. Sherlock took the service in Church this afternoon. Mary's baby was baptized (Anthony William). Clem and our Tom were godfathers and Ethel godmother. Clem cycled back to Rowland tonight.

March 2nd   Rather milder. The snow seems to be going nicely. Received a letter from Miss M. Whitehead saying she would send the 5/- reward for finding her silver flask.

March 3rd   Rather dull but milder. The snow has disappeared. Mr. Weadon came to see us tonight. Read in paper that our fleet and the French are making progress in the Dardanelles. Mr. Sherlock came and churched[1] our Mary this afternoon and afterwards had tea. Mary gave two shillings towards church expenses. Received 5 shillings for Tony finding Miss M. Whitehead's flask.

March 5th   Fine but dull and rather windy. Anthony and Thos. Wm. Brocklehurst went to Birmingham Bull show and sale. They each bought a bull. Ours was 13 months old and cost £40.19s. od. They got back to Sheldon about 9 o'clock and each led their bull from Bakewell station. Mr. Weadon called - something over some bill of Alf Wildgoose's.

March 7th   A nice morning but turns out rough and cold. Mr. Sherlock celebrated Holy Communion in Sheldon Church at 9.30. There were 8 present. Mr. Weadon took the Service this afternoon. The collection amounted to 8 shillings.

March 8th   Very cold and a little snow fell. Ethel and Kate Brocklehurst went to prepare the beds etc. for some more wounded soldiers who are coming to Bakewell hospital. I was not well today, very sick. Sent a letter to Miss M. Whitehead thanking her for postal order 5/- (reward for flask).

March 9th   A very fine day. 5 lambs. Our Ethel had a telegram to be on duty at the Red Cross Hospital at half past one today. Ethel and Kate had got as far as Ashford when they met Uncle W. Brocklehurst with the telegram. They were going to be on at 10 o'clock. Received a receipt for 7s.9d. from Mr. Sherlock. This was a contribution from the Parish of Sheldon for the Southwell Diocesan Sunday Fund.

March 10th   Rather dull and cold today. Another lamb this morning. The Germans have sunk three more British vessels (in this morning's paper). Our Ethel and Kate Brocklehurst have gone on duty (Red Cross) for 1.30. Evelyn and Tony are very busy baking oatcakes this afternoon. They have done well. Closed our house at 9 tonight. The policeman brought a paper - new closing order (9 p.m.).

March 11th   Very dull and almost dark this afternoon. Burgon's man took 448 eggs at 11 for a shilling. The British have sunk a German submarine U12.

March 12th   Rather dull but fine. Ethel and Kate got home between 10 and 11 o'clock tonight. There are now about 33 wounded soldiers at the Bakewell Red Cross Hospital.

---

1   Conducted Prayer Book Service of Thanksgiving after Childbirth

March 13th   Fine and dry. Sent Wm. Kitson a box of eggs (360) at 10 for one shilling. The Sheldon Minute Book (which could not be found) was discovered on Thursday last in Sheldon Church. Our Evelyn saw Mr. Sherlock come down Sheldon Church one Sunday with a parcel under his arm and no doubt it would contain the minute book for Evelyn found it in vestry.

March 14th   Very fine. Read in paper that the British Force in France had gained some ground but the Pirates are at work sinking ships. One was sunk off the Ayrshire coast and about 200 lives lost. Mr. Sherlock took the service in Sheldon Church this afternoon.

March 15th   Very fine. Anthony went to Bakewell to a meeting (Cheshire milk association). He bought a foot bath. I have been reckoning up church accounts.

March 17th   Very fine. Our Ethel and Kate went to meet two of the soldiers who are in Bakewell hospital. These men said they would like to see Sheldon so they came and had tea at Mrs. Ed's. (got back at 8.15). Read that the German ship *Dresden* had been sunk by the British, who saved about 350 of the German crew. There are a many British vessels being torpedoed.

March 18th   Cold but fine. Read in list of killed the name of H. Dixon (Sherwood Foresters) Gt. Longstone. Very cold and the roughest night I ever knew. Mr. Beaven came to Sheldon night school and started for Taddington between 9 and 10. We were all very concerned and wondered whether he would reach home. The wind and snow were something awful. Anthony and Tom sat up and were nailing some more boards in front of top shed where the sheep were.

March 19th   Very cold and frosty. Evelyn and Ruth B started just after 7 o'clock this morning to be on duty (Red Cross) at half past 8. Tom and his father did not come to bed until just before four o'clock this morning as they durst not leave the sheep and lambs.

March 20th   A nice day. Anthony sent cheque (church) for insurance Fire.

March 21st   Rather cold but a very fine day. Evelyn came off duty earlier as she had to play in Church. Mr. Weadon took the service in Church this afternoon. He keeps them so long 2 minutes to four today.

March 22nd   A nice day. 16 soldiers leave hospital at Bakewell.

March 24th   Rather misty but mild. Our girls have been very busy every minute this last week getting ready for the night school examination. Our Tom is ploughing on moor a field that no one in Sheldon can remember being ploughed before. George Briddon (for John Frost) fetched coke for Sheldon Church. He was given half a sovereign out of the Church funds. Our girls went to school before 7 o'clock tonight and arrived home as the clock struck 10 after a stiff exam. The boys were there from 8.30 until after

10 o'clock. The Austrian fortress surrendered 120,000 the other day amongst whom were 9 generals, 93 officers, 2,500 other men.

March 25th Very cold, wind, snowstorm this morning. Ethel and Kate Brocklehurst went to Bakewell to be on duty at half past seven and got back after 11 o'clock this morning. Another exam tonight. Mr. Sherlock came in this afternoon. He went to Wm. H. Brocklehurst's to ask if they would be caretaker of Sheldon School in place of Beatrice Wildgoose who is resigning. Anthony had some talk with S. Bramwell about taking E. Smith's place looking after the Church (caretaker etc.). Thomas Wm. Brocklehurst had asked Edwin Smith if he really wanted to give up looking after the Church and he said *Yes*.

March 26th Very cold. G. Briddon gave Anthony half a sovereign back that was given him for coke (There was none to be got).

March 27th Very bitter cold and frosty. Anthony knocked his head on a beam over balks[1] in barn and it threw him backwards. The barn door was open and as he fell he caught his back on the door which somewhat broke his fall and helped him to clutch hold of a ladder before he fell to the floor. Had he fallen straight to the floor he would have been more seriously injured. As it is he is bad enough as with knocking his head he has such pain down his neck (back) and the bottom of his back is so painful. He has had a bath and been rubbed (embrocation) and gone to bed. We have sent some wood and coal on to the Church from our house. We had a fire in my bedroom for the first time this winter.

March 28th Very frosty and cold, snow storm at intervals. Mr. Weadon took the service in Sheldon Church this afternoon. He keeps the congregation so late (4 o'clock today). Two strange young men came in this afternoon. Anthony seems a little better but has a headache. I told Kate B that I had heard about their Doris being seen walking with a postman.

March 30th Very frosty and cold. Anthony and Tom have both severe colds and Anthony's hand and wrist cause him a lot of pain. The German Submarine torpedoed the *Falaba* west of Milford Haven on Sunday night. Miss Grover called here and left half a crown for flowers for Sheldon Church (Easter).

March 31st Cold and frosty. Anthony's cold is about the same. His hand and wrist pain him very much. The following extracts from today's *Sheffield Daily Telegraph*:

The *Falaba's* End

The death roll of the *Falaba*, the Elder Dempster Liner, torpedoed by a German submarine west of Milford Haven on Sunday is 112.

An inquest has been held concerning 8 bodies including that of the commander of the ship brought ashore. The German submarine it appears

1 Upper section of the Barn

first flew the English Ensign. She fired her torpedo five minutes after the *Falaba* stopped from about 150 yards distance.

Her crew were in khaki. If the act of the Submarine was not piracy and murder said the Coroner he did not know what was. The story of the end of the *Aguila* (this ship sailed on Friday last. Crew 43 persons passengers 3) of Pembroke is not less horrifying. Murderous fire was poured on passengers and crew from two guns of the German submarine and people were killed during transfer to the boats and in the boats. (The German fiends.)

April 1st A very fine day: warmer. The German Submarines are very busy sinking our merchant ships. Nearly every day they torpedo one or two. George Briddon fetched coal for Church to the value of ten shillings. Evelyn and Ruth Brocklehurst got home at 10 o'clock tonight (Red Cross). Tom and Wm. sat up tonight with a cow. Polly Roberts begins work as caretaker of Sheldon School.

April 2nd Very wet and windy. Ethel has gone on duty with Ruth today as Evelyn has to play organ in Church. Mr. Weadon took the service in Sheldon Church this afternoon. One pound subscription came from Mr. Cockerill. Had a letter from Mr. Sherlock saying that he had written to Mr. Cockerill (agent) whether he could use £3.0.0. of the Duke of Devonshire's subscription of £5.0.0. (yearly) for the Sheldon organist and Mr. Cockerill agreed to that being done. The £5.0.0. was formerly for the Sheldon Sunday School. W. Hallows came from Caterham. The cow calved (cow calf) early this morning about 4 o'clock. £1.0.0. for Sheldon Church. Good Friday today.

April 3rd Wet at times but rather milder. Two men came and bought 17 shillings worth of eggs at 12 for one shilling. Anthony does not seem so well. His back and hand pain him. Wm. fetched coal for us. One pound per ton. He brought some fish (Smiths) which was not good. W. Hallows came in tonight.

April 4th Very fine. Mr. Sherlock administered at Holy Communion at 9.30 this Easter Morning. Mr. Weadon took the service this afternoon. The collection was for the lay reader and was not sent to the churchwardens.

April 5th Fine. Anthony went with milk and afterwards to Bakewell Fair. Anthony took the Sheldon Church bank book and found that there was no money in. He afterwards found that he had the counterfoil of a cheque made out to Thos. Wm. Brocklehurst (for Sunday School). Thos. Wm. could not remember. (Later) Thomas Wm. misunderstood Anthony. He thought Anthony meant this year's £5.0.0. He knew about last year's and had drawn it out of the bank (Church account). Anthony paid him £2.0.0. from the Duke of Devonshire (for Sunday School) and our Evelyn was paid £3.0.0. salary as organist from the Duke's subscription. Edwin Smith was paid £4.1s.0d. He settled his bill for April 6th instead of the 5th. Thos. Wm. Brocklehurst was paid 1s. 3d. for coal for Church. A little girl 7 years old, Maggie Nally, was found murdered at a station. Wm. Hallows went back.

April 6th Very wet and very windy. I have balanced up the Church accounts and am right to the halfpenny. £2.16s.3d. in hand.

April 7th Showery at times. Ethel and Kate Brocklehurst went on duty for 1.30 (Red Cross). They got off earlier to come to a dance which was held in Sheldon School in connection with the men's club. A pleasant evening was spent dancing and refreshments. Mr. J. Goodwin and E. Smith provided the music.

April 8th Rough and hail storms at intervals. A vestry meeting was held in Sheldon Church at 4 in the afternoon. Four were present. Mr. Sherlock, Mr. Weadon, Antony and Thos. Wm. B. The old wardens were proposed and elected again. Mr. Saml. Bramwell took on the duties of caretaker of the Church in place of Mr. E. Smith (resigned). Balance in hand of Church accounts was £2.16s.3d. Mr. Weadon had been here.

April 11th Very fine but dull. Mr. Sherlock took the Service in Sheldon Church. The congregation were out at 3.30. Naylor's mare foaled (filly). Our Anthony took the milk to Longstone Station this morning and got in time to see the train steaming out. The milk was left behind and Wm. Gould fetched it from Longstone station and took it to Bakewell to catch an early train from there tonight.

April 12th Very close; dull and showery. They were ploughing on moor and Tony and Wilf Goodwin were spreading manure. Mr. Edwin Brocklehurst paid Anthony £2.0.0. towards rent. He said he would pay the other when Thos. Hawley paid him.

April 16th Fine but rather dull after dinner. Tom finished ploughing on moor. Polly Roberts has been working here today. We have her two days a week since Ethel and Evelyn began Red Cross duties at Bakewell.

April 18th Fine and warm. Elsie Eaton had her little baby christened. It had been baptized before. Mr. Sherlock took the service this afternoon. Our Tony was one of the sponsors. Three men from Longstone called here. The relief station master (T. Stone), the Monsal Dale Signalman and Bernard Hambleton. Evelyn and Ruth had a day off from Red Cross work.

April 19th Fine but rather windy. Tom finished sowing a field on moor (2nd up from road). Tony took the old red cow to Bakewell and she was sold to Ben Thorpe for £24.

April 20th Dull and wet this morning but clears up after dinner. Tom and his father have gone sowing with new machine this afternoon. Tony hurt his finger with barrow.

April 21st Fine but rather cold. Sowed another field on moor. I have been at Sheldon 36 years today. Evelyn is not so well today (indigestion). Polly Roberts has been helping the girls to clean our dairy. We cannot find some books called *The banner of Israel* which Mr. Bagshaw (Moor Grange) lent me some months ago.

April 22nd Showery today. Anthony cut the lambs' tails. The war still drags on. The British took a very important hill the other day.[1]

April 23rd Fine but frosty and cold. Anthony and Tony have taken 10 young cows, 2 foals and 15 sheep on the moor.

April 24th Fine this morning but drizzling afterwards. A man and two women came in after milking time and wanted tea making. The man had been here several times last year. I think he is a German but I may be mistaken. Very severe fighting is taking place in the Front. France had to fall back owing to the Germans using some gases. Our Evelyn is not well. I want to send for a doctor but she does not want one. She has been so sick and purged.

April 25th Very rough and showery. Evelyn has had a good night and the sickness and purging has stopped a bit but she seems so full of wind and no appetite. Mr. Weadon took the Service in Church this afternoon. Late when the congregation came out (five to 4). Ruth Brocklehurst played harmonium in Church.

April 26th Rough cold and drizzly. Mr. Harry Bagshaw (Moore Grange) called here and was paid a tithe (2s.9d.). I apologised for the loss of his books. He was very nice and said we must not bother. Evelyn seems a little better but her appetite is poor. A lady called and asked if she could have breakfast here next Sunday morning. She wishes to come to Sheldon for the celebration of Holy Communion.

April 27th Very rough and cold. Evelyn is a little better. Anthony heard this morning that Samuel Nuttal one of the Youlgreave Guardians had got nearly killed yesterday. He was riding in Arthur Marsden's new motor when he jumped out and was badly injured, and died this morning. I understand he thought something had gone wrong with the car (a part of a cigarette was smoking on the car bottom) and I think he thought it (the car) had fired. Tom went to Dr. Jackson for Evelyn who sent some medicine.

April 28th Fine and dry. Dr. Jackson came up to see Evelyn this morning. He is sending more medicine (tonic). Our Tony and Wilf Goodwin on moor stone picking.

April 29th A most lovely day. Our Tony and W. Goodwin riddling hayseeds this morning. Anthony took milk and went round after to Bakewell station for small seeds. Ashford policeman called with papers about the Aliens Restriction Act.

April 30th Another lovely day. Our men are gone on moor. The small seeds were sown and afterwards Anthony and Tom went to the field at Ashford to mend some places where other people's cows and things get in

---

1 Hill 60 south of Ypres. It was near Hill 60 that Tony was to be killed in 1917.

and out of our fields. Emily went with them in float. Sam Nuttal was buried at Youlgreave.

May 1st   Rather wet at times and windy. Between last night and this morning Anthony had some violent attacks of diarrhoea. We sent by Jack Naylor to Dr. Jackson for some medicine. He sent some but I afterwards asked Peter Goodwin to tell the Dr. to come up. Dr. Jackson came up to see Anthony. He (Anthony) has been very sick since.

May 2nd   A very nice day. Tom went on Fanny's back to let the Dr. know how his father was. He (Anthony) has had a much better night and has not been sick today or purged. Holy Communion in Sheldon Church at 9.30. Mr. Sherlock celebrated. The lady who asked me last week whether she could have breakfast came and had it this morning after she had received Holy Communion. Mr. Weadon took the service this afternoon. Collection 7s. 10d. for Church expenses.

May 4th   Very cold and wet at intervals. Mr. Hartopp called to see Anthony but the latter had gone on the moor which he had no business to do as he is far from well yet. The war still goes on. We keep losing a many men and seem to make no headway. The Germans go on sinking ships, neutrals as well as ours.

May 5th   A nice growing day today. Some nice showers. Warm. Anthony seems to have diarrhoea today. I thought he was better but he does not seem so well. Tony and Wilf took 4 cows to Ashford field. Tony went to Bakewell for meat.

May 6th   Another lovely day - warm. Tony is not well (diarrhoea). Our Ethel and Polly Roberts are cleaning pantry. Anthony seems better today. The Germans have sunk two more neutrals. Mr. Sherlock and Mr. Weadon called here and had tea. Our Ethel baked 5 sponge cakes and I gave them for the tea tomorrow.

May 8th   A fine day. Heard the dreadful news that the *Lusitania* had been torpedoed by the Germans off the South of Ireland (returning from America with passengers), some of the people were saved, about 500 or 600. There was a sale of work this afternoon in Sheldon School, the proceeds to buy books etc. for Sheldon Church. The Misses Hallows and Mrs. Morton took charge of the stalls, assisted by Mr. Weadon. Mrs. Ed B and I went up to the sale and stayed to tea which was provided at 9d. each. There was dancing at night. Mr. Sherlock came in Mr. F. Cox-Wilson's car. Mrs. Cox-Wilson, Miss Ada Alice Cox-Wilson were also there and a few others from Ashford. Over ten pounds was taken.

May 9th   Very cold (east wind). Mr. Weadon took the service in Church. A collection for Diocesan Expenses (the money did not come here). According to this morning's paper (*Empire*) there were 1,457 victims of *Lusitania* and 703 saved. This large ship sank in about half an hour (or less) after being torpedoed.

May 10th Very fine but a cold air. Jumble sale at school. A man (Goddard) came from Buxton to repair Church harmonium.

May 11th Very dull and close. Anthony and Tony were gardening and Tom, Wm., Wilf were in Fallow-field. Tom was drawing out potato rows (17). Polly Roberts was helping Ethel to wash. Sangers circus at Bakewell. We lent our large umbrella to a man who came in Hick's pony trap.

May 12th Very wet and windy. Wm. emptying our tank. Read in paper of the wrecking of German premises in different parts of the country - Birkenhead, Mexborough etc. This is an indignant protest against the sinking of the *Lusitania* and other German horrors. Anthony and Fred Brocklehurst are come tonight from Caterham. The man we lent our carriage umbrella to yesterday said he belonged to the Prudential Insurance Company.

May 13th Awfully cold wet and windy with snow storms at intervals. Anthony and Ethel papered my bedroom. Fred Brocklehurst came to see us. He looks very well.

May 14th Ethel and Polly Roberts finished my bedroom. Dull and cold rather showery. Mr. Sherlock called here. There was a Managers meeting at 4 o'clock this afternoon. Our carriage umbrella has not been returned to us.

May 16th Very wet showery at times towards night. Mr. Sherlock took the service in Church this afternoon. The congregation was out at 25 minutes past three o'clock, some difference between this and Mr. Weadon's time. Ruth Brocklehurst played harmonium. Anthony and Fred Brocklehurst went back to Caterham by the 10 minutes to six train. A few young men and women went to see them off.

May 17th Windy and cold. The wind has got in the east. Ethel went to Bakewell and had a tooth stopped. It cost her 3s. 6d. Anthony called at Hicks' and got our carriage umbrella. Let that man come borrowing again. If I am able I will answer him as he deserves.

May 18th Very cold but a bit of sunshine. Tom, Tony and Wilf Goodwin are down the fields. All the men are gone setting potatoes after dinner. Ethel and Kate Brocklehurst went on duty from 8.30 until 1.30. Our men have set 9 rows of potatoes. These make 18 altogether up to date.

May 19th Frosty this morning. Plenty of sun during the day and gets a little warmer. Mr. Weadon gave me 3 shillings (from Miss Grover) to buy flowers for Sheldon Church on Whit Sunday. I gave the money to James Goodwin and told him to get some (red and white). Some papers came to be signed about Polly Roberts being caretaker of Sheldon School.

May 20th Wet and drizzly this morning but much warmer. The news of the war is not so good as there are imminent changes taking place. A coalition ministry is to be formed and I am afraid conscription is coming soon. J. Goodwin brought red tulips and white flowers.

May 21st Very close. Anthony, Wm., and Alf Brocklehurst went to Derby to get cabbage plants. Anthony got 10,000 for us at 3s. 9d. per thousand. All the young men in Sheldon from 17 to 40 had their names put down at a meeting in Sheldon School for military purposes. The men were leading manure in cabbage rows. Our milk cows lay out first time tonight.

May 22nd Very fine. Our Anthony went to Longstone Station to fetch the cabbage plants.

May 23rd Very fine. Celebration of Holy Communion in Sheldon Church at 9.30 (Whit Sunday). Mr. Sherlock celebrated. Collection in Church was 7s. 3d. Two men came in and had tea: These men have been before and I think they are Germans (one came on April 24th).

May 24th Very hot sun and cold wind. I think the crops will be light while the wind stays in the east. Anthony, Tom, Tony are gone to the fair.

May 25th Very warm and sunny. Our men were carting manure for cabbage rows. A whist drive at the Sheldon School. There were no outsiders and only 4 tables. Our Ethel won first prize (sugar basin, jug and tray). Our Tony won the booby, and Mrs. Craven booby for ladies.

May 28th Very fine and hot sun. We are having some terrible disasters. The train collision a few days since. A many soldiers lost their lives as one train contained troops. The *Triumph,* was sunk (torpedoed in Dardanelles), and this morning I read that the *Majestic* had been torpedoed in Dardanelles, and *HM Ship Princess Irene* auxiliary ship was blown up in Sheerness harbour. It is believed that over 200 lives were lost. The *Princess Irene* was a mine-layer and formerly a Canadian Pacific liner. Nothing remains of the ship. Our men are working in the fallow. Tony and Wilf Goodwin planting cabbages. Anthony burning twitch. Tom drawing turnip rows and Wm. Gould leading manure. We have a cheese today as the milk was stopped last night and this morning. Mrs. Hallows had a daughter born at Ashford. W. Hallows came to Ashford from Caterham.

May 29th Very cold. A shower of rain towards night. Our men finished planting cabbage (30 rows of about 370 in a row). Tom finished drawing rows for swedes (about 40). Wm. Hallows came in our house tonight. Sam Wilton came on sick leave from Caterham. He is recovering from pneumonia and pleurisy.

May 30th Hot sun and cold air. Mr. Weadon took the service in Sheldon Church this afternoon. Ashford Wakes. Tom Wildgoose came in just before 2 o'clock with a soldier. They went out without having a drink as we could not fill soldiers, it being after time for them.

May 31st Fine but cold. Tom Critchlow came in our house between 12 and one o'clock (dinner time). He was over from Newcastle.

June 1st Read that there has been a Zeppelin raid near London. Since Italy has joined the Allies (above a week since) they have made good progress on their side. The Turks are losing heavily. The Germans keep on with their dastardly torpedoing of neutral ships and are quite insulting in their note to U. States over their sinking (torpedoing) the *Lusitania* (which had over 100 American citizens on board). The Germans are also using gas against our troops in France and Belgium.

June 3rd   Rather dull but the rain keeps off. All the people who have sheep in Sheldon are having them washed at Ashford today, and the lambs dipped when the men come back. We had some dip left over after the last dipping so Anthony did not charge anything for the lambs today.

June 6th   Very fine and warm. Dull at times. The long looked for rain does not come. We are wanting it badly. Holy Communion at 9.30 in Sheldon Church. Mr. Sherlock administered (came in Cox's car). Mr. Weadon took the service this afternoon. Four o'clock (within a minute or two) when over. Collection 9s. 7d. for Church expenses (brought here).

June 7th   Very fine. Another Zeppelin raid over East coast (on Sunday night). Ethel and Kate B went on duty for 7.30 this morning. Came back and went to the hospital again and were inoculated for Typhoid. Kate was bad coming home. The white faced puppy dog of ours was taken with a fit on moor and our Tom, Tony and Wm. had to drown it.

June 8th   Very close. The rain does not come. Everything is drooping for want of it. There were 5 persons killed and 40 injured through Zeppelin raid (Sunday night). A splendid feat was performed by a British airman yesterday. He attacked and brought down a Zeppelin between Ghent and Brussels and 28 of the crew were killed. In falling the Zeppelin alighted in an orphanage and killed 2 nuns and 2 children. The airman had to alight in the enemy's quarters but righted his machine and was able to get back to our aerodrome. The airman's name was Flight Sub. Lieutenant R.A.J. Warneford R.N. Our Ethel does not seem so well. Her arm seems stiff.

June 9th   Very hot. I was brought downstairs and taken straight out of doors. I sat in front until nearly nine o'clock and then was carried up to bed. (Tom, Tony and Wm. cleaning mere). During the time I was sitting outside Mr. Wm. Brocklehurst (uncle) was brought to the window of his bedroom (middle) and I was able to have a word or two with him.

June 10th   Very fine. People in Sheldon are busy leading water and there is none in the meres. We have borrowed a hose and are putting some in our mere in yard (the one that was cleaned out). Mr. Hartopp, Mr. Robertson and Mr. Twelves came and had lunch. I had a long conversation with Mr. Hartopp over the war. A number of Yeomanry or engineers went up Sheldon on mules.

June 11th   Very hot, no rain. Mr. Barnes and three workmen (Chatsworth estate) called here and had bread, cheese and beer. Mr. Sherlock also called. He was on horseback. The Germans have sunk two of our Torpedo ships off the East coast.

June 13th Very hot this morning, but the wind changed into East. Mr. Weadon took the service this afternoon. Two men, one of whom I always think is a German, the other is a stranger very tall and brown faced, came and had tea.

June 14th The sun is hot but the wind is in N. East and towards night became so cold that (being starved) I had a fire lit in house. Commenced sheep shearing, 6 with maggots. Heard that Arthur Cuthbert Taylor had been killed in action (Dardanelles).

June 15th Very hot sun and cold wind. Anthony fetched a new machine from Bakewell station (swath turner etc. which cost £15.5s. od.). Tom and Tony are gone on moor sheep shearing.

June 16th They have finished and are taking their greasy things off to have a bath. They have had their bath and feel all right. Tom and Tony have shorn all our sheep this year. Anthony took the dray and fetched the wool from moor. I paid Mr. Weadon £1 10s. 9d. (proceeds of organ fund). Sheldon organ has been done up at a cost of £1 10s. od.

June 17th Very cold wind NE. Evelyn paid Ruth Brocklehurst 3 shillings for playing harmonium in Sheldon Church during the Sundays she (Evelyn) was away at Grindleford and one Sunday when she was ill.

June 18th Cold wind, very hot sun, wind N. East. One hundred years today since the *Battle of Waterloo.*

June 20th Very fine. The wind gets a little more South. Mr. Sherlock took the service in Sheldon Church. There were prayers for rain.

June 21st Very hot sun. Anthony and TW Brocklehurst attended a meeting at Bakewell (recruiting). These two had been elected to represent Sheldon.

June 23rd Dull at times, wind N. I also acknowledged receipt of letter and posters[1] (recruiting) to AWJ Eyre Esq., The Mount, Longstone. The fall of Lensburgh has been announced (the Russians had taken it from Austria early in the war).

June 24th Very cold. The wind continues in N.E. Dull at times but no more rain comes. Anthony had a letter from Mr. Sherlock hoping that more young men would offer themselves at the recruiting meeting at Sheldon next Saturday. Polly Roberts and our girls finished cleaning kitchen. Mr. Lloyd George brings out his Munition Bill and gives 7 days for voluntary workers to come forward. Thos. A. Brocklehurst and Fred came from Caterham.

[1] An all-party Parliamentary Recruiting Committee arranged for the distribution of forms to every household. The aim was to compile a National Register of those willing to enlist. These men would then be attested by the nearest Recruiting Officer. See Introduction page xxiv.

June 25th Fine but rather dull. Mr. Weadon brought a signed paper for £1 10s. 9d. (organ fund). Two men and motor chauffeur called here. I heard someone say they were Government officials.

June 26th Our Mary's birthday (28 years). Some grand refreshing showers of rain came during last night and this morning. I think people throughout the country will be most thankful to our Heavenly Father for sending it as almost everything was parched up. Captain Seymour spoke (Recruiting Officer).

June 27th Close but keeps fine. A strange clergyman took the Service. Mr. Weadon was there. Some leaflets were distributed to the men who had not recruited. A collection (Temperance). The money was not brought here (our home). Ethel and Kate B went to Taddington.

June 28th During the night and early this morning some nice showers of rain came. I heard thunder during the night. Sam Wilton went back to Caterham. Anthony and Fred Brocklehurst went back to Caterham by the quarter past 6 train tonight. These two went by a later train than S. Wilton. Jim Goodwin was greatly offended at our Ethel. He said that she had served him with such a little gin for twopence. He got up and went out of the house. Perhaps our serving of gin is like his greengrocery. He will not give much away.

June 29th Thunder and slight showers. Very grand growing weather. Alf Wildgoose came in tonight with Jim Goodwin. Anthony gave Alf some cigars and Billy Naylor gave him some cigarettes.

June 30th Thunder and heavy rain today. Alf Wildgoose went back to his company (Notts and Derby near North Shields).

July 1st Fine. Our men have been setting cabbage plants in place of those dead for want of rain. Our Ethel received a letter from Fred Brocklehurst. Anthony and Tom finished the hay barn with corrugated iron. Mr. Sherlock called here. He had been to a wedding at Taddington.

July 4th Very wet. Thunder and rain and hail all day. Mr. Sherlock administered Holy Communion. 11 present. Mr. Weadon took the service this afternoon. Collection 8s. 9d.

July 6th Very dull and close. Showery at intervals. Read in paper that the Turks etc. have lost (in killed and wounded) over 20,000. Also read that there went from Youlgreave (yesterday) about 30 more recruits. Captain Seymour was Recruiting Officer.

July 7th Very dull and showery at times. Mr. Sherlock called here as he wanted a Managers' meeting. This meeting was adjourned because Lomas had not sent his coal bill.

July 8th Very dull. The National Register Bill is passing through House of Commons. The Kaiser says *Calais at any cost.*

July 9th   Very dull and cold towards night. Ethel and Kate B went on duty for 7.30 this morning. These girls have to rise at 5.30 each morning. Lord Kitchener's speech at the Guildhall for Men, Money and Munitions.

July 11th   Dull and showery towards night. Mr. Sherlock took the service in Church this afternoon. Young Cox-Wilson brought him up in car. I was out in my chair tonight.

July 12th   Dull and windy, a good shower this afternoon. Anthony went with milk and afterwards to Bakewell. He brought blue overalls for himself, Tom and Tony.

July 13th   Dull and close. After getting downstairs I sat out of doors in front until teatime. Three women and a man came in horse and trap and had refreshment here. They sat and chatted with me an hour or two. They said they were the daughters and son of the late Wm. Gregory who between fifty and sixty years ago had a windmill at the top of Sheldon village. One of them said she was the eldest and would be 74 next birthday. She lives near Bristol. The other two sisters and brother (Peter) live at Tansley, Matlock, where they went after leaving Sheldon over 50 years ago. Evelyn showed them Sheldon Church.

July 14th   Dull and close. Our Tom and Tony had a book etc. telling them to enlist either for munitions or military work. I believe all the young men have had one. A Managers' meeting. Mr. Sherlock did not call here. Anthony did not go to the meeting as Mr. Thacker and he were bargaining over a cow (did not bargain).

July 17th   Between last night and this morning the rain fell in torrents. Very rough wind all day. Sam Wilton came to Sheldon today. He has got his discharge from Army. The doctors (Caterham) wanted him to have an operation. Something that the pneumonia etc. had left on him.

July 18th   A delightful sunny day. Mr. Weadon took the service this afternoon.

July 21st   Dull. The weather is very unfavourable for the hay. The war is still dragging on and poor Russia seems to be retreating. There is a possibility of the South Wales coal strike being ended. Mr. Lloyd George (Munition Head) and Mr. Runciman have gone there to see what can be done. This strike began last Thursday and a great shame it is. The poor soldiers cannot strike and cease fighting when they like.

July 22nd   Very dull and very heavy showers at times. The S. Wales miners have settled strike.

July 23rd   Dull and showery at times. The Germans are closing in on Warsaw.

July 24th Rather brighter today. Big Jimmy and another Irishman called here today. I let him have one pint (on strap) but told him I was not accustomed to do so.

July 25th Dull and a shower came on this afternoon. Mr. Sherlock took the service in Sheldon Church this afternoon. Young Cox-Wilson brought him in car.

July 27th Very bright and sunny first thing but there is thunder and some rain later. I was bad with the wind early this morning. Just before three o'clock, Anthony had to open the door and window wide as I felt suffocated. I had eaten some cucumber and onion. We opened tin of salmon steak (Orme's) it was bad (threw it on midden).

July 28th Dull and showery at times. The Russians are making a stand against the Germans. Mr. Weadon called and was making preparation for children's tea on Friday.

July 29th Bright at times and dull at times. All the sheep and lambs in Sheldon are dipped today on Gytes' premises. As follows

				Sheep	Lambs
Gytes	82	sheep and lambs		46	36
B. Naylors	8	sheep and lambs		6	2
A. Manderfields	16	"	"		
John Brocklehurst	36	"	"		
Thos. Wm.	30	"	"		
Herbert Frost	4	"	"		
John Frost	7	"	"	2	5
Alf Brocklehurst	13	"	"	8	5

There were five dogs dipped

July 30th Very fine this morning. When I got up I was taken out of doors and sat in front until teatime, when a heavy shower came on. Sheldon children had their annual school treat and toys etc. Miss Grover gave all. Mrs. Tinsley and her sister called and sat at the door talking with me a short time. Miss Grover, Mrs. Kenworthy and Mr. Weadon called and had a chat with me. Mr. Sherlock rode up in a carriage with Mrs. Tinsley and her sister. He called out to me and asked if I was going up to the tea. I did not go. He did not call here. I was picking red currants which Anthony had bought off Elias Oldfield (a poor lot at 6d. per lb.). Sheldon school children broke up for holidays this morning.

July 31st A very bright and hot morning. Anthony tried our new swath turner. It acted pretty well and would have done better if the crops (Hicks) had been heavier. Anthony filled up return for the sheep dipping. The Germans have not taken Warsaw yet but I am afraid its fall is only a question of a short time.

August 1st   Rather dull and showery in afternoon. Holy Communion in Sheldon Church. Mr. Sherlock administered (9.30). Mr. Weadon took the service in the afternoon (collection 8s. 4d.) for Church expenses. A nice lot in the house tonight.

August 3rd   Very wet. Thunder and the rain came down in torrents. Tom and Tony went to John Bank Wood to fetch out one of our cows which had got out of our field at Ashford. They found her and put her back.

August 4th   There is very little hay got in Sheldon as the weather is so unfavourable. We have only mown 2 of Hick's fields at present. Our men viz. Anthony, Tom, Tony and Wm. Gould are gone in hay this afternoon. There was a meeting up at school the anniversary of the Declaration of War. The resolution was passed that we should go on with war until Germany was vanquished. There were meetings all over England. Mr. Weadon took the chair. He also said there were more men who ought to go out of Sheldon.

August 5th   Dull and showery at times. There are some people staying in Miss Hallam's house. The man has been in army and travelled in 5 countries. In India, Egypt etc. He is still working under Government. It is very interesting to hear him talk over things as he did tonight in our house.

August 6th   Very dull and heavy thunder showers. Our Ethel and Polly Roberts have cleaned dairy and cellar today. The Germans have entered Warsaw.

August 7th   Very dull and showery. We have not got a bit of hay yet. We expected our Mary and Aunt H. Ethel and Tony went down to Ashford to meet them but they did not show up and I was very pleased as it came on so wet. Ethel and Tony got wet.

August 8th   A miserable dull and wet day. All at our house attended Church with the exception of Tony and I. Mr. Weadon took the service this afternoon. A full house tonight.

August 9th   Very dull and showery this morning. Anthony and Tony took 3 cows to market. Anthony sold one cow for £27.0.0. and the other two made £49.10.0. and he bought three off John Frost for £22.0.0. each.

August 10th   Dull and close and a bit showery. John Frost and Ed B brought registration papers.

August 11th   Very close. Evelyn and Ruth went on duty for 7.30 this morning. Mary and the baby seem very well. Mr. Weadon called here tonight.

August 13th   Very fine and bright but a shower came on about dinner time. The notorious *Smith* who drowned his wives in baths (3) was hung this morning. The anniversary of Anthony's and my wedding (29 years). Wm Gould began mowing top field on moor.

August 15th Thunder and showery. Evelyn and Ruth B went on duty for 7.30 this morning. Mr. Weadon took the service in Sheldon Church. Our Mary played organ. Evelyn got back from Bakewell but she stayed at home to rest a bit. Some of the men in Sheldon went fox hunting and one (vixen) was shot (by S. Rowland). Sunday was rather a queer day for that. We all filled National Register papers.

August 18th Fair today. Read in paper that the *Royal Edward* a transport ship with 1350 reinforcements was torpedoed in the Aegean Sea by the Germans. About six hundred were reported saved.

August 20th Dull first thing but clears out in afternoon. Another liner was torpedoed (*Arabic*) yesterday belonging to the White Star Line off the Irish coast. There were 391 saved out of 423. This vessel was torpedoed without warning and was bound from Liverpool to New York with a valuable cargo. Got top field on moor.

August 21st Dull but fine. We mowed Grindlow Knoll. Read that *E13* British submarine went ashore on Danish Island Saltholme.

August 22nd Dull but keeps fine. Alf Wildgoose came this morning from Sutton on Hull. Mr. Weadon took the service in Church. Joe Carson came for beer and stood talking to me in houseplace passage, 1st time since Dec. 31st 1914.

August 23rd Very fine today. Willie Needham came over from Hasland and called to see us. He is a corporal and has been 11 months in training. He expects to go to France in a fortnight. The war news is better this morning. A German cruiser has been torpedoed by a British submarine in the Baltic. Three German torpedo boats were damaged by mines in the Gulf of Riga. A British airman (Lieut. Edmonds) dropped a heavy bomb on Turkish troopship and the vessel went down. This was done from a seaplane over the Dardanelles. The crew of the *E13* were shot at whilst they were in the water by Germans.

August 25th A lovely day. Alf Wildgoose went back to his regiment to Sutton on Hull. Mr. Weadon called tonight.

August 27th A very good hay day, plenty of sun and wind. Wm. mows Waterlands and Croft heads. Fall of Brest Litowsk (Russian Fortress).

August 28th Another very good hay day. Plenty of sun and wind. Tom was using the new machine in Croft head and Waterlands. The Russians keep falling back and we had a repulse in the Dardanelles a few days ago. Mr. Sneap came in tonight.

August 29th Wet and has been during the night. Mr. Sneap and Anthony went on moor. Mr. Weadon took the service in Sheldon Church this afternoon.

Sept. 2nd Dull and windy. There are only 11 soldiers in hospital at Bakewell. Eggs are selling at 8 per shilling. A lot of soldiers (Chatsworth Rifles) stationed at Bakewell marched through Sheldon between 8 and 9 tonight towards Bakewell.

Sept. 3rd Very dull. A poor hay day. Wm. Gould mowed the Pingle and part of Big Butts. The National Register certificates were brought here by John Frost for all at our house.

Sept. 5th Another good day. Celebration of Holy Communion by Mr. Sherlock at 9.30 this morning. Mr. Weadon took the service this afternoon. Collection for Church expenses (10s. 8d.).

Sept. 7th A very fine day. We began getting the Big Butts. I was taken in my chair into the stack yard and enjoyed watching them put the loads of hay under the new hay shed. The *Hesperian*, a British liner, was torpedoed last Saturday night without warning off the Irish coast. The boats were lowered and people were saved. Today's paper tells us that one person was drowned and 25 missing. The men got 12 loads of hay out of Big Butts.

Sept. 9th A very good day, plenty of sun and wind. Ethel went to Holme Hall to a party connected with the Red Cross. She sent in a camisole for competition at the above place. In the last air raid (over London) there were 10 killed and 46 injured according to this morning's paper. Our men (this afternoon) got Hannah Croft 3 good loads and this finished our hay harvest. Our Ethel got 1st prize in competition needlework: a soldier's (back) bag of different things viz: one towel, one handkerchief, one pair of socks, one tablet of soap, one pipe, one tobacco pouch, one tin of vaseline.

Sept. 12th A very grand day: glorious sunshine. All of us went to Church this afternoon. I had not been for months. Mr. Sherlock took the service. Between 4 and 5 o'clock the man whom we always think is a German came with a young woman and had tea here. Ethel, Evelyn, Tom and Tony went to Longstone Church (Wakes). Tom and Tony did not go in Church.

Sept. 15th Rather dull first thing but clears out into a lovely day. Mr. Sherlock paid us a visit, on horseback. Having fastened his horse to the ring at our end of house, he came and had a cup of tea. Some lads kicked a football into the horse and it (the horse) bolted and ran into the Bland Croft. Our Ethel and Aunt H were helping Mr. Sherlock to mend the bridle which was broken in two places.

Sept. 19th A fine day. Mr. Sherlock took the service in Sheldon Church. Mr. Weadon is away. Our girls went to Monyash Church tonight. They took Emily in Mrs. Ed's chair.

Sept. 22nd Finished leading the corn and clover field. Rather misty. The Budget came out (Mr. McKenna's). A tax was put on tea, sugar, coffee, chickory, tobacco, income tax, imported cars etc. none on beer and spirits. As soon as the budget was known all shopkeepers etc. put up their wares. We have not put our tobacco up yet.

Sept. 23rd Misty and showery. Our men are gone on moor. Wm and Tony thistle mowing and Tom thatching stack.

Sept. 24th A very good day. Tony and Wm Gould gone thistle mowing. I sat out of doors this afternoon and was enjoying my tea when Mr. Weadon popped up. I invited him to have some and he went and had tea with them in kitchen.

Sept. 25th Rather misty and drizzling. The Russians who have been retreating for weeks seem to be giving some counter attack and retaking a few of their lost places. Anthony took Fanny and the dog-cart to meet the 4.58 at Bakewell. He brought us some damsons and two guinea-hens for Tony.

Sept. 26th Rather dull but turns out a good day. Mr. Weadon took the service in Church this afternoon. A full house. A horse of Mr. Charles Critchlow's ran away. Evelyn and Ruth met it coming at a furious rate down the dale. A. Brockley and G. Wall stopped it.

Sept. 28th A slow corn day. Not much sun and no wind. The churchyard was mown. Jack Naylor, George Brocklehurst, George Briddon, John Brocklehurst etc. were helping and the grass was carted away. Great victories by the allies in Russia and France.

Sept. 29th A very good day for fielding the corn. Our men are leading from the moor to stackyard at home (9 loads). The war news continues good in France. There are over 20,000 prisoners taken (German). Evelyn and Ruth B have finished their week at Red Cross hospital. (There are 30 soldiers there.)

Sept. 30th A very good day for the corn, plenty of sun and wind. The news continues good from France. Bulgaria has mobilized and Greece has mobilized as a reply. Sir E. Grey has uttered grave warning to Bulgaria and said that the Allies will help Servia etc. Our men were leading the corn (in sheaf) from moor (3 loads). An Italian Iron Clad lost with 400 men. The Excise Officer called (Moss) and took our licence.

Oct. 1st A pretty good day. Our men leading corn. Read that 121 guns have been taken from the Germans. Mr. Sherlock walked to Sheldon and had tea here.

Oct. 2nd Dull and drizzling rain. Anthony went with milk and called at Miss Grover's for grapes and flowers for Harvest Thanksgiving. Ethel and Aunt H went with others to decorate the Church. There was not such a profusion of things as other years but the Church looked very well.

Oct. 3rd Wakes Sunday. Rather dull but fine. We all went to Church this afternoon. The congregation was not a large one as on former occasions. Miss H. Grover and her brother were there. Mr. Grover's motor also brought Mr. Sherlock and Mr. Weadon. The collection amounted to £2. 2s. 1d. for Church expenses. Wm. Hallows, Fred and Anthony Brocklehurst went back to their barracks. A many went to the station to see them off as they are under orders for France on Tuesday next.

Oct. 4th   Rather dull. A very poor Wakes. No one in the house this morning. Fred and Ethel Brocklehurst (Potteries) came in this afternoon. Mr. Weadon called and had tea here.

Oct. 5th   Rather dull. A dance was held at the school (for club) 6d. each. There were a good many there.

Oct. 6th   Fine. A few in. Service in Church tonight (Mr. Weadon). People only in house place. A poor Wakes. We close at 9 o'clock and no dancing.

Oct. 7th   Fine. Another dance at the school (for Red Cross). Chelmorton youths came again.

Oct. 8th   Very fine. All sheep and lambs in Sheldon were again dipped. Mr. Sherlock and Mr. Weadon both called here and had tea. Mr. John Frost gave 5s. 0d. to Mr. Weadon towards Church expenses. Willie Needham is missing since last battle in France (Loos etc.).

Oct. 9th   Fine. Our men are getting potatoes (Bole Piece). The ending of the poorest Wakes I have ever known in Sheldon. The houseplace has been big enough for all home people and visitors as well. Other years we have had the parlour as well full at times. Whoever lives to see another Sheldon Wakes I hope things will be brighter and this terrible war ended. The three Sheldon men have landed in France and are all together. I have been in parlour all week.

Oct. 10th   Rather dull drizzling and cold. Mr. Weadon took the service in Church. Our Tom, Ethel and Evelyn went to Ashford Church (Harvest Thanksgiving) tonight. A cow (bought of Mr. J. Frost) calved a cow calf.

Oct. 12th   Rather dull. The men and Wilf Goodwin and Vincent Hallows are getting potatoes. Our licence was returned today by post. Eggs are selling at 6 for one shilling. The Germans are at Belgrade (Servia).

Oct. 13th   A very fine day. Our men are getting potatoes. Emily and Aunt H went to the potato field (Bole Piece). I went (in my chair) to see the potatoes in bottom cart shed. A very nice lot. (My new diary came from Grattons).

Oct. 15th   Very fine. Mr. Sherlock called here over some correspondence he had had from the Derby Education Authority over some bills. (Alf Wildgoose's and some things that Miss Hallam had ordered on her own). I signed a paper as witness to his signing.

Oct. 17th Very fine. Mr. Sherlock took the service in Sheldon Church. Young Cox-Wilson brought him up in trap. Tom, Ethel and Evelyn went to Taddington Harvest Thanksgiving (Church). Dr. Ford[1] preached and his surplice got on fire. Mrs. Roberts called out *Dr. you are on fire.*

Oct. 18th Very fine. Our Flag Day (Red Cross) at Sheldon and Ashford. Flags are being sold here. Our Ethel and Tony etc. are very busy trying to sell some. We have a box with the Red Cross on it for anyone who wishes to drop anything into it. The Vicar of Burbage called and Mr. Lowthian and bought Flags off our Ethel (gave her four shillings amongst them). Tom, Ethel and Evelyn went to Ashford to concert (Red Cross).

Oct. 20th Lord Derby's[2] scheme for recruiting was in paper. Ashford and Sheldon got over £21 for *Our Day.*

Oct. 23rd A dull day. The hunters turned out at Sheldon. There was not much sport as the hare scent was poor. The weary war drags on and the allied fleets are bombarding the Bulgarian coast. Servia is fighting very well but is outnumbered.

Oct. 24th Very rough and wet and has been during last night and this morning. Sam Bramwell lit a fire at Church as it was so cold and dashing. Anthony and Evelyn were busy with the organ as a note would not play. Mr. Weadon took the service in Church and as usual it was very long and tiring. A collection was taken for the Red Cross (11s. 9d.).

Oct. 25th Very rough. Anthony went to market. Mrs. Ed had a letter to say that Willie Needham is wounded in the knee and a prisoner. Received a cheque from Mr. Archer for milk (Oct. 16th) value £21 17s. 6d. The milk was 3/- per doz; such a price we have never reached since we began sending milk to Manchester over 28 years ago. We tied up our milk beasts tonight. They will be warmer, as the weather is so rough and dashing.

Oct. 26th Rather cold but the wind has settled. Mr. Hartopp, Mr. Robertson and Mr. Twelves came and had luncheon. I charged them 8d. each for bread and butter and cheese. Things are so dear to buy. I had a nice chat with Mr. Hartopp over the war. Goodwin had a letter from Lord Derby over enlisting. Tom ploughing (Hicks).

Oct. 27th Rather frosty, but turns out a nice day. The milk cows go out during the day but are kept in at night. I am busy knitting a scarf. I do a little every day and I hope to finish it soon (for the soldiers). Mr. Weadon called here. Miss Hallam had half a load of potatoes.

Oct. 30th Misty and cold. William Gould fetched coke for Church 12 cwt for 10 shillings. Eggs are very scarce now (5 a shilling).

1   The Revd. Dr. William Henry Ford, Rector of Taddington from 1897, author of *The Art of Extempore Speaking* (11 editions) and *The Art of Preaching* (4 editions).
2   See Introduction page xxiv

Oct 31st   Very wet and cold. Mr. Sherlock took the services in Church. Daybell brought him up in trap.

Nov. 2nd   Fair but very cold. Tom is ploughing on moor. Our Tom received Lord Derby's letter.

Nov. 3rd   Very cold. Tom ploughing on moor. Elsie Eaton had a little son. (Fanny Thorpe was there and no doctor). A Managers meeting at Sheldon School. Mr. John Frost is now a manager and was at the meeting. Mr. Sherlock came on horseback. He did not call here. Anthony had the young horse (Fanny) down in Shady Lane. It slipped as it had been frosty. Read some papers from C. White which J. Frost had about enlisting.

Nov. 4th   Cold. Anthony and Tony commenced pulling turnips. Girls are off duty for a week. I finished a scarf (for soldiers).

Nov. 5th   Miss Hallam paid for the potatoes she had here.

Nov. 6th   Frosty and cold. Tom is ploughing on moor and the others are pulling and pitting turnips. Thos. Wm. B. does not take milk on Saturday nights and as we do not take ours we shall miss having an evening paper.

Nov. 7th   Cold and rather rough but later on the wind settles. Holy Communion in Sheldon Church administered by Rev. H.E. Sherlock (9.30). Mr. Weadon took the service this afternoon, collection (7s. 8d.) for Church expenses. Monyash Wakes. Tom, Ethel and Evelyn went with others to Monyash Church. Tom was too late for the service.

Nov. 8th   Cold. Tom and Wm Gould took three carts to Ashford and brought manure from the Bulls Head. Anthony met Mr. Archer at Bakewell and bargained for winter months (milk).

Nov. 9th   Very wet this morning but clears out later. Anthony and Tony are digging in front garden. Anthony's birthday (52).

Nov. 10th Very wet. Tom and Tony and Anthony were putting up potatoes for H. Frost.

Nov. 11th Cold but finer. Two strangers came in and I had a talk about war etc. with them. Mr. John Frost called with paper over recruiting.

Nov. 12th A most awfully rough and wet day. We have a many wet coats etc. The young horses and young cows got out of our moor and Tom and Tony had to go after them in the rain. Mr. Asquith in the House of Commons said that if the single men did not come up as they ought there would be some form of conscription.

Nov. 13th Very frosty and the fields are covered with frost and snow. Our Tony's birthday (18). Dr. Tom Fentem says that Jenny Brocklehurst has got Typhoid fever and there is going to be a bother over the water. We are drinking river water.

Nov. 14th Very frosty and slippery. Mr. Weadon took the service in Church this afternoon. A full house tonight.

Nov. 15th Bakewell fair. A rough day. Snowstorms. Red Cross Sale at Bakewell. The following were sent from Sheldon:Three lambs from Gytes, Wm Naylor 1 cheese. John Brocklehurst 1 cheese. Mr. Craven 1 cheese. Mrs. Carson potatoes. Thos. Wm. Brocklehurst potatoes. Alf Brocklehurst potatoes. Thos. A. Sheldon fowls. John Frost £1.0.0. Wm. H. Brocklehurst 2s.od. L.E. Elliott 1s.od. Anthony went to the Guardians' meeting and explained about the water and afterwards went to the Red Cross Sale. Tom and Tony went to Bakewell. Mrs. Craven bought a donkey and an Airedale terrier from the Red Cross Sale.

Nov. 17th Very cold. Lord St. David spoke in the Lords about Sir J. French's general staff and other charges viz Ladies visiting headquarters, Officers playing bridge late at night and not being at their duties in the morning. Mr. Weadon called here tonight and we had quite a huffy conversation over items which had appeared in the paper over Lord Derby's recruiting scheme. Sam Rowland asked him a few questions and I asked how it was that clergymen would be exempt from serving. Mr. Weadon said a few things that I did not like. Ethel and Tony went to Bakewell for a coat and waistcoat.

Nov. 18th Cold. Jenny Brocklehurst is improving a bit with Typhoid fever. Read in paper that a hospital ship struck a mine and about 100 soldiers were drowned. The ship was the *Albania* and the soldiers were wounded. This catastrophe happened in the Channel.

Nov. 19th Very cold. Anthony has a bad cold yet. A Managers meeting was held in our houseplace. There were present Mr. Sherlock, Mr. J. Frost, Mr. Thos.Wm. and Mr. Wm. H. Brocklehurst and Mr. Gyte.

Nov. 20th Very cold. I have been reading the leaflet (Lord Derby's scheme) and I find there is a deal of difference between starred and unstarred men. The starred men may not be approached by the Recruiting Officer and if they enlist they can be sent to their employment, but the unstarred at the discretion of the Recruiting Officer may be sent back as if on leave whilst his papers are sent to the War Office. If he appeals he has not the same privilege as the starred (as I read it). We had quite a good laugh when the policeman (Dennis) brought the new licensing regulations after nine o'clock tonight.

Nov. 21st Cold. Mr. Sherlock took the service in Church this afternoon (collection for foreign mission). We had quite a row with Billy Naylor, Sam Rowland and Alf Brockley.

Nov. 22nd Very cold. Anthony and Tony took 3 cows to market and sold them. The new Licensing Act came in force today. We kept open until 9.30 tonight.

Nov. 23rd Very cold. Our men have been in turnips today. People are discussing Lord Derby's scheme. I do not know what the country will be brought to over this cruel war.

Nov. 26th Very cold, frosty. Mr. Skidmore called and had a teatotal (sic) drink. Very few have intoxicants at night. Mr. Sherlock called and had tea and a very heated argument I had with him over the war.

Nov. 28th Very cold. Mr. Weadon took the service in Sheldon Church this afternoon. Our Tom cycled over to Joe Haywoods (Dudwood). Joe and he went to Robin Hood's Stride and Cratcliffe rocks. Tom had not been to these places before and he was quite surprised to see such wonderful rocks etc.

Nov. 30th Rather milder. Mary and the baby seem very well. He is getting a rough little customer.

Dec. 1st Misty. The men were spreading manure on moor. Anthony was mending gaps. Alf Brocklehurst, Sam Rowland and Fred Carson went to attest at Bakewell recruiting office. Sam Rowland passed the doctor, but the other two did not.

Dec. 2nd Foggy in the bottom (Ashford) a little sunshine upon these hills. Misty towards night and rain. Willie Carson went to attest at Bakewell but did not pass the doctor. George Carson also went and did not pass, also John Pursglove and he did not pass.

Dec. 3rd Awfully wet and miserable. George Goodwin and our Tom went to attest. Our Tom passed for active service on the field but George Goodwin did not pass, he has varicose veins. Our Tom drew 2s. 9d.

Dec. 4th Very wet. Elsie Goodwin called to say that there would not be Holy Communion tomorrow as Mr. Sherlock was not well.

Dec. 5th Wet and miserable. No celebration of Holy Communion. Mr. Weadon took the service in Church this afternoon. There was a collection which was said to be for the Layman's stipend but whether it was taken by Mr. Weadon or not I do not know. The money was not brought here. [In pencil] The collection money was afterwards brought here (7s. 10d. for Church expenses).

Dec. 6th A most wet and miserable morning. Wilf Goodwin went to attest under Lord Derby's scheme but was medically unfit.

Dec. 7th Very wet. Fred Goodwin attested at Bakewell and was passed for active service in the field. There are four young men in Sheldon who have not attested yet. G. Briddon, G. Brocklehurst, J. Brocklst and J. Naylor. Our Tony has not but he is only just 18. Ben Naylor killed a pig for Billy Naylor.

Dec. 8th   Very heavy showers came on at intervals this morning but got fair and was frosty tonight. Our Ethel got very wet when coming off duty (Red Cross Hospital). She finished her week's work. The Duke's men are busy taking up the water pipes at the Pot Boil[1] etc.

Dec. 9th   Very frosty and cold. Eggs are very scarce 4 and 5 per shilling. A snowstorm came on after dinner and if it keeps on snowing as it is doing now there will soon be a great depth.

Dec. 11th   Wet and windy at times. I heard today that H. Wallwin had attested and passed the doctor also Jim Skidmore's son. The time for enlisting under Lord Derby's scheme is extended until tomorrow.

Dec. 12th   On getting up this morning people found that snow had fallen about 3 inches and it was very frosty; it continues so and is very winterly. Mr. Weadon took the service in Church this afternoon.

Dec. 14th   Ethel's birthday (23 yrs). Very raw and cold, thawing. Snow came this morning and afterwards turned to rain. I hope the frost will keep off as it is now slippery in the roads. Ethel had a letter from our Mary which said in it that Clem had attested last Wednesday at Bakewell. Dr. Jackson said that Clem was as good as they made them and so of course was passed. Men could attest under Lord Derby's scheme until 4 o'clock last Sunday.

Dec. 15th   A wet miserable day. Evelyn and Tony went to Bakewell to buy presents for Xmas. Some were bought for Anthony and Fred Brocklehurst who are in France and in the trenches. Anthony sent a letter to Mr. Hawes asking for information about starred and unstarred men (and about Tom).

Dec. 16th   A brighter and better day. Our Tom had a letter come back which he had sent to Anthony B. This letter was insufficiently addressed. Elsie Eaton's little baby died. Wm. Gould took some sand down to the waterworks (Pot Boil) and he also went to Cox-Wilson's for cement and pipes. Anthony is carting these free of cost. Our girls have been busy packing the things for Anthony and Fred.

Dec. 17th   Very misty. Mr. Sherlock called to see us today. Seven of the Duke's men came and took down the ruins of Haslam's old house. They came in here for their dinner hour and I had some talk to them over the war. Anthony filled up forms for our Tom viz. Employer: Anthony Gyte Occupation: Agriculture and Dairy Farmer Exact occupation of our Tom: Milking, ploughing, sowing, stacking, thatching, sheep shearing, attention to sheep at lambing time. Skilled in any of the above branches of farming. How long in present occupation - 13 years. How long will he remain - while able.

Dec. 19th   A very nice frosty day. Ernest Taylor and his wife came to see us (from Tideswell). Our Tom, Tony, Ethel and Evelyn went with them to

---

[1]   This was part of the Magpie Mine's drainage system.

Longstone Station at night. Mr. Sherlock took the service in Church this afternoon. All went from our house except Mrs. E. Taylor, Tony and myself. Mr. Harrison and Mr. Wilson came from Sheffield and had dinner here. They have not been here for a long time. Mr. Harrison's son was sailing (today) from Plymouth to Egypt. He had been in training for a soldier on Salisbury Plain.

Dec. 21st   Rather drizzly and dull (shortest day). Tom and Tony took our young horses from Sheldon moor to Ashford. Read in paper that our forces had been withdrawn from Anzac and Suvla Bay. What a costly failure this has been. Mr. Asquith's speech over the Derby Scheme cannot be made today. Miss Grover sent 5/- for flowers.

Dec. 22nd Wet and drizzling at times but mild. J. Goodwin brought some lovely white flowers from Manchester with the 5/- Miss Grover sent.

Dec. 23rd   Rather wet at first but clears out later. Sent Xmas cards to a few.

Dec. 24th Misty. Some flowers were sent for Sheldon Church (from Derby) and Ethel, Clarice etc. decorated. Anthony went to Bakewell for rum, tobacco and cigarettes. Evelyn and Tony put up the evergreens in houseplace. Our men sent a hare and Mr. Sneap a turkey.

Dec. 25th Xmas Day. Wet at times but mild. A few singers went round after 12 (midnight) and sang Christians Awake. Celebration of Holy Communion (Mr. Sherlock) at 9.30 this morning. Mr. Weadon took the service this afternoon collection for lay reader (7s.9d.). Jim Goodwin, John Purseglove, Sam Rowland and F. Goodwin formed a band and played in our house. The singers went round Sheldon tonight.

Dec. 26th Drizzling but clears out later. Mr. Weadon takes the service in Sheldon Church this afternoon. We had hare to dinner today, it wanted cooking. Mr. Weadon had tea here after service.

Dec. 27th A most awful wet and windy day. There was a dance at the school but very few were there as the weather was so stormy.

Dec. 28th A calm day after the stormy one. Three niggers came in tonight and were singing etc. Sheldon band went to Dirtlow tonight. Alf Wildgoose is in Birmingham (Edgebaston) hospital. Alf is improving slowly from fever (Dardanelles).

Dec. 29th A wet and stormy day. A tea and dancing was held up at the school. There were not many men dancing, no outsiders. Mr. Weadon was there. Wm. Gould was doorkeeper and our Tom was reckoning up things. Jim Goodwin was paid 6/- and half a gallon of bitter beer.

Dec. 30th Fair. Emily and Ethel received a letter from F. Brocklehurst. When he wrote he and Anthony had just got out of the trenches (France) and were going for a rest about 5 miles out somewhere. Anthony has got a headache tonight.

Dec. 31st The last day of the year is a most stormy one. An intercession service in Sheldon Church at 7.30 tonight. Tom, Tony, Ethel and Evelyn were there. A few in the house tonight.

1916

Jan. 1st Just before 10 o'clock this morning, Jim Goodwin, Fred and J. Purseglove were playing their horns outside our house and then wished us a happy New Year. An awful wet and windy day. I read in paper that a British cruiser had been blown up in harbour by an explosion. The name of the harbour was not given. Above 300 lives were lost. The name of the cruiser was the *Natal*. Our Tom's birthday (27). Children's Service in Sheldon Church taken by Mr. Sherlock who called and had chat with me. Anthony and T.W. Brocklehurst have just been up to school and given out the flannel dole. Only 3 children at Church so they dispersed.

Jan. 2nd Wet at intervals but the wind is calmer. Holy Communion in Sheldon Church at 9.30. Mr. Sherlock administered. He also came up and took the afternoon service. Evelyn did not go on duty. The collection went towards the Red Cross funds. Loss of another ship P and O Liner *Persia* (nearly 400 lost) torpedoed in Mediterranean on Dec. 30th. We had the turkey and plum pudding to dinner.

Jan. 4th A most wet, wintry and miserable day. We had a letter from Edith Limer wanting to borrow a sovereign.

Jan. 5th Calmer and fairer today. I sent Edith Limer a one pound note and wrote telling her that Mr. Gyte lent it her for the period of one month. The Number of the note was T15 no 95062. Mr. Weadon called here.

Jan. 7th Very rough and wet at intervals. I had a letter from Edith Limer thanking us for lending her the £1 note. Our girls are rendering fat. A dance at the school. All our children went. J. Goodwin and Fred were there.

Jan. 8th Finer rather colder. There was a talk this morning that someone had broken into J. Goodwin's building at the top of Sheldon and a strange thing was that a pick and a hatchet of ours were found there. It is evident that the someone or ones knew where to find our tools. The hatchet had been left by our men on the top of a cabbage cart and the pick was taken from the new building up back yard.

Jan. 9th Rather finer. Mr. Weadon took the service in Church this afternoon. All went besides Anthony and myself.

Jan. 11th The wind has settled a bit and it drizzles a little at times. Anthony had a paper to tell him to appear before the tribunal at Bakewell (for Tom) on Saturday next at 1.30.

Jan. 12th   Rain first thing. Clears out later. The debates in parliament are chiefly about compulsory service. I could understand it better if it was for all, but parsons are exempt and those who have conscientious objections, and Ireland must not have compulsion. Only the United Kingdom must have it. I do not see where we are winning on land. Sir Ian Hamilton's report was issued last week about the Gallipoli Peninsula and very sad reading it is. Just about victory and had to give in (inertia). Sir Frederick Stopford was blamed. As I understand there was no water and no reinforcements. They got all the men who were left from Anzac and Suvla Bay away without any loss of life whilst getting them away, but what a failure after the awful sacrifice of so many of our brave men. The ship *King Edward* was sunk by a mine last week but the crew was saved.

Jan. 13th   Windy and cold. Our Ethel started from home at 6.30 this morning to be on duty for 7.30 at hospital. On getting back she said the soldiers were leaving tomorrow so she has not to go again yet as the Red Cross hospital is to be cleaned. Mr. Sherlock called here and had a chat.

Jan. 14th   Very frosty and cold. Read in paper that 4 of our aeroplanes started out a day or two since and did not return. The Germans claim to have shot some of them down. The Compulsion Bill is bitterly resented by the South Wales miners and also the miners in other parts of United Kingdom. *John Bull*[1] calls it a miserable little Bill.

Jan. 15th   Cold. Anthony went to Bakewell Union to appear before the tribunal to appeal for Tom. The gentlemen asked questions. How many acres the farm was? How many acres were ploughed? How many cows we milked? How many sons and how many daughters etc. The tribunal then said that Anthony would hear in a few days. Sam Rowland paid for building etc. £1.0.0. I settled the bill as Anthony had to go to bed with a sick headache.

Jan. 16th   Cold but a nice day. Mr. Sherlock took the service in Church. Daybells brought him up. Ethel played harmonium in Chapel.

Jan. 19th   A very windy day showery at times. The old haystack at the bottom of the fields which was such poor weathered stuff was chopped this morning in the machine (T. Bird). There were 5 loads chopped. Anthony paid all the men. The thresher and all were off our premises before 3 o'clock this afternoon. He paid Mr. Bird £3 10s. 0d. (£2.0.0. for threshing and £1.10.0. for chopping, 1 day threshing and 1½ days chopping.) Naylor 1 day = 3s. 6d. Lewis E Elliott 1½ days at 3s.6d. per day = 5s. 3d. Alf Brockley 1½ days 5s. 3d. Ed Brockley 1½ days 5s. 3d. Jack Brockley 1½ days 5s. 3d. and Watercress Jack 5s. 3d. and 12 and a quarter cwts of coal 12s. 3d. = £2.2.0 + £3.10s.0d. = £5.12.0. There were about 16 qr of heavy oats and some light ones (over 40 bags of oats). Anthony Wm. Wager is one year old today.

---

1   *John Bull* was a weekly magazine.

Jan. 20th A very rough and stormy day, snow storms at intervals. Mr. Sherlock called and had tea and we had some very serious talk. There came an invitation yesterday for the Sheldon choir and churchwardens to the annual supper which is held at Ashford for both choirs. Sam Bramwell had not been included in the invitation and Mr. Sherlock came up to ask him but I believe T.W. Brocklehurst had threatened to resign (Vicar's Warden) and had sent him a letter (Mr. Sherlock). It seems that Mr. Stubbs[1] had found himself grieved because Sheldon had not subscribed to the supper, but it was only today that we thoroughly understood how matters were and we can now understand why Ashford people look askance at Sheldon choir, as the supper for some time seems to have been paid out of the Ashford Church funds. I told Mr. Sherlock about mugs being put on the supper table at Ashford and the Sheldon choir drank out of them whilst glasses were on the Ashford choir's table. Mr. Sherlock said he himself had a mug which was correct, but when noticed he was asked to have a glass but did not. S. Rowland brought us a hare tonight.

Jan. 21st A very rough day wet at times. Wm Gould fetched us some coal from Bakewell station and had the horses (two) shod. The choir suppering is at Ashford tonight. None went from Sheldon, neither churchwarden, choir nor caretaker. I wonder if the Ashfordites will be satisfied now. Wm Shimwell (monumental mason) and Ben Brassington (Botham) came here yesterday. I think they were doing something in Sheldon Churchyard.

Jan. 22nd A very nice day, but the wind rises this afternoon. Anthony and Tony went to Mr. Sneaps by 1st train. They took the guinea fowls back and the hare that S. Rowland gave us. Wm Gould had a letter this morning about the Sheldon Letter box being broken with a stone. The letter was from the postmaster at Bakewell (Thompson) and wanted Gould to say if he saw it done and what sized stone it was etc. Gould said he did not see it broken. I answered the letter for Gould and put the following viz.

> Mr. Thompson,
>
> Dr Sir,
>
> As Wm Gould cannot write himself I am writing for him. Your letter was read to him and he says that he did not see anything of the occurrence you name.
>
> I am sir Yrs. truly,
>
> M. Gyte.

A post card came for our Tom from Recruiting Officer saying that he (Tom) was to fetch his armlet on Tuesday next (between 2 and 8 o'clock). Mr. Weadon came here. He was giving out tickets to people 60 years old and upwards to a tea at Ashford on Feb. 4th given by a lady (Churchdale). Mr. Weadon and I had a conversation over the choir suppering. He did not

---

[1] Mr. Stubbs was the schoolmaster and choirmaster at Ashford

go to supper but just looked in after: did not join Ashford lot but went back when he saw that there was not one from Sheldon.

Jan. 23rd Fine but rather windy towards night. Mr. Weadon took the service in Church. He asked the members of the choir if they would have a suppering at Sheldon but they told him they thought they would not bother about one. Mr. Sherlock wished to know if they would have a supper at Sheldon. Anthony and Tony got back at 10 minutes past nine tonight.

Jan. 24th A fine day, a bit windy later on. Compulsion Bill passed by a majority of 347.

Jan. 25th Rather rough. Polly Roberts was helping us to wash. The clothes line broke and let the clothes down in the mud up the croft. Tom went to Bakewell for his armlet[1]. The Recruiting Officer did not say anything to him about being starred or whether he had been put in a later group. Fred Bramwell and Fred Goodwin have had their papers to present themselves at Bakewell. Fred Bramwell on the 8th of Feb. and Fred Goodwin on the 9th of February. A cow calf came this morning from our pedigree bull.

Jan. 26th Drizzling this morning but fine and mild this afternoon. The Compulsion Bill was read a second time in the Lords. The war drags on. Thousands of our brave men are either killed or wounded and still no definite results for the lives lost. Tom is ploughing in bottom Grindlow Knoll.

Jan. 27th Calm and mild today. Tom ploughing. Anthony knocking manure. Tony spreading manure. Wm Gould carting manure. The Military Service (Compulsion) Bill has passed the House of Lords. Mr. Sherlock called here. He came to see Anthony about the Flannel (dole cheque). This cheque came here the other day and ought to have been sent to Stewarts (Bakewell). Anthony had said that it must be sent to Uncle W Brockley and then forgot about it. However Ethel found it and posted it tonight to Stewarts.

Jan. 29th Very fine and mild. Tom ploughing in Grindlow Knoll. A paper from the Recruiting Officer (Mr. Sweeting) came to Anthony over Tom. Anthony signed that Tom was indispensable and posted it tonight. A many in the house tonight.

Jan. 30th A very mild day. Mr. Sherlock took the service in Church this afternoon and was very early (2.10). All from our house went except Tony and myself.

---

1 "*The Derby armlet* was in evidence today. It is a band of dark khaki cloth, about four inches wide, with a red crown on it. Arthur Thos. Stoddart had it on in Church. I passed, on my way back from morning service, a lad, bicycling with it. It is for men who have been *attested* for service." 26/12/15 Andrew Clark *Echoes of the Great War.*

Jan. 31st   A most lovely day. Tom is ploughing and Wm is leading manure. Tony is working about the farm. Read of an air raid in Paris in which 13 bombs were dropped and there were about 48 casualties.

Feb. 1st   Very misty. Anthony took the milk to Longstone Station but did not load it as the train was very late owing to a Zeppelin raid over the Eastern and Midland counties which occurred sometime between 9 and ten last night. Various places had been visited viz. Norfolk, Suffolk, Derby, Leicester, Nottingham and Staffordshire.

Feb. 2nd   Very wet and rather rough. Read in paper that there were about 220 bombs dropped over different places especially in Staffordshire. In all up to this morning there were 54 people killed and 67 wounded and damage to property. Mr. Locke came and was paid. I also bought a few things and paid him, as well as ordering Flannelette for Tony's shirts and stair carpeting.

Feb. 3rd   Very rough and wet. Mr. Sherlock called here and had a chat. Miss Hallam called with a subscription 2s. 0d. towards the refreshments for tomorrow night. Read in paper that there were 59 deaths and 101 wounded in Zeppelin raid the other night.

Feb. 4th   Dull, drizzling and snow storms at times. Wm. Naylor, Tom Brocklehurst and Gould have just gone to the tea at Ashford. A very good affair. Read in paper that a Zeppelin had dropped in North Sea.

Feb. 6th   Very wet, and at times a flinkering of snow. Cold. Cox's motor brought Mr. Sherlock to Sheldon to administer the Holy Communion at 9.30. There were 7 present. Mr. Weadon took the service in Church this afternoon. He came with a bad arm. A collection in Church (9s. 2d.) for Church expenses.

Feb. 7th   Very raw and cold. Anthony went with milk and then to Bakewell workhouse. The local Tribunal for the Military Service Act was chosen and consisted of the same gentlemen acting as Tribunal under Lord Derby's scheme. George Briddon received his papers calling him up on the 22nd of Feb. Fred Goodwin has been put back a few groups. A good many in the house tonight. Fiddling by J. Goodwin and a song or two were sung as a send off for Fred Bramwell who is called up for tomorrow. Wm leading manure.

Feb. 8th   Very cold and frosty. Tom leading manure and Anthony digging garden. Fred Bramwell left Sheldon this morning to join his group. He had to be at Bakewell not later than 9 o'clock. He left for Derby later on. Miss Grover called with the magazine.

Feb. 9th   Very frosty and cold. Sprinklings of snow now and then. Mr. and Mrs. Young and two children called here and had tea. Serjeant Young was formerly a policeman at Ashford. He is now serving in France but is on leave for a few days. I wrote to Miss Grover and sent her the measurement of the tables at school viz. 12 feet long and 2 feet 8 in. wide and one inch deep for each table. Mr. Weadon called here. His arm is still painful and is in a sling (fluid in) and has been painted.

Feb. 10th　Cold. I hear that Fred Bramwell is drafted to Watford. He went yesterday to Chesterfield for his uniform. There has been a raid by two German sea planes. Mr. Sherlock called here and had tea.

Feb. 11th　Very frosty and cold. Snowing nearly all day. I had a letter from our Hannah and she said that she and people in Middleton heard the Zepps on the Monday of the last raid but they thought they were our aeroplanes etc.

Feb. 12th　Cold and frosty. The Military Service Bill comes in on March 2nd and they have to give notice of appeal to the Tribunals.

Feb. 13th　Fine but cold. Sam Bramwell went to Dr. Fentem who took a bit of steel out of his eye. Mr. Weadon took the service in Church this afternoon. Mr. David Frost preached at Sheldon tonight. Ethel and Evelyn went to Ashford Church and Tom went to Monyash Church with G. Briddon tonight.

Feb. 15th　Very wet morning. Read in paper that the ship *Saucy Arethusa* had struck a mine on the East Coast and that 10 of the crew were drowned. The captain (Domville) was on his honeymoon.

Feb. 16th　A very stormy, rough day - snow storms. The war news today is not very bright. The British have lost about 600 yds of trenches to the Germans. I do wish the terrible war was over but it does not look at all bright. I had a letter from our Mary and she says that people about there have had orders to get dark blinds to their windows on account of the Zeppelins.

Feb. 17th　Snowstorms and a very rough day. The Russians are doing very well. The forts at Erzerum (the chief Turkish fortifications) are falling. Sam Wilton, Jack Naylor and Jack Brocklehurst received cards about the Military Service Act. Our Tom and a few more went to a whist drive and dance at Monyash. (Tom got second prize) a mirror (shaving).

Feb. 18th　Snow storms with a little sunshine in between. The best news we have had for some time is the Russian capture of Erzerum (the key to Turkey in Asia) with 1,000 guns and 100,000 prisoners.

Feb. 19th　Very wet. Anthony took the milk to station and he says that the morning was the wettest he was ever out in. He was to have called at Miss Grover's (Grange Cottage) for a parcel of material for tablecloths (school tables) but he did not call as he thought it would get so wet. Tom was ploughing down the fields in the afternoon. The hunters were busy going through where he was ploughing. It is a pity they cannot find something else to do especially during this terrible time of war. PC Dennis brought us papers regarding the lighting and air raids. Everybody has to get dark blinds to their windows.

Feb. 20th Finer and milder. Uncle Will Brocklehurst brought Tony 3 guinea fowls from Longstone station which Mr. Sneap had sent. We had Brussel sprouts to dinner which cost twopence halfpenny per lb off Jim Goodwin. Mr. Sherlock took the service in Sheldon Church this afternoon and the congregation were coming out just before half past three. This is much better than keeping them so long like Mr. Weadon. Anthony, Tom, Ethel and Evelyn went to Church.

Feb. 22nd A very stormy day, snow and wind. Our Tom, Tony and Wm were carting manure on to the moor with 3 carts and were caught in the storms. I did not get downstairs until 2.30. G. Briddon went for training for a soldier. T.Wm B brought the material from Miss Grover for the tablecloths.

Feb. 23rd Bitterly cold, frosty, snow storms and wind. Jack Naylor and G. Brocklehurst attested at Bakewell. The Allies' forces in France do not seem to be gaining anything, rather the other way as the other day the British lost about 600 yds of trench and by today's papers the French have lost similarly. The French though have brought down a Zeppelin and two other aircraft. Anthony bought a mowing machine and reaper and self binder. The mowing machine and reaper cost 32s/6d and the self binder cost £14.0.0.

Feb. 24th One of the most bitterly cold wintry days we have had this year. Frost snow and wind. The snow pundered in great drifts. Our Tom received a paper from the Central tribunals to say that he would be treated as being *starred*. Billy Naylor went to Bakewell over Jack. The Dr. had put *medically unfit* on Jack's paper and then the military authorities gave him 2/9 and another paper.

Feb. 25th A very deep snow and the wind is rising again. The French are retiring before the Germans who have taken 3 villages in the Verdun district.

Feb. 26th Another awful wintry day. Snow storms and wind. Pundering and drifting. It is thought some drifts are 8 or 9 feet deep. Some at the top of the village are very deep and one against Mrs. Morton's. There are a many people in Sheldon who have no meat for Sunday's dinner.

Feb. 27th Frosty. Snow storms and wind, pundering and drifting. I think we shall be snowed up if much more comes. Anthony and Tom took two horses with the milk (Navvy and the old grey mare). A whole lot of parcels of meat etc. were waiting for them to bring up from Ashford. Mr. Weadon took the service in Church. I think there are a many people in Sheldon who are short of coal and if this storm lasts long I do not know how we shall get some from the station.

Feb. 28th Very winterly. There are men in Sheldon cutting snow in different parts. Carts cannot get the top road to Bakewell as Twig Lane is completely blocked. John Frost had word from the tribunals about G.

Briddon saying that his appeal could not be heard unless he had attested. George had attested long ago. George Ward came in tonight. He is on leave from Longmoor Camp.

Feb. 29th (leap year) More snow has fallen during the night. People in Sheldon say they have never seen such an amount of snow before. There are great drifts many feet deep - there is no getting to the stations especially Parsley Hay, Hurdlow and up that way. Men are snow cutting in different places. Some Monyash way, some up Harrock, and the snow plough came up Ashford Dale and through Sheldon. The men with the snow plough were from Youlgreave viz. Jim Shimwell's son and Ben Shimwell's son and Fred Oldfield, the road man. I think the horses were Jim Shimwell's. Anthony and Tom took the milk to Longstone station with two horses (Navvy and the Grey mare). Billy Naylor and John Brocklehurst have to face the Tribunal today about both Jack Naylor and Jack Brockley. They went but did not get on very well and Billy has to go again. We had a row with Jim Goodwin and Billy Naylor tonight over snow cutting. Jim Goodwin wanted the roads cutting for his carts to go and was blaming Billy for setting men on and not him and his sons.

March 1st Very misty. I think it is thawing a little. Anthony and Thos. Wm are going to the Military Authorities over Tom and George as the paper says that married men must take the place of single ones in reserved occupations. The Derby scheme is nothing but a farce and the tribunals no better, there are very few exemptions and no notice is taken of the widow and one son. The farmers are shown no favour. Copy of the paper which came from the Tribunal C.T. 13b (Central Appeal Tribunal)(copy)

> Local Government Board
> Whitehall SW
> Feb 22nd 1916
>
> Please quote Local Tribunal
> No 1208 Bakewell R
> Notice of Decision
>
> Sir,
>
> With reference to the application made by you I beg to inform you that the Central Tribunal have decided that
>
> Name   Thomas Gyte
> Address   Sheldon Nr. Bakewell
> Occupation   Farming
>
> is entitled to be treated as starred.
>
> Yours faithfully
>
> J.W. Reading
> For Central Tribunal
>
> Mr. A. Gyte.

Anthony got Tom's name put on the military register as *starred*. George Brocklehurst's starred card had been sent to Charley White. Mr. Weadon called. His elbow is not better.

March 2nd   Very winterly. Snow storms and wind. Men are out cutting the snow drifts. Tom and Wm went to Hassop Station for Soya Cake and had to come up the Dale. They left one cart at the Devonshire Arms (Ashford) loaded with cake and Tony took the old Grey mare Fanny to meet them so they had four horses to pull them up. Our Tom is getting ready to go to a dance at Ashford (Rawsons) for Red Cross. He and Jack Naylor went. According to the paper the bombardment of Verona has stopped, the Germans have had fearful losses. A many vessels are being sunk either by mines or torpedos. A French transport was sunk the other day with great loss of life.

March 3rd   Very frosty and cold. On going to milk, our men found one of the best milk cows down and could not get up. Her chain was broken and Anthony thinks she had been trying to jump over the boskin.[1] They poulticed her back but she was not able to get up. Wm Gould fetched coal for us. He managed to go the top road (the road had just been cut).

March 4th   Very frosty and cold. The cow is no better and Anthony told Joe Johnson and he has been and killed her at our place. She had bruised her back and I do not think she would ever have got better. Joe Johnson bought her for £7.0.0. Wm Gould went for coal for the Church which cost 10s. 10d.

March 5th   Very frosty. On getting up this morning Anthony and Wm were surprised to find Clem had arrived (about six o'clock). He started from Grindleford at 4.15 this morning. Holy Communion at Sheldon Church (9.30). Mr. Sherlock administered and he also took service this afternoon. Collection for Church expenses (10s. 10d.). Mr. Sherlock had some talk with Anthony and T.W.B. what must be done with refugees if they should come inland out of Air Raids etc from East Coast.

March 6th   Very frosty. Clem went back this morning. Anthony took the milk and then went to Bakewell. Later there were snow storms (pundering) wind etc. Verdun is not taken yet but an air raid has been reported on North East Coast.

March 8th   The weather is worse than ever this morning. Snow storms, pundering and wind. Snow cutters are out again. The roads are blocked in many places. The High Peak Line has been blocked a week or two. J. Goodwin cannot get to Hurdlow for any green groceries to go round with. I read in the paper that 17 persons were killed in the north East Air Raid last Sunday. The Germans are gaining a little ground around Verdun.

---

1   Partition in cowshed

March 9th Snow storms. Men are out clearing the roads. Billy Naylor made a tunnel under the drift at Mrs. Morton's gate. People say it ought to be photographed.

March 11th Most bitter cold weather, frost and snow. I do not remember such a time for so much snow. Joe Oliver and Ned Wibberley called here and had a drink. Anthony gave them one quart as they with Sam Bramwell and Joe Carson are filling up old mines in our fields about Magpie mine. Wm Naylor has gone before the tribunal about Jack.

March 12th Very cold, snow storms during this afternoon, very large flakes. Mr. Weadon took the service in Church this afternoon. Anthony went to bed about tea time with headache.

March 13th Very misty, windy and I think it thaws a little at times. Anthony filled another paper over Jack Naylor.

March 14th Very misty. Poor Jack Brockley went this morning. He was to be at the recruiting office at 9 o'clock this morning. I feel very sorry for his father and mother, both sons having to go to the war. Read in paper that *starred* men are going to be unstarred. I think this is over the agitation of the married men all over the country who are trying to shove their responsibility on the single man's shoulders.

March 15th Very wet, rained in torrents. Mr. Sherlock came up to see Anthony about the refugees from the East Coast (if they come). Anthony is chairman. John Frost, T.Wm Brocklehurst, Alf Brocklehurst are on Committee. The above had a meeting at T.W.B's tonight. Mr. Sherlock got stuck in a snow drift.

March 19th Awfully misty and showery day after day. The snow is going fast. Mr. Weadon took the service in Church this afternoon. He keeps the congregation so late and it is very tiring. I heard that Jack Brocklehurst was at York.

March 21st Very cold, sleet at times. Anthony and Tony got places ready for bringing in the lambing ewes. Anthony made books up (refugees) and wrote a letter to Mr. Sherlock saying that Sheldon Committee would not be responsible for food for refugees, only that promised.

March 22nd One of the most bitter cold days we have had this winter. Emily is poorly today (more than usual) her elbow is so bad. Mr. Sherlock called here today and has gone to measure the Church, Chapel and School dimensions in anticipation of refugees coming from East Coast. Brought in lambing ewes tonight.

March 24th A fine day some sunshine. Our first lamb was born today (an ewe lamb). The fowls are laying better (80 in today). Eggs are 8 a shilling. Alfred Loftus and his sister came to Eds. He has had trench feet.

March 25th Very cold and windy, some sleet. Anthony and Tony have been boarding up part of the shed in yard to put the ewes in. The single men are being well badgered to suit the married men under the detestable Derby Scheme. They are about to unstar men who have been starred. It is abominable how they pester the poor single men who are chiefly from 19 - 20 - 21 etc.

March 26th Cold and frosty with flinkerings of snow. A theave[1] had two lambs this morning. Wm Gould posted a cheque (4s. 6d.) for the Sheldon Church fire insurance. Mr. Sherlock took the service in Sheldon Church this afternoon.

March 29th Finer and milder. Tom is emptying tank and Tony is busy looking after the lambs and ewes. We are not having very good luck as two or three lambs are dead and some look like dying. Anthony had to help an old ewe. She had two very good lambs but she is bad and has not much milk.

March 30th Fine but dull. Tom and Wm have gone for hay to Haddon. Anthony and Tom did not come to bed until 1.20 this morning as they were looking after the old ewe and lambs. We have brought one of her lambs into the house as it seems weak and panting.

March 31st A lovely day. There was a Managers meeting. Mr. Sherlock did not call to see me. The old ewe that was so bad is dead. Anthony killed her as she was so bad with inflammation and would have died.

April 1st A lovely day. Anthony and Tom sat up with the sheep. Another had two lambs. They have sat up for four nights altogether until 1 or 1.30. Ethel took Emily on to the moor in Mrs. Ed. Brocklehurst's chair. Heard that Jack Needham (rabbit) of Flagg had eloped with a young girl (Saml. Robinson's daughter of Wardlow).

April 2nd A lovely day. There was a celebration of Holy Communion this morning. Mr. Sherlock administered. Mr. Weadon took the service in Church this afternoon. Collection 9 shillings for church expenses.

April 3rd Very fine but rather frosty towards night. I heard that man out of Burgon's shop named Lawless had been fetched by the police (under the Military Service Act) handcuffed and taken to the police court where he was fined £5.0.0.

April 4th Very fine but rather cold. Washday. There have been three Zeppelin raids since last Saturday. A many people killed in England and Scotland and a many injured. I was busy with the Church accounts and could not make them balance right. However later on I found out that the pound we were short of was in an envelope in the green box where we keep all church money etc. Tom is ploughing today.

---

1   Theave = a ewe which has not yet borne a lamb

April 5th   Fine but frosty. The buildings are covered with white frost early in the mornings which clears off when the sun is out. Mr. Sherlock rode through Sheldon on horseback but did not call here. Little Benny Sheldon was taken very ill and the Dr. (Tom Fentem) was fetched. He said that the little fellow had got appendicitis and must be taken to hospital at once (Sheffield). A motor came and he was taken away tonight. His mother and Miss Martha Hallam went with him.

April 6th   Fine but very frosty. Billy Naylor and Jim Goodwin are gone to Derby to appeal for Jack Naylor and Fred Goodwin under Lord Derby's Scheme.

April 7th   Dull but fine. Our fowls are laying better 120 eggs in today. Billy Naylor and Jim Goodwin have not come back yet from Derby. The Duke of Devonshire's subscription of one pound came this morning towards the Sheldon Church funds.

April 8th   Fine but cold and frosty. The five pounds which come yearly as a subscription towards the Sheldon Sunday School was sent to Anthony by Mr. Sherlock who receives it from the agent of the Duke of Devonshire. Mr. Cockerill (last year) said that three pounds of it could be used in payment of the Sheldon church organist. Evelyn and Tony went to Bakewell tonight for medicine (Dr. Jackson) and Tony went to be measured for a new suit. He went to the wrong place. He ought to have gone to old Mr. Hill's but he went to Mr. Hill's sons. However young Mr. Hill is making them.

April 9th   Fine, but frosty in early morning. Dr. Jackson came to see the invalids. He said that Ethel must take nourishment every hour. Her mouth and tongue are awfully nasty and sore. Tom went on his bicycle for something to gargle Ethel's mouth. Billy Naylor came in tonight and was telling us how Wager, Goodwin and himself went on at Derby with their appeals which were all dismissed. I do not see where we are winning at all in the war. Fred Brockley and Anthony have been in an awfully hot shop in the front line trenches in France. Sam Rowland's dog was caught running and worrying John Brocklehurst's chickens this morning. They have found 73 dead and altogether there are about 96 dead and missing. John called our Anthony who saw the dog carrying chickens in his mouth. Ethel is a shade better tonight. Mr. Weadon took the service in Church this afternoon.

April 10th Very fine but still frosty first thing. Tom and Tony have been sowing oats in Bole Piece this morning. John Needham's (Flagg) case is heard today at Bakewell. He was let out on bail and committed to Derby Assizes 3 sureties of £50 each.

April 11th A bit showery at times, rather cold. Tom and Tony went to fetch the two young horses from Ashford and took them round by Bakewell and had one shod. Jack Naylor had a paper this morning to go on the 26th of this month.

April 12th Wet, some sunshine but showery and not very warm. Fred Goodwin had his paper to present himself for a soldier the day after Jack Naylor. Alf Wildgoose and Jim Goodwin have been in our house this afternoon.

April 13th Showery at times and rather cold. Tom has been chain harrowing on moor and Wm Gould has chain harrowed the Waterlands. Ethel is a little better but she does not eat very well, she takes a little milk and beef tea etc. Mr. Sherlock called and the topic of conversation was *The War*.

April 16th Showery and cold towards night; not much sun for April. Mr. Sherlock took the service in Sheldon Church this afternoon. Anthony, Tom, Tony and Evelyn went. Ethel is improving nicely. Emily is so sick.

April 19th Rather dull at times but a little sunshine later in the day. Anthony has the headache and is out of sorts. I have been putting the papers together out of the green box where we keep accounts. Paid Mrs. Carson 1s. 4d. for paraffin. Read in paper of the fall of Trebizond the great Armenian port of the Turks (to Russia). The relief party to Kut has had a set back and General Townshend is reported to be in a critical condition. Mr. Weadon called here and gave me half a crown (from Miss Grover) to buy flowers for Sheldon Church for Easter. Burgons man took 363 eggs of our children at 11 a shilling.

April 20th Very dull. Showers of rain mixed with snow. Tom has been chain harrowing in Bole Piece and Waterlands and Croft Head. Wm. has been emptying tank. Some books came for me from Sheffield. Mr. Goodwin sent flowers for Church (daffodils) and he was paid half a crown (Miss Grover).

April 21st Dull and showery at times. Good Friday. Mr. Weadon took the service in Church and it was as usual. People get tired of his long addresses.

April 23rd Dull. Holy Communion at Sheldon Church (9.30). Mr. Sherlock administered. Mr. Weadon took the service this afternoon. All went from our house except Hannah and myself. (Frosty). Tony had his new suit on. A little too tight under arms. Collection in Church for the Vicar's Easter offering 11 shillings.

April 24th Fine. Wash day dried clothes out of door. Anthony took the 11 shillings collected in Church on Easter Day to Mr. Weadon to be given to Mr. Sherlock as an Easter offering. I made up the Church accounts from Easter 1915 to Easter 1916 and the balance in hand is £5 1s. 3d. Mr. Bagshaw called and he was paid 2s. 9d. (tithe). He had tea here and Mrs. Ed. also came in to tea. A dance was held at the school in aid of the Red Cross. A few young men came from Flagg and Monyash. People in Sheldon gave cakes etc. James Goodwin charged five shillings for Fred and himself playing for dancing.

April 26th A lovely day. Our men have gone sawing. Read in paper of a riot in Dublin yesterday. The Sinn Feiners mostly armed occupied Stephens

Green and took possession forcibly of the Post Office where they cut the telegraphic and telephonic wires, about 12 lives were lost and about 20 wounded. Sir Roger Casement the Irish Traitor had been caught a day or two since trying to land arms and ammunition in Ireland in a German Cruiser with a German submarine in attendance which had the arms on board and was sunk. Sir Roger is now under military custody. A German squadron of battle cruisers accompanied by light cruisers and destroyers appeared off Lowestoft yesterday. The local Naval forces engaged it and in about 20 minutes it returned to Germany chased by our light cruisers and destroyers. Two of the British light cruisers and a destroyer were hit but not sunk. Jack Naylor went off this morning. He had to be at the Recruiting Office at 9 o'clock. The secret Session over recruiting took place yesterday in parliament. Our men were sowing oats. A Vestry meeting was held at four o'clock this afternoon (in our parlour) to appoint Church Wardens. The old ones were put in office. Mr. Sherlock, Mr. Weadon, Thos. Wm. B and Anthony were there. Mr. Sherlock proposed a vote of thanks to Mrs. Gyte for keeping the Church accounts. The Vicar and Mr. Weadon had tea at our house. Balance in hand was £5 1s. 3d. Our stirks[1] lay out for 1st time this year. Mr. Weadon told me he was leaving at Whitsuntide.

April 27th A most lovely day warm and plenty of sunshine. Poor Fred Goodwin went this morning. He was rather downhearted and no wonder. Dublin is under martial law. Tony and Vincent Hallows are picking up stones out of field on moor. Mr. Ed took the Red Cross money boxes (one from our house) to Ashford to be counted. The money got by dance up at school and sale of flags amounted to £1 11s. 6d. Our Girls cleaned Wm's room (whitewashed) today.

April 28th A most lovely day. The men are gone sowing the other part of Grindlow Knoll and harrowing. Tony and Vincent Hallows are gone stone picking on moor. Alf Wildgoose went today to Sutton on Hull. The Military Service Bill (in secret session) has been withdrawn. I daresay compulsion all round will follow. There are 9 more groups of married men have to report by May 29th and if 50,000 of the unattested married men have not voluntarily joined the army by May 27th then compulsion may be brought in (further). The Irish rebellion (Sinn Fein) is spreading and all Ireland is under martial law. Our Tom had a post card this morning from Jack Naylor saying that he had passed for labour at home. Our girls and aunt H cleaned the bar this afternoon.

April 29th A very fine day. Evelyn and Tony went to young Hills of Bakewell to fetch his coat (Tony's) which had to be altered (too tight under the arms). Jack Naylor came on tonight in Khaki. Fred Goodwin and Tom Wager are gone to Guernsey. Troops are being sent to stop the rebellion in Ireland.

1 Yearling bullocks or heifers

April 30th Fine but a cold wind. Matthew Gregory called in here this dinner time. He has a son in France (Charlie). Mr. Sherlock took the service in Church this afternoon. The rebellion in Ireland is being checked.

May 3rd Very nice and warm. Clem and Tony are gardening. A bill for general compulsion is to be brought in today.

May 4th Very wet and rough. Anthony and Tony sowed artificial manure on moor. In the afternoon they turned potatoes over in chamber. Clem went back to Grindleford.

May 6th Wet at times but milder. A lady came to Sheldon school to give a lesson in cheese making (small cheese). Mr. H. Frost had the job in hand but it was as usual left to the last minute in getting things ready. Miss Hallam bought the cheese made at the school. I believe it is 34 years today since Lord F. Cavendish and Mr. Burke were assassinated in Phoenix Park.

May 7th Showery and cold at times. Mary's little boy seems cross. His teeth is (sic) bothering him. Mr. Weadon took the service in Church and was as usual late coming out. Mary went to Church. Some people came here for eggs from Sheffield (Buying eggs on Sunday). Pearson (dentist) was one.

May 12th Mild but dull. Anthony has been gardening. Ethel is cleaning bath room. Anthony drew turnip rows (Hicks). Evelyn and Tony are very busy taking chickens out as they hatch. We have had good hatches but we lost a hen with 14 chickens (hen killed with coop) and either a cat or crows or some other vermin have taken about six chicks. Read in paper that the situation in Ireland is very grave. Mr. Asquith has gone there himself. Tom, Tony, Ethel and Evelyn went to a circus at Bakewell tonight (Bostocks) and got back about 11 o'clock. All got wet as it rained heavily.

May 13th Dull and showery. The British have lost about 500 yards of trenches. We do not seem to be winning in this awful war. Many thousand lives are being lost. They have shot two more rebels Connolly and McDermot. The Irish traitor Sir Roger Casement is going to be tried next Monday. George Briddon called to see us and had a nice chat. He is stationed somewhere in Kent and expects to go to France at the end of this month.

May 14th Dull and a bit showery. Holy Communion in Sheldon Church at 9.30 this morning. Mr. Sherlock celebrated. Mr. Weadon took the service this afternoon. Collection for Church expenses (5s. 9d.).

May 15th Dull and showery. Some of our chickens have been taken lately and the keepers Sam Rowland and John Pursglove killed three hawks today.

May 18th A most lovely day. Very hot in sun. Our men were on the fallow, drawing rows and sowing swedes. I was sat out nearly all day in front. Mr. Sherlock joined us and had tea and talked a bit. He brought the report about Sheldon School and it was a serious one. I think Miss Hallam will find it so. A Managers meeting was held (in our room). There were present Anthony, Thos. Wm. B and W.H. Brocklehurst. Mr. Sherlock did not stay for the meeting and Mr. John Frost was away from home.

May 19th A lovely day. Tom is drawing cabbage and turnip rows up (Hicks). Wm on moor getting potato ground ready. Tony was getting pea sticks and Anthony brought them, gardening this afternoon (Tony and father). Emily was very ill during last night and this morning. Better later on.

May 20th A very fine day. PC Dennis came tonight and told us to put our clocks faster by one hour (Day light saving). Jack Naylor and Jack Brockley came home for the weekend. A full house tonight.

May 21st A lovely day. Our people were up an hour earlier and Tom took milk to station starting before 7 old time, before 8 by clock. I was taken down the fields and on to the moor in float. Anthony drove and Emily and Tony went as well. Had dinner at eleven (old time). Mr. Sherlock took the service 1.30 old time. The fields looked beautiful. The corn is springing up nicely and the things in general looked very well.

May 22nd Fine but rather gloomy and colder. There has been some thunder about. We have not lit our lamps so far this week (2 nights) so that will be a saving of paraffin.

May 23rd Fine but dull now and then. Tom and Wm were leading manure on to the potato ground (moor). Anthony went with milk and then on to the moor getting potato ground ready. Ethel, Evelyn and Aunt H have washed today as Polly Roberts could not come. She has not been very well. Received a letter from our Mary. Clem has not had his papers yet for the army. The British have lost 1,500 yards of trenches in France. Our men have planted 12 rows of potatoes on moor.

May 25th Dull and showery at times. Orme's traveller called (not Mr. Ronston as he has gone away for his health) and was paid up to date. He had got a statement saying that we owed £2. 3. 10. This was paid last month and was stated on bill, the date as well, which was March 3rd which was the date on bill which the traveller had. I very soon told him we did not owe it and he tore the statement up. Anthony, Tom, Tony, Wm, Billy Naylor and Ed B went on moor. The two last are having a row with us. 15 rows were set today.

May 26th Fine but came on showery between four and five. Anthony went to Derby for cabbage plants. Our Tom, Tony and Wm finished setting potatoes on moor. Ethel and Evelyn cleaned the house place and patched the paper, ceiling and wall. Our men set six rows of potatoes and carted six loads of manure. They had some from J. Goodwin. We had a telegram to say that Anthony was coming home on Sunday night. Spending the interval at Mr. Sneaps. Cabbage plants came on to Longstone Station with Mr. J. Woods.

May 27th Fine. A bit frosty this morning. Our Tom took the milk and brought cabbage plants. Tom, Tony and Wm working down Hicks, leading manure and drawing up cabbage rows (12).

May 28th Fine and warm. Mr. Sherlock took the service in Church. Collection for Foreign Mission (11s. 0d.). Sarah Brocklehurst's baby was christened (Edith Millicent). Anthony came back from Mr. Sneaps tonight.

May 30th Dull at first but brighter later on. All the sheep in Sheldon were taken to Ashford to be washed. Papers came this morning to challenge our Tom's *star* on June 3rd.

May 31st Fine but cooler. Men leading manure to cabbage rows. Not very good news from Verdun. The Germans keep gaining a little at a great cost to themselves. Men keep going into training every day.

June 1st Very rough and a little showery at times but not enough rain to do any good. Our men are planting cabbages (15 rows). Mr. Weadon called and there was service in Church. Ascension Day.

June 3rd Dull and rather rough. Anthony went to Bakewell to appear before the tribunal (rural) over Tom's *star*. Tom was put back four months. The paper gives an account of a terrible naval battle (on the coast of Jutland) between the British and German Fleets. A many ships were sunk on each side and the loss of life was very heavy. Sam Bramwell went this morning to go into training. He was to be at the recruiting office Bakewell by 9 o'clock.

June 4th Very wet and rough. Holy Communion at 9.30 administered by Mr. Sherlock. Mr. Weadon took the service in Church this afternoon. Collection for church expenses (4s. 6d.).

June 5th A most miserable wet day. Anthony took Tony to Bakewell. Tony attested and drew 2s. 7d. There were a few more aged 18 who attested. Ernest Stubbs etc. They did not get back until tea time. I think there are a few in Sheldon who are very bitter about our Tom getting put back four months among whom are Sam Rowland and Alf Brocklehurst and I do not care about Sam Wilton's talk. Sam Rowland was very sleering tonight saying that Jack Armit would not get off because he was not a milk seller and other things.

June 6th A very nice day, sunny and a bit rough. Our Tom had a post card this morning with a man on and army in khaki and a few words: *This little pig stayed at home*. On the address side was written *Do not be the pig who stayed at home*. We have our suspicions that it is S. Rowland, Alf Brockley and Sam Wilton as they were looking at something and laughing the other night. The PC had Darley Dale and Matlock postmarks on and Arthur Tunnicliffe was here on Sunday. Mr. Weadon called with an invitation to attend a mission[1] in the schoolroom *To make England better*. The awful news

---

1   This was the National Mission of Repentance and Hope. See Introduction pages xxii-xxv

that Lord Kitchener was drowned and all his staff was brought to us by Mr. Craven. The ship called the *Hampshire* was conveying Lord Kitchener and about 650 troops and officers to Russia and was either torpedoed or struck a mine off the Orkneys. Everybody seems depressed and wonders where the war will end. Anthony is not well (indigestion).

June 7th   Fine, but a shower comes on towards night. We have had a cheese today. Tom went for artificial manure to Bakewell and brought back the tea service for Sheldon C.E. School. Hannah has been scrubbing out a box (calf meal box) to put these pots in ready to be taken up to school. The papers seem full of mourning over Lord Kitchener. The Russians seem to be advancing and 25,000 Austrians are reported taken prisoner, but the British do not seem to be making much progress in France.

June 8th   Fine. Mr. Sherlock came to see us and he had dinner about a quarter to 7 (stew, mashed potato and sago pudding and cheese, butter etc.). He then went to school when a meeting was held (about the Mission of Repentance and Hope) in the Schoolroom. About 12 persons were present. There ought to have been a meeting over Miss Hallam but none of the managers could go only T.W.B. as the others were away at work.

June 9th   Dull and showery. In France the Germans have taken Vaux and are about 3 miles from Verdun. A meeting was held in the schoolroom (Managers). Jim Goodwin brought some red flowers from Derby for Sheldon Church. Miss Grover gave half a crown to get some.

June 10th Dull and cold. Thunder and lightning and heavy showers at times during the day. Alf Brocklehurst used some abusive language about Mr. Sherlock, cursed and swore about him because of something that Mr. Sherlock was reported to have said to Bertha Bramwell about the bell-ringing at Sheldon Church. I spoke up for the Vicar but told AB that I should not tell Mr. Sherlock what he had said. He must tell him himself.

June 11th Whit Sunday. Dull and showery at times. Holy Communion in Sheldon Church administered by Mr. Sherlock (7 present) at 9.30. Mr. Weadon took the service this afternoon. Collection for Church expenses (8 shillings). It was after 4 o'clock when the congregation came out. We had five people for tea, some of whom had been before. The Russians are making good progress and are taking immense numbers of Austrian prisoners. 70,000 this last week or two.

June 12th Whit Fair. Dull and very rough and bitterly cold. The grass seems to be going back instead of growing. The weather has been awfully cold this week or two and no progress seems to be made in the growing department. Anthony, Tom and Tony went to the fair. The Russians have taken more prisoners of the Austrians and some Germans amounting now to about 107,000. Memorial services are being held in the Churches, but the chief one is being held tomorrow, when the King and Queen will attend.

June 13th Awfully rough and cold. We had a cheese today. There was only one cow so we kept the milk at home. Memorial Service to Lord Kitchener in St. Paul's Cathedral.

June 14th Dull and very cold. We have had another cheese today. Clem arrived here from Grindleford just before six o'clock this morning to see us before he goes into Training. He has to be at the recruiting office Bakewell at 9 o'clock on Saturday morning. Wm Gould went to the club feast (Monyash) and drew £1 os. od. Tom and Tony walked over to Monyash tonight. Tom took his cycle.

June 15th Cold winds and a little sun now and then. I think Sam Rowland went today (for training). The Russians are still sweeping the Austrians before them and have taken about 121,000 prisoners this last week or two. The Huns are still hammering at the forts before Verdun and Ypres. I have heard that Jack Brockley is going into France. The old concertina chap came today. He comes very often.

June 17th Warmer as the sun has shone beautifully. If the wind would shift from the NE we should see the things grow better. Clem went to Derby today. Our Evelyn saw him off at the Station (Bakewell). Evelyn paid Mr. Thacker what we owed him for next Sunday's beef (tomorrow) as well so we do not owe him anything. I think he is very near as we pay him 1s. 1d. per lb for beef and he charged us for half a pound of suet and we actually cart his beef from Ashford for other people and never get a copper for doing it. The Germans are still hammering at Verdun. PC Dennis has been to our house enquiring how much we were mowing, how many acres, seeds etc. He had tea here. A good many men in our house tonight. Sam Rowland was talking about how he got on at Derby. He, Jack McCrindle and Richardson (Longstone) got into the R.G.A.[1] and are going to Yarmouth.

June 18th Fine, some sunshine but a cold NE wind. Anthony took me down the fields and on to the moor in float. Tony went with us but Emily did not go. The land seems to want rain and warmth. The stock on the moor looks well. I enjoyed the outing very much. Mr. Weadon took the service in Church this afternoon. Sam Rowland said *Good-bye* to us.

June 19th Very dull, looks very much like rain but none comes. S. Rowland had to be at Derby by nine o'clock so he would have to start early from Sheldon. HM Inspector of schools called and had a pint of tea to his own food. It was the same gentleman who called here about 3 years ago. We had some very interesting talk and he said he should call to see me again when he came to Sheldon.

June 20th Finer and warmer. Tom and Tony are busy sheep shearing etc. Tom has shorn 5, Tony 2 and their father 2. They have also dipped 11 lambs and given a pill to 10 (each). Evelyn and Tony are gone to Ashford with

1 Royal Garrison Artillery

sheep and lambs. Aunt Hannah has whitewashed and scrubbed out the milk shop. I wrote to our Mary.

June 21st Dull but the rain does not come and it is wanted badly. We finished sheepshearing (30). Our Tony managed to shear 8 and Tom and his father the rest. A prayer meeting was held at our house tonight just before 9 o'clock. Mrs. Ed, Ruth and Doris, Mrs. Craven, Aunt H and our girls and I were there. A man came in tonight and I recognised him as the man who called a year or two ago with an owl and ferrets and rabbits and he is supposed to have taken other people's ferrets and dogs. Some men followed and watched where he went to. Papered the big room where Tom and Tony sleep (Ethel and Evelyn did it).

June 22nd Dull. Our people finished dipping lambs and others dipped theirs up our back yard. Tony and Tom helped Uncle John Brocklehurst to finish shearing his sheep (Tony sheared 2 and part of one and Tom sheared one and finished one). Our Tom took Fanny to Middleton to Walter Needham's horse. Wm fetched coal for us and afterwards the beer from Bakewell station. Our Mary wrote to say that Clem was at Sunderland. Mr. Sherlock held a service in Church tonight. There were 10 or 11 present.

June 23rd Warmer and more sunshine. Wind in South. We want rain. Wm Gould started about 7 o'clock this morning with Naylor and the old grey mare to W. Needham's horse (Middleton by Youlgreave) and got back between two or 3 this afternoon. Jack Brockley arrived home this morning. He got to Ambergate late last night and could not get any further by train so he stayed all night with a porter at the P. House. He had supper bed and breakfast there and they would not let him pay anything. I believe Jack is going to France shortly. Naylor's had word that their Jack was in hospital either with measles or fever. I feel very sorry for them, as they had word only yesterday that he would come for a month to help in the hay. John Pursglove put some poison on a chicken.

June 24th Dull, and some nice showers this afternoon. Eggs are 7 a shilling, farmers cannot sell their wool until the Government thinks fit. We have had a many chickens worried by rats or cats or something.

June 25th Fine. Mr. Sherlock took the service in Church. We keep finding big chickens taken and worried. Our Ethel, Ruth and Doris B went to Monyash Church.

June 28th Dull but no rain comes. Our girls cleaned their bedroom (over pantry) patched the paper etc. They went to Ashford for a walk and bought an evening paper. The British have penetrated into 10 different parts of the enemies' lines in France.

June 30th Showery. During last night and this morning the rain came down in torrents. This is just what we want especially if warmth comes but everything suffers for lack of sunshine. Anthony, Tom, Tony, James Frost went to the Royal Show at Manchester; Billy Naylor also went but our people did not see him in the show ground. Anthony and the boys arrived home all right between 9 and 10.

July 1st   Showery. No sun to speak of. Our Tom and uncle Brockley (Thos Wm) heard the cuckoo today. This is rather late to hear her. Anthony and I heard her on Midsummer day. The Allies are doing well on all fronts. Our Ethel fetched Tom's new suit from old Mr. Hill.

July 2nd   Dull and a bit showery this morning. Holy Communion in Sheldon Church. Mr. Sherlock administered, 7 present. Mr. Weadon took the service in Church this afternoon. 3 minutes to four when the congregation came out. Collection for church expenses 8 shillings.

July 3rd   Warmer but a bit dull at times. Anthony took milk to station and Tony took a fat cow to market. Dora Brocklehurst is going to live at Mr. Greenshields[1] (Vicar of Youlgreave). Elsie Goodwin also lives there as servant, she went two or three weeks since. Sarah Ann Wilson lives there as cook. Emily had a letter from Clem. He does not seem so well and is rather dull over being in the Army. He had to join the 10th North Staffords which are in training at Penkridge Camp in Stafford.

July 4th   Dull and misty. Our Tom, Tony and Wm were in the turnips. Wash day. Ethel and Evelyn went to Bakewell and brought stewing beef for which they paid. The British and French are doing well in France taking prisoners and villages, guns etc.

July 5th   Dull, not much sun. On getting downstairs this morning our men were surprised to see Mr. Sneap had arrived. He had come last night after we had gone to bed and he did not call us up and had stopped in our buildings all night. Our Ethel, Evelyn, Tony and Aunt H were busy rudding[2] and cleaning our living kitchen. Anthony took Mr. Sneap for a drive to Monyash, Flagg and Chelmorton Church and churchyard and he took some names from gravestones of the Gytes.

July 6th   Dull and very little sun. Emily is bad with neuralgia and has been for some days. Mr. Weadon called here before taking the service in Church.

July 8th   Showery. Wm took old Naylor to Middleton (Walter Needham's horse). Emily's tic is a little better. Tom and Tony were thinning turnips. Emily and Ethel went to Bakewell for a few things. The British and French are advancing in France.

July 9th   Dull and rather windy. Mr. Weadon took the service in church, late out as usual (4 o'clock). Our Tom went on his bicycle for Dr. Fentem to attend Miss Hallam who is in a very low nervous state. He came and said that she must be kept quiet and not be left as he was afraid of Brain fever

1   The Revd. L.W. Greenshields became vicar of Youlgrave in 1907 after curacies at Stanton by Dale and Bakewell.
2   Applying rudd, a red ochre, to flagstones

setting in. He (Dr. Fentem and son Tom) called upon Mr. Sherlock and said that she (Miss Hallam) had better have her holidays now. Mr. Weadon came up at about 10 o'clock tonight to see about Miss Hallam.

July 10th Dull and showery. My sister Hannah and Mrs. T.A. Sheldon stayed with Miss Hallam all night and she is in a poor way. Anthony telegraphed to Mr. Hallam and Mrs. Hallam came this afternoon. A meeting of the Sheldon School Managers was held at our house. There were present Mr. Sherlock, Mr. Thos Wm Brock'st, Mr. John Frost and Wm H Brocklehurst and Mr. A. Gyte. Our Tony was mowing the rakes on moor.

July 11th Rough and showery. Tony and Wm mowing rake on moor. Mr Hallam came and Miss Hallam went home with him and her mother. Her mother came yesterday. Miss Hallam seemed worse excited this morning and our Tom went to the Dr. but he sent word for her to be taken away. Mr. Hallam paid for telegram which Anthony sent.

July 12th Wet and windy. I did not get up until nearly 4 o'clock this afternoon as I was not well. Eggs are 7 a shilling. The British and French are making good progress, 8 miles of trenches have been taken by former.

July 13th Very dull and wet, but a nice growing day. Tom went with Fanny to Middleton (Walter Needham's horse). Service in Church (Mr. Weadon).

July 14th Very dull and this afternoon it went very dark but clears out towards night. Our men have been in the turnips thinning and transplanting, also in cabbage. The British are advancing in France but at a heavy cost both in officers and men. Our Mary had a letter from Clem and he complains of the poor food they have had this week in his camp.

July 15th St. Swithins. Very dull but no rain. Our men found that the crows had been busy taking potatoes out of the rows so they put some knitting cotton and twined it about. This has to be done every year and it seems to be the best way of stopping crows taking the potatoes. Ethel and Evelyn went to Ashford for an evening paper. The news from France continues good. The Germans' second line of trenches is broken into. We are having some heavy casualties, officers as well as men.

July 16th Very dull and heavy showers this afternoon. Mr. Sherlock took the service in church and there was a baptism, Sam Rowland's baby boy John Stanley. Our Tom and Wm Hallows stood sponsors.

July 17th Very dull and gloomy, not a ray of sunshine (drizzling). Anthony went with the milk and afterwards to Bakewell Board of Guardians. Beatrice Needham applied for relief for herself and family as her husband John Needham is in prison having been sentenced at the Derby Assizes to four months imprisonment (second division) for eloping with a girl Doris Robinson who was only about 15 years old. Miss Martha Hallam came to Sheldon today. She says that Miss Ann Hallam is a little better. Mary sent Clem a cake etc.

July 19th Very fine, plenty of sunshine and wind. We started cutting our hay, the field on moor next to road opposite the Red House. Mr. Sherlock called here and said that the Sheldon Sunday School tea would be held on Friday next.

July 20th Very dull and gloomy first thing this morning. Anthony, Tom and Tony are gone on moor in the hay and Ethel and Evelyn have taken their dinner. The weather clears and is very sunny.

July 21st Very dull this morning and about dinner time the rain came down in torrents and thunder was frequently heard. The showers came on at intervals, very heavy. The Sunday School treat was held today. Mr. Sherlock, Mrs. Tinsley and Miss Grover came up in a carriage and pair. Mr. Weadon also came and other gentlemen, prizes were also given. Miss Grover and Mrs. Tinsley called to see me.

July 22nd A very good day, plenty of sun and wind. Anthony, Tom, Tony and Wm were in the hay turning by machine the two fields and hobbling the grove rakes which had been mown some days ago. Ethel, Evelyn, Tom and Tony went to Bakewell tonight to a circus.

July 23rd Dull and misty first thing but turns out a very good day both for sun and wind. I was taken in float down the fields and on to the moor. Mary and the baby, Emily and Tony went as well with their father driving us with the old gray mare (her age is 23). Everything looks very well and if we have good weather I think we shall have better crops than we had last year. Mr. Weadon took the service in Church this afternoon. Anthony and all our girls went. Tom and Tony stayed at home and Aunt H was minding little Anthony. Wm Gould took our old Navvy to Walter Needham's horse.

July 24th Rather misty first thing but turns out a lovely day for sun and wind. They are doing up the house at Magpie (Coxs) and putting things in order at the mine.

July 25th Very fine and a lovely hay day. Sergeant Tipper has just called and told me he was after a man who had taken Jake Lomas's dog. It was fastened up last Saturday night all right. The man who the police want to take out a warrant for is the man who called here sometimes. Once he had a ferret and owl and next he had rabbits. He called here about a month since.

July 26th Very hot. The men are gone into the hay. A few in at dinner time viz Joseph Sellors of Bakewell who has been two or three days repairing Sheldon Church roof and his man, Mr. Potts, J. Berresford, Arthur (the slater). These last three are working at Magpie House. Tommy Morton had to report at Bakewell at 9 o'clock for military service.

July 27th Very hot. Thunder came on after dinner and a slight shower of rain about tea time but there was no rain on moor where the men were in the hay. Anthony and Tom finished topping stack opposite Red House and Tony was turning the seeds next to potatoes. The Russians are making splendid progress in the war and the British are holding Poizieres in France. Joseph Sellors called and said they were finishing today at Sheldon Church (repairs to roof).

July 28th   Very fine, plenty of sun and wind. Wm. Gould finished mowing Bramwell field and our men got 18 loads of seeds (moor). Ben Handley and Mr. Ed B help us after they have done their days work at Magpie Mine. Three men called and had bread and cheese and beer, they had brought a tractor engine to Magpie.

July 29th   Very fine. Sam Bramwell came home from Sunderland until Tuesday.

July 30th   Rather gloomy at first but clears out into a lovely day. Plenty of sunshine and wind. Mr. Weadon took the service in Church. Mrs. Eyre (Mrs. Morton's stepmother) attended service. Mrs. Craven and Ruth B took the children in Sunday School. Miss Hallam is away ill.

July 31st   Rather gloomy and a bit drizzly but clears out. Our men finished topping stacks on Sheldon moor and towards night they got 5 loads of hay from Top Hicks field. Ethel and Evelyn fetched their bicycles from Bakewell.

Aug. 1st   A most lovely day. Splendid sunshine and wind. Our men and Arthur B in hay, finishing Hicks, and brought it home. S. Bramwell returned to military duties (Sunderland). Air raids are getting common again. A considerable number of airships (Raiders) cruised over Lincolnshire, Norfolk, Suffolk, Cambridge, Essex, Kent, Huntingdon. Bombs were dropped off Thames Estuary. Wm. finished mowing the Waterlands and the other men including Mr. Ed, Ben Handley and Arthur B got 11 loads out of Bramwell field (we have put 16 loads in buildings). Arthur B stayed at our house all night (little room over pantry).

Aug. 2nd   A lovely day. Our Tony and Ethel went to drive our young horses out of Alf B's land on moor. All the farmers in Sheldon are very busy in their hay and it is glorious weather, good crops. We got 4 more loads of hay out of Bramwell field. This makes 15 out of Bramwell field this year. There were 4 or 5 out of the same field last year. Ethel went on bike for two pairs of trousers for Tom and Tony. She had a spill coming back. This is the second spill since having her new bicycle.

Aug. 3rd   Very dull this morning but turns out brighter towards night and very windy. Yesterday Anthony received the bill for repairing the Church roof. This morning Joseph Sellors called. I suppose for the money but he was not paid. The work was only finished a week since. The bill amounted to £3. 16. 0.

Aug. 4th   Very dull and gloomy but turns out quite sunny and a nice wind this afternoon. Miss Hallam (Ann) came to Sheldon and Ethel went to pay her salary, also Miss Martha's who came as well. A big demonstration at Bakewell on the 2nd anniversary of *Declaration of War*.

Aug. 5th   A most lovely day. Hot sun and a nice wind. Our Emily was very ill just before 5 o'clock this morning and Tom went on his bike for Dr. Jackson. Her nose bled and she seemed in a poor low way, fainty. She revived a bit before the Dr. came and she told him she thought she was done. Evelyn went on her bike for medicine and other things. Our men, Mr. Ed, Arthur B and Ben Handley are in the hay. They finished the Waterlands getting 4 more loads. These make 19 loads out of Waterlands. Our Tom had a letter from Ernest Taylor, poor lad he seems full of trouble. He joined the army about 7 weeks since. About a week ago his wife was confined of a baby girl which was born dead and its mother was in a very serious condition. Then his sister Edith is in hospital very dangerously ill, not knowing anyone. He himself was on route march and had to fall out of ranks owing to exhaustion. I think it is most cruel to march men in training in such hot weather for so many miles. Where Clem is a man dropped dead the other day. The men also got 8 loads of hay out of Croft Heads and three out of little Butts.

Aug. 6th   Very gloomy, no sun. There was no celebration of Holy Communion today nor a collection. Mr. Weadon took the service in Church and it was 10 minutes past four when the congregation came out. Emily seems a little better.

Aug. 8th   Another grand day plenty of sunshine and wind. Only our men are working in hay today. Anthony paid Arthur B, Ben Handley and Ed B at the rate of 6d. per hour with tea and beer and other meals at times. Tony fetched 3 sheep and 3 lambs from field at Ashford. Clem's brother James died yesterday (Longstone).

Aug. 10th   Another most lovely day. Very hot. Our men thinning turnips which want rain very badly. There will not be much hay left in a day or two. I think there are only T.A. Sheldon and Richard Bonsall who have a bit to get. Mr. Weadon called in house place and invited all the men to go to Church next Sunday having had such a favourable hay harvest. The Italians and Russians are pushing on and taking a many prisoners. Made out milk bill and sent it to end of July. James Wager was buried at Longstone today. I had a letter from Clem saying they would not allow him to come to his funeral. I think soldiers in training are harshly dealt with when they are not allowed to come to a brother's funeral.

Aug. 11th   I think this is the hottest day we have had. Our men are gone to the moor pulling and topping the stacks. Clem got off after all and came to his brother's funeral. He has to be in camp on Saturday night at 12 o'clock.

Aug. 12th   Dull and towards night a bit drizzly but no weight of rain. Our poor Tony received his military papers to report himself at Bakewell on Aug. 26th. All sheep and lambs belonging to people in Sheldon were dipped today at our premises. We dipped 38 sheep and tups and 32 lambs. McDougalls dip, solid and liquid, and Coopers were used.

Aug. 13th A bit dull but no rain comes. Mr. Weadon took the service in Church this afternoon. There was a collection. Showery this afternoon. The collection for Church expenses amounted to 10 shillings. Clem went back this morning from Grindleford.

Aug. 14th Gloomy and rather showery at times. Anthony took the milk and afterwards went to Bakewell where he met Mary and baby and Aunt H who came from Grindleford. He (Anthony) called at the Recruiting Office to see Mr. Sweeting about Tony and he told Anthony that he had better appeal for Tony as he was not able to say whether lads of 18 would be sent home until they were 19. Mr. Advent Hunstone advised him as well so he got an appeal form from the Union and appealed which he sent off tonight. Our wedding anniversary (30 years). Three men who brought a traction engine called here.

Aug. 15th Dull and showery at times. The three men (tractor engine) came here and had breakfast (ham and eggs) for which we charged 1s. 3d. each.

Aug. 16th Dull and showery. The three men called and had breakfast again. Anthony had word to appeal at Bakewell for Tony. Mary had a letter from Clem to say that he had arrived at camp and had walked 13 and a half miles from Stafford to his quarters. He writes not very cheerful. I wonder who can be cheerful. The Russians are doing very well also the Italians. A man and woman called here tonight and had tea. We always call them Germans, they have been here several times and look like foreigners.

Aug. 17th Dull and showery, thunder frequently heard. Our men are on moor. Tom and Tony thatching stacks and Anthony and Wm Gould mowing thistles.

Aug. 19th Showery. Anthony went to Bakewell to appeal for Tony. He (Tony) got put back for 2 months (final). I believe many rejected men are now being accepted.

Aug. 20th Showery and rather windy. Tom went with milk and called at the P. office where there was a letter from Clem for Mary saying that he was very likely coming for six days before going to France. Mr. Weadon took the service in Church. I think Miss Hallam is acting very high handed over the Sunday School. Mr. Sherlock asked Mrs. Craven to take the Sunday School while Miss Hallam was away ill and I hear that the schoolmistress put a lad through the window (this was when Miss Hallam commenced teaching again) who opened the door and she took her place in the school (Mrs. Craven had the key to the school door). Today the children marched to the Church with no one to look after them and there was no teaching in school this afternoon. I think Miss Anne Hallam is like the dog in the manger. She does not want to teach in the school nor does she wish anyone else to do so.

Aug. 21st Fine. August fair. Anthony and Tony took a fat cow to market but did not sell her. There was only one bid of £28.0.0. for her so she was brought back. A lady inspector came to school and had tea here. Tom took Mary, little Anthony and Aunt Hannah to meet the Grindleford conveyance as they went home so as to be there if Clem comes. Ethel and Evelyn went on their bikes to Bakewell. (Uncle John Brockley sold a cow for £40 and 10s. returned.) We have lost two British light cruisers which were torpedoed in N. Sea. They were the *Nottingham* and *Falmouth*. Tom went to a dance (Monyash).

Aug. 22nd Fine. Some of the men were drawing thatch, Tony in turnips. A good many in house tonight. Mr. Craven set sail for S. America. Mrs. Craven and George went to Liverpool to see him off.

Aug. 23rd Fine this morning but comes on showery at tea time. I received a letter from our Mary saying that Clem had received fresh orders and was not coming to Grindleford this week. Our Tom and Tony were thatching on moor. They have finished 2 stacks and one more (opposite Red House) wants thatching. I read in paper that the elder son of Mr. Cockerill had been killed in action. Russians and Italians have landed at Salonika.

Aug. 24th Fine. Anthony, Tom, Tony and Wm went on moor to rail the stacks round and put the tup lambs in clover.

Aug. 26th Fine first thing but thunder and very heavy showers came on this afternoon. Anthony and Tony went by first train to see Mr. Sneap and family taking with them a little white kitten. The air raids are becoming frequent again.

Aug. 27th Fair this morning but very heavy showers come on about four this afternoon. Mr. Sherlock took the service in Church and afterwards called here and asked me to tell Miss Hallam to send the absentee sheet (for June, July and August) at once to him.

Aug. 28th Showery. Miss Hallam had to come out of school owing to illness and there is a holiday this afternoon. Mr. Sherlock called here and said that he was going to telegraph to the Education Authority that she is unable to go on teaching owing to her nervous breakdown. Roumania comes into the War on the side of Britain and her allies.

Aug. 29th Dull and showery at times. Anthony and Tony took some calves on moor. The girls are making jam. The Misses Hallam went away from Sheldon today.

Aug. 30th Cold. Dull and gloomy. Mr. Sherlock's brother came to see Anthony this morning.

Aug. 31st Rather dull. Anthony and Tony were walling gaps in the morning and weeding in the turnips this afternoon. A Managers meeting was held at our house over Miss Hallam and the school. Mr. Sherlock was here and he brought his brother's wife and introduced her to me. They both had tea here. Fred Goodwin has landed in France.

Sept. 1st A very grand day. Plenty of sunshine and wind which will be good for the corn. There were no daily papers to be got at Ashford. The Romanians are doing good work. The Austrians are retreating. I had a letter from Mary saying that Clem had been drafted to Newcastle-on-Tyne and that he had come yesterday to Grindleford for a few days leave. Mrs. Morton has received a letter saying that Miss Hallam is very ill and that the Dr. had been twice a day and they were expecting him again. Ernest Stubbs called here to see if Anthony could bring his sister in float if she came teaching to Sheldon.

Sept. 2nd A lovely day. Sunshine. I hear that J. Goodwin has killed his cat and kittens and time too for the cat has destroyed chickens wholesale and taken them to the kittens. It has taken a many of ours and Alf Brockleys, Joe Carson's, Wm H. Brocklehurst's, Mrs. Morton's, Mrs. Banks and Lewis Elliott's and I think it ought to have been destroyed long since. Jack Naylor went back today to his regiment. There are about 23 of the Allies ships before Athens (anchored).

Sept. 3rd Very misty. During the day thunder and rain, heavy showers. Mr. Sherlock administered Holy Communion at 9.30 in Sheldon Church. Mr. Weadon took the service this afternoon. Collection which amounted to 7s. od. was for Church expenses. Tom heard there had been another air raid.

Sept. 4th Very dull and gloomy. Anthony and Tom took a fat cow to market and sold her for £26. 10s. od. Clem came to see us this morning and went back after tea. He goes to Newcastle tomorrow night. Anthony paid for the girls' bicycles. 13 Zeppelins are reported to have been raiding about London and the Eastern counties. One of the Zepps was brought down and fell in flames. About 15 bodies were recovered out of the mass of wreckage. There were about 25 or 30 in the Zepp. People in thousands cheered when they saw its destruction. Ethel went to Bakewell and she had Clem's company as far as the new road. Miss Ethel Stubbs commenced teaching at Sheldon School.

Sept. 5th Fine. The men were doing various work on the farm viz walling gaps, weeding etc. Wilf Goodwin went before the medical board (Derby) and passed for home service. Our Tony is not well, headache and sick.

Sept. 6th Very fine. Plenty of sunshine and wind. The 1st partridge shoot of the season. We got 7 luncheons, half gallon beer, 4 mineral waters also 3 teas for the gentlemen. Our Tony is not well and is in bed with a bilious attack. Mr. C. Ollerenshaw called in at noon and said he was trying his new teeth as it was the 1st time he has had them in. They look well. Our men are putting oil of coal or something on the hay barn and it took fire and nearly suffocated us with the smell (the pitch etc took fire not the barn). George and Joe Carson went before the medical board at Derby. George passed for something abroad and Joe for Home Service. Mr. Wood, Mr. Lowthian and Mr. Lees came here for tea. Bill for luncheon viz 7 luncheons at 1s. 9d. each = 12s. 3d. Beer half gallon 1s. 4d. and 4 minerals at twopence halfpenny each = 10d. 3 teas = 3s.0d. Total = 17s. 5d. Tony has been in bed all day. He was very sick during last night.

Sept. 7th Fine but rather gloomy. Alf Brocklehurst and Fred Carson have gone before the medical board at Derby. A motor load of furniture has come to the Magpie house for Mr. Moody. Anthony bought a cow from Mr. H. Frost £30. 10s. 0d.

Sept. 8th Rather gloomy. Miss Martha Hallam came to Sheldon and went back again. I think her sister Miss Ann is a little better. Our Tony is a little better. Evelyn cycled to Bakewell and ordered a shoulder of mutton for next Sunday and paid for it.

Sept. 9th Dull not much sun. Tom, Ethel and Evelyn went to Buxton show (cattle etc.). The two girls cycled there and back. Tom went by train (hurdles). Alf Wildgoose came home for the weekend from Withernsea. The police were demanding to see the papers of eligible men for the army.

Sept. 10th Very misty and afterwards a bit drizzling. Mr. Weadon took the service in Church this afternoon. A good many in the house tonight.

Sept. 11th Dull and drizzling. Mr. Weadon paid Anthony £4.0.0. to pay Mr. J. Sellors bill for repairing Sheldon Church roof. John Pursglove and Wm Carson went before the medical board at Derby. They have not passed for active service.

Sept. 12th Dull and cold and wet at times. Orme's man brought us rum and stout. Evelyn and Tony went to Bakewell to fetch some butter.

Sept. 14th My birthday (59). Very cold but some nice sun and wind a good corn day for drying and ripening. We shall begin cutting soon. The old concertina chap also came on his weekly round. I filled an appeal paper for Mrs. Carson for Fred.

Sept. 16th Fine. Our Emily went to Bakewell with her uncle Will Brockley and she had her portrait taken. Thos Wm B appealed for George who got put back for 4 months. We had several tourists called today. Alf Wildgoose came for a few days leave before being drafted somewhere else.

Sept. 17th Very dull and cold no sun. I went on moor with Fanny (in float), our Mary and baby and Tony and Anthony who drove us down the fields to look at swedes, cabbage and corn and on to moor to see the corn and potatoes and stock and hay etc. We got back about dinner time. Mr. Sherlock took the service in Church this afternoon. Alf Wildgoose came in tonight.

Sept. 18th Very wet and cold today. The rain came on this afternoon. Tom and Tony and Wm went corn cutting with self binder but had to come home owing to the wet. Our armies in France are doing very well and on the other fronts as well. Our new motor or armoured car is said to be doing very good work.

Sept. 19th Very rough and wet. Between last night and this morning the rain came down in torrents and the wind was so rough that it blew down the rose trees in front of the house. Anthony took the milk and he and Tom went forward to Wagers at Longstone and bought a young filly which had been Jim's (Jim died a few weeks ago). Tom and Tony went with it on the moor. The other two young horses kicked at it and it had to be put in a field to itself. I had some words with Billy Naylor and Jim Goodwin (last night). Jim Goodwin let Billy drink out of his pint after I had stopped the tap on Billy.

Sept. 20th Fine and more sun. Our men have gone into the cornfield and Tom is cutting with self binder and the others are setting up. Our Tom's military papers came this morning and he has to report at Bakewell recruiting office on October 4th before 9 o'clock.

Sept. 21st Fine. Our men (Anthony, Tom, Tony and Wm) finished cutting corn in Bole Piece and set it up. They also began opening out Grindlow Knoll. Anthony sent in an appeal for Tom. Thos Wm Brocklehurst had a field Postcard to say that Fred had been wounded and was in hospital. Fred wrote it himself. Mr. Sherlock came up to Sheldon for the Mission. It was held in the school room. There were only 7 present. Anthony and our three girls, Mr. Craven, Ruth Brockley and Mrs. Craven.

Sept. 22nd Fine. Our men are cutting corn (Grindlow Knoll). Mary had a letter from Clem (from the base in France). He is well. Thos Wm had a letter from Fred to say he was wounded in the shoulder by a bomb. John B had a letter from Anthony to say that he (Anthony) had been wounded in the thigh. There have been a many casualties in the last battle on the Somme (Sep. 15th) amongst whom are killed Mr. Raymond Asquith and the Earl of Faversham. A many of the guards were in the last action. Sheldon school boys broke a gate and knocked down stump and broke it this afternoon.

Sept. 23rd Fine, but not much sun. Our men are in corn in Grindlow Knoll. Alf Brockley has been before the Rural Tribunal at Bakewell and has been put back six months. Mr. Carson has appealed for Fred. A policeman in private clothes called here and made enquiries about the man who called here with ferret and owl. He seemed to know the man. Wm Bramwell (Monyash) was in our house and he gave him some information about a man answering to description who had gone through Taddington on Wednesday night last.

Sept. 24th Fine. We have heard that there has been another Zeppelin raid during last night and early morning. Mr. Weadon took the service in Sheldon Church this afternoon, the congregation were late out as usual it being after 4 o'clock. I was taken for a drive this morning in the float down Monyash and through our moor. Emily, Tony and little Anthony went. Anthony drove us with Fanny. Joe Sheldon (sugar)[1] was in our house tonight in khaki .

1   Sugar was a nickname for members of the Sheldon family.

Sept. 25th Fine, a good day for the corn. Sun and good wind. Anthony took the milk and then went to Bakewell. Tom, Tony and Wm were cutting corn and Anthony went this afternoon. Finished Grindlow Knoll. Read in paper of the Zeppelin raid over the Eastern counties and London. It is thought that about 12 were in the raid. A good many killed and injured but two of the Zepps were brought down and 22 of one were burned to death and 19 of the crew of the other were taken prisoners, it is said by a village policeman. Evelyn received a letter from Fred Brocklehurst from a hospital at Rouen in France and he described the battle he was in on Friday Sept 15th.

Sept. 26th Very foggy this morning: clears out after dinner. Another Air Raid. We have to go before the Tribunal on Saturday over Tom. The second partridge shoot. We provided 8 luncheons at 1s. 9d. each = 14s.0d. Two glasses were broken for which the charge is 8d. 1 gallon beer 2s. 8d.; 3 minerals 7$^{1}/_{2}$d; 4 teas (one for motor man) 4s. 0d. = £1 1s. 3$^{1}/_{2}$d.

Sept. 27th Very misty clears out a bit after dinner. Our men made a start in the corn on moor with self binder but the day was not a very good one. A Managers' meeting was held in the schoolroom. Miss Stubbs called here to see if our Mary would play the Ashford organ next Sunday.

Sept. 28th A fine day. Anthony and Tony went to Ashbourne horse show. They drove to Hurdlow station with Fanny and put her and trap up at Wm Horobins. They got back just after six o'clock. Tom and Wm cutting corn on moor. Our Emily had a very bad attack last night (late) and Dr. Jackson came this morning.

Sept. 29th Very dull, rough and cold. The men are in the corn on moor. Our Mary had a letter from Clem. He is well and has met in France with some men he knew and has found a mate with a Buxton man. The British and French have had great victories on the Somme during the last few days. Combles, Thiepval etc. are in their hands. We have had some dreadful damage in lives and property during the last Zeppelin raids. Sheffield suffered very much the other night. Emily is a little better. Ethel and Evelyn went to Bakewell and bought each of them a pair of boots which cost 14s. 6d. per pair.

Sept. 30th Fine. Anthony went before the Tribunal on Tom's appeal. Tom said he would go if they would let Tony off. Tom got off a month and Tony had leave to appear again. Finished corn cutting.

Oct. 1st   Fine. Wakes Sunday and Harvest Festival. Celebration of Holy Communion Mr. Sherlock at 9.30. There were 8 present amongst whom was Annie Haywood. Mr. Sherlock also took the service in Church this afternoon. The collection for Church expenses amounted to £1 8s. 7d. The Church was very nicely decorated with flowers that people sent. Mrs. B. Morton (Bakewell) sent flowers for the altar.

Oct. 2nd   Very misty. There has been another Zeppelin raid according to what the postman brought word. Sam and Fred Brockley (Potteries) and

Sam's lad Fred came today and are staying at Carsons. The Wakes is very quiet. We had no music and this is the 3rd Wakes we have had no dancing. The war is making everyone so sad and weary.

Oct. 3rd Our Tom's paper came this morning for one month's exemption until the 30th of October. Very wet this morning but clears out a bit after dinner.

(The following four entries were written by Tony)

Oct. 4th Very rough and wet. Mr. Sherlock called today, with the new lay reader, they had tea. Tom went to Ashford for sheep but could only find three. I found the other 4 in G. Smith's ground, not much Wakes. Hodgekinson from Calver came for Cock-chickens, had 11 couples at 5/- a couple.

Oct. 5th Very rough and wet, thunder about. Harry Buxton and Sid Brocklehurst went home today. Mother came to bed very poorly. Mr. Weadon took service in the School.

Oct. 6th Rough and wet all day. Sam and Fred Brocklehurst went home today, not many folks in tonight. Mother no better, still in bed.

Oct. 7th A bit brighter this morning, but very rough and showery this afternoon. Ethel received a letter from Clem, he says it is a nice part where he is. Cow calved a dead bull calf. Tom's exemption card came. George Eaton took the other sheet of wool to Bakewell Station. Ethel walked to Bakewell today. Mother still in bed, not much better. Tony

Oct. 8th Rough and cold. Mr. Weadon took the service in Church. I did not get up until after tea, and I do not feel so grand.

Oct. 9th Very rough, but a good corn day. Anthony and Tony took a fat cow and 7 fat sheep to market. The sheep were sold for £2 16s. 6d. each but the cow was brought back. £29 was offered for her but was not taken. Miss Ethel Stubbs came teaching to Sheldon again.

Oct. 12th Very rough. Mr. Weadon called to say *Goodbye* as he has to join the Army on 26th of this month and John Pursglove on the 24th. Mr. Weadon left £2.14.4. here, balance of money on sale of work.

Oct. 13th Very close and drizzling. The men are colouring some of our lambs ready for sale. I made out Mr. Wood's bill and sent him a letter over his enquiries over the two broken glasses I charged for (8d.).

Oct. 14th Very rough. I had a letter from Clem this morning. He is well. A very singular thing happened tonight. We had three cows calved before 10 o'clock tonight (from milking time) two bull calves and one cow-calf.

Oct. 15th Very heavy showers this morning and on Anthony and Tony going on moor they found two hen cotes very much damaged by the wind which was awfully rough last night and in the night. One hen was killed.

We had hare to dinner but I cannot taste or smell and have been like this for above a week. Mr. Sherlock and the new lay reader (Mr. Hayward) took the service in Sheldon Church this afternoon.

Oct. 16th Dull and showery. Anthony, Tom and Tony went to market with a cow, 3 bull calves and some tup lambs (S. Wilton drove lambs). Alf Brocklehurst bought our best tup lamb for £5.10.0. Two other others made £5.0.0. each, one 4 pounds. We have made a good start with the lambs, a record price. The cow was not sold. Ethel cycled down to Bakewell for green blinds for the front bedrooms as people get fined very often for showing too much light during the war, and also to get new strong boots for herself and Evelyn. Filled up and sent an exemption paper for Tony.

Oct. 17th Very dull, wet and miserable. Tony was thatching haystack in front of Red House.

Oct. 18th Dull and drizzling first thing but clears out and a bit of sunshine. Anthony, Tom and Tony were thatching corn stacks and Tony finished haystack on moor (Red House). Arthur Strong and Wm Twelves (soldiers) called here.

Oct. 19th Our Tony's papers came calling him to the colours on Nov. 2nd. Rough and cold but the corn was not dry enough to lead. Sam Bramwell came home for a few days. He was in our house tonight.

Oct. 20th Rather cold. Mr. Wood called and paid for the last shoot. He told our Ethel he was greatly amused over the letter I sent him last week but I do not believe that tale. If he had said greatly annoyed I should have believed him. Miss Grover and Mrs. Kenworthy called to see us and brought some papers about the mission and a book called *Captain Desmond VC*. Miss Grover ordered from us 1 bag of potatoes and 1 cwt of swedes.

Oct. 21st Fine and dry. The school piano was tuned today by Goddard from Buxton. Anthony Brocklehurst came home for 10 days leave from Herefordshire. George Carson joined the army this morning.

Oct. 22nd Very cold. The wind is in the east and there has been rather severe frost. Mr. Hayward took the service in Church and the congregation was out in good time, 20 minutes to four.

Oct. 23rd Very cold and rough, drizzling with rain. Sam Bramwell ought to have gone back to camp but he had a letter saying he could stay a day or two longer for getting his potatoes. Mr. Towers[1] and Mr. Sherlock took part in the National Mission tonight. A pretty good congregation. Our Tom went to Ashford to a whist drive and dance.

Oct. 24th Dull but fair. Our men were catching our hens ready for sale to Hodgkinson who came later and took forty at 2 shillings each which

1 The Revd. John Robert Towers came as Curate at Buxton in 1916 following curacies in Hoylake (1909-12), Stirling (1912-13) and Glasgow (1913-1916). He had been a student at Kelham College (1904) and was a Licenciate in Theology of Durham University (1909).

amounted to £4. o.o. (paid). There was Holy Communion in Sheldon Church at 9 o'clock this morning. The missioner celebrating 11 present. There was another service at 12 o'clock midday and another tonight. This afternoon Anthony, Tom and Tony went on moor getting potatoes. Mrs. Tinsley called in to see me also Mr. Towers the missioner who is lodging at Bramwell's (Polly). Wm Gould went for coal for the Church which cost 11s. 7d. A good attendance at school. The missioner seems to be very well liked. Anthony, Tom, Tony, Emily and Evelyn were there.

Oct. 25th Very showery. We provided the following for Mr. Wood and Mr. Lowthian's shoot

12 luncheon at 1s.9d. each	£1 1s. 0d.
1/2 gallon of beer	4s. 0d.
4 minerals	10d.
Total	£1. 5s. 10d.

Our Tony was one of the beaters (his 1st time) he got 3s.6d. Holy Communion at 9 o'clock, service at 12 (noon) and a service for women at 3 o'clock. Practice for choir at 7.30 and a service for all at 8 o'clock. A good number present in school tonight.

Oct. 26th A cold fine day. Our own men and Cecil Brockley and Herbert Newton were getting our potatoes on moor. Service (Holy Communion) in Sheldon Church, service at 12 (noon) and Mr. Towers came and celebrated Holy Communion for Mrs. Ed and myself in our parlour at 2.45. He afterwards called and had a nice chat with me. G. Carson came back from Derby and is going to work at Friden (by order of the military). Mr. Towers conducted service in school tonight and afterwards went to Ashford by motor (Coxs). Mr. Sherlock and Mr. Hayward were at Sheldon service. We killed two of our cockerels for Miss Stubbs.

Oct. 28th Very wet this morning but is fairer afterwards. Anthony went to the Rural Tribunal Bakewell and appealed for Tony. He got him off for 3 months on the understanding that Tom went in his place when (Tom) was called up. John Pursglove appealed for himself but the Tribunal could not do anything for him. Read in paper that there had been a naval battle in the Channel. Ten German destroyers came. We had an empty transport sunk and it is feared that the ship *Flint is* lost and another of ours. We sank two of the German destroyers and the others got away. Mrs. Ed's birthday (59). I was to have gone to tea but did not go as I cough so.

Oct. 29th A most miserable wet day. Holy Communion this morning in Sheldon Church 20 present. Mr. Sherlock and Mr. Towers celebrated. Service this afternoon by Mr. Sherlock and Mr. Towers. All went to Church from our house except myself and William. Collection for Church mission £1 1s. 7d. which was brought to our house by Uncle W Brockley.

Oct. 31st   Another most miserable wet and windy day. Sam Rowland and Anthony Brocklehurst went back to their regiments. S. Rowland to near Winchester and Anthony to Chelsea.

Nov. 2nd   Fine and fair. Our Mary received a letter from Clem. He is in the trenches. Jim Goodwin said that Fred was in two attacks and got back all right, but he wanted a razor as his had disappeared.

Nov. 5th   A most miserable rough and wet day. The rain came down in torrents all through the night and during today. Our Emily had a very bad attack between 3 and 4 this morning, such awful pain which struck through to her back and down her left arm. Tom went on horseback (Fanny) to fetch Dr. Jackson this afternoon who came in his motor and afterwards Mary and Ethel went to Bakewell for some medicine. Holy Communion this morning in Sheldon Church administered by Mr. Sherlock. Mr. Hayward conducted the service this afternoon very few present but the day was so wet. Collection for Church expenses 6s. 1d.

Nov. 6th   Fine and fairer but very rough. Emily is a little better. A cow calved a cow calf and Tom, Tony and Wm were emptying bags of potatoes this morning. Orme's brought 6 cases of stout and one dozen bottles of special whiskey. Our Tony posted cheque for licence (after post time).

Nov. 12th   A fine day. All at our house seem to have an influenza cold. I received a letter from Clem this morning. He is in the trenches up to the knees in mud. Our Tony had word to report at the recruiting office on the 1st of Jan. Mr. Hayward took the service in Sheldon Church this afternoon. Tom, Tony, Ethel and Evelyn went to Monyash Church tonight. It is Monyash Wakes.

Nov. 13th   Fine early in the day but a thick mist came on in the afternoon. Our Tony's birthday (19 years). Mary received two letters from Clem, in one he said he had been buried (by a shell). He was bruised but not otherwise hurt. His steel helmet was knocked off. Mr. Hayward called and had tea at our house.

Nov. 14th   A thick mist all day today. Our men have been getting potatoes, got one row. There are 11 more. Tom, Tony, Ethel and Evelyn went to a social at Monyash tonight. Got back just after 12 o'clock.

Nov. 15th   Fine. Tom, Tony, Wm H Newton and Cecil Brockley are getting potatoes for us on the moor. Mr. Mann came to see about Sheldon waterworks. John Brockley killed a pig.

Nov. 16th   Very cold. Tom, Wm, Herbert Newton and Cecil Brockley went getting potatoes on moor. Tony went with the young bull to Bakewell station. His uncle Billy went as well. They trucked it off to Mr. Sneap. Cecil Brockley was so starved on moor that our Tom sent him home. Evelyn took the horse and cart on moor after dinner for potatoes.

Nov. 17th Very frosty and most bitterly cold. Covered the potatoes up with straw and bags. Poor Victor Bonsall has been called up to be a soldier a day or two since.

Nov. 18th Keen, rough and bitterly cold. Some snowstorms. We could do nothing on the land and there are 5 rows of potatoes and many swedes want getting. Tom and Tony went on moor and gave the stock some hay, have cut in one of the stacks on moor. They brought two cotes with the hens nearer home. Emily has had a fire in her bedroom. She is very poorly.

Nov. 19th Very keen and more snow. Mr. Hayward took the service in Church. Emily seems very poorly. Her nose bled a little but I think it is with coughing or influenza cold. John Brockley received a field P. Card to say that Jack was wounded and going on well.

Nov. 21st Very cold and frosty. Anthony was pulling a few swedes this morning. Tom and Wm were carting lime and Tony is spreading it. The government have taken over milk and wheat supply and have fixed prices. The Roumanians are being pressed by the Germans etc. The Allies have taken about 7,000 prisoners and the Bulgars are in flight. Emily is about the same and is in bed.

Nov. 22nd Cold and a bit frosty. It is not fit to go on moor getting potatoes. Mr. Hayward called and had tea.

Nov. 23rd Cold and rather windy. Anthony was pulling swedes. Tom and Tony spreading lime and Wm was leading cabbages out this morning. Our men are going getting potatoes this afternoon. Our hospital ship *Britannia* has been torpedoed in the Aegean Sea. There are 1106 survivors and about 50 lost. Nothing more has been heard of Jack Brockley since P. Card came last Sunday.

Nov. 24th Our Emily's birthday (26). She got up a little while, she has been in bed since last Sunday. Cold and rough winds with snow and then a shower. Tom, Tony, Wm, Herbert Newton and Cecil Brockley have been on moor getting potatoes. We finished getting them and we are very glad as the weather has been so unfavourable. We have to finish getting swedes. Sam Rowland came home tonight.

Nov. 25th Very rough and cold. Our men are gone on the moor to clear up and pick up any potatoes left on field. All got wet through. Read in paper that another hospital ship has been sunk called the *Braemar Castle* in the Aegean Sea. Jack Naylor and Tom Morton came home for the weekend. There was a shoot in Shacklow - 100 pheasant and 5 hares.

Nov. 26th Cold and heavy showers of rain and sleet. Tom went with milk. Tom Morton and his brother in law were in at dinner time. Jack Naylor and Anthony Brocklehurst came here to tea. Sam Rowland was in tonight. He expects to go abroad before long with his regiment. Mr. Sherlock took the service in Church, collection for Mission was taken by Mr. Sherlock.

Nov. 27th Very frosty and cold. Mr. Hayward came in to tea and I had some conversation with him over last year about the choir supper etc. Jack Naylor started from Sheldon at about six o'clock this morning as he had to be at his camp at 10 o'clock. (I think Tom Morton went to Derby.) Jack Brockley sent a letter saying he was wounded in the arm and leg. Roumania is in a very grave position.

Nov. 29th Fine, rather cold. Men pulling swedes. Mr. Sherlock called here for a few minutes and then went up to school where a Managers meeting was held to appoint a schoolmistress. Miss Hallam has left and Miss Stubbs has taken her place for a few weeks. The managers present were: Mr. Sherlock, Mr. A. Gyte, Mr. John Frost, Mr. T.W. Brocklehurst and Mr. Wm H. Brocklehurst. Alf Brocklehurst brought us some pork with the understanding that we send him some when we kill a pig.

Nov. 30th Fine but dull. Our men have been getting swedes. Mr. Mann (Road surveyor) called to see Anthony over the Sheldon pumps. John Brocklehurst had a telegram to say that Jack was dangerously ill at Rouen in France. He was wounded a week or two since.

Dec. 1st Misty and cold. Our men and H. Newton and Cecil Brockley are pulling and getting swedes. They have brought 189 loads into the turnip place and made some pits in the field. Poor Jack Brockley died yesterday at Rouen in France. His parents had a telegram tonight. Sam Rowland went back to his regiment today.

Dec. 2nd Awfully misty and cold. Our men and H. Newton have been pulling swedes. Everybody seems so gloomy and sad over the death of poor Jack Brockley and are very sorry for his parents. Our Tom drowned old Gyp today. She was getting very old and in pup, so we thought it best. Miss Grover called with the magazine and wanted Anthony to let her have the potatoes and swedes she had ordered some time since.

Dec. 3rd Fine. Holy Communion celebrated in Sheldon Church. Mr. Sherlock came at 9.30. Mr. Hayward took the service this afternoon. Collection for the choir suppering amounted to 11s. 10d.

Dec. 5th Very cold and frosty. Tom and Wm leading manure. Anthony and Tony picking and putting up potatoes. Tony took Mrs. Morton some swedes. There is a cabinet crisis, members are resigning.

Dec. 7th Cold. Mr. Asquith has resigned the Premiership. The King sent for Mr. Bonar Law but he was unable to form a ministry. Mr. Lloyd George was summoned by the King and he consented to form a ministry. The situation in Greece is very grave. King Tino and his gang have led the Allies into a trap and it was only by a French warship dropping a shell or two on the Palace at Athens that somewhat saved our forces from being annihilated.

Dec. 9th Cold and misty. Tom Morton was over from Derby. He ought to have gone back but did not. Eggs are 4 for a shilling.

Dec. 10th Very slippery. Tom went with the milk. Mr. Sherlock conducted a funeral service this afternoon for poor Jack Brockley. A pretty fair congregation. All went of our family except Emily and myself. Wm stayed in kitchen.

Dec. 11th Snow and mist. Anthony went to Bakewell and took Mr. Archer's milk cheque to bank and also took (for Sheldon penny bank) £1.2.5. He had some talk with Mr. Tinsley who said that there were 500 substituted at Derby waiting to be sent to different jobs. I expect he means farming etc.

Dec. 12th Misty and cold. Slippery in places. Matthew Hodgkinson killed one of our pigs and cut it up the same day. We estimate its weight at about 20 stones.

Dec. 13th Misty and cold. Our men have weighed and picked 4 loads of potatoes which are ordered. We have sent pork out to Alf Brockleys, John Brockleys and Billy Naylor in return for what they sent to us. Our girls have been rendering fat.

Dec. 14th Cold, frosty and rimy. Our Ethel's birthday (24). Anthony was baking oatcake. Mr. Lloyd George and other members of the government are ill with influenza etc. There is a deal of talk about German peace proposals.

Dec. 15th Very cold and slippery. We had a word or two from Mary saying that she had not heard from Clem (for over three weeks). She also sent a bit of fish for Emily. I have just heard that Mr. Albert Wager (Clem's father) is dead. Three of his sons will not be able to come to the funeral as Tom and Clem are in France and Joe is in Salonica. Thos Wm Brockley fetched coal for Church (12s.6d.).

Dec. 16th Very cold frosty and slippery. We had a letter from our Mary saying that she had had word from the War Office saying that Clem had been missing since Nov. 18-19 last and that if they heard any more particulars they would let her know. She wanted to come to Sheldon so her father fetched her and the little boy and aunt H. We are all very sorrowful as missing might mean anything. A woman came to see Sheldon school and house. She is teaching at Taddington and very likely she will apply for the post of mistress at Sheldon School. She told me she had been 21 years in one school. Her name is Broadhurst and she says she was born at Matlock and that her grandmother formerly kept the hotel at Ambergate.

Dec. 17th Cold and slippery. Mary and Ethel have gone to Longstone to see Clem's mother and relatives. I hear they will bury old Mr. Wager tomorrow. Mr. Hayward took the service in Church this afternoon and offered a prayer for Clement Wager who is *Missing*. Mary and Ethel got back between 8 and 9 o'clock.

Dec. 18th Milder but very slippery. Anthony took the milk to the station and afterwards went to Bakewell market. Tony met him there with two of our calving beasts which were sold one for £35.10s. and one for £27.10s. Mary has gone to Longstone to attend the funeral of Clem's father who is to be buried at 2.30 this afternoon. It is very slippery down Ashford Dale. Anthony says it is the worst day he was out for being so bad travelling.

Dec. 21st Cold and frosty. This is the shortest day. I hope the future will bring us better news; we seem to be very gloomy and depressed over the war. Little John Joseph Eaton is very ill and Dr. Jackson wished him to be taken to Sheffield to have an operation. George Eaton went to Bakewell to get a motor car but was unable to get one as the roads are so slippery. Our Ethel (according to the Dr.'s orders) gave the little boy an injection.

Dec. 22nd Very frosty and slippery. Dr. Jackson came twice today to John Joseph Eaton and he was taken by motor to Derby. The little boy's father, his aunt Alice Brocklehurst and our Ethel went with him to Derby Infirmary where he was to undergo an operation. They started from Sheldon at about 7 o'clock. Mary received another letter from the War Office saying they had no further information over Clem being missing and that she could draw 30 weeks allowance money from the date of missing.

Dec. 23rd Quite a deep snow and has been snowing all day. Our Ethel and Alice got back about 2 o'clock this morning. The motor had broken down in going to Derby last night and they got to the infirmary at 10 o'clock, stayed two hours there and then came back. Our Tony is poorly with influenza. Very cold and snowing. Little John Eaton is no better and our Evelyn and Alice Brocklehurst went to Derby by the 6.13 train at Bakewell (to the Infirmary). Our Tom took them in float as far as J. Skidmore (Bakewell).

Dec. 24th Quite a deep snow and cold. George Eaton started from Derby to come home by 1st train. He got as far as Ashford where he found a telegram (sent by our Evelyn) saying that John Joseph was worse, so he turned back and went to Derby again. Evelyn and Alice stayed at Mr. Ollerenshaw's last night and George stayed at the Infirmary. Mr. and Mrs. C. Ollerenshaw were most kind to the girls and G. Eaton giving them their meals as well as providing lodgings. Little Jack had gone through the operation the night that Alice and our Ethel and his father took him to the Infirmary but his heart is so weak. Miss Wager (Clem's sister) came to see us. She brought a letter from Tom Wager from France saying that an officer had told him that Clem was supposed to have been taken prisoner by the Germans. Our Evelyn and Alice B came back by last train from Derby. Mr. Sherlock took the service this afternoon in Sheldon Church.

Dec. 25th Xmas Day and Xmas weather but nothing else. No singing in the night or going round. I think everybody is depressed and war weary. We did not decorate a bit as we are accustomed for Xmas. Mr. Sherlock administered Holy Communion in Sheldon Church at 9.40 this morning. We had turkey and sausage for dinner. Mr. Hayward took the service this afternoon. Collection for Church expenses (6s.10d.). Mr. Hayward called here and had tea. Wm Gould was paid and off he went somewhere.

Dec. 26th Plenty of snow. Another telegram came today saying that little John Joseph Eaton was much worse. Our Ethel went with Elsie to Derby to see him. Uncle Wm Brockley took them to the station. Anthony Brocklehurst went back to Chelsea tonight. Joe Handley and Joshua Millington joined him at Bakewell Station and they all went back together.

Dec. 27th Very slippery and winterly. Gould came back tonight. He had spent two nights away, I think at Monyash. Ethel, George and Elsie Eaton came back from Derby. Little John Joseph is about the same. Mr. Sherlock called here and had tea. He had been to baptize Elsie Eaton's baby girl.

Dec. 29th Wet and thawing. Much of the snow is gone. Our Tony had word that his papers calling him up on Jan. 1st were cancelled and he was to report when he heard again. The cow that calved before its time has not cleansed. We are giving it some ivy tea. Anthony filled up a paper and returned it to Captain Sweeting about Tony's employment and for how long he had been so employed.

Dec. 30th Nice and mild. We got 12 bread and cheese luncheons for Messrs. Lowthian and Woods' beaters and one gallon bitter beer. Mrs. Carson appealed for their Fred but he was not granted exemption. Our Tom had a paper saying that he was not to report at the Recruiting Office on Jan. 3rd but to wait until he heard again from Captain Sweeting. There was a Managers' meeting at school to appoint a new mistress.

Dec. 31st Wet but milder. Our Mary played in Church this afternoon as Evelyn has such a cough. Word came that little John Joseph Eaton was dead in the Derby Infirmary. Mr. Hayward took the service and the congregation were out at a quarter past 3 o'clock.

1917

Jan. 1st　Wet and mild. Our Mary had a postal order returned which she had sent to Clem on Nov. 16th last. The envelope said on it *Missing*. Fred Brockley came on leave. Little J.J. Eaton was fetched from Derby Infirmary by motor.

Jan. 2nd　Rough and wet. Our Tony had a paper (from Recruiting Office Bakewell) authorizing him to go before the medical board at Derby on Jan. 10th next. His paper paying his fare came as well. Our Mary and little Anthony are not so well.

Jan. 3rd　Rough. Little John Joseph Eaton was buried at Sheldon today. The bearers were Fred and George Brocklehurst, and our Tony and Sam Wilton. Ethel and Evelyn walked. Mr. Sherlock had tea at Mrs. Cravens.

Jan. 4th　Rough and sleet at times. Gould and Tony spreading lime on Grindlow Knoll. T.W. Bckst and Anthony gave flannel out at Sheldon School.

Jan. 5th　Fine. Tom is ploughing on moor. Bertie Hollinshed was snap-shotting Ethel and Evelyn.

Jan. 6th　Showery at times. We received a letter from Anthony Brockley from Le Havre (France). Tom ploughing on moor. Eggs 5 for 1s.0d.

Jan. 7th　Snow and sleet. Early Communion. Mr. Sherlock officiated. Service this afternoon (Mr. Hayward) collection for Church expenses 9s.2d. Our Emily has been in bed all day with influenza.

Jan. 8th　Quite a blizzard. Snow and wind all day. Dr. Jackson came to Emily and we paid him his bill £4.6.6.

Jan. 10th　Very frosty and more snow fell towards night. Several of the roads are blocked in the Peak District. Our Tony went to Derby and went before the Medical board and passed for General Service (A1). He went from Bakewell station and there were several others whom Tony knew - Harry Sutton and Cyril Mellor from Over Haddon and one from Pilsley etc. C. Mellor forgot to take his registration card and has to go again. H. Sutton, our Tony and the one from Pilsley passed for General Service (Normanton Barracks). Tony got back something about 7 o'clock tonight. Wm took some bags of potatoes to the co-op stores Bakewell.

Jan. 11th　Very dull, thawing a little but there is plenty of snow. Aunt Hannah is helping Mrs. Craven to cut out and sew. Mrs. Craven is expecting to leave Sheldon for S. America tomorrow to sail on Saturday. Clement's name is in the casualty list as missing in today's paper. I said *Goodbye* to Mrs. Craven who called in to see me tonight.

Jan. 12th Very winterly, cold and snow. Wm Gould took Mrs. Craven's luggage to Longstone Station also George and Piccareet. These two sat upon the boxes in the cart with shelvings. Mrs. Craven walked. The luggage and train fare cost above £3.0.0. going to Liverpool by the 11.19 train(morning). Mrs. Craven and the luggage had to go before the permit officer. Our Mary had a letter from Mr. Burdekin (Clem's employer) saying that he had made enquiries to the CO of Clem's regiment and that he had had an answer back from the CO saying that officers and men had been taken prisoners in the attack on Nov. 18th last and that doubtless Clem would be amongst them. Mary answered the letter of Mr. Burdekin (Baslow) thanking him for his kindness.

Jan. 13th Very cold, plenty of snow. Mrs. Craven sets sail in the *Saxonia* for Columbia (S. America). Later on a telegram came to Eds saying that the Cravens were setting sail at 11 a.m. (this morning) and that they were all right. She did not pay us anything for taking her things to station, only gave Wm Gould sixpence for himself.

Jan. 14th Very winterly. More snow comes at intervals. Mr. Hayward took the service in Sheldon Church this afternoon.

Jan. 15th Plenty of snow up here on these hills but not so much Ashford and Bakewell way. George Brocklehurst went to Derby before the medical board and passed for general service.

Jan. 16th Snowing again. The roads are pretty bad to travel on. We (our men) cannot do any work on the land so at times they make a fire in the chamber and pick potatoes. A man came to repair the pumps at Sheldon waterworks. He comes from Birmingham and called here for bread and cheese and a drink. Anthony afterwards took him to the waterworks where Mr. Ed was waiting.

Jan. 17th Very winterly, cold east wind. Mr. Hayward called. Miss Stubbs finished teaching at Sheldon as she has got another post. She brought the keys to our house.

Jan. 18th Misty and snifting of snow at times. There is no working on the land as all the fields are covered with snow. A fresh order has been issued that more farm workers are to join the colours. Some have only had 24 hrs. notice. Mr. Beaven (Taddington) commenced teaching the children of Sheldon for a period (until a schoolmistress is at liberty). Mr. Sherlock called here and had tea. He was at school.

Jan. 19th Very cold and winterly. Our Tom had his calling up papers to join the colours tomorrow. I do not know whenever this terrible war will end. It is awful to think of the thousands who are killed and wounded or ill, and the bad weather makes it so much worse. Little Anthony Wager is 2 yrs old today. He can say anything.

Jan. 20th Very cold. East winds. Our poor Tom went off this morning about 8 o'clock as he had to be at the Recruiting Office at 9 a.m. He came home tonight at about half past nine and had not been examined. There were three went, one from near Ashbourne and one near Hartington and our Tom. One of the youths who mated with Tom had two brothers in the trenches, he would make the third who had been called up and he had one brother left on his father's farm. The father milked 40 cows and a substitute had been sent to him (a schoolmaster). Billy Naylor brought two cheeses weighing 42 lbs and I paid him £2.2.0. (a shilling a lb).

Jan. 21st Most bitterly cold and frosty. All our children except Emily went to Church. Mr. Sherlock took the service. Mr. Sherlock had fallen and hurt his little finger which was swollen.

Jan. 22nd Very cold and frosty. There is much snow lying about. Our Tom started from Sheldon just after six o'clock this morning to go to Normanton Barracks Derby. We filled up Tony's appeal form as his time expires on the 28th of this month and sent it in after our Tom had gone. What was our surprise (getting on for 10 o'clock) to see our Tom back home again. He had been before the Medical board and they passed him CIII as a substitute for agriculture. He called and reported at Bakewell Recruiting Office. Tom seems very downhearted as Dr. Jackson had passed him for active service. He was asked some questions at the Recruiting Office. Both the youths who went to Derby with Tom on Saturday were put in khaki and went into the Notts. and Derby.

Jan. 23rd Very severe and winterly. I think every day gets colder. A fire was lit in Church to keep the water in pipes from freezing. Anthony had a letter from the substitution officer at Bakewell asking him if he would release our Tony to go into the Army if a substitute was found. Anthony wrote back that he would not release him as he was more use than two or three substitutes, and that if Tony was compelled to go he should certainly give up milk selling. A Managers meeting was held in school. There were present Mr. Sherlock, Mr. John Frost, our Anthony and Mr. W.H. Brocklehurst present. Mr. Thos. Wm Brocklehurst did not attend as he had gone away for the day. Mr. Sherlock's finger proved to be broken in the fall he had the other day.

Jan. 24th Very frosty and severe. Hannah's birthday (67). Tom seems a bit more cheerful. Tony's appeal paper came and Anthony has to go before the Tribunal on Saturday at 11 o'clock. Thos Wm has to appeal for George at 11.30. Our Tom had a railway pass and an order to go before the Medical Board on Friday next. I do not know what the officials are about as I should think he ought to have gone before the medical board before being called up.

Jan. 25th More severe weather than ever. Fires are lit in the Church almost every day as the pipes seem frozen so soon. Mr. Mallison addressed a meeting in Sheldon schoolroom at 7 tonight about the War Certificates. There were six present.

Jan. 26th A more severe frost than ever. Tom Morton went into Lincolnshire as a substitute. I did not come downstairs until nearly teatime as it is such bitter cold weather. A fox killed 13 or 14 fowls belonging to Joe Carson.

Jan. 27th Very severe frost. Everybody seems shivering with cold. Anthony and Thos Wm Brocklehurst went before the Tribunal at Bakewell over our Tony and George Brockley. Our Tony has to join the colours in about a month and George Brocklehurst got off for four months. A letter had been sent to the Tribunal from the Recruiting Office saying that our Tom was a substitute for Agriculture and Tony must go.

Jan. 28th Very severe. The wind is rough. There has not been a service in Church. Mr. Sherlock and the Misses Grover were distributing prizes in the schoolroom. Miss Grover gave our Ethel the money for the potatoes and swedes she had some weeks ago. Both Miss Grovers called to see me after the service in school. I settled the bill and put it in the post box (at least Tony did).

Jan. 29th A little warmer. The wind is not so rough. The roads are slippery and there is some sledging at Sheldon. Mr. Hayward called here. Read that the cruiser *Laurentia* had been sunk off the coast of Ireland.

Jan. 30th Very frosty. Our Tony had a paper from the Tribunal saying that he would not be called to join the colours for a month. Our Tom took the young horse (Wager) to George Frost's Bakewell to have it shod. Mr. Hayward called this morning to see Anthony over school business. Wilf Goodwin went before medical board and passed C3.

Jan. 31st Very severe with frost. The wind is not so rough. The roads are slippery and the sledges are continually at work. Some gravel was put down the street yesterday and stopped them a little. Wm Gould fetched a load of coal (cost 16 shillings) for the Church this morning and went for a load for us this afternoon. Our Tom had word this morning that he was put on the Army Reserve. The meres are thick with ice and the turnips and cabbage are so frozen that we cannot give them to the cattle and as a consequence we have much less milk.

Feb. 1st Cold and frosty and the snow does not go, but we had a bit of sunshine this morning. We had a letter from our Mary saying that she had had word from the War Office that Clem was suffering from a bullet wound in the right shoulder and a twisted knee and that he was a prisoner of war in the Military hospital at Cambrai. Miss Martha Hallam called and paid the rent of the school house up to Dec. 25th 1916. A sewing and knitting party was held at Mrs. Ed Brockleys. The following were there: Miss Lees, Jenny

Brockley and Bertha B., Beccy Ward, Kate, Ruth, Doris and our Ethel and Amy Goodwin.

Feb. 2nd   Very cold. The snow still lies on the tops of these hills. Sledging goes on among the young folks. Mr. Harry Bagshaw Collector of Income and Land Taxes called and Anthony paid him and also 2s. 6d. for the school house. We have been taxed on £50 profits of public house. Anthony had put the case into Goodwin and Cockerton's hands; before, the authorities had not taxed the profits of our public house. We got some reduction of tax of land and buildings and now we have this bother over profits. Tom and Tony went to a children's concert at Monyash and got back about 11 o'clock.

Feb. 3rd   Cold and snifting of snow at times. Our girls and myself were busy looking and copying the bills for the years 1913-14, 14-15, 15-16 to try to find out what profits we made. It was a very trying affair and we put it by until another day. Ormes van was very late (9 o'clock) in delivering things. They did not bring in any bottled stout or beer but it is charged on bill. A meeting was held in Sheldon Schoolroom about the War Savings Certificates. Only three persons attended viz Mr. Ed Brocklehurst, Mr. H and Mr. John Frost.

Feb. 4th   Snow has fallen during the night and the weather looks more winterly than ever. The sky seems very dull and leaden as though there was more to come. Celebration of Holy Communion in Sheldon Church (Mr. Sherlock officiated). There were 9 present, Ethel and Tony were present. Collection this afternoon amounted to 7/- for Church expenses. Mr. Hayward took the service. Clarissa Brocklehurst brought 6d. towards the collection so the collection will be 7s.6d. Ethel and others went to Monyash Church tonight. Snowing tonight and very cold.

Feb. 5th   Very keen with frost. The coldest day we have had this winter. Miss Broadhurst came here tonight and looked through the schoolmistress's cottage. She had tea here.

Feb. 6th   Keener than ever. It is very difficult for cattle to get a drink at meres as they (the meres) are frozen in solid blocks of ice.

Feb. 7th   Very frosty and severe. I think during last night was the keenest we have had. The Germans are fulfilling their threat of submarine warfare as vessels are sunk every day[1]. Our Mary had a letter from a Miss Harrison in connection with prisoners of war parcels fund (The North Staffords). It seems that 6 parcels per month can be sent to prisoners of war of the value of 6 shillings per parcel. In addition 7 lbs of bread can be sent weekly and the lady in her letter said that anybody could subscribe 5 or 10 shillings a month and could be sent in subscriber's name. Our Mary and little Anthony are gone to Longstone to spend a few days with Clem's mother and sister so they will be able to talk over what to do about Clem's parcels. I read that America had given Bernstoff his passport to leave and that Mr.

1   On February 1st, Germany had declared unrestricted submarine warfare against all shipping regardless of flag or cargo.

Gerard had been recalled from Berlin. Miss Broadhurst sent 30/- to buy wood and coal for school house.

Feb. 8th   More severe than ever with frost. Nearly all the taps in Sheldon are frozen. Ours keeps running but we have to keep putting hot bricks etc. to the pipe in Dairy to keep it thawed so that the cattle can drink. A letter came from War Office saying that our Mary could go on drawing her separation allowance and Clem was a prisoner of war, and her paper saying that she could draw for 30 weeks was cancelled.

Feb. 9th   Very severe with frost. Our water tap is frozen. I do not know whatever people will do for water if this weather continues. Our Tony received his calling up papers for Feb. 26th. A young man called here from Pilsley (he went to the medical board when Tony did) and he has to join the colours next Tuesday. Mr. Morton has heard that Frank Gray is seriously wounded and dangerously ill. He has only been in France 3 weeks. Read in paper that the *California* ship had been torpedoed after leaving America and there are 43 lives lost.

Feb. 10th   The weather is very severe with frost. Our water taps are all frozen up even that that comes into the trough. We have to fetch all the water we use both for the cattle and our household. There are a few of the cottages where the water is still on and we have to trouble them to let us have some and Alf Brockley's bottom trough is not frozen so he lets us fetch as well. Mr. Sherlock called this afternoon and had tea. He came about the schoolmistress's cottage. Miss Broadhurst had been to see him and she wanted a new wood floor and the pavers taking up and other things. Mr. Sherlock had written to Mr. Cockerill who said they could not do it now the war is on so I think she will have to be content with things as they are for the present. Mr. Beaven is still teaching at Sheldon School.

Feb. 11th   Very frosty and severe weather. The men are very busy fetching water for the cattle etc. The girls have to fetch some as well. Emily and her father are not well. Anthony has such pain in his back and shoulders and Emily has attacks of palpitations. Mr. Hayward took the service. Tom and Tony went to Monyash Church tonight.

Feb. 12th   Very cold and rather rough winds. Anthony took the milk and then went to Bakewell. He attended a meeting in response to Colonel Taylor's invitation to subscribe towards a wedding present for Lord Hartington and Lady Mary Cecil. The Germans keep up their sea piracy sinking many ships and disregarding the Neutrals protest. Mr. Gerard (American Ambassador at Berlin) has had his passports and left Berlin on his way to Berne. Anthony put some money in War Loan. It was between 5 and 6 o'clock when he got back tonight.

Feb. 13th   Not quite so frosty but the water pipes are still frozen and people are carting water from those whose pipes are not frozen both for cattle and household uses. Matthew Hodgkinson killed our other pig and cut it up as well as this will save him a journey again tomorrow. Stanley Brockley fetched coal for Miss Broadhurst.

Feb. 14th Valentine's day. Cold and raw. Still carting water. We have a burst in our yard owing to the pipes being frozen. Our Evelyn is not well. Her throat is very sore. Mr. Hayward called in for a few minutes.

Feb. 15th Very cold. Carting water for everything is a job. Mr. Sherlock called and brought a letter he had had from Miss Broadhurst and one from Mr. Cockerill. Miss Kate Grover called with the magazines.

Feb. 16th Frosty and cold as usual. Anthony took the milk and brought our Mary and little Anthony who has been staying with Mrs. and Miss Wager. Our Ethel has been bad today. I think it is influenza and a sore throat. The men have picked some potatoes and Tony took half a load to Mrs. James Frost and half a load to Mr. John Frost's. These were paid for. Our Mary sent a postal order for 10/- to Miss Harrison towards Clem's parcels.

Feb. 17th Cold. Still carting water. Our Ethel's throat was swollen and so we sent for Dr. Jackson. He came and said it was a Quinzy. She is in bed. Mary went to Bakewell for some shin beef and mutton chops. Ethel can swallow some beef tea but cannot eat a deal. Tom Morton was in house tonight. He is at Scunthorpe in Lincolnshire.

Feb. 18th Thawing a little. The sun was very hot. Emily was taken out in Mrs. Ed's chair. Tony took her down the lane a bit this afternoon. Mr. Sherlock took the service in Church. Miss Broadhurst came to Sheldon and attended the service. She called here and had tea.

Feb. 19th Very misty indeed. Our Mary received a postcard from Clem written by him and dated Nov. 28th 1916. This card was postmarked Jan 25th 1917. He said on the card that he was out of hospital and on his way to Germany. Mary gave the card to PC Dennis to take to Clem's mother at Longstone. Inspector Tipper came up to see J. Goodwin. I think it was about Wilf being on Robinson's premises and having something to drink during prohibited hours.

Feb. 20th Very misty and rain fell during the day. Mary, Evelyn, Tom and Tony went to Monyash to a concert and got back at 20 minutes to one. I never saw such a quiet Shrove Tuesday as it was today. Ethel is not well yet. Dr. Jackson called to see her this morning. Mr. Charles Ollerenshaw called in. Our little Anthony broke his steel tape measure.

Feb. 21st Very misty and depressing weather. Our Ethel's throat is bad on the other side. Our Mary and Polly Roberts have been clearing up at the Schoolmistress's house. They whitewashed two bedrooms. Mrs. Smith swept two chimneys which cost 1s.0d. She swept them very well. Edwin Smith is working on the road. We paid Mrs. Smith. John Pursglove received his calling up papers for 10 of March. Also George Carson for same date.

There must be something queer about G. Carson as he is working at Friden and has been for some time being sent by Captain Sweeting.

Feb. 22nd Very misty and slight showers. Polly Roberts and our Mary have been clearing up at the schoolmistress's house. Little Anthony Wager is not so well as he has such a croupy cough. Ethel is a bit better.

Feb. 23rd Misty as usual. Little Anthony coughs very much and Mary has not been able to go cleaning. Mary received a postcard from the Central Prisoner of War Committee, 3 and 4 Thurloe Place, SW viz of Clem's changed address as follows:

Name	27652 Pte. C. Wager
Regiment	8th Batt. North Staffords
New Address	Gefangenau Lager Citadelle Cambrai

Robinson's trial (Bulls Head Monyash) of serving drink during prohibited hours at Bakewell. He was caught it is said by Super. Lakin. Mr. Sherlock came up to Sheldon but did not call at our house. Robinson was fined £5.0.0. Wilf Goodwin was fined £1.0.0. and another man was fined £1.0.0. for having drink during prohibited hours at Robinson's. Miss Kelly (Peacock Bakewell) was fined on a similar charge at the same court. Mr. Lloyd George makes a long speech in House of Commons over our grave situation in regard to our food supplies.

Feb. 24th Very misty and very depressing weather. Little Anthony Wager is a deal better. Our Evelyn and Tony went to Bakewell to do a bit of shopping. They bought a wristlet watch and also a belt for Tony. There were a good few in the house tonight. Mr. C. Ollerenshaw was there. We (Anthony, Ethel and I) were busy finding and reckoning what profit we made out of sale of drink from 1912-1913 (to April 5th).

Feb. 25th Very misty and slight shower during the day. Mr. Hayward took the service in Church. Our Mary went to Longstone this afternoon leaving little Anthony while she went.

Feb. 26th Milder. Our Tony started from Sheldon about 8 o'clock to report at the Recruiting Office at 9 o'clock. His father went with the milk and then on to Bakewell where he spent the time with him (Tony) until the train went off with the recruits. I think there were 77 marched off and people cheered them as they went along. Anthony met Joseph Hutchinson and the latter advised him to go to Derby with Tony and to try to get him off, if not altogether (for a bit). They (Anthony and J. Hutchinson) travelled with some of the recruits (Tony as well) and Joe drove Anthony to Normanton Barracks where they saw Colonel Taylor who wrote a note and gave for them to give to another officer. This officer said that they could only give a fortnight so Tony got off for another fortnight but stayed all night at Mrs. Ollerenshaw's (Nottingham Arms) as he had to report himself at Normanton Barracks tomorrow morning at 9 o'clock. Anthony got back to

Sheldon between 8 and 9 o'clock tonight. John Frost brought the float back from Bakewell market.

Feb. 27th Mild but very dull. We are gaining ground in France but the submarines are still at work and some German destroyers raided the Kent Coast Towns. One woman and a baby were killed and two others injured (all of the same family). Tony got back between 8 and 9 o'clock tonight. He went to Normanton Barracks at 9 this morning and was there all day and was just able to catch the quarter to six train to Derby. He has got until 13th March. The water came on to our trough and very glad we are as we have been fetching water for days. Tom is ploughing on moor today. Fred Brocklehurst came home tonight for a fortnight.

Feb. 28th Mild but dull. Anthony and Tony have been putting some breaking tackle on the young horse (Wager) and have turned it out in Frost Croft. Tom is ploughing on moor. Mrs. Ollerenshaw called in today. I thanked both Mr. and Mrs. Ollerenshaw for their kindness to Tony and to the girls when they went to Derby.

March 1st A very nice mild day. Miss Lees called to see me and brought a book for me to read. She came up to the sewing and knitting party at Mrs. Eds. Mary is baking oatcake. We borrowed a bit of meal from Thos. Wm. Brocklehurst. Tom is ploughing on moor. Anthony has had the young horse Wager in lines for the first time this afternoon. Evelyn went up to the school with paysheet. Miss Kate Grover called to see me. She had been to the class next door (Mrs. Eds).

March 2nd Rather misty but mild. Tom is ploughing in bottom Grindlow Knoll. Mr. Sherlock called here and as usual we got on the war topic. He and I do not agree in all things over the war. He took the paysheet back with him. Mr. Beaven has done teaching (today) at Sheldon. Mr. and Mrs. C. Ollerenshaw went back to Derby today. Ethel and Evelyn went to Bakewell to buy a few things.

March 3rd Very dull, mild. The Germans are still retreating on the Ancre. Tom and Wm ploughing (Bottom Grindlow Knoll). Joe Carson went to Alport for their oatmeal and took our oats. Miss Broadhurst came to Sheldon with more of her furniture. Two men who brought it came here for tea. I charged them 1s.0d. each as they had two eggs each and bread and marmalade. Our young horse Wager was put in to plough first time and went very well with our Naylor horse.

March 4th Very cold and frosty. Holy Communion at Sheldon Church 9 present. Mr. Sherlock officiated and also took the service this afternoon. Collection for Church expenses (7s.1d.).

March 5th On getting up this morning there was quite a snow and a most bitter East wind. I thought we were going to have some better weather but it does not look like it. Vincent Hallows[1] started work for us at 4/- a week and his board (food).

March 6th   Very bitter cold east wind and frost. The men can do nothing on the land and I do not know how all the ploughing will get done. Wilf Goodwin had his papers. He has to report on the 20th. Everybody seems depressed over the war and the weather and also the scarcity of food which is threatened.

March 7th   Most bitterly cold and frosty. The water has gone out of some of the taps in Sheldon. I expect it is through the frost. I wrote to Colonel Taylor asking him if Tony could have an extension of time as we are having such severe weather that we cannot get on with ploughing and our ewes are due to lamb some of them next week.

March 8th   I think during last night and this morning the weather has been more severe with frost and cold than any time this winter. I have been cold in bed though we have had a hot brick every night. Mr. Sherlock called here about a bill that he could not find. It was his mistake as all the bills were fastened together and sent to him. The boiler at Church cracked and let the water out. Anthony went in and raked out fire and let the pipes run.

March 9th   As keen and cold as ever. Another fortnight (from March 13th) has been granted to our Tony. Word came this morning. Wm Gould has been for coal this morning and our Tom and Wm have gone for hay this afternoon on moor. Tom and Tony slipped with the milk on barrow going to uncle Wills and spilt some quarts.

March 10th Thawing, very wet and shifting the snow. Miss Broadhurst brought two photos of her parents for us to look at. They were very good ones. John Pursglove appeared at the Recruiting Office as he was called up for today. A good many went off by train this afternoon. Mr. Brocklehurst (New Mills) bid £55.0.0. for our big bull but Anthony did not sell.

March 11th   Some snow is left under the walls but the weather is milder and better. Mr. Hayward took the service in school as the boiler has burst in Church.

March 12th   Nice and sunny some parts of today. Tom has been ploughing with young horse (Wager) and our old Naylor. Wm has also been ploughing with the other two old ones. Official news that British had occupied Bagdad (Sir Stanley Maud, General). Thos Wm Brockley had two lambs born.

March 13th   A lovely day. The sun shone and everything is very nice if this terrible war was over. Tom and Wm are ploughing (Grindlow Knoll) (two teams). We are ploughing 23 acres this year. Fred Brockley went back to Chelsea.

---

1   Vincent Hallows eventually married Ethel Gyte.

March 14th Another lovely day. Tom and Wm are ploughing on Grindlow Knoll (two teams). The young horse Wager does very well in plough. Mr. C. Ollerenshaw called in. He is staying at his house in Sheldon. Tony and Vincent Hallows look after and water cows etc. Mrs. Smith came up as we had sent her word to sweep our chimneys, but she has to have testimonials before she can get a licence. I wrote her one out and our Mary has taken it. Mary has gone to Longstone to see Clem's folk.

March 15th Rather cold, but a good dry day. The British troops have got 30 miles beyond Bagdad and the Germans are still retreating in the West. Tom and Wm are ploughing this morning and this afternoon the young horse has been working for an hour or two for Thos Wm Brockley. Miss Lees, Miss Kate Grover and Mr. Sherlock came to see us this afternoon. Mr. Sherlock was paid 4s. 6d. for Church fire insurance which he had sent. Mary and Ethel were cleaning Wm's and the bathrooms. Mr. Sherlock went upstairs for a bit of fun just to see what they were doing. Anthony and Tom went on moor to set out a field to plough. This field has not been ploughed that anyone in Sheldon can remember.

March 16th Fine. Tom ploughing on moor. Miss Broadhurst paid for milk (fortnight) and bread. Mr. Joe Hutchinson and others came to look at the young horse Wager. Revolution in Russia. Abdication of the Czar. Mary had a letter from Clem. They have shifted him again and he does not write very cheerful. He only weighs 9 stones and he used to weigh over 14 stones. He would like some parcels. I do hope he will get some as Mary has been seeing about them for over a month.

March 17th Very fine and dry, rather windy. Our Tom is ploughing on moor. Tony looking after things about home (cows and sheep). Anthony has a headache. Bapaume taken by British troops.

March 18th Fine. Tom took milk to station. The service was in school this afternoon as the church boiler is not mended. Mr. Sherlock officiated. Ethel and Evelyn went to Ashford Church tonight.

March 19th Very rough and showery. Anthony and Tony took our big bull and a fat cow to market. Tony led bull by staff and it went very quietly. He made £59.10s. od. and the fat cow made £34.15.0. Robert Boyd bought the bull. The news from the battle front is very good this morning. Peronne and about 60 villages have fallen into British hands and our cavalry are after them (the Germans).

March 20th Very cold and snow storms. Our men were picking potatoes, lashing corn and Tom and Wm went on moor for hay. It was very rough for this job. Our Mary had another letter from Clem. This letter was written on Feb. 18th 1917 and poor lad he wrote it in bed in the hospital.

His address is

> Kriegs - Gefangenen lager
> Wahn (Rhld)
> Pte Clement Wager
> No. 27652 8th North Staffs
> 57 Brigade
> British Prisoner of War
> Res Lazarett
> Julich
> Rheinland Germany

Mary sent for a few things by Ethel and Evelyn to Bakewell for Clem. Mary and I wrote to Clem. The first lamb came this morning.

March 21st Bitterly cold. NE winds and snow storms. Ploughed cabbage stalks off today. We have two more lambs (single ones). Miss Broadhurst signed an agreement at our house.

March 22nd Bitterly cold and snow storms. All ploughing stopped. I wrote to Colonel Taylor asking for a further extension for our Tony. We shall be very backward as the time for work on the land is going. Potatoes are very scarce and we have had several asking if we had any to sell. The British and French are advancing in the West. We heard that Joe Handley had got killed about a fortnight since.

March 24th Misty and milder. Tom has gone ploughing on moor with Naylor and Wager. Wm is ploughing for uncle John Brocklehurst. We have not heard about any extension for Tony so I suppose he will have to go next Tuesday.

March 25th Cold. Poured with rain tonight. Mr. Hayward took the service in school as we cannot have a fire in Church owing to the boiler being burst.

March 26th Very cold. Snow storms and blizzards. Colonel H.B. Taylor wired to say that Tony's leave was granted to April 15th next. G. Brockley passed A1 again.

March 27th Very cold and snifting at times with snow. Received a letter from Colonel Taylor about Tony. Mr. Hayward called and had tea. Eggs are sold at 7 a shilling. The girls cleaned pantry today.

March 28th Cold. Snow at times. Tom was ploughing on moor. Mr. Sherlock called here with a cheque (for school) and other papers. He had tea. Ethel and Mary started cleaning parlour.

March 30th Cold and snow storms at intervals. Ploughing stopped. Our men were sorting potatoes. We could have sold many more if we had had them to spare. Our girls and Aunt H finished cleaning parlour. I have been bad with influenza and am still bad enough. We keep losing plenty of ships by submarine and we are gaining some villages in France, at least what is left of them as the Germans destroy all they can in the retreat.

March 31st When people got up this morning they found plenty of snow which has stopped the ploughing. Anthony and Ed and Mr. Moody have been trying to mend the boiler at Church but it did not act very well.

April 1st Very winterly. Plenty of snowstorms and frost. Holy Communion in Sheldon Church at 9.30. Mr. Sherlock officiated. Service in school this afternoon as the heating apparatus in Church does not act. Collection for Church expenses 5/-. I am not much better with my cold.

April 2nd Very severe. Snow and frost. I think this is one of the worst days we have had this winter. Whenever the ploughing and sowing will be done I do not know as the snow lies inches deep and the frost is so severe we had the milk frozen when cooling in trough. Anthony went to Bakewell market and was enquiring where he could buy some hay but could not hear of any.

April 3rd The snow lies on the ground and all ploughing is stopped. The sheep are lambing. We have a good many single ones and a lamb or two have died owing to the mother's shortage of milk. Read President Wilson's speech in Congress and which means the coming into war on the side of the Allies by America.

April 4th Dull and the fields are still covered with snow. Anthony did not come to bed until 20 minutes to 4 as he and Tom sat up with a cow calving. Tony sat up until 11 or after with a sheep lambing. Mary whitewashed cellar. Fred Brockley came home tonight for a bit to help on the farm.

April 5th Very frosty. The sun is bright during some parts of the day which melts the snow a bit but it freezes at night. We are getting on with the lambing. Some of the theaves bring two. Eggs are selling 8 for a shilling and corn is £2.0.0. per bag. I think there will be a famine before long as everything is going up in price terribly. There are scarcely any potatoes to be got in the country. Ours have kept well.

April 6th Good Friday. A lovely day in the sun but the mornings are very frosty. The service has to be held in school as the heating apparatus is not mended. Colonel Taylor has had a son wounded. He was in The Flying Corps. George Wallwin has another son wounded. Received £1.0.0. from the Duke of Devonshire towards Sheldon Church accounts. Mr. Hayward took the service in school at 2.30.

April 8th Cold. Holy Communion in Church (Mr. Sherlock officiated). Mr. Hayward took the service in Church this afternoon; there was no fire. The collection which I suppose will be for the Vicar or lay reader amounted to 11s.9d. Our Mary and little Anthony went to Longstone and Tony went tonight and brought them back. Tom, Ethel and Evelyn went to Monyash Church tonight and got wet through, blizzards of snow coming back.

April 9th Snowing in blizzards. Anthony went with milk and then to Bakewell fair. The British have had a great victory on the Western Front. Many thousand prisoners and guns taken.

April 10th Quite a deep snow. Anthony went to see Mr. Bingham of Monsal Dale over buying a stack of hay. He bought it if the Government would allow him, Mr. Bingham, to sell. We wrote to Derby for a pass. I wrote asking for an extension of leave for Tony.

April 11th Snowing in blizzards. The sun came out and melted it a bit but more comes at night. A vestry meeting was held at Church. There were only three viz Mr. Sherlock, Anthony and Thos Wm Brockley. Mr. Sherlock had tea here. He told me that his uncle General Sir Henry Horne was fighting in France. There was £10.2.0. in hand at vestry meeting. I gave Mr. Sherlock 11s.9¹/₂d. the Easter Sunday collection.

April 12th More snow but sunny at times. I did not get up so early. Anthony had a letter from Derby over hay buying. The British in the recent fighting got 11,000 prisoners and over 100 guns etc. Our Tom and Wm have had to fetch hay from moor and the snow lies deep. Tom, Tony, Ethel and Evelyn went to a concert at Monyash tonight.

April 13th Snow storms at intervals. All work on the land is stopped. I do not know when the ploughing will be finished. We have not heard anything about Tony having any further leave. The war news continues good. A few days ago the United States of America came into the war on our side.

April 14th Rain came down pretty heavily this morning and at intervals this afternoon there were hail storms. Anthony was poorly with sick headache and he went to bed between dinner and tea time. I have been looking anxiously for a letter to say that our Tony could stay at home a little longer but none came so he will have to go. The British troops are winning on the Western front but the German submarines are sinking a many ships and have torpedoed two of our hospital ships this week.

April 15th Very dull at times, snifting of snow at times. Our Tony's time is up today but he has not gone. He is going tomorrow morning all being well. Mr. Sherlock took the service in Church this afternoon. Anthony is a little better today. Snowing heavily tonight. If it continues there will be quite another big snow by tomorrow.

April 16th Heavy snow storms during the day. Our Tony started from home at a quarter past six this morning to catch the first train from Bakewell to Derby where he reported (Normanton Barracks). He came back tonight in khaki and had been supplied with all new things which looked and felt very good. The shirt, pants, socks and boots were very nice. Brown boots. I wrote to Colonel Taylor telling him that I had written to the Commanding Officer Sherwood Foresters A Company asking him if he could give Tony another extension of leave as the weather was so severe and we were very backward with the work on the land and that no answer had come. A man who got Tony's things asked him: *Gyte, is all the work done?* Tony answered him *No*. I saw in the paper something about Category A men on furlough having their leave extended to May 10th. Mary received a PC from Clem.

April 17th Very rough and cold and has been all night. Tony went off again to get by first train from Bakewell to Derby where he had to report (Normanton barracks) at 9 o'clock. He was told yesterday that very likely he would be sent to Sunderland with 5 others. The war news continues very good. The French have taken over 10,000 prisoners in one day and we have taken very substantial war material. Our Ethel went with Tony to the station. I paid Mr. Bagshaw (Moor Grange) a tithe which amounted to 3/- and it used to be 2/8 or 2/9.

April 18th Rather misty. We received a letter from Colonel H.B. Taylor saying that he had laid my letter which I had written to him before the Commanding Officer and he hoped that Tony would get a further extension. A letter also came from the Officer Commanding B Depot Derby saying that Tony could be spared until the 30th April. We thought that Tony would be sent back but he did not come. I wrote to Col. Taylor thanking him. Ethel and Evelyn went to Bakewell Station.

April 19th Very dull. Tom and Wm were ploughing on moor. Tony does not come. Mary and the girls started cleaning houseplace, distempered the ceiling which looks well and papered some of the wall.

April 20th Fine and better today. More sun. I had a letter from Tony. The poor lad had been drafted to Cleadon Camp, Sunderland by the 12.45 train from Derby after he had walked to Bakewell station and reported at Derby at 9 o'clock. On getting off the train, they had a six miles march with full packs and got into camp after 9 o'clock. This was last Tuesday and he does not say that the officer sent him word that he had an extension of leave. I wrote to Colonel Taylor and to the Officer Commanding B Depot, Derby. Anthony started off to Derby and there he had no difficulty in getting his permit to fetch hay. He (Anthony) also went to see Mr. Sneap and found that he had been very ill with influenza and bronchitis. He had also many losses among his cattle and sheep. I wrote to Tony.

April 21st Rather misty but clears out. Tom and Wm fetched some hay with dray and cart and 4 horses from the stack we had bought. Anthony made out a cheque for £30 and sent it to J. Bingham, Monsal Dale. Evelyn wrote to Tony. Lord Hartington married Lady Mary Cecil daughter of the Marquis of Salisbury.

April 22nd Rather misty and dull. Mr. Hayward took service today. Collection in Sheldon Church for the Prisoners of War 15s. The war news continues to be good and two of our ships have sunk two German destroyers and damaged another. There were 5 Hun destroyers in Dover district.

April 23rd Fine but rather dull. Anthony did not go to Bakewell but sowed part of Grindlow Knoll with white oats. I received a letter from Tony and I wrote to the Commanding Officer of 3rd Sherwood Sunderland sending him copies of letters from C.O. Derby and from Col. Taylor and asking for Tony to be spared until 10th May. Mr. and Mrs. Craven came to Sheldon from S. America.

April 24th Fine and sunshine but dull afterwards. Sowed next part of Grindlow Knoll and finished harrowing it. Another letter from Tony. He has got a cold. Stirks[1] and calves turned out in the day time. Anthony received PC from Bernard Hambleton who is in the trenches in France. Received a letter from Col. Taylor saying we had better write to C.O. Sunderland and lay the facts of our Tony's case before him. Cleaned dairy today. Sent the letter to C.O. Sunderland.

April 25th Fine but dull. Men working in fields. Tom and Wm fetched all the hay from moor and this is the finishing of the three stacks there. Anthony was gathering the cabbage stalks etc of the field (Hicks). Mr. Sherlock called here and had tea. He brought a paper about a concert.

April 26th Fine but dull. Our Tony landed home just after 10 o'clock this morning after travelling all night from Sunderland. They gave him a free pass and he got until the 10th of May. He has got a very severe cold and is very tired. Our Anthony cut all the lambs tails and belted the sheep. The men dragged Hicks field etc. where the cabbage and swedes had been. Our Mary and Ethel finished cleaning and papering my bedroom. Tony went to bed for an hour or two this afternoon. Alf Brockley heard the cuckoo on Sheldon Moor.

April 27th Fine but dull and cold. Tom sowed Hicks field and Wm was ploughing on moor. Our Mary and Ethel papered my staircase. Tom, Ethel and Evelyn went to Ashford to a concert. A cow calved this morning about 4 o'clock. Wm sat up all night and Tom got up. Our Tony seems tired and full of a cold.

April 28th Fine but rough. Tom and Wm went for hay from the stack bought of Mr. Bingham, Monsal Dale. This stack is up Scratter and it is a heavy road to bring the hay up Ashford Dale. They took four horses to draw up. Our Tony is full of a cold and besides he had been vaccinated the same day he left Sunderland (Cleadon Camp) and he is very tired. Anthony, Tony and Vincent Hallows have been gardening setting potatoes, lettuce, parsnips, onions etc. There is a tobacco famine in Sheldon. Orme's did not bring us any and our Mary went to Bakewell. She could only get 2lbs of Shag.

April 29th Fine and sunny. Our Tony has had a poor night with his cold and his arm is painful through vaccination. Mr. Sherlock took the service in Church (walked up). Ethel gave him the 15s. 9d. which was the collection

---

1   Stirk = young bullock or heifer

last Sunday for the Prisoners of War. Emily went to Church this afternoon and out tonight in chair.

April 30th A very fine sunny day. We had 104 eggs today. Eggs are selling 7 a shilling. News came that Eric Morgan was killed last Saturday and a few days ago word came that Victor Bonsall was killed (both in France).

May 1st A lovely day, warm and sunny. Tom and Wm went for hay up Scratter. Tony and Evelyn took 14 stirks on to moor and afterwards Tony took 3 cows to Ashford and afterwards went on moor again to feed fowls and gather eggs. He brought 110 eggs which are selling 7 for a shilling. I hear that Miss Polly Bramwell commenced teaching in Sheldon School. Neither Anthony nor Thos. Wm B knew anything of this and I do not believe any of the Managers knew except Mr. Sherlock. This is a nice state of affairs to go over the heads of the Managers like that. Started cleaning bar.

May 2nd A most lovely day. Plenty of sun. Our men were on moor. Tom was ploughing ley[1] and he says he never had such a pulling towzing job as owing to it being so dry the plough could not work well. Anthony heard the cuckoo on moor.

May 3rd A lovely day. Our men are gone on moor, ploughing etc. The budget was in this morning's paper. Tobacco, excess profits and places of amusement were taxed. The submarines are doing deadly work with our shipping and food shortage is imminent. Tony is a little better and his arm seems to be going on all right.

May 4th Another lovely sunny day. Ethel, Evelyn and Tony went off by the 7.30 train this morning from Bakewell and got back between 9 and 10 tonight to see Mr. Sneap. Anthony on going to feed fowls on moor found six worried (by a fox he supposed) and others bitten.

May 5th There is quite a change in the weather. Today there is a rough cold wind quite different from the last few days. I had no fire at all yesterday (1st time without this year) in the house place but I had one lit today. Our Tom has gone sowing oats on moor and Wm and Vincent Hallows are harrowing. Gave one of the worried fowls to Ed and one to Elsie E and sold one for 2/6 to Jim Goodwin. Anthony and Tony have been sowing clover and hayseed in Hicks field.

May 6th Cold winds and hot sun. There was celebration of Holy Communion in Sheldon Church, Mr. Sherlock officiated. Mr. Hayward took the service in Church this afternoon and collection for Church expenses. Fred Brockley handed round the box. Our Tony and James Frost went to Monyash tonight and had supper with Mr. and Mrs. David Frost.

May 7th Cold winds and hot sun. Anthony went with milk and then to Bakewell market. Tom and Wm went for more hay from the stack Mr.

---

1 ley : untilled grassland

Bingham sold us. Tony and Vincent were gardening also Anthony this afternoon. Sold a bull calf for 50 shillings (Alf Brockley had the buying of it). We put up our spirits and beer today.

Spirits (special whiskey)	6d	per	glass
Ordinary whiskey and Rum	5d	”	”
Beer mild	6d	per	pint
Bitter	7d	per	pint
Bottled Beer and Guinesses Stout	6d	per bottle in, 5d. out.	

May 9th Cold winds and hot sun. Tom and Wm have been getting the potato ground ready on moor, dragging etc. Anthony has been rolling ley and Tony and Vincent clodding. Anthony also finished Grindlow Knoll (rolling). Tony's things are being got ready for tomorrow.

May 10th Nice shower of rain. Our poor Tony went this morning by the 10.33 train from Bakewell Station for Cleadon Camp Sunderland. Ethel and Evelyn went to see him off. There were other soldiers going to Sunderland viz Joe Prince (Flagg) Ralph Mellor etc. They got in the same carriage as Tony so he would have company all the way. Fred Brockley went by the 6.13 train (for Chelsea). Wm Gould has been in bed all day (sickness and diarrhoea). Anthony and Vincent working on moor. British retake portion of what Germans took yesterday.

May 12th Beautiful weather. Slight shower towards night. Tom and Wm fetched the last of the hay from Bingham's stack. I received a PC from Tony saying that he had arrived all safe. Mr. Luxmoore[1] died at Buxton.

May 13th Between 12 and 1 o'clock this morning we had a heavy thunderstorm lightning etc. and rain. Very nice growing weather with the sun. We received a letter from Tony. Mr. Hayward took the service in Church. Collection for Diocesan purposes 11s. 6$^{1}/_{2}$d. Received a letter from Mr. Sherlock saying that the funeral of the Revd. J. Luxmoore would take place on Tuesday next. Our milk cows lay out tonight for 1st time. Very close.

May 14th Very close, nice growing weather. Anthony complains of feeling queer about the heart. He did not go to Bakewell as we are so busy on the land. Our Tom and Vincent are leading manure to Hicks field. Wm is chainharrowing. Thos Wm Brockley received a telegram signed *Luxmoore* saying that he hoped the Wardens would join in the funeral procession (old Mr. Luxmoore) at Ashford tomorrow. Mr. Hayward came up to ask about two bearers being wanted to go to Ashford tonight at 8 o'clock as Mr. Luxmoore's body was being brought from Buxton and would stay in Ashford Church all night. Wm Henry and Alf Brockley are going for bearers. Our Ethel cycled to Bakewell to order a wreath for Mr. Luxmoore. We heard that poor Arthur Stubbs had been killed in action and that Victor

---

1   The Revd. J. Luxmoore, former Vicar of Ashford and Sheldon

Turner was seriously wounded. Received a letter from our Tony. He is not settling very well.

May 15th Bitterly cold. Our men working on moor and spreading manure. Ethel and Evelyn walked to Bakewell to get the wreath for Mr. Luxmoore. On getting it they took it to Ashford and was in time for the funeral. The inscription on the wreath was as follows: *In loving remembrance of our late Pastor and friend. From the people of Sheldon.* Evelyn had been to ask a few in Sheldon to subscribe for wreath and she got 23 shillings. The wreath cost a guinea, the box one shilling and the other shilling is being used to buy flowers for altar. Mr. Luxmoore's funeral took place at 2.30. There were many present, 8 clergymen, The Bishop of Derby and many local people. Anthony and Thos Wm Brockley joined and led the procession with the Ashford Church Wardens. The Ashford choir walked and the hymn *Abide with me* was sung. (Our milk cows lay in tonight as it was so cold).

May 16th Very cold but a little more sun. Our men have been getting the potato rows ready on moor and manuring them. Received a letter from our Tony. He says he is trying to settle and has been inoculated again. Our girls papered and cleaned the room over pantry.

May 17th Very rough, wet at times and cold. Our men took some manure and set 5 rows of potatoes on moor. We sent a good parcel to our Tony to Cleadon camp. We had two letters from him, one for Tom and one for Ethel.

May 18th Very cold and misty. Our men have been on moor and set 7 rows of potatoes this morning. Mr. and Mrs. Craven and family have just gone off to Matlock to a hydro or something.

May 19th Very misty and drizzly first thing, clears out later in the day. Our men working on moor. Anthony and Wm Hallows gapping and the others working on potato ground. There were 7 hens found worried with a fox, laying hens that were on moor. Heard that Victor Turner wounded in France died last Saturday. Sam Bramwell had written to his parents and told them.

May 20th Dull and nice growing weather. Mr. Hayward took the service in Church. Our Ethel and Evelyn and Tom went to Monyash Church to a service to the memory of Victor Bonsall and Eric Morgan (night service). Received a letter from Tony saying that he had got the parcel all right and what a grand one it was. Our Mary took Emily out a bit in chair. Another hen was found worried on moor.

May 21st Some nice rain came today and it is grand growing weather. Billy Naylor bought 5 pigs (about 9 weeks old) from Mr. Littlewood of Wardlow. We are having three of the pigs. Heard that the Revd. D. Steele-Morris, Vicar of Stanton and Birchover had died of Pneumonia.

May 22nd A lovely day. Plenty of sunshine and very nice growing weather. Our men are gone setting potatoes on moor. There are 22 rows of potatoes set now. We had a letter from Tony. Ethel cycled to Bakewell. Anthony, Tom and Billy Naylor carried the three pigs each in a bag from Naylor's.

May 23rd Fine, nice growing weather, cooler towards night. I think there has been thunder about. We did not receive a letter from Tony today. Ethel and Evelyn started cleaning the kitchen (colour washing).

May 24th Showery this morning but turns out lovely this afternoon. Our men leading manure. The young horse Wager was put in cart and was leading manure. He went well. This afternoon they have gone selling potatoes. Fred Carson (top of Sheldon) is helping us today in return for us lending them different things.

May 25th A lovely growing day. Sun and warmth. The men are carting manure on to moor for swedes. Fred Carson has helped us again today. We have been eating the fowls that the fox killed this week and they have been very nice, boiled with a bit of ham. The girls received the brooches (Notts and Derby badges) this morning (silver and enamel) which are very lovely from Tony. Read in paper that another British Transport had been sunk in the Mediterranean Sea with above 400 troops on board. A dark roan cow which had been fetched from Ashford 2 or 3 days since calved a very nice red cow-calf out in the field. Eggs are selling six a shilling. Evelyn has gone to Bakewell to buy a few things for Tony's parcel.

May 26th A most lovely day. Plenty of sunshine and warmth. Our men on moor in turnip ground. Sowed 20 rows of swedes. Received a letter from Tony. He has been on coastguard on the cliffs near the sea. He sent a few violets. We sent him a good parcel this morning weighing 9^1/$_2$ lbs.

May 27th A lovely growing day, rather dull and like rain at times. Whit Sunday. Celebration of Holy Communion in Sheldon Church this morning at 9.30. Mr. Sherlock officiated. At dinner time Joseph Gregory and his son Ephraim called here. His son who was in khaki is in the army (Canadians) and has been twice wounded in France. Joseph has three daughters in Canada and each of their husbands are fighting in France. These three daughters are living in one house. Mr. Hayward took the service in Church this afternoon. Collection for Church expenses 11s. 0d. Our Ethel gave Mr. Hayward 11s. 6d. that had been collected for Diocesan Fund. A man and woman called and had tea. It was the same man whom we always think is a German. He told me he was working in munitions and he showed me a card red at the corners. This card was signed with the name H. Sumersgill. An air raid on South E Coast yesterday in broad daylight. A many killed and wounded at Folkestone.

May 28th Whit Monday. Bakewell Fair. Anthony and Tom went taking two cows to the field at Ashford. A most lovely day. Wm was leading manure on to moor and chain harrowing and Vincent was also working on land. Our Emily has been very ill through the night, so sick and such dreadful pain. The girls were up nearly all night. Anthony got up two or three times and went to her. They put the hot water bottle to her. Tom got up between 3 and

4 to go for the doctor but she went a bit easier so he cycled to Bakewell about 8 o'clock this morning, and then came back and went to the fair. Dr. Jackson came and he said Emily had got inflammation on the coating of stomach. He ordered her to have a mustard poultice and Ethel put her one on. Received Tony's photos from him. I consider them much too sad and serious looking.

May 29th A lovely morning but a thunderstorm came on this afternoon. The rain will do good. Everything seems to be growing well. Emily seems a shade better but is still very weak and ill. A lady and gentleman who are staying at Ashford (from Nottingham) called here. They lived quite close to young Ball[1] the airman and knew him quite well. The Germans have now got young Ball a prisoner. He is only 20 years old and has brought about 42 German aeroplanes down. Our men have been carting manure on to the moor for swedes.

May 30th Very fine, cooler. Our men are carting manure on moor. Fred Carson is helping us. Anthony is gapping. Two women came in at dinner time and wanted a pot of tea. They have been before and one of them is one we call a German as she has been here with the man who was here last Sunday who we always think is a German. The following called here as well viz. Dr. Jackson, Mr. Hayward, Mr. Sherlock and Mrs. Fanny Thorpe. Mrs. Ben Morton's man also came for potatoes which he paid for.

May 31st Dull and cooler. Our men and Fred Carson are gone on moor spreading manure etc. Received a letter from Tony who said he had received his parcel. He was on coastguard with six soldiers, a lance corporal and a serjeant major. Emily is a little better but not much. We sowed 20 more rows of swede and manured and drew up more.

June 1st Colder and showery. I have a fire in the houseplace. Anthony received a paper saying that he could draw the 1st interest on the £200 he put in war loan (£2.17.6) on June 1st. Anthony and men on moor getting turnip ground ready and sowing 22 more rows of swedes. Our Evelyn took 6 lbs of butter and sold it to Mr. S. Ashton at 1s.10d. per lb.

June 2nd Fine first thing but thunder rain came on after dinner. All the sheep in Sheldon except Frosts were washed at Ashford this morning. Our Tom got wet with getting a sheep out that was drowning. Emily seems a little better. She has had a better night not so sick.

June 3rd Showery. Mr. Sherlock took the service in Sheldon Church this afternoon. Collection for Church expenses 5s. 4½d. Mr. H. Shimwell and another man called here and had tea. They were motoring round to see

---

1 "In April 1917, the life expectancy of British pilots was 17 ½ flying hours. But of those who survived through skill and luck, many became 'aces', the qualifying number of 'kills' varying from country to country. (A notable ace was) Albert Ball who destroyed 43 aircraft before being killed when not yet 21. Captain Albert Ball VC DSO MC was one of the small band of flyers whose exploits and heroism captured the imagination of the British public. A watercolour by Norman G Arnold depicts his last fight on 7 May 1917 when his SE 5a was attacked by German Fokkers and he was shot down near Annoeullin." *Great Battles of World War 1* Anthony Livesey pp 136, 142. Also see Introduction p.xix

farmers and tell them how much land would have to be put under the plough for 1918. These two men came from Chatsworth. Fred Brockley went by the 5.55 train from Bakewell on his way back from home after having a few days leave before going to the front again.

June 4th   Fine but dull and rather cool. Anthony appeared at the Town Hall to appeal against taxing our profits on public house. They put us on to be taxed on £20.0.0. profits. I was very bad with rheumatics and had to go to bed about 7 o'clock.

June 5th   Fine and sunny first thing but dull in the afternoon. Mrs. Banks was showing our girls how to make cheese her way. We had two new vats and 4 new cheese cloths, one new screw cloth and a thermometer which cost 3s. 9d. The vats were 4s. 3d. each (15 size). She (Mrs. Banks) salts the curd and does not rub any outside. Our men finished the fallows, sowing 40 rows of turnips.

June 7th   Very early this morning I heard the thunder and afterwards the rain came down in torrents. Very misty but a lovely growing day. Our Mary sent a letter saying she had had two post cards from Clem but he had not received a line or parcel. A mission for children was started at 7 o'clock tonight. A procession marched from school to Church, singing hymns. A cross was carried in front. Our Ethel and Evelyn and other choir girls joined in procession. Mr. Sherlock and Mr. Hayward were in attendance. Mrs. Tinsley and the Misses Grover were there as well.

June 8th   A lovely growing day. Our men are working on moor. Ethel and Evelyn are baking cake as we are sending Tony a parcel. We received a letter from Tony and his singlets to wash.

June 10th Very fine. Mr. Sherlock took the service in Church this afternoon and finished the mission for children. Miss Grover called to see me after service and we had a chat over the Roll of Honour. Our Tony's name had not been put on Sheldon Roll in magazine.

June 11th Very fine and hot. Tom started shearing sheep on moor (10 today). We sent Tony his singlets washed. We have not heard from him for three days. Billy Naylor brought me a pair of spectacles from Bakewell which cost 1s. 3d. We received word that Mary had had another letter from Clem (Germany) and he had received two letters, one from Mary and one from Evelyn.

June 12th Very hot. I had a letter from Tony saying what poor food and little quantity (one round of bread and marmalade) to breakfast. After the men made complaint another round was given them and then they went on a route march of 18 or 19 miles. Our Tony's feet were in such an awful state that he had to go to the doctor who ordered him 2 days leave from marching (and this in England). I wrote to him and we will try to send him another parcel this week. Our Tom has shorn 16 sheep today.

June 13th Hotter than ever. Tom went on moor and finished shearing sheep (19). Mr. Hayward came to see me over Sheldon Roll of Honour. In the magazine for June the name of Clifton Cox-Wilson was put as having joined up but our Tony, though he had been gone longer than he, was never mentioned. After talking, I was of the same opinion still.

June 14th As hot as ever. Miss Grover sent 15/- for buying 4 tea pots for Sheldon School. Received a letter from Tony saying that he had been firing on miniature range and testing (wearing) a gas helmet. The men set 16 score plants in garden, cabbage, cauliflower, brussels etc. Richd Skidmore brought us some Pixie plants yesterday. There has been another awful air raid over London, more than ever killed and wounded, above 90 killed and over 400 wounded in E end. We sent some food etc. to Tony in two parcels.

June 15th Very hot. Our men were working on moor. Anthony was putting wire and wire netting round the corn. Mr. Sherlock came and had a cup of tea. Received a letter from Tony. He was pretty well but his feet were still sore.

June 16th Still very hot. Some rain is badly wanted. There is a plague of caterpillars in the Edale, Chapel-en-le-Frith and Woodlands (Hope) district, thick over in thousands, eating up everything green and spoiling cornfields etc. The British in France are still gaining ground after the Messines[1] victory of a week ago.

June 17th Very hot, thunder came on but only one bit of a scud. We received a letter from our Tony and he said he had received the parcels we sent. Mr. Hayward took the service in Church.

June 18th Very close, no rain and it is badly needed. Anthony went to the doctor for himself. He told him to rest and put him a belladonna plaster on. He also said that he had a valve (heart) leaking a little. We had a letter from Tony this morning. The little postman forgot the keys and so the letters had to stay in box tonight.

June 20th Dull, grand growing weather. Thunder at times and some nice showers frequently. Our young horse (Heathcote) had breaking tackle on. Ethel went to Bakewell tonight shopping (a few things for Tony). Mr. Hayward called about the Roll of Honour.

June 21st Rather dull, showery at times. The bull that we turn out with cows died suddenly this morning about milking time. Nothing had been noticed about its being ill. They gave it a drink (warm ale etc.) and it died just after. Tom went for Mr. Marrison (vet) who did not know whether it was speed or what so he ordered a post mortem exam. We sent Tony two parcels.

1 On June 7th, a million pounds of high explosive were detonated under the Messines Ridge; see Introduction p.xxx

June 22nd Dull, very much cooler, showers at times. Received a letter from Tony and I wrote one back to him also one to the Commanding Officer 3rd Sherwoods Sunderland asking if he could grant Tony leave to help in hay harvest. Anthony saw Marrison and he said the young bull had pneumonia and pleurisy and it had collapsed in 1st stages. Heard that Richard Bonsall's son John had been wounded.

June 23rd Dull and cold. Dipped lambs (all in Sheldon except H. Frost). Our young horse Heathcote in lines, went pretty well, shied a bit. Mary had another letter from Clem. Heard that Tom Wager had been wounded in 3 places on 10th June and is in a London hospital.

June 24th Dull and showery at times, nice growing weather. Mr. Sherlock took the service in Church. We have had comfrey boiled as a vegetable for two or three Sundays. Beef is 1s.6d. per lb.

June 25th Dull, slight showers at times. Received word from Commanding Officer, Sunderland that we must apply somewhere else for soldier labour (to some Council or committee).

June 26th Dull and cooler. Some men had been trying to get an engine on the road which had got fast when bringing it to Magpie mine. Mr. Hayward brought frames for the Roll of Honour. One for those serving and one also for those who have fallen. Mr. Hartopp came to Sheldon to see what land the farmers could plough up this year. He had refreshment here.

June 28th Dull, slight showers and very rough and cold wind. NE. Our Tom and Wm went for coal as we are having a bit extra. The young horse (Heathcote) was put in harness and taken to help draw the coal between two old horses. Tom took it to be shod first and it was very awkward but was all right when in chains drawing up. The Rolls of Honour were put in Sheldon Church porch on the baize doors.

June 30th Very cold and dull. Received a letter from Tony that he was coming tonight, and afterwards a telegram came put in at Cleadon at 3.50 to say he was coming on leave. He will not be able to get through. Men working on moor in potatoes and swedes.

July 1st Dull and cold. The wind keeps in N. East. Our Tony came up to Longstone by milk train from Derby. He had arrived at Derby at 2 o'clock this morning and had stayed at the YMCA in an easy chair until the train started. About 20 soldiers from his lot had come on leave. Tony went on moor after going to Sheldon Church and came back and then went to Monyash with Tom and James Frost. Ethel and Evelyn also went to Monyash. Mr. Hayward took the service in Sheldon Church. Collection (Church expenses) 5s.6d. Celebration of Holy Communion at 9.30 this morning. Mr. Sherlock officiated.

July 2nd Finer, more sun. Anthony took milk and then went to Bakewell market. Tony went to Bakewell. We wrote to the C.O. Sunderland for an extension of leave for Tony as we had not heard from Mr. J.R. Bond. Tony went for a ride on Evelyn's bicycle and James Frost went with him on his bike. They went to Monyash, Sheldon and Bakewell. Our Anthony sold the young horse Wager to Thos Wm Brockley (for £50).

July 3rd   Very hot in sun but a cold wind (N. East). Tony, Ethel and Evelyn went on bikes to Middleton. George Brockley lent Tony his bike.

July 4th   Very dull and very much like rain. Anthony had a letter from Sunderland saying that Tony could not have his leave extended. The Russians have again taken the offensive taking 10,000 prisoners yesterday, and 7,000 in today's paper.

July 5th   Very fine. Our poor Tony set off from home just after nine o'clock this morning to catch the 10.55 train. Ethel and Evelyn went with him to Bakewell station and saw him off. There were 3 other soldiers got into the same carriage bound for somewhere. A lady bought our Tony and 3 other soldiers a book each about General Smuts. Our girls brought home stewing meat and kidney and paid for same from Mr. Thacker. We do not owe him anything. Our men have been on moor in swedes (thinning them) and potatoes.

July 6th   Fine, but rather heavy and like thunder. Our men on moor in turnips. Mr. Sherlock called here and he seemed annoyed when I spoke about the managers not knowing about Polly Bramwell being appointed teacher. She has been on the paysheet for this month and not a word has been said about it to the other managers. Our Tom took Fanny to Mr. J. Dicken's horse. Mary, Ethel, Emily and little Anthony went down Monyash Dale, through Monyash and back to Sheldon. Emily had Mrs. Ed's chair. Heard that Sam Bramwell is wounded in the leg and is on his way to Liverpool.

July 8th   Fine but very cold. N.E. wind. Two letters came from Tony this morning. He seems homesick and expects to be sent out early this week. I think it is a most cruel shame as he has only been in training about 6 weeks. He got three days CB and one day's pay stopped because he overstayed his leave by a few hours. Mr. Hayward took the service in Church. Fred Goodwin was wounded a fortnight (today) since. Severe gun shot wounds I think in the eye.

July 9th   The wind keeps in the NE and with a very hot sun there is not much growth of pastures. Men working in turnips on moor. I wrote to Mr. Beaven (Taddington) about the (belated) soldiers allotment. Ethel went to Bakewell and posted a letter and parcel to Tony. Mary and Evelyn went to Bakewell tonight and bought some little suits for Anthony W. Wager who was very awkward to have them on as these are his first trousers etc. Sam Bramwell has arrived in England and is at Whalley (wounded).

July 10th   Dull and cold, wind NE. Looks like rain at times. Instead of our poor Tony coming to help us in hay etc. he has been given his outfit for

France where he expects to go today or tomorrow. We received a letter from him this morning to that effect.

July 11th   Very fine: hot sun. We commenced mowing 2nd seeds on moor. Received two letters from Tony. In one he expects to be sent to France or somewhere else today. A managers' meeting at 4 o'clock: only two present viz our Anthony and Rev. H.E. Sherlock. The others could not leave their hay. Mr. Sherlock did not call here. The Russians have taken the offensive and are doing well.

July 12th   Very hot, good hay weather. Our men were on moor. Will Hallows was helping us after he had been at the mine, and our Tom was stacking. They got six loads of hay. Evelyn and Mary were milking. We had no draught beer for sale today. Wm fetched the 3 kils allowed us (from Bakewell station). He also called at Orme's and got 1 case of bottled Bass and 2 cases of Guinness, stout. They let him have about 3lbs of sugar and the bag burst and the contents came on the barrels and cart bottom. Mr. Beaven called to see us and explained how we were to proceed to draw soldiers' allotment money. He said he drew for both his sons and put it in the war loan for them. Our Tony has got to Folkestone en route for France. We had a letter from him this morning.

July 13th   Hot sun and a good wind. Looks like rain at times. Sheldon school broke up for holidays this afternoon. Our Tom shot his uncle John Brockley's old horse.

July 14th   Very fine. Hot sun and plenty of wind. Miss Grover called with magazine and said the children's tea (Sheldon school) might be put off until September as her sister is away and she expects to go next month. Miss Hallam came to Sheldon (Mrs. Morton). Our large Dreadnought has been sunk while lying at anchor (*Vanguard*) with between 700 and 800 casualties.

July 15th   St. Swithins. Very fine 1st thing but showery this afternoon. Mr. Sherlock took the service in Church.

July 16th   Very dull and showery at times. No hay day. Received a field PC from Tony dated July 12. A sailor was in at noon with T.A. Sheldon (from *HMS Excellent*).

July 17th   Fine first thing, but dull and threatening for rain. The afternoon and evening we led 14 loads which were put under the hay barn. I was taken in rickshaw into stackyard.

July 18th   Very wet and this will do such a deal of good. I had a letter from our Tony from France and I have written back to him this afternoon. Our Tom found 4 hens killed by a fox. Bertha and Polly Bramwell and little Clarice went to see Sam in Whalley Military hospital and found he was worse wounded than they at first thought.

July 19th Dull and wet first thing but turns out brighter later on. Received another letter from Tony.

July 20th Fine first thing but very close and dull in afternoon and slight drizzle of rain at times. Anthony is not well at all and really is not fit to be in the hay. Received a letter from Tony.

July 21st Very fine, but rather dull at times. Received a letter from Tony saying that he was all right and that Joe Gregory (Taddington field) was at the same place as he.

July 22nd Very fine and very close. Anthony, Tom, Ethel and Evelyn went to Church this afternoon. Mr. Hayward took the service. We have nearly sold out of beer etc.

July 23rd Very fine. Our men are gone to the hay. Received a letter from Tony and I am just answering it. There has been another air raid over Harwich, 11 killed and 26 injured. The Russians are giving way completely. The soldiers won't fight. PC Dennis and his brother have just called and had lunch. Got 4 loads of hay out of Hicks field and 2 out of Bramwell field.

July 24th Very close dull at times. Got one more load out of Top Hicks field and Gould finished mowing Waterlands this morning. Received a letter and Ethel a card with the Notts and Derby badge in silk from Tony. He says he keeps alright and is well. We got 5 more loads of hay out of Bramwell field.

July 26th Very close. Wm Gould mowed Croftheads and started in Little Butts and finished (Little Butts) and Pingle. Received (Evelyn) a card and letter from Tony saying that the parcel we sent was received by him in a damaged condition, jam over everything. We got 3 loads of hay out of Waterlands.

July 27th A stop is put to getting any more hay today as showers are frequent but this will do such a deal of good because other things want rain so much, the pasture and roots, corn etc. We received a letter from Tony.

July 29th Cold and drizzly at times. A children's flower service was held in Sheldon Church. Mr. Sherlock took the service. Lovely bunches of flowers were brought and a collection was made which amounted to twelve shillings. Our Ethel and Evelyn packed them in three big hat boxes and carried these to Longstone station en route for Derby Infirmary. James Frost helped to carry the boxes of flowers to the station and they saw them off by the last train. I put a note in one of the boxes saying that the money would be sent tomorrow to the infirmary. Our Tom received a letter from Tony.

July 30th Rough and cold, a bit drizzly at times. Received a letter from Tony and I wrote back to him. I sent a 10 shilling note and a two shilling postal order to the Secretary, Derby Infirmary.

July 31st   Rough. Our men, James Frost, Billy Carson and Sam Wilton were in our hay this afternoon. Ben Handley and Wm Hallows also came after their work at the mine. They got 13 loads of hay, 8 out of Croft Heads and 5 out of Little Butts. Received a letter from Tony. We have no beer to sell but there were a good few in tonight drinking spirits.

Aug. 1st   A rough wet miserable day. Had a receipt for 12/- from Derby Infirmary.

Aug. 2nd   Drizzly, rough and dull. No hay day. Our men went on moor working in swedes. Received a letter from Tony and he said he had seen Ralph Mellor in France. We have no beer neither draft nor bottled. People have been drinking all spirits at night. Another offensive began in France a day or two since and we have had a set back with our advanced posts but before this we took about 5,000 prisoners.

Aug. 3rd   Wet and dull this morning but clears out later. Mr. Sherlock called here and had a little conversation. Our men are gone on moor.

Aug. 4th   Dull and showery at times. Our men are in turnips. Mary and Evelyn went to Bakewell tonight (shopping). They called at the P Office and found two letters from Tony. He also sent two lovely cards one for me and one for little Anthony Wager.

Aug. 5th   Dull at times. Holy Communion in Sheldon Church at 9.30. Mr. Sherlock officiated. Mr. Sherlock took the service in Church this afternoon (anniversary of war) 3 years. All went from our house (visitors as well) except Wm and myself. Collection 16/- for Church expenses.

Aug. 6th   Dull but turns out a fine afternoon. Anthony took a calf to Bakewell auction. Mary and Anthony also went but Mr. Sutton dentist was not there so she could not have her teeth seen to. As it was Bank Holiday the shops were shut. I received a letter from Tony saying that some of his mates had been moved down the line but he himself was still at the base owing to him having to do some more firing. Jack Naylor went back this morning.

Aug. 7th   A lovely day. We finished our hay today. James Frost and Billy Carson came to help us this afternoon and Wm Hallowes and Ben Handley came after leaving off their work at the mine. We got 11 loads out of Big Butts and Pingle. Anthony paid Wm Hallowes and Ben Handley the sum of 25/- each. I sat out of doors after tea until 9.30. We had stewed hare, cabbage and new potatoes for dinner today. Tom caught the hare last week. The hay crops were not as good as last year's. We got the following loads:

2nd seeds and other field	30
Bole Piece (next to Johnson lane)	25
Top Hicks field	5
Level Bramwell field	7
Waterlands	12
Croft Heads	8
Little Butts	5
Big Butts and Pingle	11

Total   103   loads of hay

Number of loads last year 137.
34 loads less this year.

Finished hay on Aug. 8th last year. This year Aug. 7th

Aug. 8th   Dull first thing and afterwards turns out very wet. Received (Mary) a letter from Tony. He is lonely as two of his best mates (Shrewsbury for one) have been moved up the line. Tony has another course of firing to do.

Aug. 9th   Dull and showery. Our men went for manure to Ashford (Uptons). Anthony bought this manure for 27s. 6d. I received two p. cards in envelope from Tony and he said that he had no writing paper so had had to use these instead. He had received the parcel we sent last week. Aunt Lizzie is sending him one today. Tom took young Heathcote to be shod at Bakewell. Arthur Sheldon had 13 or 14 fowls worried.

Aug. 12th   Very showery at intervals today. Mr. Hayward took the service this afternoon. We received a letter from Tony.

Aug. 14th   Anniversary of Anthony's and my wedding day (31 years). Thunder and rain came on at intervals. The weather is very unsettled. We are getting a few mushrooms. Harry Buxton and Billy Naylor got about 4lbs in Billy's field this afternoon. Wm Gould went twice to Bakewell for coal for us. We are getting some extra for winter as it is supposed there will be a shortage. There were about 30 killed and 53 injured in last air raid (Sunday). Ethel is not very well. Her face is swollen owing to having her teeth out.

Aug. 15th   Dull. Two letters came from Tony today, one to me posted on August 12th and one for Evelyn posted on August 9th so some are longer on the road than others.

Aug. 16th   Dull and during the night the rain fell in torrents. Our Tom received a letter from Tony. He keeps pretty well and is still at the base (France). We have had a very busy day. All sheep and lambs in Sheldon were dipped (in our yard) 241 in all belonging to the following:

Mr. Herbert Frost	38
Mr. Carson	3
Mr. Manderfield	9
W.H. Brockleys	1
Mr. T.A. Sheldon	7
Alf Brocklehurst	20
Anthony Gyte	79
John Frost	5
John Brocklehurst	28
Thos. Wm Brockley	34
Wm Naylor	17
	241

241   sheep and lambs

Our numbers were 44 ewes and 35 lambs = 79. We used McDougalls dip. Sent Tony a letter and a parcel. The old concertina chap (Ellis) came.

Aug. 17th Rained in torrents all day. Anthony went with milk and also went to Bakewell for paint, oil and turpentine which have all gone up very much in price. The paint is 10d per lb. Everything you have to buy is gone up in price. The farmer is restricted in everything he has to sell. It is a wonder there is one patriotic farmer the way he is being treated by the Government and the majority of people who know nothing of farming. Wm went to Bakewell and was charged 2s.8d. for a lb of Kiel Butter; eggs are 5 per shilling, sugar what we can get 6d. and 6½d per lb; lard 1s. 3d., sultanas 1s.4d., big raisins 1s.0d., dates 8d, flour 3s.4d. per stone which is beastly stuff. All cotton goods have gone up and are going still higher in price also woollen and other commodities. Anthony and Tom were busy painting the binder getting it ready for the harvest. They had put on a new bottom part a few days ago.

Aug. 18th Showery at times. Anthony and Tom finished painting the binder. We are getting a nice lot of mushrooms nearly every day.

Aug. 19th Showery at times and then sunshine. Emily received a letter from Tony and he said that Shrewsbury (his mate) had been sent to the base again as his heart is bad (he was sent to the lines before). All our girls and little Anthony are gone to Church this afternoon. Mr. Hayward took the service. I suppose Mr. Sherlock has gone away. There has been some sort of a naval battle between the Germans and our ships in North Sea. I think there was not much damage done to either side. The Germans say our ships ran away.

Aug. 20th Rather dull. Bakewell fair. Received a letter and a handkerchief from Tony. The handkerchief was for Emily. Tom shot a hare. There was an accident at Magpie this morning early. The rope broke and let the chair down but no one was injured. Wm Hurst was at the engine.

Aug. 21st Fine but dull at times (rained in torrents tonight). Mr. Hayward called to see us.

Aug. 22nd Shower, thunder at times. Tom started painting our windows and had finished one when heavy rain came down.

Aug. 23rd Very showery and very rough this afternoon. Our men are gone on the moor. PC Dennis called to see how many dogs we have as we only applied for one exemption this year. We drowned old Gyp last December. Received a letter from Tony and Mary a PC from Clem saying that he had received a parcel at last which was dated March 12th. He is not well.

Aug. 24th Showery. I wrote to Tony. The church boiler was sent to Mr. Bennett Needham.

Aug. 26th Dull and very showery this afternoon. A few young people are gone to Eyam (Cucklett) to the Anniversary sermon on the *Plague of Eyam*.

Tom, Ethel, Evelyn, Clarice B and Alice B, James Frost and George Brockley went. I am afraid they would be wet. Mr. Hayward took the service in Sheldon Church and Mary presided at the harmonium. There was only Ruth Brocklehurst belonging to the choir. Received a letter from Tony and one from Fred who was in hospital (sick) when he wrote acknowledging the parcel which our girls sent him. I saw it in *Derbyshire Times* where Mary Jane Hawley's husband had been killed in France. He was named John Stephenson. Our girls etc. got back just before 7 o'clock and were drenched to the skin. They had tea at old Godbers and were charged 2/- each. James Frost had a spill and hurt his thumb.

Aug. 27th Finer during the greater part of today but heavy rain came on tonight. Anthony went with the milk. Tom took 3 cows to market (his uncle Billy Naylor helped him). He took 2 cows from Sheldon to the field at Ashford and the three were fetched out of the Ashford field and taken to market. There were a blue cow, a light roaned one and a white faced one. These three cows were sold for £40 10s. 0d. each to Arthur Brassington. Billy Naylor went from Bakewell on his holidays. I received a letter from Tony and I wrote back to him.

Aug. 29th Showery. Received a letter from Tony (to his father). Anthony wrote him a good long letter and sent it. Billy Naylor came back from his holidays. He went to Manchester and stayed all night at Roberts and then went to North Road to his sister Mary's.

Aug. 31st The last day of August and it has been finer. Our Mary has been baking a cake and buns for Tony. I wrote to him. Ethel and Evelyn are gone to Bakewell shopping. They called at the Post Office and there was a letter from Tony. In it he said what rough and wet weather they were having where he was (at a base in France) and that the wind had blown many of the tents down and it was all wet and mud. Turns out wet tonight.

Sept. 1st Another very wet day. Our Mary received a letter from Clem. He said he was improving a bit in health and that he had received another parcel but that he was expecting to be moved again.

Sept. 2nd Finer, towards 10 o'clock tonight a shower came on. Holy Communion this morning. Mr. Sherlock officiated and also took the service this afternoon. Collection for Church expenses 11s. 8d. Tom, Ethel, Evelyn and others went to Monyash Church tonight. Our girls (Mary and Ethel) took me in Mrs. Ed's chair first in our yard and then down as far as Naylors. The chair was lowered to the ground by taking the steering wheel off. I was then lifted in and the wheel put on when I was sat in chair.

Sept. 4th Very fine. Began cutting corn in Hicks field, Anthony, Tom, Wm and Vincent. The reaper and binder worked well. Ethel and Evelyn took me in Mrs. Ed's chair to watch the men and binder at work. Little Anthony went and was asleep all the way there and back.

Sept. 5th Fine but the dew was on corn until late. Partridge shooting began today at Sheldon. We had five gentlemen to tea viz. Mr. Wood, Mr. Lowthian, Mr. Lees, Mr. R. Dixon and another. I charged them 1s. 6d. each. Mr. Wood asked if we could provide luncheon for beaters at Partridge shootings. I told him I would rather not. Received a letter from Tony saying that he was going to be shifted from base. I think we are doing badly in the war. The air raids are coming very thickly and often. Sheerness, Chatham and London have been raided again and there are many casualties. The Russians have also retired from Riga. Wm Naylor killed 4 pigs today. Anthony was called up to go to a cow of John Frost's just before 11 o'clock tonight. It had calved and was putting her belly down. He took some laudanum from our house.

Sept. 6th Very misty until late in the day. Our men went opening out in Grindlow Knoll Cornfield. Billy Naylor started between five and six o'clock this morning to Buxton taking the four pigs killed yesterday. Made a bit of jam with 3lbs of sugar. The man that Billy Naylor took his pigs to did not pay him as there was a bother over price.

Sept. 7th Misty at first but clears out later. Our men started with reaper and binder in Grindlow Knoll. Mary went to Bakewell and called at the P. Office where there was a letter from Tony. I wrote to him leaving out 14th I.B.D. Section 24th A.P.C. as he has been removed to somewhere else from the Base. I hope the letter will find him allright. Alf Brockley finished cutting his corn.

Sept. 8th Rather misty with slight showers. The Government binder is at work in Thos W Brocklehurst's corn. A man named Wood is working it. Emily had two teeth extracted at Dr. Jackson's. Tom took her and Ethel down to Bakewell in float.

Sept. 9th Dull and v. close. Very poor weather for drying. Mr. Hayward took the service in Sheldon Church and called here afterwards. I had a very short talk with him. We do not always agree.

Sept. 11th Dull but clears out later and is a lovely day. Tom, Wm and Vincent in corn on moor. Anthony went to Chesterfield (by a train just after 9 o'clock) to look for a bath chair. He went to Eyres and paid £8.0.0. or more, the chair to be sent or brought in a fortnight. Anthony started back from Chesterfield at 12.18. Mr. Sherlock came up to attend a managers meeting. There were only two present, himself and Anthony so the meeting was adjourned. Received a letter from our Tony.

Sept. 12th Dull at times mixed with sun and wind. Cutting corn on moor with binder. Mary went to Bakewell and brought some stewing meat from Mr. Thackers (did not pay) and also a letter from the P. Office from Tony.

Sept. 13th Very wet. Anthony, Tom and Thos Wm B started mowing churchyard but had to stop as the rain came on. Mr. Ronston came and was paid up £11 2s.6d. I had quite a straight talk to him of how Orme's had treated us over bottled beer etc.

Sept. 14th Fine. My birthday (60). Evelyn went to Bakewell to Mr. Duckmanton's for her first music lesson. Bought me a shawl and a book for my birthday. Mr. Hayward called here and had tea.

Sept. 16th Fine. Mr. Sherlock took the service in Church this afternoon. He told Thos Wm B that he was going away on the 7th Oct to preach at the Harvest Festival where he used to be. As it is our Wakes Sunday and we have always had our Harvest Thanksgiving on that day I do not know who will come here. Ethel and Evelyn went to Longstone Church tonight (Harvest Festival and Wakes). We put our clock back one hour tonight.

Sept. 17th Fine first thing but came on dull and a bit drizzly at dinner time. Anthony did not go to Bakewell as the corn is ready for leading. We have not heard from Tony since last Wednesday night. He then said he had used his last envelope and he had not received the parcel which contained writing paper and envelopes. Ethel went to Bakewell and brought a letter from Tony.

Sept. 18th Fine first thing, a bit drizzly later on. The hay was led out of churchyard. Thos Wm Brockley had one load and we had one. Our Evelyn and Annie Haywood were turning it with rakes last night. A managers' meeting was held in the schoolroom. Mr. Sherlock, Anthony, TW Brockley and Wm H Brockley were there. We sent our Tony a parcel this morning.

Sept. 20th Very rough and wet. Mary received a letter from Tony this morning dated Sept. 11th. In it he said he had received the parcel sent a week or two since and the contents were all crumbled up. Gould fetched 2 kils of ale from station and Anthony tapped one and the men had some. I wrote to Tony.

Sept. 21st A good corn day, wind and sun. We received a letter from Tony. When he wrote it (Sunday last) he had just come out of the trenches after being in 3 days. I feel very depressed about it. There was another great push on the Western front yesterday. There were about 2,000 Germans taken prisoner and some guns.

Sept. 22nd Fine first part of the day with a nice wind. Our men and Louis E Elliott got 9 loads of corn when the rain came on drizzling and stopped them. These 9 loads were got out of Grindlow Knoll. Two men and two women called here and had tea. They brought their own food. Ethel and Evelyn walked to Bakewell. Evelyn went for a music lesson to Mr. Duckmantons. This is the second lesson she has had. Ethel took a cheque and paid Mr. Thacker for all we owe him (tomorrow's meat as well). We got a letter from our poor Tony written on Monday last.

Sept. 23rd Very dull and misty, drizzling a little. Our Tom and Gould sat up all night with a cow which calved early this morning (cow calf). We have had five cow calves following each other but have to sell them as we do not want to be short of fodder and we want the milk. Mr. Harkness[1] (formerly Vicar of Edale) took the service in Sheldon Church this afternoon. All ours went besides Mary, little Anthony and myself. Ethel and Evelyn went to Ashford Church (Harvest Thanksgiving) tonight.

Sept. 25th Rather dull but keeps fair. Our men are gone on moor for corn. Fred Bramwell arrived at Sheldon on leave from France. We have not heard since Saturday from Tony. Mr. Sherlock called here.

Sept. 27th Fine, but dull. Anthony and Tom put the young horse (Heathcote) in the dray and dragged Grindlow Knoll and afterwards it was put in trap and they went down Monyash Dale and home. It went all right. Mr. Knight (the old hunting chap) called and had refreshments. Sheldon school treat was held today. Miss Kate Grover, Mrs. Tinsley, Mr. Hayward, Mrs. Kenworthy and Mr. Sherlock were there. Our Ethel and Evelyn went. Our men went on moor for corn and brought two loads (all). Received two letters and a field card from Tony. One letter was dated Sept. 22nd and one Sept. 23rd and he had just gone out of the trenches again. Walter Brocklehurst brought us two cases of bottled beer.

Sept. 30th Very fine. Sam Bramwell is on crutches and cannot put his foot to the ground. He looked through our window and I had a word or two with him. He looks well. Anthony and Tom put young horse Heathcote in trap and took the milk to Longstone station with him. In the afternoon, Anthony took me and little Anthony on moor for a drive. Vincent went with us to open the gates and feed hens. Dedication Service at Sheldon Church. Mr. Hayward took the Service.

Oct. 1st Very fine. Anthony took the old red cow to Bakewell and made 39 pounds of her. Our men went on moor and commenced getting potatoes. Ethel went to Bakewell to have her teeth seen to. A young man brought our new chair (bath) by motor. No letter from Tony. I wrote to him. Orme's brought 1 kil ale, 6 doz Guinness and whisky, rum and gin.

Oct. 2nd Very fine. Our men are gone on to moor getting potatoes. Mr. Squires' eldest girl came to help in picking them up. Our Ethel went this afternoon to help as well. Mary and I have got severe colds. Another air raid on London. This is the fourth in succession. Sam Bramwell went back this afternoon to Burnley. No letter from Tony. Evelyn took the Church linen to Miss Grovers.

Oct. 3rd Fine first thing but turns out wet this afternoon and stops the potato getting. Our Tom was dragging bottom Grindlow Knoll. Our girls, Mary, Ethel and Evelyn, Ruth B, Clarice Brockley and Alice, Bertha and Polly Bramwell, Mrs. Craven were cleaning the Church. Tonight, Mary and I picked the damsons which came from Mr. Sneaps yesterday. Mary made 6 quarts into jam with 6lbs of sugar but we had no more sugar and so we put them in a stewpot in the oven. Received two letters from Tony, one

---

1   The Revd. Edward L Harkness left Edale in 1915 to become Vicar of Fairfield, Buxton

dated Sept. 26th and the other Sept. 29th. He says he is fairly well and is out of the trenches. He got the parcel we sent on Sept. 17th. Mr. Hayward called here and he said that Mr. Sherlock and other clergy had gone into *retreat*.

Oct. 4th   Very wet. The men have been lashing corn and getting chopper ready and drawing thatch. We have been boiling plum puddings and are going to send one to Tony. Mary and Evelyn have been cleaning the Church, Clarice, Alice and Bertha have also been. Wm has been leading turnips out.

Oct. 5th   Drizzly this morning and rather rough. Tom, Wm and Vincent were carting lime from Hindlow to the moor. Our Mary went to Bakewell sugar hunting. She got 2lbs from Skidmore, 1lb from Ormes and 1lb from George Frosts. She bought a tin of glucose (3s.6d.) and we put most of this into the damson jam with 3 lbs of sugar. I had a letter from our Tony. He wrote it on Oct. 1st and is still out of the trenches. There has been another advance on the Western Front.

Oct. 6th   Fine but very cold. Anthony brought some very nice flowers which a few people from Ashford sent to the Harvest Thanksgiving tomorrow. Maggie Naylor sent some Michaelmas daisies. Evelyn received a letter from Tony. Our girls, Mary, Ethel and Evelyn and others are decorating the Church this afternoon. Tonight Ethel and Evelyn went to Bakewell. The Misses Grover sent two beautiful bunches of grapes for the Harvest Thanksgiving.

Oct. 7th   Sheldon Wakes Sunday. Very wet. Thunder etc. Holy Communion at 9.30. Mr. Sherlock celebrated and also took the Service. The Harvest Thanksgiving. A good congregation. Collection for Church expenses £2 0.0. Polly Bramwell's and J.R. Gregory's banns were published first time.

Oct. 8th   Wet. Anthony took a bull calf to market. A good many in our house tonight. There was singing for some time and then a collection which was for *the boys who have joined the army*. The sum of £1 15.6. was got. Our girls were selling button holes and flags sent by Miss Lees.

Oct. 9th   Wet with intervals. Wm Gould fetched 12 cwts of coal for the Church and took Mr. Squires' potatoes. Mr. Sneap went back. He bought some lambs from Anthony and some from Alf Brockley. He did not buy Billy Naylor's. A social was held at the school room for the Red Cross. Received a letter from Tony who thought he was going into the trenches again. Jim Goodwin was paid 5/- and 1/2 a gallon of beer for playing at social.

Oct. 10th   Finer but showery at times. Wm was carting manure from Ashford to our field at Sheldon. Mr. Hayward called here. Our Bessie has been knitting a pair of socks for Tony. A good many in house place tonight. Mr. Dennis (P.C.) had tea and brought a lb of tea yesterday. No letter from Tony today. Flowers and grapes and a basket of vegetables were sent to the Derby Infirmary (carriage by rail 1s.9d.) and we gave Wilf Goodwin 6 pence for taking them to the station. Mrs. Squires and daughter came to pay Anthony for carting potatoes and for some more potatoes, £15.0 altogether. They had tea.

Oct. 12th   Showery in the morning part. Tom, Wm and Vincent went for lime to Hurdlow with 3 carts in morning. Tom and his father went to the foal show at Bakewell in the afternoon. A dance was held at the school for the Red Cross. Jim Goodwin as usual was paid 5/- and beer. Eben Ollerenshaw and Fred Brockley were in our house. Evelyn received a letter from Tony dated Oct 7th. He was then in fairly good health and had not been in the trenches again. The war drags on and we keep hearing of bright young men falling in action. F. Beaven and Hubert Fotherby have been killed recently.

Oct. 13th   Drizzling rain at times. Anthony is not well. He has such a cold. George and Alf Brockley have each got off for six months at the Tribunal today. Ethel and Evelyn rode to Bakewell with Eben Ollerenshaw. He was going to fetch Charlie who had been to Derby for a few days. The horse slipped and fell down somewhere about the Rutland stables, throwing out Eben and Evelyn. Eben stuck to the reins and some young man helped our Evelyn up. Polly Bramwell and our Ethel sat behind and were not thrown out but a glass shade of Polly's was smashed to pieces. The girls called at the Post Office and there was a letter from Tony. Matthew Gregory and a man and dray took Polly Bramwell's furniture to Dove Holes.

Oct. 14th   Frosty and very cold. Mr. Hayward took the service in Sheldon Church and called out the banns for the second time between John R. Gregory and Mary Ann Bramwell. Tom, Ethel and Evelyn went to Taddington. It was the Wakes and Harvest Thanksgiving.

Oct. 15th   Very frosty and cold but fine. Anthony and Tom took 8 ewes and 4 tup lambs to Bakewell fair and sold them all but one. The 8 ewes and 1 tup made £34.10.0. G. Goodwin came up with Anthony from the fair to our place to look at one of our lambs but did not buy one. No letter from Tony. The night school started. There were 12 present. French was taken.

Oct. 16th   Drizzling first thing but turns out finer. Sam Swindell brought 3 of his ewes to our tup. We turned our ewes to the tup. Sent a parcel to our Tony. We have not had a letter from him. The postman brought a letter from Tony tonight dated Oct. 11th.

Oct. 17th   Dull and misty with drizzling showers at times. Tom and Vincent have been spreading lime on moor and Grindlow Knoll. Wm has been twice to Bakewell Station for dried grains. Anthony has taken the young filly Wager out a bit this afternoon. Very sad news came from France this morning. Poor Anthony Brocklehurst got killed with a shell on the 10th of this month. Fred Brocklehurst sent word to Clarice and asked her to break the news to John and Louisa. I do not know how ever they will bear up as they have lost both their sons. What a cruel wretched war this is and we are losing the flower of the country as there are so many grand young men being killed.

Oct. 18th Drizzling with rain and cold this morning. Two girls of Mr. Squires (Lumford) came to help us to get some potatoes. After having some refreshment they went back home as we thought it would be too wet. However it turned out quite a good afternoon and our men got nearly three rows of potatoes. Received two letters from Tony. One to Emily dated Oct. 11th or 12th and one dated Oct. 14th to Mary. He had got his parcel containing pudding and cake. Mr. Beaven came to take the night school at Sheldon. Mrs. Ollerenshaw paid her subscription and attended the class. Received a box of apples and pears from J. Naylor (Wales). Anthony and Ed Brockley put the boiler in the Church apparatus.

Oct. 19th Fine but cold. Our men have been getting potatoes on moor (Mayfield blossoms) which are very good. Mary went to Bakewell to get something to send to Tony.

Oct. 20th Fine. Our men were getting potatoes on moor. Ethel and Evelyn went to Bakewell and bought new black hats from Barratts 4s.11d., 5s.6d. and 5s.11d. They were more reasonable than Broughtons. They paid Thacker all we owe, for tomorrow's as well. Tom had a letter from Tony.

Oct. 21st Fine in morning, drizzling towards night. Poor John and Louisa and family and people in Sheldon went to Church thinking there would be a memorial service for Anthony. Mr. Sherlock did not come and Mr. Hayward never mentioned the poor lad in his address (just a bit in the prayers) but a sort of service and address was given about Nelson and Trafalgar Day and finished up with *God save the King*. There is not a deal of sympathy for people who are shedding their life's blood. We received a sad letter from Tony over poor Anthony.

Oct. 22nd Dull and cold, rough winds. It had a bad ending the last week what with the Zeppelin raid killing and injuring people on the N.E. coast and the loss of ships. Two of our destroyers were sunk and a many other vessels carrying merchandise. Anthony took the milk and then went to Bakewell. He bought a shoulder of mutton at a shilling per lb, tobacco from Ormes which he paid for. Our men were getting potatoes on moor. Mr. Wood and Mr. Lowthian were shooting and came here for tea. They never told us they wanted tea until about 2 hours before it was wanted. Jack Armit came to Sheldon and bought a tup lamb from Anthony for £6.0.0.

Oct. 24th Snow had fallen during last night and this morning. The fields were covered. Later in the day the rain fell heavily. Getting ready for tying calves up as it is really not fit to turn them out at night. The men are winnowing this afternoon and Anthony is soldering cans. Mr. Burley sent the milk cheque (£40.10.2$^{1}/_{2}$). Evelyn received a letter from Tony. We tied up all milk cows and calves.

Oct. 25th Showers. Awfully cold. No potato getting. Tom, Wm and Vincent went for lime to Hurdlow. Anthony went to Bakewell station for 4 kils of ale. He tapped one kil and we sold some at 5d a pint. We have to sell the beer at 5d per pint beginning on Oct. 28th by order so we have begun before the time. The night class commenced at 6 o'clock. The lads are taking fretwork. Aunt H and the girls are busy making black costumes.

Oct. 26th Snifting of snow and very cold and rough. Tom, Wm and Vincent have gone to Hurdlow for lime which they are putting on the ley field on moor. Evelyn received a letter from Fred Brockley. He does seem bothered over poor Anthony. We read Anthony's name in the casualty list this morning *(Sheffield Independent)*. The French have been very victorious over the Germans in Flanders, over 11,000 prisoners and a great many guns. The Germans are retreating. Ethel and Evelyn went to Bakewell and changed a black blouse for 9 yds calico. Jack Broomhead's little girl was christened Elsie, also Sarah Brocklehurst's baby girl also called Elsie tonight by Mr. Sherlock who also held a confirmation class in the school.

Oct. 27th Very frosty, also snow and very cold. The snow melted away as the sun shone. Polly Bramwell and John Gregory were married (2 o'clock). Mr. Sherlock officiated and afterwards called here and had tea. We had a conversation over different topics. Our men were spreading lime. The hounds turned out at Sheldon. Only two called in here to have a drink. Mr. Knight and Wm Bramwell and John Gregory called and had a drink before the wedding. Evelyn went to Bakewell for her music lesson. The Italians have had a serious reverse. No letter from Tony.

Oct. 28th Very frosty and snifting of snow. Mr. Sherlock took the service in Church. A young man called and had dinner. He was dressed in navy blue with cap. He said he was stationed at Sleaford or near and belonged to the naval flying corps.

Oct. 29th Very cold and very rough especially towards night when the rain came down very fast. Anthony took 5 lambs to Tideswell fair in float and sold out. Two at 4 guineas each. One at £4.0.0. and two for £7.10.0. the pair. We received a letter from our Tony. He had been in the trenches for four days. We have to sell our beer at 5d per pint. We began doing so a few days ago but the right time for beginning selling at that price was yesterday. Our Mary went to Bakewell and bought us some stewing meat which she paid for at Thackers.

Oct. 30th Cold and dull. Showery at times. Anthony did not go to the Haven Fair but all the men same as yesterday were getting potatoes and finished getting them. There were six rows. The Agricultural potatoes (war) turned out pretty well. Mr. Hayward called.

Oct. 31st Fine and milder. Anthony fetched two loads of potatoes (in bags) from moor which had been got out and left on moor last night. The others were pulling and cutting swedes. Brought two loads home. A meeting was held in Sheldon school room to appoint a committee (Food control). There were only five attended and these agreed to act. They were as follows: Messrs. H. Frost, Ed Brocklehurst, Thos Wm Brocklehurst, W. Hallows and Anthony Gyte. There were several in our house but none of these attended the meeting. Aunt H received a letter from Tony.

Nov. 1st   A most miserable misty day. Does not clear at all. Tom was dragging Grindlow Knoll with Navvy and young Heathcote. Wm and Vincent were pulling and pitting swedes. Received a Field card from Tony. I made out the milk bill to end of October and with carriage this bill amounted to £36.8s.10½d. The carriage was £1.2s.3d. The station master at Longstone had made out an account of what we paid every morning.

Nov. 2nd   Very misty. Received a letter from our Tony saying he had received the parcel with the 5/- in. Tom was ploughing Grindlow Knoll and Anthony was dragging on moor. Wm and Vincent were pulling swedes. Mary and Evelyn went to Bakewell shopping. Rode back with Mr. Craven in motor. Anthony, Mr. Herbert Frost and Thos Wm B went round Sheldon to ask the farmers what they were going to plough.

Nov. 3rd   Mary received a letter from our Tony saying a young man from Bakewell named Elliott had joined his battalion. Very misty. Anthony went by the 9.15 train to see Mr. Sneap and took a cheese from Billy Naylor for him. Tom was ploughing Grindlow Knoll with Heathcote and Navvy. Freddy Carson was with him. Ethel wrote to Tony. Lady Maud Cavendish's wedding day.

Nov. 4th   Fine. There was a celebration of Holy Communion at 9.30 in Sheldon Church. Mr. Sherlock officiated. Mr. Hayward took the service this afternoon. Collection for Church expenses (9s.1d.). Anthony came back from Mr. Sneaps. Clarice, Leah and Alice went to Youlgreave Church tonight.

Nov. 5th   Cold. Anthony took 4 lambs to market and sold them at 3 guineas each. Tom was ploughing. The others swede pulling etc. I wrote to Tony and we sent him a parcel containing 10/-. Anthony and Thos Wm B attended a meeting at Bakewell about ploughing.

Nov. 6th   Cold and showery at times. Tom was ploughing. Anthony is not well (indigestion). A letter was sent to our Mary from Gertie Frost saying that Mr. James Elliott had received a letter from his son in France and that our poor Tony had been wounded last Friday. We got a letter from Tony tonight dated Nov. 1st the day before he is said to be wounded.

Nov. 7th   Very cold and storms of sleet and snow come on at intervals. Tom is ploughing and the others are getting swedes. Anthony is not well. We have not received any more news of Tony. Ethel and Evelyn went to Bakewell and called at the P. Office. No letter about Tony but the girls called at Mr. James Elliotts and read the letter from his son which said that Tony was badly wounded.

Nov. 8th   Very stormy, rain. No letter from Tony. Our Anthony went to Mark Clays (Over Haddon) and bought a ram lamb for £6.0.0. and half a crown back for luck. Turned this lamb to our theaves as well as that from S. Swindle.

Nov. 9th   Very cold. We have not heard anything more of our poor Tony. The anxiety is dreadful. Miss Grover called with the magazines. She wanted me to let her know when we heard of Tony. Rain came on at intervals and thunder and lightning tonight.

Nov. 10th   Very wet at intervals. Tom was ploughing and Anthony was dragging on moor. Wm and Vincent were pulling swedes. The weather was very cold this afternoon. Anthony had his top coat and gloves on when driving the horses. Ethel and Evelyn went to Bakewell to do a bit of shopping.

Nov. 11th   Fine but cold. The girls and little Anthony and Anthony went to Church. Tom and Emily did not go. Mr. Hayward took the services in Church. It is Monyash Wakes. Ethel, Evelyn and Tom went to Monyash Church tonight.

Nov. 12th   Very cold. November Bakewell fair. Anthony went. Tom ploughing. The others pulling up swedes. Anthony saw Mr. James Elliott, the father of the young man who wrote saying that our poor Tony had been badly wounded, but Elliott said that they had not heard any more from their son. There were five hens worried by a fox today on moor.

Nov. 13th   Fine. The dreadful news came (officially) that our poor Tony had died in the field ambulance on Nov. 2nd. We are all in a sad way, poor lad, it is only six months since he went into training and now killed in the beauty of his manhood. What makes it so sad the news came on his 20th birthday. We are all in a dreadful way. Mr. Hayward came and sympathized with us and afterwards Mr. Sherlock came and had a nice talk and a prayer with us. My poor dear Tony, gone for ever and we shall never see his face any more on this earth. How shall we bear it? Poor Mrs. Ed wrote a note of sympathy to me. Tom went and was measured for a new suit of black at Mr. Hills (Bakewell) tonight. Miss Broadhurst called and said how sorry she was about poor Tony.

Nov. 14th   Drizzling at first but clears out and is fine and sunny. Anthony and I have had a poor night. We can scarcely realize about our poor Tony. Tom is ploughing and the others are in swedes.

Nov. 15th   Rather misty first thing but clears out and is a fine day. Tom finished ploughing Grindlow Knoll and Anthony and he set out part of level Bramwell Field and began ploughing there. Uncle Will Brockley was helping them in swedes and Fred Carson (senior) has been a few hours for a day or two. We received a few letters of sympathy about our poor dear lad Tony viz Mr. Sneap, Miss Grover, Mr. A. Wilson, Mr. Alfred Buxton, Miss H. Buxton, Mrs. Morton; and Mrs. Ed called to see me.

Nov. 16th A fine day. Our Tom is ploughing in Bramwell Field and the others are on moor in swedes. Anthony has made a place to put some in just through the top yard gate and they will begin to cart some from moor (starts drizzling). Mr. Sherlock called in tonight. Our Mary went to Bakewell to do a bit of shopping. She bought 5 yards of Black Cashmere to make me a dress and some crepe lace.

Nov. 17th Drizzling first thing but turns out a nice day. Tom is ploughing in Bramwell Field. Wm went for coal and 2 cwt of straw to Bakewell (Frank Lomas's). Vincent and little Freddy Carson are clearing up the yard. Richard Bonsall is getting a few swedes in. I made and sent the milk bill to Mr. Burley to Nov. 15th which came to £40.1.6. with carriage. Anthony saw Tom Wager at Longstone Station. He was come for a few days leave.

Nov. 18th Dull but fine. A memorial service was held in Sheldon Church for our poor Tony this afternoon. Mr. Sherlock preached a very good sermon and referred to *Tony Gyte*. A very sympathetic sermon. Anthony, Tom, Mary, Ethel, Emily and Evelyn went to church. Aunt H, I and little Anthony stayed at home. After the service, Mr. Sherlock called here and prayed with me. He left me his sermon to peruse. A good many people were at church and special hymns were sung viz. *On the resurrection morning, Jesu Lover of my soul* and *Abide with me.* Ethel and Evelyn went to Ashford church tonight and Tom went to Monyash. There was a memorial service there for poor Hubert Fotherby who got killed a week or two before our dear Tony. It is rumoured that G. Bridden is killed.

Nov. 19th Dull but fine. Anthony is not well at all. He is fretting so much for our poor lad. He as well as myself dread the night coming and then thinking of our poor lad, how he used to get up in a morning to go working on the farm. It is awful to think we shall never see his dear face again in this world, but we have to keep living somehow and poor John and Louisa have lost both their lads. Anthony did not go to Bakewell today. The men are getting swedes and leading them home from the moor.

Nov. 21st Drizzling. We killed a pig (Matthew Hodgkinson). I was talking a bit with poor John about his lads and our Tony being killed. He is in a poor way as well as we.

Nov. 22nd Fine. Tom is ploughing in Bramwell field. Wm and Vincent carted 6 loads of swedes home. I received a letter of sympathy from Miss Stubbs and answered it. The sad news came that poor Alf Wildgoose had died of malaria. So there are five dear lads who went from Sheldon have found graves in a foreign land viz

Jack Brocklehurst died of wounds on Nov. 30th 1916
Thomas Anthony Brocklehurst killed Oct. 10th 1917
George Bridden died Oct. 21st 1917 of wounds
Tony Gyte died of wounds Nov. 2nd 1917
Alfred Wildgoose died of malaria Nov. 15th 1917.

Matthew Hodgkinson cut up pig and Anthony salted it.

Nov. 23rd   Fine. Tom is ploughing in Bramwell field. Wm and Vincent are carting lime from Hurdlow. Anthony took some potatoes to the station, (Bakewell). He took little Anthony with him. We received several letters of sympathy from people. I answered two of them viz Joe Needham and Sam Bramwell. Tom finished ploughing Bramwell field. Ethel and Evelyn went to Bakewell tonight. Mr. Sherlock called here tonight. Rain and wind came on and was very rough at bed time.

Nov. 24th   Very rough winds and showers. Too rough for Wm and Vincent to cart lime so they carted 7 loads of swedes from the moor. Our Emily's birthday 24th of Nov. (aged 27 years).

Nov. 25th   Rough winds and snow storms with frost towards night. Received a letter from Pte Ernest Rawlinson who was in training with our poor Tony at Cleadon. A very nice sympathetic letter and I wrote back at once to him at Ripon. We had also a letter from Fred Bramwell. Ethel and Evelyn, Clarice and Leah went to Ashford Church tonight. Leah was sick.

Nov. 28th   Rough and wet at times. Anthony and Tom went and set out ploughing for Billy Naylor. Tom started ploughing. Thos. Hawley, Mr. Mann and Billy Naylor were in our house settling about what should be done to the Sheldon Waterworks. I wrote a letter of thanks to Mr. Roper in reply to his letter of sympathy about our poor Tony, and Mary wrote to Mr. Frank Lomas.

Nov. 30th   Very mild, dull. Ethel and Evelyn and Leah B went to Matlock to have some photos struck from Tony's, also one enlarged. Anthony went on moor helping to pull swedes. Tom Frost brought one kil of beer, 1 case Bass and 1 case Guinness. It is just one year today since poor Jack Brockley died of wounds and 4 weeks today since my poor Tony died of wounds and still the war goes on. Our men brought six loads of swedes from moor and put them through the top yard gate. The girls got back between 7 and 8. Leah brought poor Jack's enlarged photo. It is a very good one.

Dec. 2nd   Keen Frost. Awfully cold, snifting of snow. Celebration of Holy Communion in Sheldon Church (Mr. Sherlock) at 9.30. Mr. Hayward took the service this afternoon. A Memorial Service for the poor lads George Briddon who died of wounds Oct. 21st 1917 and Alfred Wildgoose who died of Malarial Fever on Nov. 15th 1917. Nellie Wildgoose, Maria and her husband and Beatrice Wildgoose were there. Cissie Robinson and Mary came from Monyash. Collection at Church amounted to 13/- for Church expenses.

Dec. 3rd   Winterly. Frosty and snifting of snow. Anthony took the milk to Longstone station and then went to the Board of Guardians meeting. Tom took the rent to Ashford. Mary went to Bakewell shopping and she paid Mr. Thacker all we owe (yesterday's as well). Mary Gregory (late Polly Bramwell) called to see and sympathise with us over our poor dear Tony. What a blow

The Devonshire Arms

Anthony and Maria Gyte with four of their children: Mary, Tom, Ethel, Emily. (This is the only photograph of Maria)

Anthony Gyte

Tony in his pram (Church of St. Michael and All Angels in the background)

Evelyn Gyte in fancy dress
(see April 6th, 1920)

Tony with John Brocklehurst

Sheldon School 1916

Key to school photograph

1	Winnie Brocklehurst	12	Kathleen Rowland	22	Jim Rowland
2	Addie Hallows	13	Charlie Brocklehurst	23	Frank Goodwin
3	Amy Brocklehurst	14	Herbert Frost	24	Clarice Bramwell
4	Vera Carson	15	Henry Frost	25	Arthur Bramwell
5	Connie Goodwin	16	Ben Sheldon	26	Jim Bramwell
6	John Frost	17	Dick Rowland	27	Mabel Hallows
7	Leslie Carson	18	Jean Brennan	28	not known
8	Clarice Goodwin	19	not known	29	Ida Ward
9	Ethel Brocklehurst	20	Betty Sherwin	30	Elsie Brocklehurst
10	Jessie Goodwin	21	Nancy Brennan	31	not known
11	Dorothy Roberts				

Alice Brocklehurst

Leah Brocklehurst

John and Leah Brocklehurst sheep shearing

John Brocklehurst working with horse   John Brocklehurst shearing sheep

John Brocklehurst, Anthony Gyte, Thomas William Brocklehurst, Tom Sheldon

The Methodist Chapel (now demolished)

John Brocklehurst on Sheepwash Bridge, Ashford-in-the-Water

Tom Gyte (left) and William Gould(?) harvesting

Tom Gyte in garden

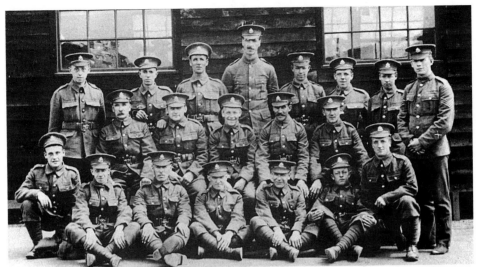

Probably Cleadon Camp, Sunderland. Tony is standing on the left

Standing left to right: Evelyn, Ethel and Mary
Gyte and (seated) Ruth and Kate Brocklehurst in
VAD uniform

Ethel Gyte wearing the Notts and
Derby brooch given to her by Tony
(*see* May 25th 1917)

Evelyn wearing the Notts and Derby
brooch

Wedding of Mary Gyte and Clement Wager, April 13th 1914
Clarice Brocklehurst, ? Wager, Ethel, Evelyn, Anthony, Emily,
Clement Wager, Mary

Clement and Mary Wager with little Anthony

Making up the 'thraves'; Tom Gyte on the left and Anthony

Harvesting in Bole Piece Field, Tom Gyte leading, Anthony behind

At the Sheldon Waterworks 'Pot Boil'
Tom Gyte, Billy Carson, Jack Naylor, Stanley Brocklehurst, ?, John Brocklehurst,
Anthony Gyte, William Brocklehurst

Mrs. Edwin Brocklehurst

James Stephenson the Lay Reader, in the doorway of Sheldon Church

A formal portrait of James Stephenson

Sheldon Church today

14

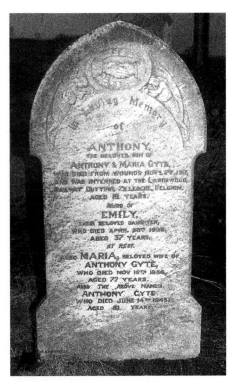

Tony's memorial stone in Larch
Wood Railway Cutting Cemetery,
Zillebeke

Tony's gravestone in Sheldon
churchyard today

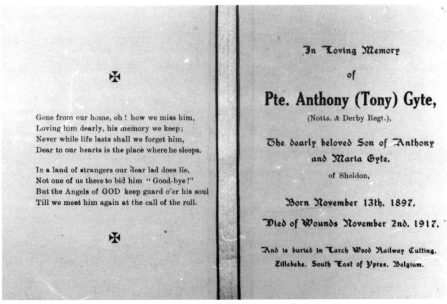

Gone from our home, oh ! how we miss him,
Loving him dearly, his memory we keep;
Never while life lasts shall we forget him,
Dear to our hearts is the place where he sleeps.

In a land of strangers our dear lad does lie,
Not one of us there to bid him " Good-bye!"
But the Angels of GOD keep guard o'er his soul
Till we meet him again at the call of the roll.

In Loving Memory

of

Pte. Anthony (Tony) Gyte,

(Notts. & Derby Regt.),

The dearly beloved Son of Anthony
and Maria Gyte,

of Sheldon,

Born November 13th, 1897,

Died of Wounds November 2nd, 1917.

And is buried in Larch Wood Railway Cutting,
Zillebeke, South East of Ypres, Belgium.

Memorial card (see entries 14, 21 and 28 October 1918)

The tablet, by William Shimwell of Youlgreave, 'which they considered very beautiful' (see November 27th 1919)

Interior of St. Michael and All Angels Church, Sheldon after the installation of the war memorial

it is for us all. Sam Bramwell is over for 10 days leave. He came home last Friday from a Military hospital at Burnley. He seems pretty well but cannot put his foot to the ground. Wm and Vincent fetched the stirks off the moor to lie in.

Dec. 5th   Finer and not quite so cold but rather raw towards night. Our Tom took 3 bags of oats to Alport Mill to be made into meal. Billy Naylor has been busy at the Sheldon Waterworks for a day or two. Wm leading manure and Vincent wheeling out lime on moor. Anthony received a letter from Mr. Hawes on behalf of the members of the Board of Guardians, a beautiful letter of sympathy on the death of our poor dear Tony. We are overcome by grief at times.

Dec. 7th   Fine. Tom is ploughing for Billy Naylor. I answered Mr. Hawes letter, also Mr. Hills, which we received yesterday. The war news has not been so good. The Germans have a third of the ground back again which we had gained from them around Cambrai. The Russians are agreeing to an armistice for a separate peace.

Dec. 9th   Cold and a thin sprinkling of snow on the ground this morning. Received a letter from the Register of Soldiers graves saying that Tony's grave had not yet been located. Mary received a PC from Clem written sometime in September. Mr. Hayward took the service in Sheldon Church. A Memorial service was held in Monyash Church for George Briddon. Tom, Ethel and Evelyn went to the service there. Our Tom was paid for the potatoes we sent by rail.

Dec. 10th Very frosty and cold. Anthony went to Bakewell and Sam Bramwell rode there with him. Sam was going to Derby Barracks, his leave was up. Lady Hartington confined of a son.

Dec. 12th Misty at first but cleared out and the sun shone. A letter of mine that I had written to Tony and one that Evelyn had written to him were returned to us. Mr. Hayward called and had tea. He told us he was leaving Ashford and going to Cornwall. Ben Handley's daughter died of appendicitis.

Dec. 13th Very dark and misty. A letter was returned that I had written to my poor dear Tony on Nov. 5th. Tom has gone ploughing for his uncle John B. I think we have so many orders for potatoes that we shall have to pause a bit and think. There is no getting anything scarcely and what a price everything is. There is such a shortage of the following articles viz. butter, bacon, tea, lard, margarine, sugar, jam, currants, raisins, candied peel, dates, figs. Eggs are 7 for two shillings.

Dec. 15th Snow. The men were sorting potatoes. Ethel and Evelyn went to Bakewell. Sam Rowland came into our house this dinner time. He arrived home about midnight last night from France. I received a letter from Ernest Rawlinson and I received one from Lizzie Bacon about my poor Tony. I wrote back to E. Rawlinson at Ripon, York. Billy Naylor brought us two cheeses (60lbs) cost £3.15.0. and was paid.

Dec. 16th Snow storms and rough. A deep snow. Hannah went to Mrs. Morton's to tea. Doris Melland went to Monyash.

Dec. 17th Awfully keen with frost and deep snow. Anthony took the milk but did not go to Bakewell. Tom and Wm went on moor for sheep and found 10 buried in snow. They brought them all home. Doris Melland did not come back last night. The men are picking potatoes and getting hay in.

Dec. 18th Keen frost and snow. The men were sorting and taking out potatoes. Some to Mr. Herbert Frosts etc. Willie Twelves called in our house tonight. He is over from France on leave for a fortnight. Our Mary and Bertha Brocklehurst went to Bakewell. Mary bought herself a new jacket. Anthony lit a fire at the Church.

Dec. 19th Frost and snow. Received a letter from Ernest Rawlinson giving his home address which is at Brimington near Chesterfield. I wrote a letter and got a little parcel of tea and cocoa ready to send to Lizzie Bacon. We also put in half a crown and Hannah one shilling. Mary baked a loaf etc. to send to Ernest Rawlinson who is at Ripon.

Dec. 21st Some rain, thawing a bit, rather rough wind. Anthony took milk and came round by Bakewell. He came back by Bakewell Moor as the roads by Dirtlow are not cut and very deep snow lies. Tom and Anthony watered the cattle as Wm and Vincent went this afternoon to Bakewell station for oat and straw and they had to come by Bakewell moor, owing to the roads not being cut on the top by Dirtlow. Mr. Sherlock called.

Dec. 23rd Rough and cold. Mr. Sherlock took the service in Sheldon Church this afternoon. Mr. Hayward left Ashford last Thursday. I hear he is going into Cornwall (St. Mervyn). Mr. Sherlock's car stuck in the snow coming this way from Crowhill Lane and he and another man had to walk to Sheldon which caused them to be late (5 mins to 3 o'clock).

Dec. 24th Some rain which took quite a lot of snow and enabled Anthony to come back by the top road (Dirtlow). This road had not been opened by the Bakewell snow cutters. Mr. Sneap came back from Bakewell with Anthony and he brought us a turkey. Anthony took Miss Broadhurst to Bakewell this morning. All beer and all intoxicants was finished tonight so we have only mineral waters for Xmas day.

Dec. 25th Xmas Day and such a sad one. My dear lad Tony was missing from the family circle first time for 20 years. Oh Dear! What a dreadful war and what awfully sad homes there are this Xmas. The worst I have ever known. No joy. No singing Xmas hymns. No decorations. The singing will be in Church. Ethel, Evelyn and Aunt H went to Church. The others stayed at home. (Collection for Church expenses 7s.10½d.) Mr. Sneap went home this morning. Anthony took him to Bakewell station. Wm Gould was paid and went off somewhere after dinner. Anthony and I have no heart for anything, only grief for our dear lost lad; and poor John and Louisa, how sad they must feel, as poor Anthony was with them as our dear boy was with us this time last year. Mr. Sherlock took the service in Church. There was celebration of Holy Communion at 9.30 in Sheldon Church. Mr. Sherlock officiated.

Dec. 26th Cold and dull at times. Young Billy Twelves went back tonight on his way to France again where he has spent nearly 3 years. We do not seem to be getting any nearer the end of this terrible war. The Russians are nothing to be depended on and the Italians are having a severe struggle to hold back the Huns. I am afraid there will be a famine before long as there seems to be no getting things for money and people are standing by thousands outside the shops in the large towns. Our Tom went to Alport for our oatmeal which he brought and it is very good. We have nothing to sell, only minerals and very few of them are left.

Dec. 27th Very cold and dull at times. Sam Bramwell went back to Derby this morning. He walked to Longstone Station on crutches. Sam Rowland was in our house. He said *Goodbye* as he has to go back to France tomorrow.

Dec. 28th Very cold and dull. Anthony took the milk to the station. It was not our turn but he took it for Thos Wm as the latter went to Manchester yesterday. Anthony went round by Bakewell to see if he could get any beer, spirits or anything to sell as we are without. (What an awfully sad and dull Xmas we have had.) He brought 2 kils of ale and 1/6 of a gal of gin. This bottle of gin cost 8/- and contains little more than a pint. Anthony is not well. He has such a headache.

Dec. 29th Very cold, snow at intervals and rough. Anthony is a little better and is putting new wires in winnowing machine riddle. A clergyman called here. He thought of seeing the hunters but they did not turn out at Sheldon. Three British destroyers have been sunk with 13 officers and 180 men.

Dec. 30th Very cold, rough winds and dull. Mr. Sherlock took the service in Church. Mary and little Anthony went also Ethel and Evelyn. We had turkey and sausage for dinner.

1918

Jan 1st   Bitterly cold, rough winds and snow storms at times. Mary made some sausage rolls and she bought a cake yesterday. She made up a parcel for E. Rawlinson which contained a cake, some sausage rolls, shortbreads, chocolate, cigarettes, an envelope with a 2/- book of stamps, money (2/6). I wrote to him and also to Miss Adams. The letters and parcel did not go tonight as no post came.

Jan. 2nd   Cold and very dull at times. Anthony went with the milk and round by Bakewell and got some treacle and salts to give to a cow of ours that is not well. Ethel and Evelyn took the parcel and letters (9) to Bakewell post office as we could not trust to anybody fetching them. I wrote to the Chaplain of the Notts and Derby about our poor Tony.

Jan. 3rd   Very frosty and cold. Vincent has been to Bakewell. He is having a bit of a holiday, as he had none last week. Mr. Ronston came and was paid up £14.17.0. We paid for mincemeat (2/-) and he owes one penny for saccharine. Jenny Brocklehurst was confined of a baby girl. Mr. Herbert Frost had a cow calved which put her belly down. They sent for Joe Johnson and Marrison and they put it up again. Mr. Sherlock called here.

Jan. 5th   Fine but cold. The annual distribution of flannel took place in the Sheldon schoolroom. Thos Wm B and Anthony gave it out. Mr. Sherlock seems to have put this duty on the churchwardens as he was not there to give it out. There were four or five taken off the usual list as the flannel is so expensive to buy.

Jan. 6th   Cold. Epiphany. There was a Celebration of Holy Communion at 9.40 by Mr. Sherlock. There were 19 communicants. Most of the licensed houses in the country were closed today. Ours was closed all day, the first time in anyone's memory. Mr. Sherlock took the service in Sheldon Church this afternoon. It was called the Intercession Service. Special prayers and lessons were used on account of this most terrible war. A collection was made which amounted to £1.0.3d. in Church. Miss Broadhurst had given 5/- before to go to the Red Cross and as the collection in Church was for the same object we shall put it to it making £1 5s. 3d. Tom called at Ashford P Office and brought a letter from Ernest Rawlinson. A very nice letter saying that he had received the parcel we sent and how very much he appreciated it.

Jan. 7th   Very severe with frost. Snow fell a little this afternoon. Anthony walked to Bakewell as Tom and Wm had to fetch some straw from the station (Bakewell) with the two horses we had sharpened. Mr. Sherlock's housekeeper called here to ask for potatoes.

Jan. 8th Another very severe frosty day. Snow storms this afternoon. The water in the pipes and radiators was frozen in Sheldon Church. Alf Brockley and Anthony covered up the one in the West end. A fire is lit every day but the weather is very severe. A cheque was sent to the fire insurance company (Wager Beardon) for our yearly payment (18.6).

Jan. 9th Very severe with frost. Snow storms at intervals. Wm fetched 2 kils of ale from station and brought mutton chops for Emily (did not pay for them). I wrote to Ernest Rawlinson (Ripon Camp) and sent him photos of our girls viz one of a group of Mary, Ethel and Evelyn in nurses uniform and one of Emily sat down with a book on her knee.

Jan. 13th Very cold and frosty snow fell at times. Mr. Stephenson took the service in Sheldon Church. He is a gardener at Church Dale and I think a very nice man. Anthony, Tom and Emily did not go to Church. Mary and little Anthony went to lie down.

Jan. 17th Snow on the ground and plenty of it. The men were lashing corn. Snowing tonight. Tom, Ethel and Evelyn went to the night school. Mr. Beaven did not come as the night was so rough. He did not attend last Monday either. Tom Riseley was in our house. They (Alf B and S. Wilton) were talking about him singing but I told them I could not do with it.

Jan. 19th Wet. The snow is nearly all gone but the ground is all sloshy. Our Mary went to Grindleford and put fires in her house. Today is little Anthony Wm Wager's birthday (3). His father has been a prisoner of war in Germany for 14 months being taken on Nov. 18/19 1916. Evelyn went to Bakewell for her music lesson and she brought little Anthony some tea things. Tom Risely went from Sheldon today to Macclesfield. His leave expires next Friday. He is a stretcher bearer in France. My letter was returned which I wrote to the chaplain of the Notts and Derby (France). Had been to Scotland.

Jan. 20th Showery and rough at times. Mr. Stephenson (lay reader) took the service in Church this afternoon and afterwards called and had tea here with me. Ethel, Evelyn, Mary and little Anthony and his granddad went to Church. Ethel and Evelyn went to Ashford Church.

Jan. 21st The wind has settled and it is a very nice mild day. Anthony took Mary and little Anthony and aunt H to Bakewell where they met the Grindleford conveyance (Goddards) and went to their home there for a time. She (Mary) sent some tea cups and saucers which I had told her to get (willow pattern). Our men were spreading manure. The *Goeben* sunk and the *Breslaw* very much shattered.

Jan. 22nd Very fine today. Jack Naylor went back early this morning to the farm he is working at in Lincolnshire. S.E. Carson has resigned being a member of the War Council. Our Evelyn went to Ashford and changed a book at the library (Grattons).

Jan. 23rd   Fine, mild. Tom is dragging on moor and Anthony gapping (walling up). The old concertina chap called after an absence of some weeks. The Misses Grover called to see me at the same time and they each gave the old man a shilling, so it was rather a good day for him 2/- at once. We received a letter of sympathy from Mr. Weadon who is in Egypt at a convalescent hospital as a nursing orderly. Mr. Sherlock called also and I let him read the letter.

Jan. 24th   Fine, mild. Tom dragging on moor. I wrote to our Mary from whom I had a letter this morning and also to Ernest Rawlinson. I feel awfully bad over the loss of my dear Tony and I can scarcely hold up when I think of him[1] my loved lad whom I shall never see in this world again. It is too dreadful to think of the thousands of grand young men who have laid down their lives in this terrible war. My sister Hannah's birthday (68). Mrs. Ed came and had tea with me.

Jan. 25th   Fine, mild. Tom dragging on moor. We had a very nice letter from France from Shrewsbury our poor Tony's chum when in training at Cleadon. Anthony took some swedes to Miss Grover (1s.6d.), she did not pay.

Jan. 26th   Fine, rather rough winds at times. Two post cards came from Clem this morning, one for Anthony and I, and one for Mary. I sent them and Shrewsbury's letter to Mary. Mr. Stephenson lay reader (who is a gardener at Church Dale) visited many of the people of Sheldon today. He called to see us here and had a cup of tea. I had a nice conversation with him and he brought me a book to read called *The Student in Arms*. Evelyn went to Bakewell for her music lesson and Emily's medicine and she called at Skidmore's shop and brought ½ lb thick twist, ½ lb thin twist and half pound of tobacco in packets which came to 11s.3d. She did not pay for it. PC Dennis brought us ½ lb tea tonight.

Jan. 30th   Misty at first but clears out later on. I wrote about Tony's photos. We have not a drop of beer or spirits in the house to sell. Mr. Sherlock, Mrs. Poe and a Mrs. Rowbotham called to see me. Mrs. Poe brought me a book to read: *A lame dog's diary.*

Feb. 1st   Fine on our hills but misty Ashford and Bakewell way, raw and cold. Tom and Wm are ploughing for Thos Wm Brockley (2 teams). Tom with Heathcote and Navvy and Wm with old Naylor and the old gray mare. Mr. Hartopp and Mr. Teddy Fearn called here and had lunch, bread and cheese and tea and a bit of oatcake. Everything in the food line is so scarce and I am afraid it will be scarcer still. I had a nice long talk with Mr. Hartopp about the war and our poor dear Tony's death. I received a very nice letter from E. Rawlinson and I wrote to Shrewsbury. I also received a letter from Mr. Statham about Tony's photos.

---

1   At this point on the page the ink is blotched

Feb. 3rd   Fine. There was a celebration of Holy Communion at 9.30 this morning. Mr. Sherlock officiated. Mr. Stephenson took the service this afternoon. Collection 10/- for Church expenses.

Feb. 5th   Very fine. Tom and Wm are gone ploughing for Thos Wm Brockley. This morning the photos of our poor Tony came this morning, also a letter from Fred Bramwell, and one from Fred Brockley to our Emily.

Feb. 6th   Rough winds this morning. Wm Gould went for 2 kils of ale to Bakewell station (Burton ale). Anthony tapped the beer (one) as soon as it came. Thos Brockley and Billy Naylor soon came for a drink. Mrs. Smith swept two of our chimneys. She charged 9 pence each. Kitchen and houseplace.

Feb. 7th   Rather rough. Fine. Tom is ploughing for Carsons. Two men brought a furniture van and took Beatrice Wildgoose's furniture to Darley Dale. One of the men's name was Allen. He had four sons in the war and two of them are killed. Tom has made two picture frames and is varnishing them when he has time. We have packed up a parcel for our Mary to go by tonight's post a bit of bacon, butter, tea, sugar and two eggs. Emily's finger which has been gathering bursted today.

Feb. 10th   Very rough winds and showery at times. We had a hare for dinner (one that Tom shot a few days ago). Anthony, Ethel and Evelyn went to Church this afternoon. Mr. Stephenson took the service and he afterwards called to see Mr. Wm Brocklehurst. He did not call here today. Our Tom has a very sore ringworm on his neck.

Feb. 11th   Rather showery at times, but the wind has quietened down a lot. Anthony took the milk and then went to Bakewell. Evelyn took the school bank books to have them balanced at the savings bank. Tom Slater (Flewitts man) had a horse down with a load of corn. Tom, Wm, Vincent and others assisted him in getting it up.

Feb. 12th   Shrove Tuesday. Nice and mild during the day. Rain came on at night. Tom and Wm took a team of horses each and were ploughing for Thos. Wm Brockley (Kirkdale). Tom and others from Sheldon went to Monyash to a concert tonight. Dr. Burne and Dr. Manver (Youlgreave) were singing, conjuring etc. My poor Tony went to a concert at Monyash last Shrove Tuesday and now he lies in a foreign grave. Some things were brought to our house from Mr. J. Frost's. I wrote to our Mary and to Ernest Rawlinson. I sent Ernest one of Tony's photos. I am not well today (cold and cough).

Feb. 13th   Very misty and drizzly. A letter came from Register of Graves enquiry office saying that our Tony was reported buried South East of Ypres, North of Hollebeke. Ethel is baking oatcake. Yesterday was the reassembling of Parliament. The King's speech. Some dissatisfaction of Mr. Lloyd George's methods about the war. Russia has quite given up fighting. Wm Gould fetched us a load of coal.

Feb. 14th Very misty. Tom and Wm were ploughing for Thos Wm Brockley. I had a letter from Ernest Robinson who is still at Ripon. Tom, Ethel and Evelyn attended the night school. Tom has finished two photo frames (fret work) and varnished them. Mr. Beaven was quite pleased with them. Valentine's day. Not much like times gone by when such fun used to be got out of sending people comic valentines. I have had such pain all over me today. My cold seems a little better.

Feb. 15th Fine, but very dull. Fred Brockley sent word to their folks that he had landed at Dover and is being sent to Liverpool. He had been gassed a week or two ago. Miss Grover called here with the magazine and paid for the swedes she had of us. I gave her some oatcake to take back with her.

Feb. 16th Fine and dry a frosty air. Read in paper of a German naval raid in Straits of Dover. Six or seven trawlers etc. were sunk and the German ships got back safely it is said. This afternoon Mr. Stephenson (lay reader) came and brought some of his friends to see me viz. Mr. and Mrs. Goodwin and a young soldier who used to be with him (Mr. Stephenson) at a place before he came as gardener to Mr. Fairholm, Churchdale hall. Mr. Goodwin is organist at Heath Church. Mr. Stephenson has been most kind in getting a friend of his to make enquiries about my poor Tony. This friend is a vicar. Mr. Stephenson brought a letter which he has received from his friend which is as follows:

> Feb.5th 1918
>
> Dear Sir,
>
> With reference to your letter asking about Pte. A. Gyte 79156 17 Sher.For. I have this day seen his company officer and the stretcher bearer who took Gyte to Clearing Station. The boy did not live long after he was wounded. He was hit in stomach, leg and arm. He was taken to the Casualty Clearing Station but I think did not live long nor was able to speak much. Gyte is buried in Bodmin Copse near Ypres. This is all that can be said. If Gyte's mother would like a photograph of the grave she should send particulars to The Director of Graves and Enquiries War Office Winchester House St. James Sq. London WC
>
> They will give what she desires, as periodically they come to take such photographs.
>
> Yours truly,
>
> J.A.A. Baker CF
> (17th Sherwood For.)

I felt awful when Mr. Stephenson gave me this letter. I gave way to my grief. Evelyn went to Bakewell and paid Mr. Thacker £2.5s.5d. all we owe him for, this morning's as well.

Feb. 17th Very frosty but very fine with sunshine. Mr. Sherlock took the service in Church this afternoon. Jenny Brockley's baby was christened (Marjorie) Tom, Ethel and Evelyn went to Church. Tom Critchlow and

Prince who used to keep the Lion at Monyash were in our house tonight. We had a full house. Jenny Brockley's brother and Tom Ridgway were here as well. George Brennan was in. He landed today from France.

Feb. 19th Very frosty and very dull later in the day. Wm Gould fetched coal for the Church. Anthony and others are gone fox hunting this afternoon. He was seen in Sheldon moor plantation this morning. We sent our Mary some sugar etc. and I wrote to the Director of Graves.

Feb. 20th Fine first thing. Tom and Wm went to Flewitts thresher and brought straw and oats back. I had a letter from Ernest Rawlinson saying that if he could get leave he would come up to see us next Monday. I wrote back to him. Tom Hannaford and another chap called today. They had come from France on leave. Mr. Sherlock called and had tea. Rain came on this afternoon. Mr. Stephenson took the service in school. He called here and had a chat.

Feb. 22nd Very rough winds. We received two letters from the War Office. One from the Director of Graves and another saying that the affairs of our dear Tony had been got all ready and a form was sent for Anthony to fill up in the presence of a minister or a magistrate. Received some fish and a letter from our Mary. Wm and Vincent are lashing corn and getting the calf place ready for calves. Mr. Sherlock called tonight after service in school and signed the paper that came about our poor Tony.

Feb. 23rd Drizzling rain first thing, afterwards dull but milder and not as rough. I received a very nice letter from Mrs. Rawlinson (Ernest's mother) saying that Ernest would come over to see us on Monday next starting from Chesterfield at 6.40 morning. Tom lit an oil stove and put it in the turnip place to dry it a little. Evelyn went to Bakewell for her music lesson. Mr. Thacker only sent us 4lbs of meat today. Sidney Brocklehurst was in our house tonight. He had come over from Sheffield to see his father who is very ill. I am not well, very downhearted. I cannot get over the loss of our poor Tony.

Feb. 24th Drizzling showers at times, finer afterwards. Mr. Stephenson took the service in Church this afternoon. He called to see Mr. Brockley and Mrs. Ed but did not call here today.

Feb. 25th Cold but fine. Anthony went to Bakewell with Fanny and dog cart to meet Ernest Rawlinson who got to the station at 8.20. He arrived at Sheldon just after nine. He seems a nice lad, like our poor Tony in his ways and is not 21 until the 9th of May next. I was very upset today thinking about my dear lad and Ernest being in training together at Cleadon, Sunderland and now our poor Tony lies in a foreign grave. Ernest went back by the last train which left Longstone at 9.2. Ethel and Evelyn went with him to the station. He took back with him a cake, a bit of cheese and a few eggs. Our girls also gave him a box of nice cigarettes.

Feb. 26th Very rough winds and every room in the house seems full of smoke which damps down. The Russians have made a complete surrender to the Germans having made peace on the German terms, so it says in the paper. Ernest Rawlinson had to go back to Ripon today. We had no customers in the house tonight.

Feb. 27th Mild but very dull, looking like rain. Vincent Hallows is still at home poorly. I sent him a bit of bacon, an egg or two and a bit of oat meal. Wm Gould took the horse and went down to the Pot Boil at the Sheldon waterworks to fill in some place where the water had burst. Mr. Stephenson called here and brought me two more books.

Feb. 28th Bitterly cold rough winds and snowstorms at intervals. Mr. Beaven did not come as it was such an awful rough night and such snowstorms. There were 7 present at night school. I received a letter from Mrs. Rawlinson and I wrote back to her tonight.

March 1st A very rough day. Very cold and intervals of snow. Our Tom had a letter to appear before the medical board (Derby) on March 5th. Anthony is writing to Mr. H. Shimwell today about it. Anthony has been with the milk for 3 or 4 mornings as TW Brockley's horse is lame. Mary sent some herrings and says they are coming to Sheldon all being well next Monday. The first lamb was born (Alf Brocklehurst) in Sheldon. I wrote to our Mary. Mr. Sherlock came up to the school and took the service.

March 3rd Most bitterly cold and snifting of snow at intervals. There was a celebration of Holy Communion in Sheldon Church at 9.30 this morning. Mr. Sherlock officiated. Mr. Stephenson took the service this afternoon. Collection for Church expenses (6s.7d.). Mr. Stephenson called here and had tea. We had a paper from Mr. Shimwell to fill up about Tom. Anthony and I filled it up.

March 4th Very dull and dark but calmer and milder. Anthony took the milk again as we have been doing all last week except Monday. He took the form about Tom to be signed either by Mr. Flewitt or Mr. Hartopp. Mr. Flewitt signed it.

March 5th Very misty, raw and cold. Our Tom went by the 9.25 from Bakewell to Derby and went before the medical board (St. Augustines). He was passed for grade one and got back early tonight.

March 6th A miserable misty raw cold day. Our Evelyn's birthday (23). Mr. Sherlock called in and had tea. Mr. Stephenson called before he took the service in school. Mr. Sherlock left 6d for our Evelyn to buy a doll for her birthday. Mr. Stephenson brought another letter from the Director of Graves.

March 8th Quite a snow and snowing at intervals during the day. We have had 5 cows calved this week; two cow-calves and 3 bull calves. Mr. Sherlock took the service in school tonight. Wilf Goodwin was fast with his cart with green groceries down the dale. Anthony and Wm took old Naylor down Hunterside with the intention of helping him up but when they got down Wilf and his father had gone up Kirkdale and on the flat. Received a letter from E. Rawlinson.

March 9th   Beautiful sunshine this morning which melted a lot of snow. Tom Frost brought us a 36 gal of ale from Ormes and our Tom fetched one kil of Burton from Bakewell station. I wrote to Ernest Rawlinson who is at Sunderland. Mr. Stephenson and his daughter called and had tea with me and a nice conversation. Charlie Brocklehurst came out of France to see his father.

March 10th   Very fine and mild. Mr. Stephenson took the service in Church this afternoon. Miss Stephenson came up with him, called to see Anthony about the Easter collection. Mr. Wm Brocklehurst is very low indeed tonight.

March 11th   Very fine. Wm Gould sat up all last night thinking a cow would calve. She calves a cow-calf this morning. Poor old Mr. Brocklehurst died this morning at quarter to 8 after being in bed 3 years on the 19th January last. Mrs. Craven is ill and Dr. Jackson has been attending her. Gertie Brocklehurst is ill and Dr. T. Fentem attends her.

March 13th   A lovely day. A cow calved (cow calf) this morning after Anthony had sat up all night. Tom and Wm are gone with corn to Flewitts thresher. They brought back the straw and 24 stones of oats. Received a letter from Mrs. Rawlinson.

March 14th   Very cold wind in NE. Mr. Wm Brocklehurst was buried today at 2.30. All his sons and all his daughters were at funeral. Ernest, Tom, Charlie, Sid and Alf and three of his daughters in law, Florence, Hannah (Sid's wife) and Jenny. Mr. Sherlock and Mr. Stephenson were at the funeral. All old uncles and sons were in our house tonight and George Brocklehurst. Anthony read the will to the brothers and sisters as he is one of the executors. Mr. Sherlock and Mr. Stephenson called to see me. We had an official letter saying what Anthony was entitled to about our poor Tony.

March 15th   A very raw cold day. Anthony received a P. office order for 6 guineas which belonged to our poor dear Tony. Fancy a life for that sum. Oh dear! My poor lad to think of it. We have not received a thing which belonged to him. He had a watch, money belt, photos etc. but none comes to us. Joe Johnson has been to look at a calf of ours which Anthony thinks has joint evil. Mr. Sherlock called tonight. Wm fetched artificial manure from Bakewell. Mr. Johnson bought the calf for 30/-.

March 17th   A very nice day, rather cold winds. We let Mrs. Ed B have 2½ lbs of pork as they had not a bit of anything for dinner. Mr. Sherlock took the service in Church.

March 18th   Fine first thing, showery later on. Anthony went to market, and to a meeting (Farmers union) which commenced at 2 o'clock. The meeting was very well attended by farmers from districts all around

Bakewell, and farmers were proposed and seconded to look after the interests of their own villages. Alf Brocklehurst proposed John Frost and Anthony seconded. Some other farmer proposed Anthony Gyte and so there are two for Sheldon. Our Anthony proposed Walter Needham for Middleton by Youlgreave. The subscriptions were up to a pound and as low as 5/- or at the rate of one penny per acre. Mr. Cutts addressed the meeting which was considered to be a very successful one. Anthony changed the PO Order for £6.6s. which was the money said to be owing to my poor Tony when he died of wounds. Mary went to Bakewell and bought 9 yds of silk (black) for the girls blouses, and some lace.

March 19th Very showery but mild. I received a letter from Ernest Rawlinson. Sam Bramwell went back to Leeds hospital after spending a week at home. Thos Wm Brocklehurst and Clarice went to Liverpool to see Fred (came back tonight). We have 8 lambs up to this afternoon. Two more lambs came tonight. The exemption paper came for two dogs.

March 21st A very lovely day. Our men were leading swedes from moor to home. We have 12 lambs up to date. Miss Stephenson called and had tea. She also went to Church with Evelyn to practise. We sent a P order for 4s.6d. for Sheldon Church fire insurance. Also a cheque for Proctor and Rylands together with a £1 note. We sent a receipt to Chatsworth for one pound which was sent for Church expenses. The night school finished for this season.

March 22nd A most lovely day, dry and plenty of sunshine. The men are leading swedes from moor. Ethel and Evelyn took me out in our chair. Today is the first time I have been out of doors since a long time before my poor Tony died. I went into the churchyard and then called to see John and Louisa. The German offensive began on the western front yesterday on a front of 50 miles before the British. We have neither spirits nor beer to sell. Our Tom had a paper to fill up over the army.

March 23rd Another grand day. We received our poor Tony's things. Letters and photos, wallet, belt, scarf, 3 religious books, 11 stamps. His watch did not come and there was no money in belt. I received a letter from Mr. Stephenson and a card with very appropriate verses on it. The weather was so fine that I sat at the house door in my rickshaw for a bit. Arthur Millington and Tom Hawley (Jun) were in our house tonight. They had ginger ale to drink as we have neither beer nor spirits. Ethel and Evelyn went to Bakewell. The war news is very serious for us as it is reported *The Germans have penetrated our lines for 8 miles.* Put on the clock one hour when going to bed. Received a letter from Mrs. Rawlinson.

March 24th Very fine and sunny. Evelyn was not so well this morning (bilious) and Mary played in Church. Mr. Stephenson took the service and afterwards called here but did not stay as he was going to see Mrs. James Frost who is very ill. A lot of men were fox hunting. They saw one or two foxes but did not kill them. I think one of them was in the Winckets. Our girls took me in my chair up the fields in Croft Heads to see lambs after service.

March 25th Fine but cold. The wind has got into the East. Anthony took the milk and went forward to Bakewell. He went to the Guardians meeting and also to a farmers meeting which was held at the Peacock. We sent a parcel to E. Rawlinson. I sent a letter to Mrs. Rawlinson. There was a service in school. Mr. Stephenson called here. The Germans are forcing us back and are taking a many of our men prisoners. Everybody seems very anxious and downhearted.

March 29th Cold, but dry and fine. Mr. Sherlock took the service in Church as it is Good Friday. There was no surplice as they had sent them to Ashford to be washed. Albert Wager told Anthony this morning that Tom Wager had been wounded. This is the second time and he was sent back to France last January. Mary went to Longstone and got back just after 9 o'clock.

March 30th Wet. Anthony, Tom and Wm took the oats on the moor with the intention of sowing but it rained so they put them in the cabin. They brought hay back from moor and were all wet through. Mr. and Miss Stephenson brought flowers and evergreens to decorate the Church. Mr. Stephenson filled the vases and Ethel, Clarice, Evelyn, Leah and Alice put moss (which they had got last night) in the windows. Miss Stephenson came and had tea with me. Mr. Stephenson called and brought Anthony and I something in an envelope which we were not to open until tomorrow.

March 31st Very showery. Celebration of Holy Communion at 9.50. Mr. Sherlock and Mr. Stephenson came in a motor and there were 23 Sheldon communicants. Mr. Stephenson took the service in the afternoon and there was a good congregation. Collection for the vicar amounted to £1.6.8½. Miss Stephenson sang alone (*I know that my Redeemer liveth*) and people appreciated it very much. Mr. and Miss Stephenson did not call here today. We opened the envelope and found a very nice card with suitable verses. Ethel and Evelyn went to Ashford Church tonight. Tom went to Monyash. Last Easter Sunday my poor Tony was here and went to Longstone at night.

April 1st Very showery. Anthony and Tom are gone to the fair. Alf Brockley had his calling up papers. Last week was a week of very unfavourable war news. The Germans massed and hurled tremendous divisions at the British Front for about 50 miles. They pressed us back. This morning there is a bit more favourable news as we seem holding them. General Foch is now in chief command over the armies on the Western Front. Our Tom and Billy Carson went to Monyash tonight to a whist drive and dance. Ethel went to Bakewell fair this afternoon.

April 2nd Showery at times and at times plenty of nice sunshine. Our Tom came back from Monyash this morning. It was about half past four. Mary was baking custards for the social tonight. Mr. Stephenson called to see me on his way to the schoolroom and recited a piece or two to me. The social began about 7.30 and was a great success. Mr. Sherlock, the Misses Grover, Mr. and Miss Stephenson, and others came. Mr. Sherlock sang a song, also Mr. Stephenson sang and recited. Miss Stephenson sang three. The others who took part in the singing were Mrs. Rebecca Ward, Miss F. Goodwin, Miss Clarice Brocklehurst, our Mary, Miss K Brocklehurst. A Dialogue went off very well. It was called *An Unexpected Entertainment*. The characters were Miss F. Goodwin, Miss E.A. Brocklehurst, Miss Clarice Brocklehurst, Miss Ruth Brocklehurst, Miss Hilda Carson and Miss Ethel Gyte. The refreshments were given by the various people in the village. There was plenty of food such as sandwiches (potted meat), cake, custard, bread and butter and tea and cocoa to drink. Some people gave sugar, tea, cocoa, milk and there was enough for all the people and children who attended. Mr. Sherlock made a good speech about Mr. Stephenson and Mr. Stephenson replied. Mr. Thos Brocklehurst and Mrs. Smith recited. Mr. Sherlock called and signed our sugar application form. Mr. Stephenson paid me 4s.6d. for Mr. Alfred Fewkes tuning piano at school.

April 3rd Very frosty first thing. The weather has been frosty for several mornings and later rain has fallen. Our Mary and the others have been making up the Church accounts. Mary has entered everything and kept the Church accounts for two years. A vestry meeting took place at 4 o'clock. Mr. Sherlock gave the Easter collection £1.6.8½d. towards Evelyn's salary as organist. The Duke's agent has not sent the £5.0.0. he annually sends to Sheldon for organist and Sunday School. The Vicar called here and he and Anthony went to the Church where they were joined by Mr. Thos Wm Brocklehurst. These three were the only ones present, so after ringing the bell they came up to our house where the accounts were audited. The balance in hand of Sheldon Church is £9.13.9. The churchwardens are Mr. A. Gyte and Mr. Thos Wm Brocklehurst as there was no opposition. Mr. Sherlock signed our sugar paper.

April 4th Fine but cold. Evelyn received a very nice letter from Mr. Stephenson about the social and offering to give a snapshot to each of the choirgirls of himself and Miss Stephenson.

April 5th Very fine and sunny, cold as wind is in East. Our men (Anthony, Tom, Wm) have gone on moor. Tom is sowing oats (the first oats of ours to be sown this year). Anthony is dragging and Wm is harrowing after Tom. Today's paper says *The Germans have started another offensive and have pressed back a little the British and French.* What with the awful war and the cost of living it is dreadful. People are not able to get necessities for money. It is very hard for poor men to do their daily heavy work; some of them can only get bread and treacle and a bit of margarine. Eggs are 7 for 2 shillings. Treacle 1.2d. per lb, bacon 2s.4d. or 2s.6d. per lb., coffee 2s.2d. Everything seems to be rising in price and I am sure the flour is simply rubbish. I eat more oatcake than ever I did in my life before. Mr. and Miss Stephenson called in to see us.

April 6th Very wet all day. Mary went to Grindleford with Johnson. She started from Ashford at half past seven this morning. There was a letter for her at the Grindleford post office and it contained a photo of Clem and four Russian comrades in a group. He said how sorry he feels over our poor dear Tony's death. When she brought the photo back with her tonight we showed it to those in the house. Ruth Brocklehurst agreed to be cleaner etc. of Sheldon Church.

April 7th Showery. Thos Wm Brocklehurst went with milk and called at Ashford P Office for letters. There was one for me from Pte G.E. Shrewsbury who was a chum of my Tony's being in training with him at Cleadon and going across with him and Ernest to France. Shrewsbury used to be called Dick by the other two and he would like a photo of my dear lad. Mr. Sherlock took the service in Church. Anthony shewed Ruth B how to do with the heating apparatus and lighting of fire.

April 8th A lovely day. The men did not sow as the ground was too wet. Mr. and Miss Stephenson called here tonight. I wrote to Clem and Shrewsbury. Sent the latter Tony's photo.

April 9th Very dull and misty. Tom and Wm took a dray load of corn to be threshed at Flewitts and had to do nearly all the work themselves. They brought 82 stones of oats back with them. Anthony cut some of the older lambs' tails, belted the hogs and took them on moor. We have 25 lambs up to date. The girls are clearing out and looking over my Tony's things. I cannot look at anything of his just yet as my grief is as fresh as ever. My dear lad always used to play on the harmonium the hymn *THY way not mine, O Lord*. I have not heard a hymn played on it since Tony died. I cannot bear it yet. Mary Jane Stephenson (formerly Hawley) received a letter from her husband last week. He is a prisoner in Germany and she has mourned him as dead for nearly 8 months. Mr. Lloyd George introduces the *Man Power Bill*. Hetty Wager went to see her brother Tom at a hospital in Guildford Surrey.

April 10th A very misty, wet and cold day: rough winds. Our girls did the top in big bedroom and papered part of the room where the bed goes. Mr. Stephenson called here tonight. Received a letter from Ernest Rawlinson.

April 11th Misty first thing: very rough and cold. Mr. Sherlock sent a letter enclosing £5 in £1 notes which he said was the Duke of Devonshire's subscription to the Sheldon organist's stipend and to the Sheldon Sunday School, three pounds to the former and 2 pounds to the latter. This subscription has come before the Easter Vestry meeting other years but had not been received this year so the books were made up without, therefore it will go in this year's account from Easter 1918. Thos. Wm Brocklehurst keeps the Sunday School funds. The Germans are pushing us back. Evelyn took £2 notes to her uncle Thos. Wm Brkly.

April 12th Very misty and dull. Mr. Sherlock came up with the intention of holding a service but he found out that he had not given notice so he did not hold one. He called here and sat and chatted with a few who were in the house about the war.

April 13th Very misty and cold. I received a letter saying that my poor Tony's grave had been registered and a wooden cross was put over it. We are very pleased his grave has been located. Mr. and Miss Stephenson called here and had tea.

April 14th Very rough and cold, wind in N. East. Mr. Stephenson called here before he took the service in Church. We have now 26 lambs off 18 sheep. How our poor Tony used to look after the sheep and now he lies at rest in a foreign grave and what thousands have laid down their lives since he died and still we are in a most grave position in regard to the war as the Germans keep forcing us back on the Western front.

April 15th Very rough and cold. About half past 4 this morning George Eaton called Anthony up and borrowed a horse and float to fetch Mrs. Fanny Thorpe. Before they got to Sheldon Elsie was confined of a baby girl.

April 16th Rough N. East winds. I wrote to Ernest and Mrs. Rawlinson. The girls colour washed the staircase and baked oatcake. Just one year ago my Tony was dressed in Khaki. He went to Derby on the 16th of April 1917 and came back at night dressed in uniform.

April 17th Bitterly cold and rough winds. One year since today our poor Tony was drafted to Cleadon. Mr. Stephenson called to see me. The girls whitewashed and cleaned the pantry.

April 19th Very frosty and cold. Our mere was frozen over.. The war is still going on very unfavourable for us on the Western front. The French are fighting and General Foch is in supreme command. Mr. Stephenson sent me some very nice verses by post. Mr. Sherlock took a service in Sheldon Church but it was soon over as it was so dark. Mr. Stephenson called tonight.

April 21st Very cold and wet. Mr. Stephenson took the service in Church. Anthony, Tom, Ethel, Evelyn, Mary and little Anthony went to Church. We heard tonight that Mrs. Sherwin had official news that her husband (Jack) was *missing*. Boden (marble works) was in our house tonight. We sold out all the beer. It is 39 years today since I came to live at Sheldon.

April 22nd A better day today, plenty of sun. If the wind would change from the quarter it is in (NE) I think we should soon have some grass and we should be able to go on with sowing etc. The Allied Armies on the Western front are stopping the German advance. Anthony went to market and Mary has gone to get the meat tickets for Anthony, Tom and Wm for extra rations. The Military Service Act calls upon all youths from 19 to 23 to send in their exemption certificates.

April 23rd Fine but very dull and dark today. Our girls began cleaning their room (what we used to call the cheese room). They did the top and papered one side. Mary helps them very well. Aunt H is honeycombing Ethel's new white dress.

April 24th A most lovely day. The wind is mostly in the NE. Our stirks lay out for the first time this year in the fields at home. Anthony fetched 1 ton of seed potatoes (King Edwards) from Bakewell station. Mr. Stephenson called to see us tonight. He wanted some eating potatoes but we have sold what we have to spare. Read in paper that our naval men made raids on Zeebrugge and Ostend with the intention of blocking them (the U Boats). They sank some of our own old cruisers which were filled with concrete. These raids happened last night and our casualties were reported as being very heavy. It was considered a brilliant affair and gave great satisfaction. Fred Brocklehurst came on 10 days leave. We have 28 lambs and 7 calves up to this date.

April 25th Another lovely day. Tom went to sow Bramwell field and Anthony went to help him later on. The girls are clearing Wm's room and they are putting new oil cloth in their room. Read in paper that the Germans have taken another place nearer Amiens. Lizzie Simpson and Edna and little Arthur came from Tideswell to see us. She was put about over our poor Tony as she was living at our house when he was born (Nov. 13th, 1897) and she was so good to him when a baby and nursed him so well. Ethel and Evelyn went to Longstone station with them tonight. Mr. Sherlock called and had tea.

April 26th Very fine. A lovely day. Another lamb (29) and another calf today. Girls cleaned the bar. Just one year today since my Tony came from Cleadon (until May 10th). He had been vaccinated and had such a cold. Whittakers brought mineral waters (£2.3s.0d.). Mr. Sherlock took a service in Church.

April 28th Very fine and sunny but rather rough NE winds. Mary received 3 postcards from Clem. In one he says he is going to be removed from Limberg into Holland. I received a letter from Mrs. Rawlinson. Mr. Sherlock took the service in Church and read the bishop's letter on the military service of clergymen. There has been no water in the taps for two or three days and it makes it so heavy to have to fetch every drop from anywhere you can get it. A year ago our poor Tony was at home from Cleadon. Anthony saw the first swallow of this year on the moor.

April 29th Very cold NE winds. Anthony took two bull calves, one that had been born without a tail, and another. The one without a tail made £2.18s.0d. and the other £3.0.0.. Ethel and Evelyn went to Bakewell and bought new black hats for them and Emily 8s.11d., 9s.5d., 8s.5d. Had a letter from Ernest Rawlinson.

April 30th Very cold. East winds continue. Our men are getting the fallow ground ready. I wrote to Ernest and Mrs. Rawlinson. We have 31 lambs and are milking 25 cows. Eggs are 4 a shilling.

May 1st   Cold. Snifting of snow this morning. Anthony went to Bakewell Station and brought 2 kils of ale, one to be sold at 4d. per pint and the other at 5d. per pint. Sheldon children went round with a May Pole. Our girls cleaned my bedroom. Mr. Stephenson called and brought Evelyn a photo in frame of his daughter Mabel.

May 2nd   Very misty. No sunshine. The men are getting the fallow ready. The girls have cleaned the staircase and passage. Hannah ironed my bed hangings. It is just six months (calendar) since my Tony died only it was on the Friday Nov. 2nd 1917.

May 3rd   Dull and cold. Anthony went to Bakewell station for some seed potatoes (Great Scots) which Mr. Froggatt had sent. Mr. Sherlock called here after service in Church. Miss Broadhurst came here with a letter she had received from Dr. T. Fentem about the children's coughs. Fred Brocklehurst went back from his sick leave. We turned our milk cows out during the day but let them stay in at night.

May 4th   Wet and misty first thing but turns out a most lovely day, grand sunshine and the wind is in S West. Mr. Stephenson called and had tea with me. Our men heard the cuckoo but I did not hear it. We heard that Ben Roberts (Taddington) had been killed in action.

May 5th   Dull first thing but turns out wet tonight. Mr. Stephenson took the service in Church. He brought a young youth named Allan Marsden with him and they called here and had tea. There was a collection in Church for the Diocesan fund (18s.8d.) which was made up to 19s.0d.

May 7th   Dull. Anthony took the young mare (Wager) to meet Beswick's horse at Longstone. Received a letter from Pte Shrewsbury who is over in England on leave as his wife and child have had pneumonia. Mr. Sherlock came up to see the schoolmistress but she had gone off somewhere.

May 8th   Cold first thing wind N. West gets warmer later on. Our men and Jimmy and Charley are busy setting potatoes. They set 10 rows of Irish up-to-dates above the pit hole in Grindlow Knoll and 5 rows of Great Scots below the pit hole. Mary, little Anthony, Aunt H and myself have colds. Mary and Anthony (little) have awful coughs. I hear that Miss Broadhurst has closed the school owing to some children having whooping cough. A year ago my poor Tony was here getting ready to go to Cleadon on the 10th of May. Mr. Stephenson called and brought me two views of Heath Church (old and new) also recipes for coughs. He read me letters from the mothers of poor boys who have fallen in this detestable war. We heard that Sam Brocklehurst (Potteries) had been killed.

May 10th   Very fine. Hot sun. The wind seems in N West. Last year on May 10th my Tony left home for Cleadon (to train). Poor lad he did not like the army and felt awful at leaving home. The men are gone potato setting in Grindlow Knoll. Ethel and Evelyn are gone to Matlock to fetch Tony's enlarged photos. They were catching the 1.22 train from Bakewell. Lloyd

George wins a majority in Commons over General Maurice's letter. Carson's young horse has got lockjaw. Anthony has been helping to give it a drink. Our men were setting potatoes. Ethel and Evelyn got back between 9 and 10 tonight bringing Tony's photos which are very good. I was quite upset and could not look at them closely.

May 11th Fine. Our men were setting potatoes, Mayfield Blossoms (7 rows). Carson's young horse died this morning and Joe Johnson fetched it. Joe Carson said it had twisted bowels and bad kidneys. Received a letter from Mrs. Rawlinson. Mr. Stephenson called and had tea. He brought me some lemons, matches and pansies. The last named were set in my Tony's garden (border). Rain came on just after five o'clock (nice shower). The Misses Grover called (magazines).

May 12th Fine. Mr. Stephenson took the service in Church. Anthony's foot is bad (on the top). He cut an old shoe so that it would not press on it as it looks like gathering. He has also got a little Erysyphalis (sic) in his nose. A notice went up that there would be a meeting on Monday to discuss Mrs. Carson's loss (signed by A. Brocklehurst). Mrs. Ed was taken bad this afternoon.

May 13th Showery today. We fetched three pigs, 2 hogs and 1 gelt from Billy Naylor's. They cost £3.5s.0d. each and five shillings for luck.

May 14th Dull and looks like rain. Our men have been leading and manuring rows for potatoes. Jimmy Rowland and Charley Brocklehurst are big men helping to knock manure in rows etc. I made out a paper about Mrs. Carson's losses. Thos. Wm. Brocklehurst and Alf Brocklehurst went round collecting in Sheldon. Several gave a pound each, others 10 shillings and some 5/-. Our girls cleaned the Houseplace. Our Tom fetched Dr. Fentem to Mr. Ed Brocklehurst.

May 16th Very fine. Hot sun. I think it has been the finest day this year so far. Our men have finished setting potatoes. We have 40 rows. We set Mr. Ed's as he is poorly though improving. Mary and Ethel took me down Johnson lane in my chair to where I could see Grindlow Knoll. I saw our little pigs for first time.

May 17th Very fine. Tom has been chain harrowing. Tom and Wm leading manure for swedes etc. Anthony getting twitch out. Mary has gone to Bakewell to do a bit of shopping. Mr. Sherlock called here tonight.

May 19th Very fine. There was a celebration of Holy Communion in Sheldon Church this morning. Mr. Sherlock officiated. Mr. Stephenson took the service this afternoon. He and Miss Stephenson called here after staying to tea at Alf Brocklehurst's. I sat outside for a bit. A collection in Church for Church expenses (18s.7d.). Little Anthony had a new suit on today.

May 22nd A lovely day but very close. The men were doing various things, leading manure and sowing artificial. Anthony and Tom sowed 32 rows of swedes; we have 54 rows sown now. Mary, Evelyn, Aunt H and little Anthony went on moor to fetch the sheep and lambs home. A lady and gentleman called here this dinner time. They were from Nottingham and came here last year. She said she was 46 and I told her she looked about 30.

May 23rd Very early this morning there was a thunderstorm and rain fell. On getting up the rain came down in torrents at times and it keeps rumbling of thunder. The sheep in Sheldon were taken to Ashford and washed. Anthony, Tom and others got very wet. Anthony wrote to Mr. Shimwell about the rookery behind Mr. Tinsley's. We have had another cheese, more milk in it. This makes 7 cheeses we have had in all. Mr. Stephenson called here.

May 25th Dull. Our men were gardening. Finished the garden next to stackyard and began the other. Wm emptied tank. Mrs. Campbell (formerly Miss Evans of the butter classes) came to Sheldon and gave a demonstration in making Peakland cheese. The girls took me up to school in my chair and there were also present Mrs. John and Mrs. H. Frost, Mrs. Ollerenshaw, Ann and Mary Frost, Ethel and Evelyn, Kate Brocklehurst, Mrs. Flewitt and her daughter Emily, Miss Broadhurst, Hilda Carson and Mrs. Thos A Sheldon. Miss Broadhurst bought the cheese (or the milk it was made of). Ethel and Evelyn cycled to Bakewell to see about the prizes won at a draw for the benefit of the Sherwood Foresters prisoners of war. I won a tea pot and our Tom a war bond (15s.6d.). I think the draw took place last Wednesday and a list of prize winners was posted up in Roger's shop. Mr. Stephenson called here and had a chat.

May 26th Fine but rather dull. Mr. Stephenson took the service in Church this afternoon. On the 26th of May last year my poor Tony sent a few violets which he had gathered on the cliffs at Sunderland when on duty and now he lies in a foreign land. Oh whenever will this cruel wicked war be over.

May 27th Very fine. Anthony took milk and then went to market. Thos Wm Brocklehurst took train to Derby. He had to be there at 11 o'clock to appeal for George. He did not get poor George off and they would scarcely hear him. I believe an appeal was sent in for him to the central Tribunal, London. Our Tom cycled to Bakewell tonight to fetch his prize which was a war bond for 15s.6d. and my prize was a tea pot.

May 28th Very fine. Our Tom's knee is very inflamed and swollen. He went to Bakewell for the Vino Sacro[I] and also the Burton beer (2 kils). He called at Dr. Jackson's who said he must rest it and go down on Thursday when it would have to be cut if no better. Tom hurt his knee about 6 or 7 weeks ago with jumping off a load of hay or straw and fell on a stone. The great German offensive has started again yesterday.

May 29th Very fine. Tom is resting his knee. It does not pain him quite as much but is still swollen. We have had to give ground to the Germans for

I   For Holy Communion

8 or 10 miles on the Western Front. Thos Wm sent a letter that Mr. Tinsley wrote over George to Mr. Hughes Hallet. Mr. Sherlock called here and Miss Wager came up to see us. I had some biscuits and a little tea sent from some one. It had the Manchester postmark. Mr. Stephenson called in tonight and brought me some tulips. Mary, Ethel and Evelyn were cleaning the parlour. I sent Lizzie Bacon some oat cakes (3). Anthony was busy in the fallow.

May 20th Very fine very hot sun. Wm and Vincent in the fallow (leading manure). Tom went to the Dr. who told him his knee was rather better and that he must go on with the same treatment. Anthony was gapping etc.

May 31st Very fine and very close, like thunder. Anthony, Wm and Vincent working in fields. Tom mending bicycles. Mary milks morning and night. We are losing ground on the Western front. Our men are outnumbered (8 to 1) and still the war goes on. Papers have come from J.R. Bond saying that the Government will call on men from agriculture from 18 to 51 and they have to fill up a form for exemption but I do not think many will be exempted. All men whatever grade will be called upon.

June 1st Very close and very fine. Our Mary went to Grindleford this morning with Johnsons. She has had two letters from soldiers who have seen Clem in Germany. One sent a portrait of Clem and a very good one it is. Clem had given it Pte J. Smith (Royal Scots) to send to Mary from Holland and he did so. Vincent Hallows went to Tom Critchlow's to plant his father's (Hallows) potatoes.

June 2nd Very hot and fine. We shall soon be wanting rain. I received a letter from Mrs. Rawlinson and one enclosed from Ernest. Celebration of Holy Communion. A young clergyman staying at Ashford for the weekend officiated. Mr. Stephenson took the service in Sheldon Church this afternoon. Collection 11s. 8d. for Church expenses. Sam Johnson came and sat with me outside our house tonight and was helping to fill our Tom's paper up.

June 3rd Very fine plenty of air. Wm and Vincent leading manure on to fallow (cabbage row). Rent day of the Duke of Devonshire at Ashford. Our Mary took our rent and uncle Will Brocklehurst's. Anthony and I filled up Tom's exemption form and sent it to J.R. Bond.

June 4th Very fine, frosty this morning and a colder wind. Anthony took Fanny (mare) to Longstone to the horse. He started just after 5 o'clock this morning and was back before 8 just when Tom was measuring milk. Tom has shorn 16 sheep (on moor). Vincent caught and held them. Anthony has been planting cabbage etc. in garden and syringed and put sulphur on roses.

June 5th Very fine until after tea when rumblings of thunder were heard and nice showers of rain came on which will do a great deal of good. Tom clipped 16 more sheep on moor. Anthony was horse hoeing in Fallow. Wm setting cabbage. I wrote to Mrs. Rawlinson. Mr. Broughton called and was paid up (£4 15s.0d.). He did not return a copper. I told him about charging 3s.11d. per yd (for Mary's dress and girls' blouses) when he gave us to understand it was 2s.11d. Read in paper that the Germans are only 39 miles from Paris.

June 6th Very fine, rumblings of thunder. Anthony received a P Card from Mr. Joseph Anthony asking him to take our wool down to Bakewell to be weighed. Tom clipped 90 sheep which finished the lot. Anthony fetched the wool from the moor and took it straight off to Bakewell and weighed it so we had not to store it at home at all. We had 41 fleeces this year and 44 last.

June 7th Showery first thing cleared out later in day. Four of our big chickens (1st hatch) disappeared completely. We think a fox is about and has taken them. Ethel and Evelyn went to Matlock (Statham studio). Evelyn had her photo taken as she said she had moved in the negative when taken before. After leaving the studio they (the girls) set off and walked to Darley Dale to see Polly and Albert Evans. There they had tea and then came by train to Bakewell where they had left their cycles. Sam Wilton is bad. I think Dr. Fentem thinks it is lockjaw as he made enquiries whether he had been about any animals. Sarah Brockley told him that he had been about Carson's horse. Mr. Sherlock took service in Church tonight, 6 present. Made out ticket for ration books.

June 8th Fine. Tom, Wm and Vincent have been dragging, harrowing and leading manure on to fallow ready for sowing lints[1] and rape. On going to the fowls it was found that something had snapped off the head of our poor Tony's guinea fowl (the cockerel) and taken the body. I expect the fox has been again. Our girls go at night to fasten the chickens and fowls up. Mr. Stephenson called to see me.

June 9th Some very nice showers. Mr. Stephenson took the service in Church this afternoon and afterwards called here with two of his friends who had come from Heath to see him. All three had tea with us. The two friends were Mr. Metcalf and son (a youth). Our Tom went to Monyash. He saw some youths who had been called up. He said they looked down. Anthony had a paper saying that our Tom's case would be tried on Wednesday next at Derby.

June 10th Dull and cold. Ernest landed at Bakewell at something past eleven this morning and rode up with Anthony. Tom took the youngest filly to Bakewell to the horse. Ethel and Evelyn cycled to Bakewell. Evelyn went for her music lesson and Ethel paid Mr. Thacker for meat up to date (£4.18.6) by cheque) and got some bacon from Ormes at 2s/- per lb which was very salt. Uncle Will Brockley has to go to Derby on Wednesday about George and the army.

---

1   lints: linseed

June 12th Very fine. Anthony and Thos Wm Brocklehurst went from Longstone (9.15) station to Derby and appeared before the War Agricultural Committee. Anthony was summoned for 10.30 and Thos Wm for 11.30. They were both successful. Tom got off (going into army for the present at any rate) and George until a suitable substitute had been found for his father. They got back about tea time. We had all been very down hearted and anxious all day, but cheered up wonderfully when the results were known. Mr. Sherlock called here about a cheque. This had been paid to Miss Broadhurst for salary.

June 13th Very dull and like rain. Tom has had the young filly (Wager) in lines and Ernest went with him all round the flat and back. Ernest went for a walk with Ethel and Evelyn. Since he has come, they have been to Monyash and through that church, through Ashford Church and the Shacklow woods.

June 14th Very slight showers at times. We want rain very much. Ethel, Evelyn and Ernest went to Bakewell shopping and went through Bakewell Church. Ethel took the tickets (7) to Skidmore to be rationed for tea. Mr. Sherlock took the service in Church. I wrote to Mrs. Rawlinson.

June 16th Slight showers but no weight of rain. Mr. Stephenson had to bring the pony and trap to Sheldon as he is so lame. After taking the service in Church he called here. He had sent a boy with some white flowers and a book of sketches about London for me. Tom and Ernest went for a walk through Flagg and Monyash and got wet as it was showery. Sam Wilton is not much better with lockjaw or something.

June 20th Showery but no weight of rain. All the lambs in Sheldon (85) were dipped this morning in our yard. Mr. Stephenson called to see us tonight. He brought 2 bottles of Sloans liniment at 1s.3d. per bottle (paid him) for which I was very pleased as it is so scarce to get. Ernest seems much better for his visit. He goes out when fine and seems to enjoy himself. The Austrians are failing in their attack on the Italian front and their men are being taken prisoners by Italy and the British. The Northumberland Fusiliers, Sherwood Foresters, Royal Warwick and the Bucks regiments have taken prominent parts in this attack. There seems to be a lull on the Western front. Men are being called up to the age of 51. There is great dissatisfaction (in the paper) of the Grading of the older men but what about the poor lads of 18. These have to go and there seems to be no pity for them. Some families have all their sons in this dreadful business (war) and others have not sent one. There is very unequal sacrifice. The village of Sheldon for its size has suffered heavily in the death roll of her best young men. We sold out of beer.

June 22nd Very showery (heavy) and rough. Anthony went in dogcart with Thos Wm Brockley to Froggatt to look at a horse. A good few in tonight and we tapped a kil of beer which Orme's sent as soon as it came. Anthony went to bed with headache. Mr. Stephenson was going to the isle of Ely today.

June 23rd Very rough and dull. Good news from the Italian Front. The Austrians appear to be failing in their attack. A lull on the Western Front. Mr. Sherlock took the service in Sheldon Church this afternoon. The collection amounted to £1.6s.3d. which was for the Derby Royal infirmary. Ethel, Evelyn and James Frost and Ernest went to Monsal Dale tonight. Tom went to Monyash.

June 26th Dull. Anthony, John Frost and T.A. Sheldon are gone to the Copyhold Court at Ashford. Our Mary's birthday (31). During the last few days the Italians have gained a great victory over the Austrians and have driven them back across the Piave. Over 45,000 prisoners are said to have been taken. The British have fought well in this. Tom took Fanny (mare) to Burlow Farm, Harpur Hill (no good). (Not as many as 45,000 prisoners). Mr. Stephenson called tonight. Came from Ely yesterday.

June 29th Misty first thing, clears out later and after is dull and close. A year ago today which was June 30 (Saturday) we received a letter and afterwards a telegram to say that our dear Tony was coming home on leave from Cleadon.

June 30th Very hot in sun but nice and breezy. Last year today was July 1st 1917. On this day (Sunday last year) our poor Tony came by the milk train from Derby where he had stayed during the night on his way from Cleadon on his last leave before going to France. I have felt very sorrowful all week thinking about him and how he came up stairs (as soon as he arrived) and put his arms round me. I cannot get over my dear lad's loss. Emily and I and little Anthony were taken for a drive in float with the old grey mare all round the flat and down Bakewell moor and up Hunterside. I had not been for years (4) that way. Mr. Stephenson took the service in Church and afterwards called to see us when he was telling us of his visit to Ely.

July 1st Very hot in sun but breezy. It would be a good thing if rain would come as everything wants it very much. I wrote to Dr. Jackson asking him to write out another certificate for Emily to try to get her a bit of white flour. He wrote one out and said it would have to go to the Food Controller. He did not think we should be able to get white flour as he only knew one case where it had been allowed and that was to a person who had cancer. Mr. H. Frost went before the War Agriculture Committee over James. He was successful in getting the lad off for the present.

July 2nd Very dull, looks very much like rain but none comes. One year ago today which was July 3rd last year my poor Tony and Ethel and Evelyn cycled to Middleton and Youlgreave and out of that time my dear lad has been lying in a foreign grave for 8 months today. Anthony wrote about Tony's money in war loan. Another hospital ship has been torpedoed by the Germans on its way from Canada. Read in paper that Pemberton Billing[1] was removed from the House of Commons by four men. He will not be

---

[1] Noel Pemberton Billing, MP, had attacked the government's handling of the war

allowed to go back this session unless he apologises which if I were him I would not do as I think all the present Government ought to be cleared out.

July 3rd   Very hot in sun; a nice breeze and at times towards night it looks very dull and threatening for rain but none comes. Eds received a letter from Kate saying she arrived safely at Fairfield, Scalecroft, Cumberland on Monday July 1st. Mr. Skidmore brought us 54 lbs of sugar for making jam. Clarice went to meet Fred's young lady.

July 4th   Very hot in sun, a nice breeze. Anthony, Tom, Wm and Vincent started the hay on moor. Our Anthony had to take the dinner. Just one year today which was Thursday July 5th last year we said our last *Good bye* to our dear lost Tony. It was awful for me his mother. He had got in the staircase after saying *Good bye* and I called him back. He put his arms round me and I blessed him and he said he would be a good lad. Oh dear! I think I shall never get over it and the war still goes on, thousands of our brave lads have laid down their lives since then. Ethel and Evelyn went with Tony to Bakewell station and saw him off on his return to Cleadon, Sunderland.

July 5th   Dull at times and very much like rain. Wm finished mowing on moor. We have no beer and have not had any for over a week. Our men have to drink minerals. Mr. Sherlock called in to see me before service at Church. I think most people are in the hay as there were only 4 present in Church. We had a cheese today. I believe it will be the last to be made this year. We have 11 made now and have sold two to S. Ashton, a small one and one weighing 30 lbs. We sold them at 1s. 4d. per lb. The last cheese we sold made £2.0.0. Just one year ago today by the day of the month my Tony went back to Cleadon.

July 6th   Very dull and very much like rain but none comes. Mary received a PC from Clem and he says he has met some Derbyshire men in Germany. Little Anthony received a PC from Mr. Stephenson asking if the girls could do the altar for him as he could not come up.

July 7th   A very good day for sun and wind. Mr. Stephenson took the service in Church this afternoon. The collection was for Prisoners of War (Sherwood Foresters). It had not been given out what the collection was for as I do believe the amount would have been more. Mr. Stephenson called in and had tea with us. There was a celebration of the Holy Communion at 9.30 this morning (Mr. Sherlock officiated). At noon there were 14 men including Mr. Roper called here from Nottingham, 13 of whom had minerals to drink as we had no beer or anything else. I received a letter from Mrs. Rawlinson.

July 8th   Slight showers which stopped the hay leading. I wrote to the Ministry of Food for some flour for Emily, and also to Whittakers for minerals. Mr. Stephenson came in our house with the Rector of a place near Ely (Cambridgeshire) whom he introduced. The rector accepted a glass of milk.

July 10th   Dull. Our men went on moor and led 4 loads of hay. In the afternoon a thunderstorm came on and they had to leave off in the midst of rain. They put the stack cover over the stack. Mr. Stephenson and the rector of a place near Ely visited us tonight. A slight thunderstorm (soon over). A paper came this morning over my poor Tony's money in war loan. We part filled it up and had to leave off.

July 11th   Dull hindering weather for hay, slight showers but no weight of rain. Wm Gould went to Bakewell station and brought us 3 kils of Burton ale. One kil we can charge what we like, the other 2 to be sold at 5d. and 4d. per pint. We gave Gould 30/- to buy boots. After we had got in bed tonight our bull got out of the Hannah Croft by breaking a fleak[1] and got into the street making an awful noise. Anthony and Tom got up and drove him up the back yard into a building. We filled a paper up and sent it off about our poor Tony's money in War loan. Mr. Ed signed it and was witness. A paper came to us over Emily's bit of white flour which has to go to Dr. Jackson to be filled up.

July 12th   Very wet this morning, nice straight rain which will do a deal of good. I have a fire in the house-place as it seems a bit chilly. Thunder can be heard at intervals. Coal has risen in price and is now 31s.6d per ton. Eggs are 3 a shilling and everything else is awfully high in price.

July 13th   Fine, good hay day, plenty of sun and nice breeze. Our men went on moor after dinner and finished getting hay there. They got six loads and raked and topped up the stack. They got home at 11 o'clock tonight. The stack on moor has 31 good loads of hay in it (there were 30 last year) and is off 2 fields. Mr. Stephenson brought a young soldier to see us. His home is in Cambridgeshire but he is in a Yorkshire camp now as an instructor. He has had a young brother (not 19) who died of fever in East Africa. Both Mr. Stephenson and the young soldier stayed to tea. Ethel took our ration books (11) which came this morning to Bakewell to have them signed. She paid Dr. Jackson (18s.6d.) and he signed and filled up a paper for our Emily about white flour and Ethel posted it at Bakewell.

July 14th   Steady drizzling showers today. I received two letters this morning, one from Ernest Rawlinson who is staying in Cambridgeshire with his relatives and one from Shrewsbury from France. I wrote to Mrs. Rawlinson. Mr. Stephenson took the service in Church.

July 16th   Showery first thing then a thunderstorm and heavier rain, close. Mr. Hudson (Food Office, Bakewell) called and asked a few questions about 4 penny beer and cards relating to supplying meals. I wrote to Mr. Stephenson about some greens to fill up in field or garden. I also wrote to Ernest R who is in Cambridgeshire.

July 17th   Very dull and close first thing. Anthony took milk and on coming back there was a hamper of green plants waiting for him so Mr.

---

1   fleak (or flake) :hurdle or gate

Stephenson had been very prompt in getting them ready. Ethel washed my head this morning. The men and Anthony planted the greens in Fallowfield etc. which Mr. Stephenson sent.

July 18th   Very dull at times and the rain comes down heavily every now and then. This will do such good if the spell of wet weather is not too prolonged. Our men are putting oil of coal and parrafin (sic) on the hay barn roof. Mr. Stephenson wrote such a very nice letter which I got this morning. Fred Goodwin who came on leave last Saturday night went back today. Mr. Ronston came tonight and was paid up. We paid him for 3 bottles of whiskey which did not come last month but which Mr Ronston says he will send on with the other order on Saturday next. We also paid for a kil of ale which came but was not on the bill. Walter Brockley brought us 2 kils of beer which we owe for. We paid by cheque which came to £10.8s.od. I wrote to Mr. Stephenson. Mr. Ronston took our ration books.

July 19th   Dull at first like rain but clears out into a very nice afternoon. Our men are gone into hayfield (Tom and Vincent have gone to Ashford with two cows). Mr. Sherlock took a service in Church: only 4 present. He afterwards called here and he and I had an argument over war and other things. I told him we would agree to differ. The Allies are doing well in France.

July 20th   Showery at times towards night. A fox worried another guinea hen of our poor Tony's. Only one left.

July 21st   Dull and showery this morning. Mr. Sherlock took the service in Church. Received a PC from Mr. Stephenson from Heath where he went yesterday. The photos of Mary, Anthony and Aunt Hannah arrived this morning.

July 25th   Finer at times and a nice wind. Several people in Sheldon had got their hay dry. Mr. Bonsall had horse and cart in field to begin leading when the rain came on very heavy (thunder). Mr. Stephenson came up with the intention of being present in School whilst the children learnt a hymn which Evelyn was going to play for them. Miss Broadhurst did not want the children to meet in school as she said the measles might be caught. The children are all running together in the street so I do not quite see how practising a hymn in school would affect them. She asked Evelyn yesterday what Mr. Stephenson wanted to teach them hymns for as she could do that (the jealousy of her!). I suggested to Mr. Stephenson that he should wait until Miss Broadhurst re-opened school after the holidays and the same night he should have the children to practise the hymn he wants. This was agreed to by him. We had hare to dinner. Tom caught or shot it the other day.

July 26th   Very dull and showery. The hay that has been cut for two or three weeks is getting weathered. As soon as it is dry the rain comes on again. Our Top Hicks field has been cut a fortnight tomorrow. Our men are busy whitewashing the outbuildings etc. We are having pigeon pie to dinner. Tom killed two the other day. I feel very depressed at times over our poor Tony. I wrote a long letter to Miss Adams and one to Pte. Shrewsbury. Thundering at intervals. Tom and his father have been mortaring and mending the roof of the old stable.

July 27th   Dull. Mr. Stephenson brought a new mat for the chancel and a Union Jack. He said the mat cost £2.10.0. He called and had tea at Billy Naylor's. E. Naylor and L. Brockley went on holidays. George and Piccareet Craven came to Mr. Ed's tonight.

July 28th   Very fine. Mr. Stephenson took the service in Church this afternoon and afterwards came here to tea. I received a letter from Mrs. Rawlinson this morning and I think both she and Mr. Rawlinson will come to see us before long.

July 29th   Frosty early this morning. A most lovely day. Our men are in the hay. They got the Top Hicks field tonight (6 loads). I sat out of doors this afternoon but the sun was very hot. Ben Handley is helping us at nights. The Germans are retreating in France. If the strikers do not go in to work in different parts of the country they will be liable to be taken into the Army and a proclamation to that effect has been published in papers by Mr. David Lloyd George. They must go to work today.

July 30th   A most lovely day. Our men are in the hay. Wm started mowing Bole Piece next Johnsons Lane (a good crop) He finished it tonight. The Jonas case has ended. Sir Jonas was fined £2,000 and Vernon £1,000. The other man was let off a few days ago. This case has lasted a week or two and was over getting and giving information to the enemy. I think many times a day of my poor Tony. He was so young to have to sacrifice his life and oh! how many thousands more dear lads have gone under in this awful war. It is said that the strikers went back to work.

July 31st   Very misty and did not clear until dinner time. Our men with Ben Handley and Ed Brockley got 9 loads of seeds out of Hicks field, 2nd from top tonight. I sat out a little while. I received a letter from Mr. Stephenson saying the rug for the Church was paid for.

Aug. 1st   Very misty again, clears out after dinner. Mary received a long letter from Clem which was written in May. He hopes to be home by Xmas. Mr. Stephenson called in tonight and had a chat over school treat and altar cloth etc. Anthony had a PC saying that the accident Insurance was overdue.

Aug. 2nd   Dull at first but clears out later in the day. Mary had a PC from Clem which was posted in Germany on the 6th of June. Anthony decided not to send the money for the Workman Insurance as there are so many questions to be asked. Heard that poor Jess Johnson was dead. He was severely wounded some months ago.

Aug. 3rd   Very wet and has been during the night. Mary received another long letter from Clem. He is working in a hospital among the fever patients etc. He says he was in camp. Our men have been whitewashing the buildings up back yard. I received a letter from Mrs. Rawlinson saying they were coming on Monday. Our Mary wrote to Miss Harrison and enclosed a 10/- note for food for Clem. Poor Jess Johnson was brought to Ashford from Newcastle (died Aug. 1st of wounds received in April last).

Aug. 4th　Fine. Holy Communion in Sheldon Church. Mr. Sherlock officiated. I went out in my chair after tea. Called at Mr. Ollerenshaw's and sat out talking with Mrs. C and Mrs. E Ollerenshaw's daughter Mrs. Hazlehurst and Sam Ollerenshaw's daughter. I had been down the lane where I could see the fallow field. Ethel and Evelyn went to Ashford where Mr. Stephenson saw them and took them round Churchdale gardens. There was an Intercession Service in most of the churches today. Mr. Sherlock took the service in Church this afternoon being 4 yrs that the war has been on. Collection for Red Cross 18s.2½d.

Aug. 5th　Dull. Mr. and Mrs. Rawlinson came this morning. Our Tom went to meet them at Longstone station. Ethel and Evelyn took Mrs. Rawlinson for a walk and Tom took Mr. Rawlinson on moor and down fields. Ethel walked with them to Longstone at night to catch the 10 minutes to six train. Poor young Jess Johnson was buried at 2 o'clock today. A military funeral (Ashford). Anthony went to market.

Aug. 6th　Showery. No hay day. Mr. Sherlock went for holidays. Mary sent Clem a photo of little Anthony. The Germans are retreating on the Western front but they sank on Saturday an ambulance ship in the Channel and two destroyers. Sid Brockley went back. He came last Saturday.

Aug. 7th　Finer. Our men (some of them) were mowing thistles on moor this morning and are in the hay this afternoon. Our three girls have been turning the hay in Waterlands. We had seven for hot water this afternoon and a man and boy for bread and cheese. Received a letter from Mrs. Rawlinson. Mr. Stephenson came up and took a service in Church. He called here and brought us a very large box of matches which was very acceptable as they are so scarce.

Aug. 8th　Very dull and looks very much like rain this morning. Anthony was undecided whether to break out the hay which was hobbled up in the Bole Piece. However, he ventured to do so about dinner time and it was a good thing he did for the rain kept off, and a good wind arose and dried it, and about tea time the men and Wilf Goodwin loaded and brought three more loads to the stackyard, then finishing the Bole Piece - 26 loads of hay were got out of this field. The boy scouts (who are staying at Ashford) called and had mineral water to drink (15).

Aug. 10th　A very bright hot morning. In the afternoon it was close and gloomy. Wm finished mowing the Waterlands and mowed the Croft heads. Mr. and Miss Stephenson called this afternoon and Evelyn went to practise with Miss Stephenson in the Church. Very good news from the Western front. The Allies took 17,000 prisoners and 300 guns. We got 5 loads out of Waterlands.

Aug. 11th   Very close and gloomy at times. Mr. and Miss Stephenson came up early to service which Mr. Stephenson took and Miss Stephenson sang in Church, *Nearer my God to Thee*. Evelyn played. A collection was taken £1.4.2. towards an outing for the choir. Miss Stephenson sang and played in school tonight to a good audience. We had Mr. and Miss Stephenson and Mr. Metcalf and son to tea.

Aug. 12th   Very fine first thing but just after dinner when our men were ready to lead some hay in Waterlands, a heavy shower came on and stopped them. Later on a nice wind arose and enabled them to go on. Mr. and Miss Stephenson called here. We gave him a lb or two of cheese. Miss Stephenson was practising up at school with the Sheldon children (hymns). Miss Broadhurst was talking to Mr. Stephenson over Sunday night. She had taken off with the keys of the school and people tried to take off the lock to get in to hear Miss Stephenson sing. However, the lady turned up (Sunday night) with keys and so she was not in a very amiable mood over things which occurred. I wrote to Mrs. Rawlinson.

Aug. 14th   Very fine and rather a rough wind which will be good for drying the hay. The anniversary of Anthony's and my wedding day (32 years). Anthony is raking up the Croft Heads. I received a very nice letter from Mr. Stephenson. He called in tonight. Got 5 loads of hay out of little Butts.

Aug. 17th   Dull, and at times very drizzling. A tea was given to the children of Sheldon and toys distributed. Mr. Stephenson and the choir girls helped and Mrs. Kenworthy and her daughter were the only ones from Ashford. Mr. Sherlock and the Misses Grover are away from home. A Mr. Terral is taking the services in Ashford Church whilst the vicar is on his holidays. Alf Barratt called with the things I ordered on Thursday last and they were an awful price. Two shirts for Anthony: the bare stuff without the lining cost £1.5s.0d. viz 10 yds of Flannelette at 2/6 per yd. We always put 1½ yards of calico in each shirt. He brought 3 yds at 1s.0½d. per yd.

Aug. 18th   Dull and rather windy but fine. Mr. Stephenson took the service in Church and called and had tea here. We had a conversation over a white cloth for the Altar at Sheldon. Mr. Stephenson has had a price list and a very plain one would cost 10 or 12 pounds so we thought it would be better to refund the money which has been collected for the purpose unless Miss Grover and others are prepared to make up the deficiency. Our Ethel had a letter from Mrs. Kell saying that Mrs. Craven had had a baby boy (at Sheffield) yesterday. Mr. Craven came to Sheldon yesterday and went back to Sheffield on receipt of the news.

Aug. 21st   A lovely day. Mary and Ethel took me in chair down as far as the Bramwell cornfield. Mr. Stephenson called and told us that Mr. Fairholm had given him £5.0.0. towards Sheldon choir trip. Clarice Brockley went on her holidays. Miss Anne and Miss Martha Hallam called to see us.

Aug. 23rd Very fine. All the sheep and lambs (except Bonsalls) in Sheldon were dipped, 187 altogether. 70 of ours with tups, 39 sheep and tups, 31 lambs. We used McDougall's dip (and Coopers). The war news continues very good from the Western front. Albert has been recaptured by British and 5000 prisoners taken. Received our Tony's war certificate back (stamped) and transferred to Anthony (his father).

Aug. 24th Fine. Our Mary and little Anthony started from here at a quarter to seven o'clock this morning and went with Johnson to Grindleford. Our Tom went to Longstone with milk cart en route for Mr. Sneaps. He was going by the 9.15 from Longstone. The war news continues very good from the Western front, about 100,000 prisoners have been taken by the Allies since July 18th and many villages have been recaptured including Albert. 14,000 prisoners in the last 3 days. Mr. Stephenson called and had tea here and then went with the Sheldon children who ran races for some things that Mr. and Mrs. Ollerenshaw had given.

Aug. 25th Very drizzling and wet. Mr. Stephenson took the service in Church. He called and had tea here. He did not seem very well. We had to have foreign meat this week and I did not fancy it so I did not eat any. I think of our poor Tony every day. What a shame it seems that so many of our grand lads and men have fallen in this horrible war and to think we shall never see them more on this earth. Very heavy showers keep falling. It is Eyam Wakes and the anniversary of the services held in Cucklet Dell.[1]

Aug. 27th Very wet and dull and windy. Our men were getting the Binder ready for cutting the corn. A motor car came tonight with officials to draw money for the war bonds and certificates. Not many put anything in at Sheldon. The following were the people who were noticed to go to the car for the purpose of parting with a bit: John Frost, Thos Wm Brocklehurst, Thos A Sheldon, Anthony Gyte, Tom Gyte, Emily, Ethel and Evelyn Gyte and Mary S. Wager. Filled a paper up about our Tom and sent it to Derby. Wrote to Mr. G. Allsop over sugar and to the Local Fuel overseer over coal.

Aug. 28th Rather drizzling and dull this morning, clears out this afternoon. Tom is thatching on moor. Anthony is thatching in Croft Heads. Wm and Vincent are opening out for corn cutting on moor. Ethel and Evelyn are shifting hen cotes and putting hay in nests. May is baking oatcakes. I have written to Hannah and Mrs. Rawlinson. Received a letter from Mr. Burley and milk cheque. He made a complaint about last Wednesday's milk being sour. Everything is very dear to buy viz eggs 4½d each, butter 2s.6d. per lb, lard 1s.8d. per lb, bacon 2s.4d., flour 2s.8d. per stone, tea 2/9 per lb, beef various price from 1/- to 1s/8d. or 1s.9d. per lb, mutton the same various price. Clothing is also very dear. Anthony paid Mr. Hill on Monday last for his new suit £6.12.6.

Aug. 29th Rather dull. Tom, Wm and Vincent went on moor opening out for corn cutting. Anthony took the float wheels to George Frost and brought

---

1   During the Plague at Eyam in 1665, Services were held in the open air in a nearby field called Cucklet Dell.

3 kils of Burton ale from Bakewell. George Ardern (old man) and another man came to look at our young horse Heathcote. They came to Sheldon whilst Anthony was at Bakewell. They went on the moor and Tom showed them the horse. They then came back and saw Anthony and Mr. Wild gave Anthony a cheque for £130. This will be ours if the Government allow us to sell the horse. Anthony wrote to Mr. Henry Shimwell, Chatsworth for him to send a form to fill up. Anthony finished thatching stack in Croft Heads. We tapped 1 kil of ale and there were a few in our house tonight. I wrote to G. Alsopp for extra sugar and filled up forms for coal for Church and school.

Aug. 30th Dull and it was drizzling rain this afternoon. The men are opening out cornfield for Binder and Anthony is finished thatching the stack on moor.

Aug. 31st Very dull and drizzling at times (cold). Anthony received a form over the horse he wishes to sell and he filled it up and sent it to Mr. J. Bond. The address of the Purchaser is:

> Mr. A.K. Wild
> Team owner Shaw and Crompton
> Nr Oldham.

Mr. Stephenson called here and had tea.

Sept. 1st A very wet and miserable day after being wet during the night. There was a celebration of Holy Communion at 9.40. The vicar who is taking services at Ashford during the absence of Mr. Sherlock officiated. Mr. Stephenson was present and he also took the service this afternoon and had tea here. A collection for Church expenses amounted to 15s.4d. Our Tom received a voucher exempting him from military service.

Sept. 3rd Dull but finer. We received a letter from the Derbyshire War Agricultural Committee viz as follows:

> Executive Committee
> County Offices
> S. Mary's Gate
> Derby
> 2nd September 1918

> Mr. Anthony Gyte
> Sheldon Bakewell
> Dr Sir,
> Sale of horses Order
> (copy of letter)

With reference to your application for a Licence to sell a four year old Bay Gelding to Mr. A.K. Wild, Team Owner, Shaw, Nr Oldham. I have to inform you that this Committee cannot grant you a licence to sell to

any person except a holder of Agricultural land. If Mr. Wild will write
to the Controller of Horse Transport 7 Whitehall Gardens, London SW
fully explaining the purpose for which the horse is required he may
receive a permit to purchase.
Yrs faithfully
J.E. Kelly
Deputy Executive Officer.

Emily and Evelyn went to Longstone Station en route for Buxton by a train
that leaves between 2 and 3 this afternoon. Wm Gould (who is not very well,
being purged) took them with Fanny and Float, and took the bath chair
which is going to Buxton for Emily's use (Evelyn walked). They have gone
to Mrs. Hollinsheads. Anthony, Tom and Vincent went on moor to cut our
corn. Received a letter about our poor Tony's watch and a form to fill about
it. We have not received his watch at present. After my dear lad has been
lying in his foreign grave for 10 months (yesterday) I feel as sorrowful as
ever about him. I wrote to Mr. A.K. Wild enclosing the letter from the
Derbyshire War Agricultural Committee.

Sept. 4th   Very miserable and wet continually today. No corn cutting. If
the weather does not take up soon, it will be very serious for the corn
harvest. Our poor Tony's watch came this morning by registered post. After
my darling lad has been dead 10 months. Mary signed the form and sent it
back to Lichfield. I sent milk bill to Mr. Burley to end of August £38
17s.0½d. Received a PC from Evelyn saying that Emily and herself had
arrived at Mrs. Hollinsheads, Buxton. They took a taxi from the station.
Anthony received a letter from Mr. Shimwell saying that if any farmer at
Sheldon wanted horses for harvest there were some to be had at
Chatsworth. The war news is very good from the Western front. The
Germans are still retreating and a number of important places keep falling
into the hands of the Allies.

Sept. 5th   Very misty, dull and wet, wind in East. Little Anthony received
a PC from Aunt Evelyn. Emily and Evelyn are not having nice weather at all
for their holiday at Buxton. Wm Gould is not so well. He is purged. Just one
year ago today we received a letter from our dear Tony saying he was going
to be removed from the Base.

Sept. 6th   Very misty and showery today. Ethel went to Bakewell this
afternoon, called to see Dr. Fentem who sent Wm a bottle of Diarrhoea
medicine. Gould seems better today.

Sept. 7th   Misty this morning after a wet night but clears out towards
noon. Our men went on moor and went 17 times round the cornfield with
Binder. Thunder and lightning came on about 6 o'clock and the rain fell in
torrents. Our men got wet through and had to change everything. Ethel
cycled to Buxton starting about quarter to 3 this afternoon, arriving at Mrs.
Hollinshead just after 4. Evelyn started from Buxton at a quarter past seven
and got to Sheldon at about 20 past eight. It rained when she started but
got fair soon after so she came between showers and did not get so wet.

There was a procession and different things at Monyash in aid of the Red Cross, dancing etc. It rather spoilt everything when the thunder and lightning came on. Our Tom went to Monyash after milking. Mr. Stephenson called here and had tea, after which he washed up tea things etc.

Sept. 8th Very showery all day. We received a letter from Mr. A.K. Wild about the horse Heathcote, and a book called *The Hundredth Chance* from Ernest Rawlinson, and our Tom had something come about the War Certificates. Mr. Stephenson took the service in Church. Mrs. James Frost died tonight.

Sept. 9th Very showery, no corn cutting. Anthony wrote to Mr. J. Bond enclosing Mr. A.K. Wild's letter over sale of horse. Viz copy of letter.

> Tel. 61 Shaw
> Moorfield Cottage
> High Crompton
> Sept. 6th 1918
> Shaw Lane

> Dear Sir,
> In answer to yours re Sale of horse I have an authority to purchase horses granted under licence by Controller of Horse Transport. My licence number is 147. What you require is a Permit which when you have obtained you send it on to me and I will return to you duly signed. Hoping you will find this quite alright.

> Yours Respect.
> A.K. Wild

> Mr. Anthony Gyte
> Sheldon
> Nr Bakewell
> Derbyshire

Sept. 11th Very showery. Thunder for days together. No corn cutting. Mr. and Miss Stephenson called here. Mr. Stephenson was put about. He had received a letter from Lord Hartington's housekeeper, Hardwick, saying she could not allow Sheldon choir through Hardwick Hall on Monday next as Lord and Lady Hartington were coming in residence. Mrs. James Frost was buried.

Sept. 12th Very showery all day. No corn cutting. Anthony received a licence to sell the horse and he sent it off to Mr. Wild to sign. Fred Brocklehurst came for leave tonight. Some more jam made from our own marrows.

Sept. 13th Very wet and miserable in the morning but turned out a good afternoon. Our men went round the cornfield 21 times with the binder.

Evelyn went to Buxton by 2.28 train and Ethel came back by the 5.10. Thos. Wm Brocklehurst was fined 15/- at Bakewell court for not having a dog exemption.

Sept. 14th Most miserable and wet all day. My birthday (61). Mrs. Ed sent me a Christian Novel and card. No corn cutting. It is a most serious time. Tom took young horse Heathcote to be shod ready for sending him off by train next Tuesday. Mr. and Miss Stephenson called here and had a little refreshment. Afterwards Miss Stephenson sang up at school to a good audience. A soldier came with a Binder with which he is to cut corn beginning for Thos Wm Brocklehurst.

Sept. 15th Very wet all day. Mr. Sherlock took the service in Church this afternoon. Emily and Evelyn returned from Buxton. Leah Brockley came back with them. She had gone to Buxton show yesterday. She stayed with her aunt Mary Hollinshead. Our Evelyn left her bag purse at the station which had £1 6s.7d. in and on going again tonight to the station the stationmaster gave it to her. She gave him one shilling. Fred Brocklehurst and Miss R. Wilson called here to see us.

Sept. 16th Very dull. A slight shower this afternoon. No corn cutting. Ethel and Evelyn and the other choir girls went off to Manchester starting from Sheldon at a quarter to eight going to Longstone station where they would meet Mr. Stephenson. Anthony went to market. The girls got back just before 10 tonight after spending a most enjoyable day visiting the Cathedral and afterwards Belle Vue. They had beef steak pie for dinner, also fruit pies.

Sept. 17th Showery. No corn cutting. Tom took the young horse Heathcote to Bakewell station early this morning to catch the 8.25 train. A horse box had been ordered by Anthony the other day and so Tom put him in the box and put the directions on his head. The station master was very nasty because Tom had not enough money to pay for him going. Anthony thought that Mr. Wild would pay but the stationmaster said he would not let the horse go unless paid for at Bakewell. Harry Ardern lent Tom 10 shillings so the difficulty was overcome. Tom had 10/- of his own; the carriage was 12/- so there was not much to refuse to send the horse for.

Sept. 18th A very good day up to 4 o'clock this afternoon when it poured with rain for a time. Our men went on moor corn cutting. Mr. Lowthian, Mr. Wood, Mr. Snieder and Mr. John Spencer called here this morning for the first Partridge shoot. I had a very nice conversation with Mr. Snieder about the war etc. Whittakers brought us some mineral waters but no soda water.

Sept. 20th Fine in morning. Our men were opening out in Bramwell field and then went off with binder and did a good piece of corn cutting. Showery towards tea time. A deal of oats are shed on the ground. Good news from France and the Balkans. The Allies have broken through the Bulgarian front positions. I have been very depressed today about our poor Tony and the other lads who were called upon to sacrifice their grand young lives in this most cruel war. Mr. Sherlock called in our house tonight. John Naylor (Wales) was in our house tonight.

Sept. 21st Dull but fine this morning. Our men went in Bramwell field and finished cutting the corn in it when rain came on again and they had to leave. The war news is very good on all fronts. General Allenby's forces have captured a many prisoners and have cut the Turks line of communication. Mr. Stephenson called here and had tea (oatcake and toasted cheese).

Sept. 22nd Dull and very showery at times. Mr. Stephenson took the service in Sheldon Church this afternoon. Fred Brocklehurst went back. He went to Church and the congregation did not come out until after 4 o'clock when it rained very heavily. His train left Bakewell at 5.15 so he would not have much time. Tom Wager went to Sheffield Hospital yesterday to have his foot amputated.

Sept. 23rd Rain again. Very showery. Anthony went to market after taking milk. Tom took a cow to the field at Ashford and then went on to Bakewell to go by bus to Grindleford. Ethel started from Sheldon just after 1 o'clock to cycle to Grindleford where she would meet Tom who has gone for Clem's bicycle. Mary received two P cards from Clem. Evelyn went to Bakewell for her music lesson and Ethel and Tom came back with her tonight, Tom riding on Clem's bike. Hannah came to Sheldon from Middleton. I wrote to Mrs. Rawlinson.

Sept. 24th Dull and showery. We have no beer or spirits for sale. The hop bitters from Whittakers are in splendid condition but we have nearly finished them. Our Mary received a PC from a man who had been with Clem for some months in Germany. This man said he had left Clem three weeks ago. He was (the man) an exchanged prisoner and said that Clem was well and jolly when he left him.

Sept. 27th Dull and wet at times this morning. Sunshine and wind about dinner time. Received milk cheque up to Sept. 15th The ministry of food has fixed the milk price from Oct. 1st at 2s.3d. per gal to the farmer, railway carriage to be put on as well, for winter months. Our men went to cornfield and brought 3 loads but could not unload as rain came on in torrents. Mr. Sherlock called here on his way up to school for service.

Sept. 28th Dull and very showery. Mr. Stephenson brought Mr. and Mrs. Wright from out of Cambridgeshire to see us. Mr. and Mrs. Wright had tea here and Mr. Stephenson had it at Mr. Alf Brockley's. A heifer (blue) pecked her calf and had a very bad time. Mr. and Mrs. Craven and family came to Eds.

Sept. 29th Dull and showery towards night. Holy Communion in Sheldon Church at 9.40 - 14 present. Mr. Sherlock officiated. A new altar cloth was used for the first time today. Mr. Stephenson took the service this afternoon. A Service for the Dedication was used as it is St. Michael's

Church. Collection in Church for Church expenses £1 14s.2d. Mr. Stephenson and Mr. and Mrs. Wright called here and had tea. We put the clock back an hour.

Sept. 30th Dull and showery. Anthony took two young bull calves which were sold in auction: one made £1.3.0. and the other £1.0.0. They were two good calves. Excellent news from all the Allies fighting fronts. Bulgaria surrendered unconditionally to the Allies.

Oct. 2nd Very drizzly. Mr. Stephenson brought a picture here which he has given in memory of the fallen lads of Sheldon. He wants it hanging in the Church. The Allies are doing well on all Fronts. Heard that Fred Bramwell is wounded and is in Leeds hospital.

Oct. 3rd Dull but very windy. Tom went with milk. Wm and Vincent getting rape and lints. This took some time so Mary and Evelyn and their uncle Billy Naylor went off to the cornfield and fetched 2 loads. Billy made the stack. When the other men had done the other work they began leading. Wilf Goodwin came to help us. In this morning's paper I read that the Allies under Gen. Allenby had got possession of Damascus in Palestine and had taken 7,000 prisoners. Also that ourselves and the French etc. had got the whole of St. Quentin. In Flanders the Belgians and British are doing well under General Plumer. People in Sheldon are very busy leading corn as it looks so much like rain. Anthony arrived home between 5 and 6 o'clock. He stayed the night at Mr. Sneaps and in the afternoon went with Mr. Ollerenshaw to the pictures. He did not succeed in getting a ram as so few were shown at Nottingham Fair.

Oct. 4th A little drizzling first thing but turns out a very nice day. Our men went on moor to lead corn. Wilf Goodwin came to help us but had to leave about 3 o'clock to meet his father. Our troops and the other allies are doing well. Lens is entirely in the Allies hands and the Germans are said to be retreating. There was another shooting party today, Mr. Wood, Mr. Lowthian and two other gentlemen. We provided tea for them charging 1/- each.

Oct. 5th Very wet. No corn leading today. Mr. Stephenson, Mary, Ethel, Evelyn and Aunt H were busy decorating the Church for Harvest Thanksgiving tomorrow. Mr. Stephenson hung the picture[1] in Church to the memory of the Fallen Lads.

Oct. 6th Very rough and a bit showery at times. Holy Communion at 9.40, 14 present. Mr. Sherlock and Mr. Stephenson were both present. A very good congregation this afternoon. Mr. Sherlock and Mr. Stephenson were both present again. Mr. Stephenson dined with us and stayed to tea at Thos Wm Brocklehursts. The collection for Church expenses amounted to £2.13.0, the best we have ever had. The Misses Grover and others were up from Ashford. Miss Wager was here for tea. She said that Tom Wager was

---

1   See Introduction pp. xviii, xix

in Bakewell hospital (came last Friday). Billy Naylor gave 1/- towards Church collection so this makes £2.14.0. A day or two since the Bulgarians surrendered unconditionally to the Allies.

Oct. 7th   A very severe storm of hail, snow and rain early (before 8 o'clock) this morning. There was a good wind and when Anthony got back from market the men went on moor and led 6 loads of corn. Eben Ollerenshaw and wife and Fred Brockley and wife (Potteries) came this morning to Sheldon and Mr. C. Ollerenshaw went to Derby. It does seem such a poor Wakes. No people in the house like as in years gone by. Formerly we used to have every room full as well as the dancing room. There seems no joy in anything owing to this awful war. The Central Powers have sent a note to President Wilson (America) for an armistice to discuss Peace proposals. I do not think people will be gulled by them as they did not want peace when the Germans were winning. A Landgirl came to Thos Wm Brockley's.

Oct. 8th   Very dull at times. Our men went on moor to lead corn. A slight shower or two came on but was soon over. Our Mary went to Bakewell hospital to see Tom Wager who is stationed there. I never saw such a poor Wakes for everything. No plum puddings, no cake. No jam. Not even a bit of treacle to be got. Our men got 13 loads of corn on moor today. They brought some home on carts.

Oct. 9th   Very wet all day. No corn leading. Tom fetched 2 kils of Burton ale from Bakewell station. Our girls were filling glass bottles etc. with different things such as flour, salt, salts, Bengers food etc. for a guessing competition for the Red Cross. A box was also put in our house. Mr. Stephenson called and gave Mrs. Ed and myself the bunches of grapes out of Sheldon Church.

Oct. 10th   Fine, rather windy. Anthony and Tom have been colouring tups and Wm and Vincent have gone on moor to set up the corn that had been knocked down. Just one year today since poor Anthony Brocklehurst was killed and today I read that Cambrai had been taken by the Allies. Our ram was put to the ewes (Mark Clays). There was dancing and a guessing competition in Sheldon School tonight, the proceeds to go to the British Red Cross. Everybody paid 2 pence to guess what the glass bottles contained and a cucumber sent by Mr. Stephenson for the Harvest Thanksgiving being put up for sale and sold over and over again made £1.11.6. The weight of the cucumber was also guessed. Sixpence was charged at the door and altogether a nice sum was raised. Altogether a most enjoyable evening was spent and Mr. Eben Ollerenshaw made a very good salesman. Mr. Stephenson was not able to be present. Mr. Ronston was paid all we owe.

Oct. 11th   Fine but the corn is not dry enough for leading. Anthony and Tom are gone to the foal show at Bakewell. It was arranged in our house to do something more for the Red Cross, so Wm H. Bramwell, W. Hallows and S. Wilton decided to go round the village tomorrow and collect anything that people would give. Ethel went to Bakewell. Miss Muriel Cox-Wilson was buried today. She died early on Wednesday (aged 16).

Oct. 12th Dull and on the whole pretty fine with the exception of a shower or two. Our men were leading corn on moor. Four loads were brought home and 5 stacked on moor. We finished getting our corn and we have 20 stacks altogether (70 loads). Mr. W.H. Bramwell came this afternoon and brought (from Bakewell) some very useful articles to be given in aid of Red Cross viz.

10 tins of sardines	Orme and Co
5 cwts of coal (to be fetched)	F. Lomas
1 tablecloth	Mrs. W.H. Bramwell
1 ditto	Mr. Clarke
1 Link of Polony	Mr. J. Nelson
1 Pork Pie	Mr. F. Naylor
Cash 2/-	Mr. Thacker
Cash 1/-	Mr. C. Critchlow

A very nice lot of things were collected from the Sheldon people and some gave cash, cabbages, cauliflowers, a drake, some cockerels, rabbits, oatcakes, candles, and other articles were sold up at the schoolroom and then a dance. When the money was added up it was found we had from all sources the handsome sum of £13.1.0. which will be handed over for the benefit of the British Red Cross. It was further decided that the people of Sheldon should get something up for our soldier lads (those that are left alive belonging to the village) and Mr. Fred Brocklehurst (Sneyd Green) contributed 10 shillings towards that purpose. Mr. Goodwin played for dancing. Mr. Stephenson called at our house but did not stay long as he was not well. The Germans are still retreating. I heard the sorrowful news that young Elliott who wrote about our poor Tony had been killed.

Oct. 13th Very fine and I hope this weather will continue as I do not remember having such a wet time for so many weeks together. I should think we have had continual wet for 7 or 8 weeks which has made such bad work with the splendid crops, so much of the corn has been shed. Mr. Stephenson took the service in Sheldon Church this afternoon and called here after service. I lent him Anthony's coat. Eben Ollerenshaw and his wife and Fred Brockley and his wife (Potteries) went back today.

Oct. 14th A most miserable wet day. Anthony and Tom went to market with some sheep. I wrote a letter to Mr. and Mrs. James Elliott about their son and one to Mrs. Rawlinson, also copied out some verses on a paper from which we want memorial cards copied.

Oct. 15th Very fine. Anthony and Tom were thatching corn stacks. Afterwards Anthony ploughed out a row of Mayfield Blossoms in our fields. Ethel and Evelyn went to Matlock for 3 new hats which cost more than they ought for what they were.

Oct. 16th Fine but dull at times. Tom is gone on moor thatching. Wm is drawing thatch and Vincent has gone home because Wm has been swearing at him so I understand. The Turks want an armistice and peace and we are doing well on the Western Front. Mr. Stephenson called here. Mr. Skidmore said what a comfort my letter had been to Mrs. Elliott of Bakewell over her dear lad.

Oct. 17th Fine but dull. Our men are getting potatoes (Mayfield Blossoms). Anthony went down to see Vincent over yesterday. The lad came back and I hope Wm will keep his tongue still. Ethel and Evelyn have got colds. Mr. Sherlock called here and had tea.

Oct. 18th Fine but dull. Our Anthony and Tom were thatching. Tom on moor. Vincent is at home as he has hurt his ankle (jumping off a wall). No potato getting today. Mr. Sherlock held a service at school. Ethel and Evelyn did not attend as they have got such severe colds. Ostend, Lille and Douai are in the Allies hands.

Oct. 19th Fine. Our men and Freddy Carson went getting potatoes this afternoon. Old Watercress Jack called in this dinner time. I received a very nice letter from Mrs. James Elliott in answer to one I sent her when I heard her boy was killed. Mr. Stephenson called and had tea. Mary and Hannah went picking potatoes this afternoon. A meeting was held in our house to see what could be got for the soldiers belonging to Sheldon for Xmas. A Committee was formed and these have to see what people will give in the shape of prizes so that there can be books printed for a draw. Fire was lighted in Church first time.

Oct. 20th Very raw and cold looking like rain. Mr. Stephenson took the service in Church and afterwards called here and had tea. Ethel and Evelyn did not go to Church as they had such colds. Mary played harmonium. Mr. Stephenson brought a beautiful gold compass pendant which he gave for a prize (soldiers) and also a ten shilling note that someone had given him.

Oct. 21st Misty and showery towards night. Mary went to Bakewell and was trying to get a few necessary things such as treacle etc. but she was not successful. It is said that Orme's had a cask of treacle on Saturday last and some people got both treacle and jam. She ordered some memorial cards for our dear Tony (Smiths).

Oct. 22nd Very misty. No potato getting as the ground is so wet. The men are busy. Vincent's foot is a bit better. Evelyn received a letter from Mr. Stephenson. He was in bed yesterday with a cold. Ethel, Evelyn and Mary and myself have got the influenza colds.

Oct. 24th Misty first thing but clears out, sunshine and rather cold. Tom, Wm, Vincent and Freddy Carson were getting our potatoes. Sam Bramwell was in our house tonight having come home on leave last night. Billy Naylor was hacking out below Mr. Eds to find a burst in the water pipes. It was found in T.A. Sheldon's branch pipe and now there is a supply for folks at the top of the village. Some people are bad with influenza. Four at H. Frosts and Billy, Pattie and Hilda Carson.

Oct. 26th Fine and a very good day for getting potatoes. Our men were busy getting them. Anthony was thatching on moor. Mr. Stephenson called and had tea and took a couple of cockerels back with him (one weighed 4 lbs, the other 4½ lbs at 2/- per lb). A meeting was held in our house to decide what should be done for the soldiers' Xmas fund. We let our milk cows lie in shippen tonight. Several contributed money and we have now the following sums and prizes:

Mr. Fred Brocklehurst (Sneyd Green)	10s.0d.
Mr. Stephenson	10s.0d.
Mr. Cox-Wilson	10s.0d.
Mr. Roger Sheldon	5s.0d.
Mr. Sam Wilton	3s.0d.
Mr. W. Brown	2s.6d.
Mr. G. Carson	2s.0d.
Mrs. Morton (Aldern House)	2s.0d.

Prizes up to now

Mr. and Mrs. Naylor	A sucking pig
Mr. C. Ollerenshaw	Box of cigars
Mr. Stephenson	A compass pendant in gold
Mr. J. Goodwin and Mr. Wm Hallows	Bottle of Whiskey
Mr. T.A. Sheldon	Couple of fowls
Mr. Ed Brockley	Two milking stools
Mr. Alf Brocklehurst	1 cwt of potatoes
Mr. Gyte	2 cwts of potatoes
Mrs. Fairholme	scarf and gloves
Mr. Moseley (promised)	rabbits
Mrs. Lees (promised)	rabbits

Sam Wilton said that his brother Matthew was killed on October 11th last by a sniper.

Oct. 27th Fine but dull at times like rain. Mr. Sherlock took the service in Church. Dr. Fentem attends Frosts and Carsons. I believe James Frost and Pattie Carson are still very ill, the others are improving. I received a very nice letter from Ernest Rawlinson saying that he had heard from Shrewsbury and that Shrewsbury had had a brother killed and the youngest brother maimed for life and poor Dick as my dear Tony and Ernest used to call him was feeling very bad. I heard tonight that Johnny Bramwell of Monyash had been killed. He joined up about the same time as our dear Tony.

Oct. 28th Fine, mild but no sun. More people in Sheldon taken with the Flu. Ethel and Evelyn walked to Bakewell and called for our dear Tony's memorial cards. Two dozen of these with envelopes cost 13/-. They are very nice indeed.

Oct. 29th Fine but dull. Anthony took 5 ram lambs to Tideswell Fair. Mr. Stephenson called here and was up at school. James and Ann Frost and two Carson girls (Pattie and Hilda) are still very ill. I wrote to Ernest Rawlinson and sent him a memorial card.

Oct. 30th Fine, rather cold. Anthony did not go to the Haven Fair with lambs but he, Tom and Wm were getting and finishing the rakings in corn fields on moor on Bramwell field. Ethel, Evelyn and Aunt H were raking in Bramwell field. No potato getting this day or two. Vincent is away with Flu and his father is in bed with a bad throat. Mr. Stephenson was up at Sheldon again tonight. He called here and had supper. The draw books came and the milk cheque (£62.6s.0d.) from Mr. Burley.

Oct. 31st Fine but rather dull at times. Little Anthony Wager is not so well (full of cold). Anthony, Wm and Tom were getting potatoes. Wm H. Bramwell was in our house tonight. He had sold 120 tickets for the Sheldon soldiers draw.

Nov. 1st All Saints day. Cold, drizzling rain this afternoon. Anthony, Tom and Wm were getting potatoes this morning. Our Mary has gone to bed again. She coughs so and is starved. Vincent is still away poorly. I received a very nice letter this morning from Mrs. Rawlinson, enclosing a postal order of 1/- from Ernest for the soldiers draw. Read in paper that an armistice was signed between the Allies and the Turkish Government at noon yesterday, General Townshend was liberated by the Turks to approach the Allies. Austria has been heavily defeated by Italy and wants an armistice. It is just one year ago since my dear Tony wrote his last letter which was to his father wishing him many happy returns of the day. November 1st was on Thursday last year. Rain tonight. Ethel went to Bakewell.

Nov. 2nd All Souls Day. Very rough and rather showery at times. Between last night and this morning the rain came down in torrents and the wind was very rough. Just one year ago today by the day of the month my darling Tony gave up his life, he dying of wounds. He must have died the same day he was wounded as he wrote to his father the day before and he was all right then. I received a very comforting letter and card from Mr. Stephenson who shows himself so sympathetic and kind to everybody. He called and had tea with me today. There are a many people all over the country in every village and town down with some sort of influenza. James Frost and Carsons are improving. People do not seem to be able to get any nourishing things like they could do formerly. Mr. Stephenson got some apples for James Frost and he said that apples were 3/6 per lb. The draw for the soldiers fund, the tickets I mean, have a very good sale. Anthony saw Wm Bramwell and told him to send some more books. Mr. Twelves has sold 1 book and ten tickets for another (sent money). A Memoriam was in the *Derbyshire Times* for our dear Tony.

Nov. 3rd The wind has dropped and it is rather showery. Holy Communion this morning. Only 5 present. Mr. Sherlock administered. Mr.

Stephenson called here and had dinner. He took the service in Church this afternoon and spoke about the lads in Sheldon who have laid down their lives etc. A hymn was sung that our dear Tony used to play so often on my old harmonium viz: *Thy way, not mine, O Lord.* Anthony, Tom, Ethel and Evelyn went to Church. Mary is in bed and little Anthony has a most severe cold. A collection in Church for Church expenses 10s. 4d.

Nov. 4th   Frosty and cold. Anthony and Tom went to Bakewell with cows. Anthony took milk and Billy Naylor helped Tom with the cows. Mary is still in bed. I think she is a little better. Ethel is not well, and Evelyn and little Anthony cough very much. Vincent Hallows is still at home poorly and there has not been any potato getting. We have about half to get and then all the swedes. Austria and Hungary is out of the war having surrendered and accepted Allies conditions.

Nov. 5th   Rough and showery at times. Anthony bought a Holstein cow off Herbert Frost giving £48.0.0. for her. Dr. Jackson came to see Mary and Ethel. Mary's stomach is bad. She is sick after taking anything. She is only having liquids. Anthony went to Bakewell for medicine and to do some shopping. Mary received a PC from our Clem. He got the photos. The 5th of Nov. passed without bonfires or anything we used to have. Arthur Goodwin called with 12 more books of draw tickets.

Nov. 6th   Fine, frosty. Tom, Wm and Freddy Carson are getting potatoes. Ethel is a deal better. Mary is about the same (still in bed). Aunt H took little Anthony out for a walk (1st time for a week). The Germans are retreating on 70 miles front. Read Mr. Lloyd George's speech over the Allies terms to Austria Hungary which are very strict. Just one year today since we heard our Dear Tony was badly wounded from Mr. Elliott.

Nov. 7th   Fine, cold and frosty. Our Anthony, Tom, Wm and Freddy Carson are getting potatoes Grindlow Knoll. Mary does not get on at all. She eats nothing and only just sips a little soda and milk, chicken broth and eats a little jelly. She is very weak and no energy at all. Mr. Sherlock called and had a cup of tea. Ethel was going to get up but he went upstairs and told her not to do so. Wm H. Bramwell called and said that the Sheldon soldiers would be included with Ashford and Bakewell in the money got from the concert in the Town Hall, Bakewell, tonight. Mr. Sherlock was going to speak at the concert.

Nov. 8th   Cold and very dull. I wrote to Dr. Jackson and Doris Brocklehurst went to Bakewell with the letter. Our Mary is no better at all, so sick and weak. Ethel came downstairs this afternoon. Clarice is in bed. Mr. Hallows went for the Dr. for Mrs. Hallows. Sam Wilton is bad and others. Our Mary did not come downstairs. Elsie and Elizabeth Wallwin are ill with the Flu.

Nov. 9th   Cold and Showers of hail and snow. Vincent is a little better. Mrs. Hallows and the other people are about the same. Ethel and Mary got up for a bit tonight. They are weak. Mr. Stephenson called. He has sold nearly 3 books of *draw tickets*. Anthony's birthday (55 years old). Hunters at Sheldon today.

Nov. 10th Fine 1st thing, showery tonight. Mr. Stephenson called and had tea after taking service. Only Evelyn went to Church today. The others seem a little better. I received a letter from E. Rawlinson.

Nov. 11th Fine this morning. We heard the sorrowful news that both Lizzie and Elsie Wallwin were dead with the Influenza. Herbert Wallwin came to Sheldon about 4 o'clock this morning to see if some one would go and lay them out. Anthony's sister Louisa went. What dreadful things are happening besides the war. The time is getting short for Germany to make up her mind to come into the Allies terms, before an armistice can be arranged. The German Government was given 72 hours to come to an understanding and the time expires at 11 o'clock this morning. Meanwhile the Allied Armies are winning all before them on the Western Front and will soon rid the Huns out of their land if things go on as well as they are doing. Tom drowned our old black cat which has been such a good one. She had sores. News was telegraphed throughout that the Armistice had been signed by the Germans at 5 o'clock this morning. Bells were ringing all round the different towns and villages and flags were out. The Armistice lasts for 35 days. Harry Cooper came up and had supper here.

Nov. 12th Very frosty and cold. When the frost had gone off Tom, Wm and Freddy Carson went on Grindlow Knoll getting potatoes. Anthony went to Wallwins to see a cow that could not calve. He tried to get the calf but could not and they fetched the vet. (Herbert Wallwin fetched Anthony in trap). A few flags were out at Sheldon but some had no heart for joy, those of us who have lost our loved ones. Mr. Stephenson brought up the two shirts which Mrs. Tinsley has given to the Sheldon draw. There were thanksgivings to GOD in St. Margaret's Westminster as soon as possible after the news was known, members of the House of Commons and Lords attending, Mr. Lloyd George and Mr. Asquith walking together. I have had today's newspaper put away as it contains the terms of the armistice.

Nov. 13th Very frosty and cold. Twenty one years ago today by the day of the month my dear Tony was born and he has been lying in a foreign grave for over one year. It is dreadful to think of. We are glad that the war is won but what sorrowful hearts there will be when some of the lads come home and so many are left behind. Poor Lizzie and Elsie Wallwin were interred at Ashford this afternoon at 3 o'clock. Our men are getting potatoes. Mr. Stephenson came up and took a service in school afterwards having supper here.

Nov. 15th Not so frosty. Our men were cutting swedes this morning and potatoes after dinner. A thick fog came on this afternoon. Our Mary had some official papers which she has to sign and she can draw £30.0.0. of Clem's back money. Clem had written to headquarters for her to have it. Ethel and Evelyn went to Monyash to buy clogs. Ethel got a pair but the other two have to wait until some are sent for. Just one year today since poor Alf Wildgoose died of fever (Salonica).

Nov. 17th Raw and cold, dull. Mr. Sherlock took the service in Sheldon Church this afternoon. I received a folded card (Chesterfield views) from Mr. Stephenson who went to Heath yesterday. A Memoriam for poor Alf Wildgoose was in the *Derbyshire Times* this week from his brothers and sisters, nephews and nieces.

Nov. 18th Raw and cold, fine. G. Carson began wood cutting. Our Tom, Teddy Lomas, Freddy Carson and Vincent (Vincent returned to work this morning) went getting swedes. C. Hall, the Landlord of the Red Lion, Bakewell, died of pneumonia. Influenza and pneumonia is making terrible work with people all over the country. Two, three and more in some places lying dead in the house at once.

Nov. 19th Fine rather raw and cold. Our men, Teddy Lomas, Freddy Carson and Thos A Sheldon have been getting our potatoes (Grindlow). A paper came with the amount of cake etc. we can have for our cows. Mr. Stephenson called and paid for the three chickens he had a week or two since (£1.3.0.).

Nov. 20th Raw, cold and frosty. Our men and Teddy Lomas were leading manure and bringing swedes back from Grindlow Knoll. They could not get potatoes as the ground was so hard. Mr. Stephenson called after service in school and had supper here. Mary had a PC from Clem. People keep dying of influenza and pneumonia.

Nov. 22nd Very raw and cold and very foggy. Our men did not go getting potatoes as it was so severely cold. Ethel and Evelyn walked to Bakewell. Mr. Sherlock called here and said he had been making soup and carrying it out to people in Ashford. Read that the German Fleet had surrendered.

Nov. 23rd Misty, gets a bit clearer this afternoon. Ethel started just after 9 o'clock to cycle to Grindleford. Our men, Alf Brocklehurst and Wm Hallows were getting potatoes in our Grindlow Knoll. They are very good potatoes and a nice crop. Harry Cox and Billy Doddimede (Longstone) died after the Flu. Ethel got back all right but said how bad the roads were. She had to walk a good bit. Mr. Stephenson called and had tea.

Nov. 25th Mild. A bit showery. Fred Bramwell went back today (4.30). He had to report at Grantham. He has had ten days leave which he has spent at Dove Holes and Sheldon. Tom, Wm, Vincent and Freddy Carson finished getting our potatoes (Grindlow Knoll). Mary drew £30.0.0. at Bakewell PO. This sum Clem had written for from Headquarters (written from Limberg). She put £25.0.0. in the Savings Bank and with the other bought herself a raincoat, umbrella etc.

Nov. 27th Mild, very slight showers. Our men and Jack Broomhead *(puff crumb)* were pulling swedes and carting them home. Mr. Stephenson called here (service at school). Fred Brocklehurst came home on Draft leave.

Nov. 30th   Very misty. Mr. Stephenson came up and brought us a few currants and 1 oz of tobacco. He told me that Mr. Sherlock's father died last Wednesday (suddenly). Mr. Stephenson and Mr. Wm Hy Bramwell (Bakewell) went round to some houses in Sheldon for subscriptions to the soldiers' Xmas fund. There was a draw in our houseplace tonight. Two bags were in use viz. one containing the number of each ticket sold (1440) and the other bag as many blanks and with the name of a prize on some (17 prizes). Mr. Stephenson held one bag (blanks and prizes) and W.H. Bramwell the other bag with numbered tickets. Ethel drew the numbered tickets and Evelyn the blank tickets and prizes.The prizes fell to the following people: viz

No	460	Pig	B. Hampshire 74 Kedleston Rd Derby
	599	Couple of rabbits	S. Wilton senior Flagg
	608	Bottle of Whiskey	J. Smith (Printer) Bakewell
	1025	1 cwt of potatoes	George Wm Hurst Ashford
	586	couple rabbits	Ethel Brocklehurst Sheldon
	1195	1 cwt potatoes	Ida Ward Sheldon
	1200	Duck	Elizabeth A Brocklehurst Sheldon
	164	couple rabbits	C Moss 70 John St. Derby
	257	milking stool	J. Stephenson Church Dale
	1266	winter scarf	Stanley Brocklehurst Sheldon
	375	1 cwt potatoes	Margaret Goodwin Haddon Grove
	1006	Box of cigars	S. Wright Church Street Ashford
	318	milking stool	Bertie Littlewood Bakewell
	561	pair of gloves	C. Benn Bakewell
	704	couple shirts	Leah Brocklehurst Sheldon
	1091	compass pendant	J. Stephenson Church Dale.

There were a good house full at the draw and we had not a drink of anything in the house and have not had for over a week. Mr. Stephenson had supper. The draw took about 1½ hours of time to get through.

Dec. 1st   A bit showery at times. Mr. Sherlock administered Holy Communion at 9.40 this morning. A good number present. Mr. Stephenson took the service this afternoon, collection for Church expenses (17s.od.). He came and had tea after service (at our house).

Dec. 3rd   Fine. Our men were pulling swedes. Received a letter from Mary enclosing some ration cards. Little Anthony wants to come back to Sheldon already. I wrote to Mrs. Rawlinson. Fred Brocklehurst went back after being on leave.

Dec. 4th   Fine. Vincent, Freddy Carson and J. Broomhead were pulling swedes. Tom and Wm went to Bakewell for manure. I got a letter from Shrewsbury. Thos A Sheldon brought us two pullets which Anthony won at the *Draw*. Mr. Sherlock called here and had tea. Mr. Stephenson called here and had supper.

Dec. 5th   Showery at times and rather rough. Jack Broomhead, Freddy Carson and our men pulling swedes. Anthony and Naylors received postcards saying that Clem was released (prisoner) and had reached Calais on his way home.

Dec. 7th   Heard from Mary that Clem had arrived at Dover. Fine, men were getting swedes. Mr. Stephenson called and had tea and brought a Xmas book for A.W. Wager.

Dec. 8th   Dull and showery. I received a letter from Mary saying that Clem had arrived home (Grindleford) on Friday night. He and other prisoners were turned out in Germany and had to find British lines. They arrived at Metz and were treated very well by the American troops and they afterwards got to Calais where they sailed for Dover. Mr. Stephenson took the service in Church.

Dec. 10th   Dull and showery. Clem came this morning by the milk cart from Longstone and is staying the night. He brought some German bread and paper money and coins. He went through awful hardships during his 2 years as a German prisoner of war and is very thankful to get back. He bears marks where the bullets and shrapnel have hit him and his left arm is not very strong through them. Charles F. White sent a telegram to Ed. Brockl. saying that he could not speak at Sheldon tonight as his car had broken down. Mr.Stephenson brought two rabbits for one of the prize draws.

Dec. 11th   Very dull and very misty. Clem left here at about half past 10 on his way to Grindleford. He was calling at Longstone. A post card came from T. Hawley about closed carriages or conveyance for those that could not walk to the poll at Monyash next Saturday. Mr. Stephenson came here and had supper. The rabbits went to Ethel Brocklehurst (prize).

Dec. 12th   Rather rough but a drying wind. Our men finished turnip pulling. The younger boys broke the porch window up at school tonight. Jenny Brocklehurst and Bertha Bramwell went round Sheldon collecting to get Mr. Stephenson a Xmas gift.

Dec. 13th   Dull, mild. Our men finished carting swedes. We had the tame rabbit to dinner. No one would eat any of it but the men. It was killed on Wednesday. Mr. Sherlock called here and had tea. He brought one piece of blue flannel to look at from Stewarts.

Dec. 14th   Fine. Ethel's birthday (26). No one sent her any cards or anything. Voting day. Mr. Warden's car came from Monyash to fetch those who could not walk very well. The women who went were as follows: Mrs. H. Frost, Mrs. Ollerenshaw, Mrs. Sherwin, Mrs. W.H. Brocklehurst, Mrs. Thos. A.Sheldon, Mrs. Banks, Mrs. Alf Brockley, Mrs. S. Bramwell, Mrs. J. Frost, Mrs. Louis E. Elliott. The men chiefly went at night. Mr. Stephenson called and had tea etc.

Dec. 15th Showery at times. Ethel received birthday cards from Grindleford. Mr. Sherlock took the service in Church today. Mr. Stephenson did not come up.

Dec. 17th Very heavy showers towards night. Fine in morning. A man and woman came and tuned the Church harmonium. Ben Naylor killed one of our pigs. Vincent has not been today. He has hurt his ankle. Sam Rowland came on leave.

Dec. 19th Snow storms. Our Tom and Freddy Carson fetched the fowls off the moor as it looks like being a deep snow. Vincent has not come back as his foot is swollen and he has got cold. Anthony has a severe cold and Wm coughs very much. Sam and Fred Bramwell came on leave.

Dec. 20th Snow storms at intervals. Another man came to tune the Church harmonium (Pearson who has a shop at Bakewell) but it had already been tuned. Ethel went to Bakewell to do a bit of shopping. She managed to get half a lb of sultanas and a few other things. Emily and I were reckoning up the Sheldon soldiers' money and putting it in envelopes. Each soldier had £2.11s.2d. and we gave some of the money to the soldiers in the house viz. Sam Bramwell, Fred Bramwell. We gave Jim Goodwin their Fred's money and Billy Naylor their Jack's. Mr. Sherlock took a service in school tonight.

Dec. 21st Wet towards night. Shortest day. Anthony's cold is no better. Evelyn took the other soldier lads' money to their homes viz Fred Brockley's, Ben Sheldon's, Jack Sherwin's, George Ward's and Jimmy Rowland fetched his father's. Mr. and Miss Stephenson and Mr. and Mrs. Goodwin called here and had tea. Mr. Goodwin (organist of Heath Church) has come to play at the organ recital at Sheldon Church tomorrow. Arthur Stroyan is on leave. I feel very upset over our poor Tony when I see the other soldier lads arriving home on leave.

Dec. 22nd A most wretched misty wet day. Mr. Stephenson and Mr. Goodwin arrived about dinner time and both dined with me (roast pork, brussels and potatoes). Mrs. Goodwin and Miss Stephenson came a little later. These two ladies dined with Alf Brocklehurst. Owing I think to being so very wet and rough the congregation was not as large as expected. After Mr. Stephenson had conducted a short service Mr. Goodwin presided at the organ and Miss Stephenson sang. The collection (for the St. Dunstan's blind soldiers) amounted to £2.11.9. Mr. Goodwin and Mr. Stephenson had tea here and Mrs. Goodwin and Miss Stephenson had theirs at Alf Brocklehurst's. Sid Brocklehurst and Mr. Goodwin set out to Bakewell station to catch the 5.43 train for Sheffield. Mr. Goodwin would get off at Chesterfield. Sid Brockley came to Sheldon last night. Prayers were offered in Church for Mr. Craven who is ill of pneumonia. Our Tom brought a turkey from the station which Mr. Sneap had sent us.

Dec. 23rd Very wet and rough at times. Anthony went (though his cold is not better) to Bakewell to meet Mary, Clem, Anthony and Aunt H. They arrived between 2 and 3 this afternoon. A telegram came to Mr. Ed Brocklehurst saying that Mr. Craven was dead (died today).

Dec. 24th Snow storms. Freezing. Our Emily was taken ill with one of her bad attacks and I sent to the doctor. Vincent went and brought some medicine for her. Our Tom and Clem were plucking and drawing the sinews out of the turkey. We have not put any holly or evergreens up. This is the 2nd Xmas that our poor Tony has been lying in a foreign grave.

Dec. 25th Xmas Day. Snow. Holy Communion. Mr. Sherlock celebrated and Mr. Stephenson was here at 9.30. Mr. Stephenson came and took the service this afternoon. Collection for Church expenses (14s.2d.). Mr. Stephenson called and had tea but did not stay long. We had the turkey for dinner.

Dec. 26th Very frosty. Mr. and the Misses Stephenson called today and are having tea with T.Wm B. Jenny Brocklehurst presented Mr. Stephenson with £4.0.0. which had been collected in Sheldon to make him a present. He seemed quite overcome about it. There has been some sledging as the roads are in nice order.

Dec. 27th Thawing, wet. Our girls were busy getting the schoolroom ready for tonight's entertainment. Mr, Miss and Miss Elsie Stephenson had tea here before going up to school. The entertainment went off very well. Songs were sung by Clem, Enoch Marsden, Ed and Miss Stephenson. Monologues by Miss Elsie Stephenson. Dialogues by our Ethel, Ruth B and Hilda Carson *(Neighbours in Gooseberry Court)*. Clarice, Alice and Mary the land girl's dialogue was called *Aunt Dorinda*. Above 50 shillings was made at this entertainment and with the collection in Church will be handed to the blind soldiers of St. Dunstan. Mr. Sherlock was present at school for a short time. Clem shot our old Navvy.

Dec. 28th Most miserable and wet at times today. A many people went to Bakewell to hear the poll declared (Election poll) which was read out at about a quarter to six o'clock tonight. Charles F White went in with a majority of 2,163 votes over Lord Henry. Wm went to Bakewell and paid Mr. Hill. He also bought himself boots, slippers and leggings. Mr. Craven was interred at Staveley cemetery.

Dec. 29th Most wet and miserable. Mr. Sherlock took a short service this afternoon for the fallen lads (in the war) of Sheldon. Clem and Mary went to see Naylors and uncle John Brocklehurst.

Dec. 31st Rough wind. Sam Rowland went back after his leave. Anthony took some oats to Alport Mill. Mary and Clem went to Bakewell. We boiled ham for Mr. Stephenson. Mr. Stephenson called here and had tea. He brought some matches for us.

1919

Jan. 1st   Rough, snowstorms. The girls are getting ready for the tea Mr. Stephenson is giving tonight. Mr. and Miss Stephenson have just arrived and are sitting warming themselves just before going up to school. One of the best calves is dying of speed. It was inoculated for that disease only last Saturday. We had 20 inoculated the same time. Tom's birthday (30 years). No ale or spirits at New Year's day. 1st time only in 30 years. Later on a full assembly at the school had tea with Mr. Stephenson and Miss Stephenson at his expense. The eatables were very good - cakes, buns and bread (from Marsdens) and ham sandwiches. There was singing and dancing after tea. Clem and Mary sang. Jim Goodwin played for dancing. All at our house went to tea except Emily and myself. Our tea was sent to us.

Jan. 2nd   Very rough winds. Mary, Clem little Anthony and aunt H went back to Grindleford. Stanley Brocklehurst took them with their horse and our float. Mr. Routledge came for Orme and Co. as Mr. Ronston was not well. Anthony paid up (by cheque). We had had 3 kils of ale last month. We paid for them all and some tobacco (1lb) as well. Nobody in the houseplace tonight as we have only minerals to sell. Sam Rowland came home (from the army).

Jan. 3rd   Keen frost this morning and a sprinkling of snow. I find great difficulty in doing much writing as I am so bad with rheumatism in my right arm. Mr. Sherlock called and had tea. Mrs. Banks flitted to Fairfield.

Jan. 4th   Deep snow. People cannot remember such a deep snow falling in so short a time as early this morning none had fallen and on getting up the walls in front of our house were piled up very high. We had a sheep (hog) buried and Anthony, Tom and George Eaton went to try to find it but were not successful. Tom had been before and got sopping wet through and did not find it. However Tom went round the fields again and at last found it overthrown at the top of the Big Butts with its feet sticking through the snow. Mr. Stephenson called and brought us some sugar and macaroons. (He had tea at Alf Brockley's). Ormes did not come to Sheldon with the order. I suppose they could not get through the snow. Sam Rowland flitted from John Frost's house into the one that Mrs. Banks left.

Jan. 5th   Snow. Mr. Sherlock did not celebrate Holy Communion in Sheldon Church this morning. There were four people waiting but no clergyman came so there was no celebration today. Mr. Stephenson had dinner with us and took the service in Church this afternoon. Collection for Church expenses (11s.6d.). He also held a service at 7 o'clock until eight in the schoolroom tonight and had a very good congregation. He stayed to tea at T.Wm Brockley's. Anthony and Tom took the milk to station with two horses, old gray one and Fanny.

Jan. 7th   Thawing. Our men were lashing straw and getting hay in etc. Night school. We have had scarcely any water as there is so much back water down at the pumps which prevents them working.

Jan. 8th   Misty. Wm went for a ton of coal for the Church. There was a sale of stock etc. at the late Fred Furniss's. We have had no beer for above a week. Mr. Stephenson called.

Jan. 10th   Finer, rather raw and cold. Wm has been carting manure on to the moor. The crows have been on to the corn stacks, and Anthony wrote to Mr. Shimwell a day or two since about it and also told him what a great number of both crows and pigeons there were about. The crows had pulled our stacks shamefully. Two youths brought two kils of ale from Ormes. Mr. Sherlock called here and had a talk with us about Mr. Stephenson and the Church services.

Jan. 11th   Fine. Our Tom was ploughing on moor (cabin field). He had done two or three half days before Xmas. A preliminary meeting was held in Sheldon school tonight (7.30) to discuss a war memorial for the fallen (in the war) men of Sheldon (7 or 8 present). Two things were put forward, either a tablet to be placed in Church or a monument and I was asked to write to Mr. Wm Shimwell of Youlgreave to send patterns etc. Fred Goodwin went back to his depot. Miss M. Stephenson went to London. Mr. Stephenson was up at Sheldon and had tea at Naylor's. He stayed for the meeting and had supper here.

Jan. 12th   Misty and raw. Anthony is not well. He was so cold and had cramp so bad in the night. Vincent was not here to dinner. He went with Harry Carson on bike. Mr. Stephenson took the service in Church and had tea at Mr. John Frost's. There was a well attended service at Church this evening (Mr. Stephenson).

Jan. 13th   Very misty and raw. Anthony took the milk and afterwards went to Bakewell. He attended a meeting of the Farmers' Union. George Haywood paid him for one cheese which he had had off John Brocklehurst and this money was given to Leah tonight. Tom Critchlow and Sam Rowland were in our house. Anthony paid Tailor Hill for our Tom's coat and waistcoat which was £4.0.0. (shameful).

Jan. 14th   Misty and wet at times. PC Young came on duty to Sheldon being the first time since joining up when the war started. PC Dennis gave up duty for Sheldon on Saturday. He came up. I am sorry Dennis has left. He has been most obliging all during the war. I wrote to Wm Shimwell about the tablet for the fallen of Sheldon. Sent £6.5s.0d. to Sir Arthur Pearson for the blind soldiers and sailors. There was a whist drive and dance at Monyash tonight.

Jan. 15th Fine first thing but turned out wet tonight. Uncle John Brocklehurst fell off the haystack and hurt his head. Our Tom went to do a bit of ploughing on moor but the ground is in such a sodden state that nothing much can be done on the land. Mr. Stephenson came and took service in school. He told us that his daughter Mabel had had a good report as to her music (singing) in Sheffield.

Jan. 16th Misty and wet at times. Tom took 3 cwts of potatoes to Mrs. Sims, Bakewell (paid) and brought 2 kils of Burton ale from station. Ben Naylor cut up Mr. Ollerenshaw's and Thos. A. Sheldon's pigs (killed yesterday). Anthony put £300 in War Loan. Received a letter from Wm Shimwell.

Jan. 18th Wet at first but cleared out a nice day. Tom and Wm were ploughing with two teams on moor. Anthony cut a tree down in Shacklow and Vincent and he brought it. Mr. Stephenson came and had tea here. He brought some plaice for Emily and one guinea for the pendant from Mr. Metcalf. I gave 4 men 2/4 each: Sam Rowland, Sam Bramwell, Jim Goodwin for Fred, and Billy Naylor for Jack. There are 5 others to have it. Posted 3 cards for little Anthony Wager.

Jan. 19th Very cold and frosty, snowed a little at night. Holy Communion was celebrated in Sheldon Church. Mr. Sherlock officiated at 9.40. He also took the service in Church this afternoon. Mr. Stephenson took an evening service and called here and had supper. Anthony Wager's birthday, 4 years.

Jan. 20th Misty and wet. George Ward came home tonight. He has been in Salonica over 2 years. Mr. Harry Bagshaw came and Anthony paid Income Tax, Land Tax, and 2/6 for Miss Broadhurst tax (out of his own pocket).

Jan. 21st Wet and misty. George Ward came in our house and I paid him 2/4 like the other soldiers. A cousin of uncle Will's and uncle John's was in our house at noon. A very talkative chap called George Goodwin. Received a letter from our Mary saying she had received the parcel (two sailor blouses for Anthony) but she had not got the P cards sent on Saturday.

Jan. 22nd Fine but cold. Received a letter from Annie Sneap saying that her father had received a hare which was sent a week or two since and two cockerels which Anthony sent on Friday last. Tom and his father and Wm are gone ploughing with two teams on moor. They took two loads of manure. Our girls are getting a parcel and letter ready to send to Lizzie Bacon.

Jan. 25th Misty. Wm and Vincent were leading manure on to the moor. Poor Cyril Mellor (Over Haddon) was buried. He died either Wednesday or Thursday of Diabetes, aged 21. Mr. Stephenson called and had tea. Fred Goodwin is at home from Army.

Jan. 26th Fine. Mr. Stephenson came here to dine and to Thos. Wm. Brockley's to tea. He took a service at night as well as the afternoon service.

Our Tom brought word that Joe Bagshaw was killed yesterday at Hindlow with a light engine. Two heifers have pecked, one last night and one tonight.

Jan. 27th Snowing. Anthony took milk and went to Bakewell market and to a Farmers' meeting. Sent a letter to Pickford to say we had lost 3 cows and gave him the nos. etc. Fred Brockley came home. Jim Goodwin ordered 4 bags of potatoes.

Jan. 28th More snow. This has stopped the working on the land. There are a many out on strike (miners) and others threatening to come out.

Jan. 29th Frosty and a little snifting of snow. Anthony and Tom are putting up bags of potatoes for Jim Goodwin. I wrote to our Mary but am suspicious the letters are not taken out of the box (very often lately) as people do not get their correspondence on the day they expect to get them. Mr. Stephenson called here and afterwards took a service in Church.

Jan. 30th Very severe with frost and snow. No working on the land. Fred Brockley called and had tea. Some of the young folks were sledging.

Feb. 1st Very frosty and cold. Trying to snow at times. Sledging goes on merrily with the young folks down the village of Sheldon. Mr. Stephenson called and had tea here. Anthony has a bad back and neck (stiff). The men are on strike in different parts of the country and others are threatening to come out. I do not think they themselves know in a many cases what for, some want shorter hours work per week etc. I think the country will be brought to ruin by such behaviour. Troops are being sent to Glasgow, Lewis guns etc. The riot act has been read and pillaging and looting going on. Why did the Government allow such things? They ought to have taken a firm stand at the commencement of the war. Soldiers cannot strike and I should like to know why men who have had the chance to stay at home whilst other poor lads have fought and died (for little over 1/- per day) are allowed to do as they like. There has been no such thing as equality of sacrifice.

Feb. 2nd Very frosty and cold. It is one year and 3 months since our dear Tony laid down his life and what a many people young and old have passed away since that day, people whom we knew so well. The influenza made terrible havoc in 1918. It seems abating but we hear of one now and then dying of pneumonia. Joseph Bennett (Longstone) who was blacksmith for many years passed away with pneumonia at the age of 68. We miss the old concertina chap (Wm. Ellis) who died towards the end of last year at Stoney Middleton. He generally came once a week to Sheldon in fine weather and I always gave him a good meal and a penny every time. There was a celebration of Holy Communion at 9.40 this morning (Mr. Sherlock came and officiated). Mr. Stephenson took the services in the afternoon and evening. Collection at evening service amounted to 17s.3d. for Church expenses. He called after service and had refreshment here. I received a long letter from Miss Stephenson and one from Mrs. Rawlinson. We had a cow calved tonight (cow calf). Tom took some of our milk to station in Alf Brockley's can as we had only one. Tom had to wash a can at the station and empty milk out from Alf's can.

Feb. 3rd   Very severe with frost and cold. Anthony went to market. His back seems a little better. Wm is emptying liquid tank. Anthony bought two buckets at 3s.6d. each. Before the war we could get similar buckets at 10d. and 1/- each.

Feb. 5th   Dull and snowstorms at intervals. Anthony and Tom took a gun each and other men of Sheldon with guns (9) went fox hunting. They saw a large fox but were unable to kill or shoot it. Mr. Stephenson called here and said he had seen two foxes making their way towards where Mr. Herbert Frost's cornstacks were down Hunterside. Service in Church tonight. Wm was leading manure on to moor.

Feb. 6th   Very dull and snowing at times. Anthony, Tom, Vincent and others went fox hunting but did not kill any. Tom and Evelyn went to the whist drive and dance at Bakewell. A good many went from Sheldon viz. Rebecca Ward, Pattie and Hilda Carson, Eliz. Ann and Stanley Brocklehurst, Fred Goodwin, Fanny, Maggie and Edith Goodwin, Leah and Alice Brocklehurst, Fred, Clarice and George Brocklehurst, Mary the landgirl and Rose Wilson, Eliza Naylor. (Clem had to report at headquarters).

Feb. 7th   Frosty and cold. Tom and Evelyn arrived home. Evelyn before 3 this morning and Tom about 3. Received PC from Mr. Froggat. Ethel went to Bakewell this afternoon and paid for the Church psalters and also Dr. Jackson's bill. I forgot to send 8s.6d. to the licensing justice. Jack Naylor came home.

Feb. 8th   Keener than ever with frost. Children keep sledging. Jack Naylor is not so well. He has got cold. Polly Naylor went to Bakewell and brought word that she had seen our Mary who had walked from Grindleford to Bakewell and had to walk back. Mary had to get some paper about Clem. Mr. Stephenson did not come to Sheldon today. There was a tea and dance at Ashford at which Mr. Charles F. White was welcomed on his being returned a member of Parliament in place of Lord Henry. No one went from Sheldon to tea.

Feb. 9th   Very severe with frost and cold. Mr. Stephenson took services in the afternoon and night. He had tea with Anthony and myself.

Feb. 11th   Very keen, thawing a bit towards night. People keep seeing foxes about and the men of Sheldon have been at a great amount of trouble in trying to trace them but have not succeeded in catching any this year. Received a letter from our Mary and she is afraid that Clem will not get off (army). He is at Lichfield barracks. Anthony and Tom keep picking over our potatoes. We do not seem to see many. I wrote to Mary asking her if she had got Clem's Scotch dress and to send it for our Tom to wear at the Sheldon ball on Friday next. Ethel and Evelyn are fixing up their dresses for that occasion and are finding Emily some things.

Feb. 12th   Sharp with frost. Anthony took milk. He said it was one of the worst days he had ever seen, so awkward travelling down the dale as it was so slippery. The girls finished their dresses ready for Friday's affair. Mr. Stephenson called. The magazine for Feb. referred to our Ethel's gift (an altar cloth of fair linen).

Feb. 13th   Keen with frost. A few keep sledging. Emily Sheldon lent Kate B a lovely old fashioned shawl (yesterday) for our Emily to wear with a dress that was my mother's. Received a letter from our Mary saying that she and Aunt H were making a kilt and cap for Tom of scotch plaid and a dress (altering) for Emily. She said that Clem was acting as orderly in Lichfield Barracks. Tom and William did not go to bed until after 3 o'clock this morning as they had sat up expecting a cow to calve which she did (bull calf).

Feb. 14th   Misty and raw with a few drops of rain. St. Valentine's Day. A fancy Dress ball was held in the Sheldon schoolroom and was very largely attended and kept up until late. People gave the refreshments, and 9 pence was charged at the door. The proceeds were given towards new lamps for the Church. The money from all sources viz door, sale of refreshments and contributions amounted to £6.5.2. + 2/- = £6.7s.2d. The characters represented were:

Mrs. Wm H. Brockley	Sister of Mercy
Mrs. Alf Brocklehurst	Milkmaid
Mrs. S. Bramwell	Pierrot
Miss Eliza Naylor	Crimson Rambler
Miss C.A. Brocklehurst	Gipsy Miss
Mary Carson	Britannia
Miss R. Wilson	Red Riding Hood
Mrs. Eaton	Quakeress
Miss Leah Brocklehurst	Daffodil
Miss Alice Brocklehurst	Flags
Miss Gyte	Night
Miss Ethel Gyte	Queen of Hearts
Miss Evelyn Gyte	Good Luck
Miss Kate Brocklehurst	Mid Victorian
Miss Ruth Brocklehurst	Indian Squaw
Miss D.M. Brocklehurst	Red Cross Nurse
Miss F. Goodwin	Peace
Miss C. Goodwin	Nurse Maid
Miss P. Carson	Modern Dress
Miss A. Carson	Victory
Mr. Stephenson	Chef
Mr. T.W. Brocklehurst	Grenadier Guard
Mr. J. Naylor	John Bull
Mr. T. Gyte	Highlander

Mrs. T.W. Brocklehurst	Pierrot
Mr. G. Brocklehurst	Cricketer
Mr. V. Hallows	Soldier
Mr. F. Carson (Junior)	Footballer
Mr. J. Goodwin	Bandmaster
Mr. F. Goodwin	Old Gentleman

A very enjoyable time was spent. Mr. Stephenson changed his clothes here.

Feb. 15th Misty and slight rain at times. Our Tom got in from ball at 2 o'clock. Evelyn and Ethel just before that time (this morning). Emily came in at 10 o'clock last night. Mr. Stephenson came up and had tea today at our house but had to hurry down as he had forgotten to post a letter.

Feb. 16th Very misty and slight snowstorms at times. Mr. Sherlock took the service in Church this afternoon. Mr. Stephenson took the service at night and had supper at our house. Three lamp glasses were broken. I do not know from what cause. A glass was fetched from here.

Feb. 17th Snowstorms and blizzards blowing. Anthony and Tom took two fat beasts and a bull calf to market and sold them. The calf was sold to Joe Eyre who did not pay for it. I received a letter from Clem. He is very upset as he says they are keeping him in the army which is a confounded shame after he has suffered so much with being a prisoner in Germany for 2 years. I wrote back to him; also made milk bill to the 14th February. Jack Naylor went back to Lincoln.

Feb. 18th A deep snow and snows at intervals. Everywhere seems blocked up and nothing to be done on the land. For about a week I have had a bit of fire lit in my bedroom about 7 or 8 o'clock but the coal is such a question.

Feb. 19th A deep snow. Not so much of it in the valley. Our men can do nothing on the land. They were winnowing oats. Mr. Stephenson came up to Sheldon tonight and took the service in Church. Sold out of beer. Wrote to Burton for more. Paid Sarah Brocklehurst 15s.10d. for tobacco etc. which she brought from Bakewell.

Feb. 20th Rather misty: thawing a little (rain). Our men picking potatoes etc. Heard from Mary. Tom and his father went fox hunting with others this afternoon. (Did not kill.) Mr. Sherlock called and had tea. I wrote to Mrs. Rawlinson. I received a letter from Ernest the other day. Anthony and Tom sat up with a cow calving.

Feb. 21st Dull, thawing a little. Wm went for coal as we are entirely without. Sent a £1.0.0. note to Mr. Goddard (Buxton) in payment of repairs done to Sheldon Church organ (Dec. 17th 1918).

Feb. 22nd Milder, drizzling a little at times. Tom, Wm and Vincent were leading manure on to the moor. They put the young horse (Wager) in with the other to lead manure. Mr. Stephenson came up and had tea. (He brought some fish). We were looking at some designs of War Memorial Tablets that Mr. Wm Shimwell had sent the other day.

Feb. 24th Very frosty. Lovely sunshine this morning. Vincent is away from work. Anthony took milk and afterwards went to market. The village water supply is very deficient lately. There must be either some leakages or something queer as the pumps have been attended to. Mr. and Mrs. Wm Shimwell of Youlgreave came to see us this afternoon and brought some more designs of monuments and tablets for War memorials. We had a nice long talk about Youlgreave people. They had tea here and afterwards went home. Mrs. Craven and baby came to Mrs. Ed's.

Feb. 25th Frosty, raw and cold. There has been a great majority among the miners to go on strike and the Prime Minister has given them grave warning about crippling the industries of the country.

Feb. 26th Very dull, raw and cold. Received a letter from Mary saying that Clem had not heard anything of coming home. Anthony has been very busy cleaning out the bakestone flue. Mrs. Smith has swept the houseplace and kitchen chimneys. Mr. Stephenson came and took a service in Church.

Feb. 28th Rather cold. Anthony went to the station (Bakewell) and found the beer (Burton) there. He brought 2 kils. The postman did not bring the letters until after 12 o'clock. There was a well attended social held in Sheldon School tonight. Our four and Wm went. Something has come to my left foot. It looks like starved blood etc. I have noticed it for above a week. This is the last day of the month and my father's birthday.

March 1st Dull but milder. Mary and little Anthony and aunt H came to Sheldon from Grindleford with Mrs. Johnson tonight. Mr. Stephenson called here. Eds owe 7 weeks milk, a quart a day at 6d. per quart. They never paid the old score off for milk which amounted to £1.8.0. (owing) and now Mrs. Craven is having a pint a day and she does not mention paying.

March 2nd Rather windy and cold. Mr. Sherlock officiated at the Holy Communion (8 present). Mr. Stephenson came here to dinner, and took the service this afternoon and evening. Collection at night service (15s.9d.) for Church expenses.

March 4th Wet and snow at intervals. Anthony had an order for 5 or 6 cwts of potatoes. There does not seem a ready sale for potatoes. Tom, Ethel, Fred, Clarice and George Bst., Mary Carson, Liz Ann and Stanley Brocklst went to Bakewell ball. Mrs. and Miss Blackwell were buried at Ashford.

March 5th Raw and cold. Tom and Ethel got back at just before 4 o'clock this morning from the Victory ball. Anthony took Sally Brockley, Jenny B and Bertha Bramwell in gig to vote for Mr. Ezra Walker to be C. Councillor. Ben Naylor killed one of our pigs. Mr. Ed B is not very well.

March 6th Slight showers towards night. Evelyn's birthday (24). Something came to my foot about a fortnight ago. It burns and itches but does not seem to get either better or worse. I have a bread poultice on now and then. Ben Naylor cut up the pig. Jack Naylor came home tonight. Mr. Mallison was returned C. Councillor by several hundred votes over Mr. Ezra Walker.

March 7th Very wet all day. Mary had a letter from Clem this morning saying that he was coming tonight for a weekend. She went to Bakewell to meet him but he did not arrive by the train expected so she came home to Sheldon again. Clem arrived here at something after 8 o'clock tonight. Gladys Brocklehurst is at home from France for 10 days leave. Vincent is no better. Little Anthony Wager has had a cold all week and so has aunt Hannah.

March 8th A bit showery at times. Tom, Clem and Wm went for hay on Sheldon Moor. They cut into the stack on moor for 1st time. We have a sheep very lame. Mr. Stephenson called and had tea. We had a conversation over the War Memorial. Clem seems to have a cold and is very much put about at having to stop in the army. Our sheep are brought in every night now as we are expecting lambs soon. Mr. Ed. Brockleys owe for 8 weeks milk at 3/6 per week which amounts to £1.6.0. There is that amount owing for milk they had a year or two since and I think it is too much to owe for milk. They never mention paying and Mrs. Craven had 9 pints for which she did not pay and went to Sheffield this week and never mentioned it.

March 9th Rather dull. We had pork for dinner. Mary, Clem and the boy went to Longstone this afternoon. Mr. Stephenson took the service in Church. Doris Brocklehurst brought 3s.6d. which pays for one week's milk out of the eight. Two sheep lambed, two each this afternoon. How my darling Tony would have looked after them if he had been alive. What thousands of grand young lives have been lost during this awful war. There are 12,000 who were reported prisoners of war who are feared to be dead (by the precious fine Government of ours) as they cannot be traced. Mr. Stephenson had tea with Mr. and Mrs. J. Frost.

March 11th Very dull and wet. Another lamb which makes five in number. Clem went to catch the 1.20 train Derby way. Mary went with him to Bakewell station. I do not know what time he would get to Lichfield Barracks. Sam Bramwell is picking potatoes for us. Gould took some potatoes to Widdowson and some to Bakewell. He brought coal back for us. Evelyn took 17s.4d. to uncle Wm Brockley to pay for coal which he fetched for Sheldon Church last week. I received a letter from Mrs. Rawlinson. The milk cheque came from Mr. Burley to end of February. There was a meeting in Sheldon school of the members of the club to discuss what they should give towards a memorial for the fallen lads of Sheldon and it was decided to give £3.0.0. from the funds.

March 12th A very stormy day, snowstorms and blizzards blowing. The men can do nothing on the land. Three men came to see if Sheldon farmers would let their supply of milk go to Sheffield and it would be fetched from their doors. Mr. McLocklen (Edensor) was one of the men. Mr. Stephenson came up and took the service in Church. Richard Bramwell buried at Ashford. Heard that Mr. Curtis had struck Mr. Frank Cox-Wilson over the head with a stick and cut him. The Dr. put 5 stitches in.

March 13th Finer. A bit frosty and the wind has calmed down. Mary had a letter from Clem saying he got back all right but it was very wet. He said that Will had written to him saying that a Mr. Bradbury would employ him (Clem) as keeper and that Mr. Burdekin and Mr. Crossland had written for him so I do hope he will be liberated from the Army.

March 14th Rather frosty. One of our sheep died of inflammation. Joe Johnson fetched it. Sam Bramwell is working for us at 5/- a day. Meeting was held in the schoolroom over the War Memorial for the fallen lads of Sheldon. Thos Wm Brockley, Mr. Stephenson and Anthony were chosen to see things carried out. Mr. Sherlock and Mr. Stephenson were present (total number there 23). Mr. T.W. Brocklehurst is to write to Mr. Wm Shimwell.

March 15th Rather cold. Mary had a letter from Clem enclosing Mr. Turner's and asking her to write to C.F. White which she did and told him about Clem being a prisoner etc. Mr. Stephenson called and had tea.

March 16th Fine, rather cold. Mr. Sherlock took the service in Church this afternoon which was rather short as the vicar had a headache. Mr. Stephenson came for tea and took the evening service in Church.

March 17th Fine. St. Patrick's Day. I wrote to Ernest Rawlinson. Mrs. Craven came back from Sheffield. Money was paid for milk she had off us.

March 18th Fine this morning. Tom went ploughing on moor. Sam Bramwell went with him. Wm went ploughing this afternoon but snow fell heavily and stopped the work. We are very busy with cows calving and sheep lambing. We have 16 lambs off 10 sheep. Mary received a very nice letter from Mr. C.F. White MP promising to write to the War Office over Clem etc. Ed Brocklehurst's keep fetching milk from our house and never paying for it. They are now going on for 9 weeks. We refused to let Mrs. Craven have milk as we are tired of such customers who keep fetching and not paying for such a length of time.

March 19th Blizzards of snow and it is again lying very deep. All work on the land stopped. The men have been weighing and putting potatoes in bags ready to take to Mr. Shenton, Bakewell. Two lambs came for the Church. Received a letter from Mrs. Rawlinson. Mr. Stephenson called and we gave him a roll of butter and some cheese which he was going to send to his daughters.

March 20th Snowing and blowing as much as ever. Anthony sent his resignation to Mr. A. Hawes as Rural District Councillor and Guardian for Sheldon.

March 21st Snow and frost. Received a letter from Mr. Hawes stating that the time was not up for choosing R.D. Councillors but that if Anthony still wished to resign he (Mr. Hawes) would prepare papers to send to the Local Government Board. A meeting was held at the school for choosing overseers etc. Ed Brockley has given notice that he will not look after the Sheldon Waterworks so Sam Rowland was proposed and he said that if he could have the oiling etc. he would do the work. The old overseers were appointed. Sent milk bill £62.4s.1d.

March 22nd Snow and frost. I had a letter from Miss Stephenson thanking me for cheese and butter. There is a parade at London of the Guards today. Fred Brocklehurst went there yesterday. Mr. Stephenson did not come up to Sheldon today. Ed Brockley's fetched the milk tonight but brought no money. They now owe for 9 weeks milk at 6d per quart and £1.8.0. was left on before which they never mention.

March 23rd The old sort of weather. Frost, snow and east winds. Bitterly cold. Mr. Stephenson took services both afternoon and night. He came here for tea, dinner and supper. All the lambing ewes are inside and all the lambs with their mothers. There is such a lot of work for all the men and girls carrying food and water etc. Tom could not go out tonight as we had a sheep lambing and other things.

March 24th Frost and flinkerings of snow. No snow at Ashford and Bakewell and we cannot get about for it here. Anthony and Tom took a calving cow to market and sold her for £30.0.0. Anthony wrote to Mr. Hartopp to ask if he would see about getting Tom put on as joint tenant with himself for the land.

March 27th Cold and frosty westerly wind. The milk cheque came £62.4s.1½d. to March 16th. Anthony received a letter from Mr. Hartopp saying that our Tom had been put down joint tenant with himself as from March 25th 1919. We have only a few bottles of beer to sell.

March 29th Raw and cold, snifting of snow. Mr. Stephenson did not come up as he has been ill all week. Tom Frost brought Orme's things but only brought 1 kil of ale (Bass) and no rum (as promised). The men like the beer which we sell at 6d. Eggs are selling at 3d each. Doris Brocklehurst was given the milk bill which amounted to £1.15.4. with an egg she had fetched and not paid for. Sam Rowland looks after Sheldon water, oils etc. the pumps.

March 30th Cold and little snow storms at intervals. Mr. Stephenson came and had dinner with us. He took the services afternoon and evening. Went to tea to Thos Wm Brockleys. Ernest Brockley was here tonight.

March 31st Cold and stormy at intervals. Other farmers began sending milk to Sheffield. Mr. Daybell brings cans and collects it. Alf Brockley, John Brockley, John Frost and Billy Naylor send their milk. Vincent Hallows began full work today. Sam Bramwell is still working for us. Mr. Moss came to examine spirit book.

April 1st   Snowing all morning, rather finer this afternoon. We had a calf with mad staggers and Alf Brockley and our Tom killed it etc. I made out milk bill to end of March 31st 1919 (£59.0.4$^{1}/_{4}$). Heavy snowstorms towards night.

April 2nd   Finer, rather cold. Mr. Wm Shimwell (Youlgreave) met Mr. Stephenson, Thos Wm Brockley and our Anthony at Sheldon to arrange about the tablet for the fallen lads of Sheldon. They went to the Church and chose out a place where it would be best to put it and they thought in the NE of Chancel. Mr. Shimwell and Mr. Stephenson came and had tea with me. Ben Naylor killed a pig (the last for this season) for us; one for Mr. Ollerenshaw and one for Mr. Bonsall. Ethel and Evelyn went to Bakewell Town Hall to a concert and dance for the VAD Nurses.

April 3rd   Dull and cold. Anthony cut up the calf that we killed and we sent and gave a piece to the following: viz Aunt Lizzie, Uncle Thos Wm B., Aunt Louisa Hallows, Sam Bramwell and Alf Brockley. We did not sell any as we did not want to run any risk. Ben Naylor cut up the pigs killed yesterday. They guessed ours at nearly 30 stones, Mr. Ollerenshaw's 24 or 25 and Mr. Bonsall's 18 or 20. Anthony fetched two kils of Burton ale from Bakewell station.

April 4th   Fine. Anthony set out this morning to catch the 9.15 train at Longstone. He was going to a farmers' meeting at Derby and afterwards to Mr. Sneap's. Tom was ploughing in Bramwell Field. He broke a swingle tree[I] and plough share and had to leave off. He struck a piece of rock. We have finished lambing and the ewes and lambs have been turned into the fields. The snow has gone well only under the walls. Our Evelyn seems dull and tired and has a cough. Mr. Sherlock called here and had tea.

April 5th   Fine but dull at times. Tom went with milk and went ploughing this afternoon. Evelyn is about the same, no appetite, starved pain in back and legs. Ethel went to Bakewell and paid Dr. Jackson's bill (10s.6d.) and asked him to send Evelyn a bottle of medicine which he did. Mr. Stephenson called. We read him a piece out of the *Derbyshire Courier* about the coal controller and Mr. Fairholm. Mr. Stephenson seemed put out over it as Mr. Fairholm's head gardener had been mentioned. I gave Mr. Stephenson a piece of pork which he made up here and was going to send to his daughters. He also made a start collecting for the Sheldon War Memorial. I filled up papers for Ethel and Evelyn of how many hours they were engaged in Red Cross Work nursing etc. at the Bakewell Hospital.

April 6th   Fine but dull. Our Evelyn has broken out with measles. I expect she caught them from Kate B who caught them from Mrs. Craven's baby. She is in bed. We had a roast leg of veal and stuffing to dinner of the calf which we killed with mad staggers. Mr. Sherlock officiated at Holy Communion this morning, only 3 present. Mr. Stephenson took both

I   Swingle tree: Crossbar holding chains attached to harness

services. Collection 13s.10d. for Church expenses. Anthony got back from Mr. Sneap's at 9.30 or about.

April 7th Fine, not much sun. Anthony went to market. Our poor old horse (Naylor) fell down in stable. Anthony left her out of doors tonight. Voting took place at Bakewell for Urban District Council. Anthony voted for 3 viz. Alf Buxton, A. Creswell and Frank Lomas. Evelyn is about the same. Mrs. Craven's furniture was brought to Sheffield today. I wrote for an exemption for Wm over minimum wage.

April 8th Fine but slight drizzles this morning 1st thing. Tom went ploughing in Bramwell Field. Mr. Buxton called and told us that A. Creswell headed the poll, himself 2nd and Frank Lomas third. The Duke of Devonshire's agent (Roland Burke) sent a £1.0.0. note for Sheldon Church.

April 9th Very fine. Wm is ploughing for Wm Naylor and Tom has finished Bramwell field. Mr. Sherlock sent 5 £1 notes which was the subscription to the organist and Sunday School, £3.0.0. to the former and £2.0.0. to the latter. He (Mr. Sherlock) had sent a receipt for the above so he stated in a letter to the Duke's agent I expect. I feel very much annoyed and hurt with the manner things are going on about the Sheldon War Memorial. It seems that some person or persons told Mr. Stephenson that it would be better to have more estimates and this after what Mr. Shimwell had been asked and after a choice had been made of the tablet. I expect Mr. Shimwell's was too much money to give for anything that the dear lads had done in giving their lives. Thos. Wm B said that Mr. Stephenson had interviewed John Lees of Ashford and Thos Wm himself has written to Mr. Shimwell about having more estimates. Why could not this have been arranged at the meetings before things had gone so far with Mr. Shimwell of Youlgreave? Mr. Stephenson called here and it seems that it was Herbert Frost who had been talking to him about having more estimates and the cost. I told Mr. Stephenson to tell him that I did not want anything from him for my Tony. I told him to make out a begrudging list. Fancy such people being kept at home in safety (while other poor men and boys had no choice but to lay down their lives) and to barter people down over a War tablet.

April 10th Dull and drizzly at times. Tom has been ploughing for Billy Naylor and Wm has taken another ton of potatoes to Shentons. We had a card from the Co-op at Bakewell wanting potatoes. They would not have any some time ago when Anthony asked them and now they are too late as they are all sold. Filled up forms over Wm Gould. Our Evelyn seems tired and not well.

April 11th Cold, windy and drizzly at times. Tom is ploughing for Billy Naylor. Jack Naylor has been leading turnips from Grindlow Knoll for us today and yesterday, and Anthony and Wm are also leading some off today. Ethel has gone to Dr. Jackson for something for Evelyn as she has no appetite and is full of wind. Sent Wm's paper and ours to Agricultural Wages Board. I received a letter from Mrs. Rawlinson. I have written back to her.

April 12th Drizzling at times and dull. I paid Albert Redfern for 7lbs of dripping (all we owe him) at 1s.4d. per lb. He had come to Sheldon for a dead calf of Louis E Elliott's and he called here. Mr. Stephenson did not come up to Sheldon today. Doris Brocklehurst paid for this week's milk and 5/4 on account of the bill which leaves them owing £1.0.0. George and Piccaret Craven came tonight. Their mother went to Sheffield to meet them. They are at Dorking with Miss Craven. This week some of the men who have been sent to work on farms but who have not had their demobilization papers have been sent papers as I understand to be called up again. I fear there is more going on in Russia than we the public knows. Some of our poor men are in great danger of being overpowered by the Bolshevicks (sic) and drafts of men are being sent to their help. I want to know what our men and lads are doing in Russia, who sent them and for what purpose. I think the country is sick to death of English Statesmen who got in at the last General Election by pledges which are turning out to be downright lies. Before the Election the cry was *Vote for Lloyd George and No Conscription* and now a bill has been read a second time to compel men to stay in the Army until April 1920, even men who have gone all through the horrors of war for 3 and 4 years.

April 13th Wet and sometimes hail and snow. Mr. Stephenson took both afternoon and night services. Our Mary played both last Sunday and today as Evelyn is bad with measles. Mr. Stephenson called and had tea. He told me that Herbert Frost and C. Ollerenshaw had each subscribed £5.0.0. towards the War Memorial which Mr. Shimwell says he can work for £65.0.0. exclusive of lettering. Mr. T Wm Brocklehurst was writing to Mr. Shimwell to say that his tender would be accepted.

April 16th Very rough. We have a lamb with bud[1] and we shall have to kill it. (We did kill it.) Evelyn is better today. It is just 2 years today by the day of the month since my darling Tony 1st put on the hated khaki. He came back at night from Derby.

April 17th Drizzling at times. Tom was ploughing on moor. Wm took half a ton of potatoes to Mr. Shenton and brought 18 cwts of coal back. Clem came for a weekend tonight. He seems pretty well and they have allowed him to put another wound stripe on his arm. So he has got two now. Poor Jack Naylor has to go up again to the army. Just 2 years ago today my Tony went off 1st thing to Derby and he was sent to Cleadon Camp Sunderland.

April 18th Good Friday A most lovely day. Clem went on bicycle to Longstone. Mary played harmonium in Church as she has done since Evelyn had measles. Mr. Stephenson took the service.

April 19th Another fine day (Primrose Day). Tom sowed part of Bramwell field and Anthony the other part and it was harrowed (oats black). Mr. Stephenson and Ethel were decorating a bit in Church. He had tea in the kitchen.

1   Bud: illness in lambs which was thought to be caused through eating wool

April 20th Easter Sunday Frosty and very cold. Mr. Sherlock officiated at Holy Communion at 9.30 this morning. Mr. Stephenson came as well. There were 23 communicants. Mr. Stephenson took afternoon and evening services. There were two collections (for the Vicar) 19s.1d. in the afternoon and 15s.10½d. at night. Daniel Harrison and a young man called and had tea here and then wanted to be put up for the night. We made them a bed up in parlour. Wm slept on kitchen sofa. We finished our beer tonight. Mary played harmonium in Church as Evelyn did not go. Evelyn is a bit better but seems languid.

April 21st Frosty but lovely sunshine during day. 40 years since I 1st came to Sheldon. Daniel Harrison and the young man went off this morning after they had had breakfast. We charged them 2/6 each for supper, bed and breakfast. Two men and a lad brought us some mineral water (Whittakers). I paid them £1.18.0. for 28 dozen. The club members were playing whist up at the school. Our Emily won 2/6. Fred Goodwin and Jack Naylor came back from the fair (Bakewell) in a very drunken condition and went up to the school after 10 o'clock. Fred Goodwin was calling folks shirkers and said he was a soldier and was talking very silly. (Clem, Mary and little Anthony went to Buxton).

April 22nd Fine, a bit frosty 1st thing. Anthony and Sam Bramwell were levelling turnip pits and Tom was dragging in Grindlow Knoll. Mr. Stephenson called tonight. We paid Miss Hawley for Ethel and Evelyn's new long rain coats which were £3.5.6. each. Not a copper was returned to us. I also paid for Flannel and toilet covers.

April 23rd Fine but dull. Anthony and Vincent were sowing artificial manure on oats in Bramwell Field. Tom and Wm finished dragging in Grindlow Knoll. Miss Orme was married at Bakewell to the Rev. Saunders Williams[1] rector of Eyam. Anthony had a letter from Mr. Sherlock asking whether the vestry meeting could be put off as he was going into Devonshire (Mr. Fairholm's house) or if the Wardens liked they could appoint a chairman and have the Vestry meeting without him (Mr. Sherlock). They decided to await the Vicar's return.

April 26th Most bitterly cold, snow storms at times during the afternoon. Tom was ploughing on moor. Mr. Stephenson called here. He is collecting for the Sheldon War Memorial. Two years ago our poor Tony came from Cleadon to stay at home until the 10th May.

April 27th Very cold, snow storms. Mr. Stephenson took services in Church and then went to tea to Mrs. Clara Morton's where the wedding was held.

April 28th Most bitterly cold, wind in E and N East. One of the coldest days we have had this winter. Our old grey mare got down in stable. Men had to drag her out. After this was done she soon got up but had knocked herself

---

1 The Revd. Howell Saunders Williams became Rector of Eyam in 1919 after a curacy in Bakewell.

about the eyes a bit. She was put in the implement place up back yard and we put old Naylor with her after she had done her work. Anthony went to Bakewell Guardians meeting and afterwards to a meeting of the Farmers' Union where the milk question and wages and hours were discussed. Italy has broken off peace negotiations because her just claims are not being met as president Wilson seems to be the dictator. They (the military) are calling up men who were sent on farms from the army and the farmers are bitterly opposed to it.

April 29th Bitterly cold and snow at intervals. Wind in E and N East. Billy Naylor went on his holidays going up by milk train to Manchester from Longstone. Our men leading manure.

April 30th Dull. Sam Bramwell is not so well and has not been working for us today. Mr. Lomas's man brought a load of manure and took it on moor ready for potatoes. Lady Blanche Cavendish was married to Captain John Cobbold and Miss Elizabeth Asquith was married to Count Bibesca (Romania). Mr. Stephenson called here. Ethel cycled to Buxton and had a tooth stopped at Suttons.

May 1st Very cold. Our men have fetched hay from moor. Tom has been ploughing there yesterday and today. The new milk prices are on today and all farmers are very dissatisfied as they can only get 4/0 per day or 1/4 per gal. If the Wages Board go on with giving farm labourers their demand I think farmers will have to get out as soon as possible. A May Day procession by the children (5 pence each). Billy Naylor landed home tonight from his holidays. He had been to F. Brockley's brother and other places.

May 2nd Dull, a little frosty 1st thing. Tom and Wm ploughing on moor. Anthony mending gates etc. Just 1 year and 6 months since my Tony died of wounds. I feel as sad as ever when I think of him. A whist drive was held up at school. There were prizes given. Ladies 1st an umbrella (Hilda Carson) 2nd Teapot (Edith Goodwin). Hidden number Vases (Evelyn Gyte). Mr. Stephenson was there and one or two servants from Churchdale. Walter Brockley brought us 2 kils of 5d. ale from Ormes.

May 3rd Rather frosty, turns out fine. Tom and Wm ploughing on moor. Sam Bramwell has been away ill since Tuesday but is a bit better. Mr. Stephenson was up at Sheldon collecting for the War Memorial. On going to Sam Rowland's he was met with a refusal to give anything. Sam was not in but his wife said they were going to give to Youlgreave. Sam Rowland has received all the benefits that the Sheldon lads have in everything and yet he has nothing to give towards the lads who have shed their life's blood.

May 4th Dull and very much like rain. Celebration of Holy Communion by Mr. Sherlock who came back from Devonshire on May 1st after about 10 days holiday. There were 9 present (9.40). Mr. Stephenson took services this afternoon and tonight. He came here for tea. Alf Brocklehurst's mare foaled. The vet (Marrison) had to be fetched and others helped.

May 5th   Dull. Anthony went with milk and Tom took our big bull and one of our fat cows to be graded at Bakewell. They were sold for £103.5.3. The bull made £63 and the cow £40. Naylors and John Brockley are making cheese these last day or two as no cans come for the milk from Sheffield. Turned 24 young stock out to grass in day time and one or two milk cows which are going dry.

May 7th   Drizzling rain. Our men were preparing to sow on moor but were stopped by rain. Mary, Ethel and Evelyn were cleaning the big room over kitchen. Miss Broadhurst sent 10/- towards War Memorial regretting she could not give more as she was going to give to Ambergate (mean old thing). She is getting about £175 a year teaching Sheldon children. We let Alf Brockley have some whiskey for his mare. A Vestry meeting was held at 4 o'clock. There were present Mr. Sherlock, Mr. Sheldon (Benjamin Senior) T.Wm Brocklehurst and Anthony Gyte. The old wardens were appointed. Mr. Sherlock called here and tonight Mr. Stephenson called. He had some seed potatoes from us this morning.

May 8th   A lovely day. Anthony and the men are gone on moor all day sowing etc. I wrote out a reference for Mrs. Craven for the post of Assistant Matron for Bakewell Workhouse. Our girls have cleaned and whitewashed Dairy. The postman brought (last night) the milk cheque to end of April (£59.18.4½). Anthony finished sowing oats on moor.

May 9th   Fine but wind in East and North East. Tom sowed the small seeds on Grindlow Knoll and Vincent sowed hay seeds. Anthony was rocking in Bramwell Field. Wm was harrowing on moor and Sam Bramwell was gapping. Farmers who have been sending milk to Sheffield have not been sent any all week. They have had no cans and have not been paid up. George and Piccaret Craven went to Sheffield. Going from there to Dorking tomorrow.

May 10th   Fine and sunny but a cold wind. Mary had a sorrowful letter from Clem. He thinks he will have to say in the Army until he is 38 years old. Mary has gone to see a doctor, and paid Thacker all we owe him £5.16.6½. Sunday's meat as well. Mr. Stephenson called and took Polly Roberts's Insurance Card as the Education Authority at Derby wanted it and Mr. Sherlock told Mr. Stephenson to get it from here. We gave him 3/- to get six sixpenny stamps to put on. I wrote to Clem. It is 2 years today by the day of the month since my Tony went back to training at Cleadon.

May 11th   Rather dull 1st thing. Mr. Stephenson came and had dinner here. The meat was off our own bull which we sold last Monday. Mr. Stephenson took the service in Church. Collection £1.1s.2d. went towards the new lamps. During the afternoon there was lightning and thunder and rather heavy rain.

May 12th   Fine. Anthony went to Alport Mill and took oats to be made into meal. He came back by Bakewell and had a good deal of business with lawyers, Taylor and Goodwin and Cockerton. Taylors handed to Anthony the deeds of the cottages now tenanted by Mr. Edwin Brocklehurst. There had been a mortgage on these which has been paid off by Anthony. Goodwin and Cockerton are getting a deed ready to be signed by Anthony and Tom as Tom is going to be joint tenant with his father for farm and Anthony opened a fresh banking account in both names. Dr. Jackson came to see Mrs. Craven's baby whose face is broken out. Mrs. Craven went to a situation at Sheffield but the baby is left at Mrs. Ed Brocklehurst. Dr. Jackson called here and gave Mary a certificate that he had attended her for Flu early in the year and now other things. Mary sent a number of letters and these certificates from Dr. Fentem and Dr. Jackson to the Demobilization Officer, Lichfield to try and get Clem off. John Berrisford hung us 4 windows and put a small door to get under stairs with minerals.

May 13th Very fine, sunny and warm. Mary, Ethel and Evelyn are cleaning Wm's room and bathroom. Mrs. Hallows washed 1st lot of our blankets. The deed which Tom and his father have to sign came from Goodwin and Cockerton. They signed and Thos. Wm B. witnessed.

May 14th Very fine, hot sun but rather cold wind. Mary, little Anthony and aunt H went to Grindleford. They walked to Ashford and Mr. Daybell took them forward and charged them 7/-. Kate B had a queer attack this morning like our Emily but she soon came round. The girls spring cleaned their bedroom today. Mr. Stephenson called and brought us a nice cauliflower. Our young calves lie out.

May 15th Very fine. Wm rolling seeds on moor. Tom in fallow. Anthony and Vincent are gardening. I wrote to the Morris Wallpaper Co. and to our Mary. Naylor and Alf Brockley have been paid up by Sheffield milk firms. Ethel and Evelyn began cleaning parlour.

May 16th Fine. Men on moor, rolling and in fallow. Ethel and Evelyn finished parlour. The milk beasts go out in day but come in at night. The Germans are whining over peace terms. Mrs. Sherwin has heard that her husband poor Jack is killed.

May 17th Fine. Tom leading manure. Wm took Old Naylor and old white mare to G. Frost's to be shod. Mr. Stephenson called and had tea. He had met Sam Rowland on his way up to Sheldon and they had a long talk about what happened when he (Mr. Stephenson) called to ask for a subscription to the Sheldon War Memorial. Ethel went to Bakewell. A thunder shower came on. Nearly all Sheldon smaller farmers began sending milk to Nestlés. Eds still owe 19s/6d. for milk but never mention it. It will be like the £1.8.0. they owed years ago. Had a letter from Mrs. Rawlinson.

May 18th Rather dull and drizzling at times, but nice growing weather. Nestlés send a dray for Sheldon Farmers milk and provide cans. Mr. Sherlock took service in Sheldon Church this afternoon.

May 19th Fine. Men dragging and rolling on moor. Anthony went to Bakewell and to the Rural District Council meeting. Mrs. Craven attended the meeting and the post of Assistant Matron was given to her. She begins work in a fortnight. Mr. Sherlock's and my testimonials were read at the meeting and the members voted her in. There was only one other applicant.

May 20th Fine. Tom and Wm in fallow getting potato ground ready. Mr. Sherlock came up and was copying from Church Book. The girls began cleaning my bedroom. Our milk cows lay out all night for the 1st time this season.

May 21st Fine. Men working in fallow and leading manure on potato ground. Our men planted 7 rows of potatoes. Mr. Stephenson called both before and after service at Church. I understand he has sent in his resignation to Mr. Fairholm. Our girls (Ethel and Evelyn) were papering my bedroom.

May 22nd Very fine and sunny. Tom and Vincent have been leading manure from Sheldon to the potato field on moor. The men have set 15 rows today. Alf Brockley, C. Ollerenshaw, Jack Naylor and old Watercress Jack have been setting potatoes in Alf's field. Our girls (Ethel and Evelyn) finished cleaning and papering my bedroom. Miss Hawley (Barratts) came and was paid up. She did not charge for the $^1/_2$ yard of matting. I told her to tell Mr. Barratt that I would pay for it if he wanted it but that I should not order anything else of him. I had ordered last month 3 yds of matting at 9s.6d. per yd and he sent 3$^1/_2$ yards calling it a remnant but charging full price. Received a letter from our Mary. Clem has not heard anything more about getting off. Little Anthony's finger nail is coming off. He trapped it when at Sheldon with coal.

May 24th Very fine. We finished setting potatoes on moor, 22 rows for ourselves and 3 rows for other people viz. 1 row for Wm Bramwell, 1 row for Frank Lomas and 1 for Eds. I sat outside a bit after tea. Poor old Abraham Manderfield was found dead in the fields. He had gone to look after his cattle and W.H. Brockley found him lain dead. James Frost (with others to help) brought him home in the (Frost's) conveyance. Mr. Stephenson was at Sheldon and he helped and saw the policeman. There will not be an inquest as the Dr. (Fentem) had been attending him. Mr. Stephenson had heard that Jack Sherwin was killed.

May 25th Very nice drizzling rain came on today which was very much wanted. Mr. Stephenson took the service in Church. He told the congregation he was leaving. Collection (Diocesan) was £1.5.6. Ethel started making cheese.

May 26th Rather misty and nice growing day. Anthony is not well, so aching in his limbs and tired. Our Ethel took Mrs. Hallows some blankets and top covers to be washed. This is the 3rd instalment this year.

May 27th Very fine. Mrs. Hallows helped to clean houseplace, papering etc. All the sheep in Sheldon were taken to Ashford to be washed. Anthony and Vincent were with ours.

May 28th Very fine. Poor old Abraham Manderfield was laid to rest in Sheldon Churchyard. Anthony was one of the bearers. The funeral was waiting outside the Church gates for nearly half an hour owing to a mistake of Mr. Stephenson as regards the time. Our men were leading manure. It is such a long way from Sheldon to the moor. The girls finished house place.

May 29th Very hot and dry. More rain is wanted. Anthony, John Frost and T.A. Sheldon went to Ashford to Copyhold Court. They had a good dinner and Anthony sang *(My Ancestors)*. He was also made foreman for 12 months. James Taylor made a good speech, also Anthony when he proposed the health of the deputy steward (Wilson).

May 31st Fine. Tom was sowing swedes and Vincent Artificial on moor. Mrs. Hallows cleaned and papered the bar. Mr. Stephenson called and had tea. He showed the girls the book with the War Memorial subscriptions in and there is over £60 subscribed. Received a letter from Mrs. Rawlinson.

June 1st Fine and dull at times but no rain comes. Holy Communion in Sheldon Church. Only 5 present. Mr. Sherlock officiated. Mr. Stephenson took the service in Church this afternoon. Collection for Church expenses 21/-. The interest on £200 War Loan came this morning.

June 6th Very fine and dry winds. If the rain does not come soon things will look very serious. I sat out a bit tonight and Mrs. King (Fanny Brockley) joined me at the door. Men were working Fallow. I wrote to Mary. Mr. Sherlock called and had tea.

June 7th Fine, dry and hot winds. I wrote to Mr. Ronston for a kil or 2 of beer. Mr. Stephenson called and had a chat. Ernest Rawlinson and Mr. Sneap both popped in tonight. Ernest slept in little room and Mr. Sneap in big room. Tom on chair bedstead.

June 9th Just a bit of a scud but nothing to do any good. Tom cycled to fair. Mr. Sneap and Anthony went in high trap. Anthony came back for float and then went to Bakewell again for 3 pigs (black) which he had bought of Chris Furniss for £24 the three, £8 each.

June 10th Very hot. Mr. Sneap went back after dinner. Anthony took him in float. We started sheep shearing. Tom and Vincent were shearing on moor. Vincent did 5 and Tom 10. Ethel fetched 3 sheep and 3 lambs from Ashford. Anthony helped with these to shear. Mr. Burley's milk cheque came (end of May).

June 11th Very close. Anthony, Tom and Vincent finished sheep shearing. Ernest went on moor for the eggs. A man with a camera took Tom, Vincent and Ernest with the sheep and wool against them. Two of the pigs that Anthony bought are not well. Mr. Stephenson called and brought two very young rabbits for Emily. He had sent two before.

June 12th A very high wind and drizzling showers but not as much rain as people would like. Anthony went on moor and found one of the shorn sheep dead. Ernest went back tonight. James Frost went with trap to meet the 9.2 (Longstone train) so Ernest rode with him. It was very rough.

June 13th Very rough winds and just a drizzle of rain. Anthony went and buried the sheep on moor. Had a reply from Burton Brewery to say they were sending us some beer.

June 14th Very close. No more rain comes. Mr. Stephenson called and had tea. Walter Brockley brought us 2 kils of beer from Ormes. I sat out (after tea) until bed time. Received a letter from Mrs. Rawlinson and our Mary.

June 15th Fine. Mr. Stephenson took the service in Church this afternoon, calling here afterwards. We want more rain very badly.

June 18th Dull and close. Anthony heard that 2 or 3 pigs were dead at Longstone. These were bought out of the same lot as ours. Saml. Johnson and George Ward bought them. Anthony reported ours to the police. Inspector Tipper came up twice today about them. Mr. Stephenson and Mr[1]. and Mrs. Greenstreet came to see us tonight the two latter having tea here and afterwards attended service at Church. Anthony ordered some currant loaves etc. from Marsdens.

June 19th Slight drizzling rain at times but no weight falls and everything is in a bad way for want of it. Mr. Howe (vet) of Buxton came to examine our pigs. He killed one and sent some of its intestines away. The others are no better. Mr. Ronston came and was paid up (£18.13s.0d.). Miss Hawley (Barratts) called and was paid up.

June 21st A bit showery at times and colder. Biggin cricketers played at Sheldon with Sheldon cricketers. Sheldon won easily their score being 101 against Biggin's 38. George Ward scored 48 runs and our Tom 24. Tom and Alf Brockley were the bowlers. Others got runs but did not score as many as G. Ward and our Tom. Mr. Stephenson called and had tea and he went to see the cricket match. We had 17 sat down to tea the majority being Biggin cricketers. We charged them 1s.4d. each which did not leave us with much profit. We ordered 6 loaves of currant bread from Marsdens, buns and plain bread. The loaves cost 2/- each. A great do at Ashford for their returned soldiers. Youlgreave band played today, and last Tuesday as well, at Ashford.

June 22nd Looks like rain at times but so little comes. Mr. and Mrs. Greenstreet (Downham) and Mr. Stephenson came to tea. Mr. Greenstreet preached the sermon in the afternoon. Tom Ridgeway and another chap were in our house tonight. They came yesterday for a few days' holiday.

June 24th Midsummer day. Dull. The women's club feast at Ashford. Dove Valley band played for them. An inspector came and asked a few questions about our pigs. Mr. Howe came and killed one of Thos. Wm Brockley's pigs. His other pig is bad. These were brought with ours from

---

1 The Revd. Clement M Greenstreet was Rector of Downham from 1907

Bakewell market in our float. Ethel went to Bakewell for something for Evelyn. Her throat is bad and she has indigestion. We have heard nothing more about our pigs.

June 25th Very dull. Ethel, Evelyn, Leah and Alice went to Chatsworth (cycled). Hannah is busy making the girls dresses (voile). All our men are working on moor, sowed rape. Evelyn was very bad tonight with her throat and indigestion. Another of our pigs died tonight.

June 26th Fine, cold towards night. The rain does not come. Mary's birthday (32). Sent a note asking Dr. Jackson to come to see Evelyn which he did and gave her a proper sounding and examined her throat. He thought that she probably had an ulcer low down which caused her to have such windy spasms. She can only take liquids. Anthony reported about the other pig and the one left he killed (shot) as it was no better. He buried them temporarily. Thos. Wm Brockley's other pig is no better. Filled Polly Roberts's Insurance card and it was sent off. Ethel went for medicine.

June 27th Dull. A small drizzle this morning but clears out. Our Tom and George Brockley took 14 children in floats to Haddon Hall at Miss Broadhurst's request. Tom's load was as follows: Addie Hallows, Vera Carson, Winnie and Ethel Brocklehurst, Clarice and Jessie Goodwin and Dorothy Roberts. Evelyn is about the same, in bed and can take nothing but slops. Mr. Howe (vet) came here to see about the other two pigs. He uncovered them and took some of the intestines to send them off. He gave Anthony 5/- for burying them with lime etc.

June 28th A drizzling shower or two. Flagg cricketers came and played Sheldon tonight, Sheldon winning easily. Robinson the postman brought word that *Peace had been signed this afternoon*. Our Tom buried the two pigs properly. Evelyn is about the same. She cannot swallow anything solid. Anthony Wager plays about and has been enjoying watching the cricket match. Received a letter from Mrs. Rawlinson.

June 29th Very cloudy and bit drizzly at times but no rain to do any good. Mr. Sherlock took the service in Church and gave out the banns of marriage between Maggie Naylor and Sam Johnson (1st time). Our Mary played harmonium at service. Mr. Stephenson has gone to Heath for weekend. Anthony Wager received a p card from him (Chesterfield Church).

June 30th Very dull but no rain. Everything seems shrivelling up and does not grow. Light crops may be looked for. Evelyn is about the same. Anthony took milk and then went to market. We have not received any milk cheque for the whole of this month. I shall have to write about it. Two years ago we received a telegram from our dear Tony to say he was coming on leave. Showers came on tonight. Anthony received a milk cheque from Mr. Burley and a letter saying that he had not received a bill. I had sent him a receipted bill up to May 31st and a further bill to June 15th. I made enquiries off Postman Robinson but I do not know whether Mr. Burley's (bills) were delivered or not to him. The cheque was about £2 more than the bill came to up to June 15.

July 1st Heavy showers today and one loud clap of thunder. Tom wrote milk bills at my dictation, one up to June 15 and another to June 30. We took off the money which Mr. Burley had sent over what he ought to have done (Ethel posted bills). Just 2 years ago today by day of month (it was on Sunday 2 yrs ago) our dear Tony came on leave from Cleadon. The leave which proved to be his last. Mr. Buxton (Burley's man) brought his statement which came to £47.6.8. to June 26th 1919.

July 2nd Showery. Wm went for lime to Sterndale. Anthony slaked it ready for whitewashing buildings. Ethel cycled to Bakewell for medicine for Evelyn and paid Thacker's meat bill up to June 28th (£5.17s.6d.). Skidmore brought us our extra sugar 100 lbs and was paid for it. Mr. Stephenson called here. He took a service in Church. Kate Brockley played. Evelyn is very little better with her throat.

July 3rd Drizzling rain. The men are whitewashing buildings. Evelyn sent (for us) a ten shilling note for Dr. Barnardo's home. July 19th has been officially fixed for peace celebrations.

July 5th Misty drizzly 1st thing dull but no rain later on. Two years today my Tony said his last goodbye to us and went to Cleadon, afterwards to France and now he lies in a foreign grave. July 5th was on a Thursday 2 yrs ago. Sheldon cricketers went to play Chatsworth. Sheldon and Chatsworth had two innings but Sheldon lost the match. Our Tom took our Fanny and float with part of cricketers and Fred Brockley took their horse and float with others. One or two cycled to Chatsworth. Mr. Stephenson called.

July 6th Dull. Holy Communion (Mr. Sherlock). Mr. Stephenson took the service in afternoon. It was a peace thanksgiving in all churches. Collection 14s.8d. for church expenses. Mary and aunt H made a lovely wreath for the fallen lads of Sheldon.

July 7th Dull, no rain. Anthony went to market. Mrs. Hallows, Mary and Ethel are cleaning kitchen. Aunt H is altering Clem a jacket and mending Anthony's coat. I wrote to Dr. Jackson and the postman took Evelyn's bottle for more medicine. Mary went to Ashford for her separation money.

July 9th Fine, warm. The men working on moor. Anthony took three of them shopping to Bakewell. Mary stayed at home. Our Tom went shooting on Frost's land with James. They killed 12 rabbits. Tom brought 6 home. It was late (after eleven) when he got in.

July 10th Fine, looks like rain at times but none comes. Men working on moor in turnips etc. Alf Brockley started mowing. Tom got hit with cricket ball at Flagg (broke his watch).

July 11th   Fine. Men finished running turnips over 1st time and then came from moor. We began mowing in Hicks field. Mr. Sherlock came to see Mrs. Carson and Wm H. Brockley both of whom are ill. He did not call here.

July 12th   Just a drizzle of rain but nothing to do any good. Wm finished mowing Hicks. Such a poor crop and everything is poor as there is such a drought. I expect there will be such a shortage of hay, corn, roots etc. as to cause a famine. Eggs are 4d. each. Mr. Stephenson called and had tea here. Mrs. Carson is very seriously ill.

July 14th   Fine. Anthony went to market and Mary went with little Anthony and came back in trap. She bought Maggie Naylor a set of dishes for her wedding present (white). Anthony's and my present to her was a cruet. Tom's : plates. Emily's : tea pot and stand. Ethel's : tea cups, saucers and plates. Evelyn's : wine glasses and cheese dish. They brought these last week when they went to Bakewell. We got two loads of hay out of Hick's top field. Mrs. Hallows was helping us today.

July 16th   Fine but dull: not much of a hay day. Our men hobbled Bole Piece up tonight. Wm mowed a field on moor. Mr. Stephenson called tonight (no service in Church). Mary made some blackcurrant and rhubarb (mixed) jam. We have some very nice black currants. Gooseberries have been an entire failure this year in our garden. Sent Mrs. Rawlinson a box of roses. We have a great quantity and such fine roses this year.

July 19th   Very close, sunshine sometimes during day. Peace rejoicings all over the country. A few flags out at Sheldon and a garland made by Bertha Brockley. I wonder how people can think of the sorrowing hearts of those who have lost their loved ones being expected to look on or join in any festivities. Some people have had a deal to say (to Mr. Stephenson) because there was not something at Sheldon for today. Miss Grover is providing an excellent tea (ham etc.) for every one next Thursday, grown up and children as well, but I should think some of them wanted two gorging do's. Sam Bramwell and G. Ward were two of the grumblers. Today Sam Johnson and Maggie Naylor were married at Sheldon Church by Mr. Sherlock who forgot to bring the marriage register and the bride and bridegroom had to call at the Vicarage or Church (Ashford) to sign it on their way to Longstone station. I think Sam's mother and aunt also went to sign as witnesses. A splendid tea was provided for the wedding guests etc and was held in the schoolroom. Plenty of everything good and plenty to spare. There was dancing tonight (Miss Oliver played piano). Jim Goodwin had gone away somewhere. Maggie Naylor's wedding dress was of champagne coloured silk and very beautiful it looked. Elizabeth Naylor and Alice Brocklehurst were bridesmaids. Emily, Ethel and Evelyn put on their voile dresses and went to church to witness the ceremony. I was taken to the door and could see the Rutland motor going backwards and forwards for wedding party. Jack Naylor gave Maggie away and Martin Oliver (Longstone) was best man. The bride and bridegroom left in the afternoon to go to Blackpool. Alex, Ena and Lily were at the wedding and had made the wedding dresses. Rain came on tonight. Anthony and Clem and the other men went this afternoon and led 6 loads of hay that was ready on moor. Anthony has a headache. Bonfire could be seen burning in the distance from Sheldon.

July 20th Wet and drizzling. This rain will do such a lot of good. I am afraid the crops will not be half as good as last year. Mr. Stephenson came here for dinner and tea, and took the service in Church.

July 21st Fine. Anthony and Tom took 2 young bulls to market and sold one for £11.10.0. and the other for £12.10.0. Auctioneer's fees 6 shillings, leaving £23.14. for seller. Mrs. Hallows is helping us wash today. Mr. Stephenson came to stay at Ed's for a week or two. I made out and sent milk bill to July 16 at 1.10. per gal. which came to £51.5.1½d. A meeting was held in Sheldon Schoolroom to discuss what should be done next Thursday as that day is to be kept for the peace celebration. A collection was arranged the proceeds to go for sports. Wm Hallows talked very excitable over mugs for the children. Clem went to Longstone and bought a gun (Herbert Dixon). A committee was formed of those who had worn khaki.

July 22nd Dull, no hay making. Men in turnips, Jack Naylor as well helping us. Tom was horsehoeing the potatoes. It was hard work as the corn which shed on the ground last year has come up quite green all over potato rows and amongst rape etc. Mr. Stephenson made a house to house collection for sports and those who had been talking most gave the least. Hallows gave 3/-, Sam Rowland 2/6, G. Ward 4s.6d. and yet those wanted two do's and Hallows wanted mugs.

July 23rd Dull no rain. Men on moor in swedes etc. Mr. Stephenson is busy getting ready for tomorrow. Only part of the committee were helping in the arrangements tonight. Clem went back to Lichfield this morning by the 9.15 train from Longstone. We boiled two hams ready for tomorrow.

July 24th Dull. Men are very busy fixing up flag on Church and making other arrangements for today. A cricket match between ladies and gentlemen was the 1st on the list of sports. After all, the children had mugs given by Miss Grover. A motor brought them about dinner time. A very impressive service was held in Church by Mr. Stephenson. The people and children of Sheldon walked in procession and G. Ward carried a laurel wreath which was made by Mr. Stephenson and deposited on the altar. The service was in remembrance of the fallen lads. Mr. Sherlock, Mrs. Tinsley and Miss Grover called to see me and my tea was sent from the school as well as to other invalids etc. A scud or two of rain came on tonight during sports.

July 26th Dull. Wm mowed seeds on moor. The men were there as well. Mr. Stephenson went to Ashford and brought Miss Broadhurst's salary. She happened to be coming down the street opposite our house and when he offered it to her she would not accept it and told him he must take it up to her house as she had a train to catch. She was most insulting to him. He left salary at our house and she fetched it tonight. Tom, Ethel and Evelyn cycled to Taddington tonight. There were sports etc. there.

July 27th Dull but no rain. Both Mr. Sherlock and Mr. Stephenson were at the service in Church this afternoon. Mr. Stephenson commenced taking the Sheldon Sunday school.

July 28th Dull. Anthony went to market. He bought 2 cows from H. Frost at £39 each. A committee meeting was held in Sheldon School to finish off giving the prize money at sports. There were 7 shillings to hand which was given to the War Memorial. The men were hobbling the seeds on moor.

July 29th Fine. Some sun and wind. Our men went on moor and were leading the seeds (16 loads). Sam Bramwell is helping us. Wm started mowing the Waterlands this morning. Mary had a letter from Clem to say he was very likely coming home (Grindleford) on Saturday next. Sam Rowland sent me two small trout. I gave Cassy 6d. A report came about our 3 pigs. It was not swine fever but pneumonia and a draft was sent for six pounds so we lost £10.0.0.

July 30th A very fine day plenty of sun and wind. Wm finished mowing Waterlands and was mowing Croft Heads. Poor Jack Naylor had to go back to the army this morning. It is a shame he is not allowed to stay and help his father in the hay. I think strikes and militarism is gone mad in England. Many thousands of miners have been out on strike this last week or two. Some have gone in to work but the Yorkshire miners are still out and many mines are flooded owing to the pump men being made to come out. An inspector from Derby called here and had some tea. He knows Mrs. Gerram and goes to inspect the homes of people (slums) and soldiers' homes.

Aug. 1st A bit dull and drizzly and rough 1st thing. Mary and little Anthony were taken (by Mr. Hawley of Ashford) to Grindleford. He came up and fetched them and a lot of luggage (crib etc.) from Sheldon. Little Anthony did not want to go back and was crying all morning. Mr. Stephenson got us some of our roses and helped to arrange them (six) for Ashford show tomorrow. No hay got today. Gladys Brockley came home from France.

Aug. 2nd Drizzling and wet. All our men went on moor into the turnips. All got wet through and had to change. Tom went to a cricket match at Ashford, G. Ward and Alf Brockley as well. Uncle Will Brockley took our roses in float to the show at Ashford. Received a letter from Clem saying that he would be home for good today. Received a PC from our Mary. Our roses got the 1st prize and a special (razor). Our Tom was playing with Ashford against Longstone (cricket). He bowled 5 out. He himself was run out (0).

Aug. 3rd Dull. Holy Communion was celebrated at 9.40 in Sheldon Church. Mr. Sherlock and Mr. Stephenson were there. Mr. Stephenson took the service in the afternoon. Collection (Church expenses) 15s.1d. and came here for tea.

Aug. 4th   Fine at 1st and a good wind. The Waterlands was all ready for leading and our men had got one load when the rain came on and the job was stopped. Anthony did not go to market. A young stirk of H. Frost's could not calve so Anthony went and put things right. The calf was dead. He stayed for supper and Mr. Herbert gave him 3 rabbits.

Aug. 5th   Fine but dull and looks very much like rain. Wm fetched us some coal which came to £1.18.0. at 37s.6d. per ton. Tom and Vincent in turnips. Anthony and Wm went on moor this afternoon. I made out and sent milk bill to end of July (£14.5.7½). Wrote to our Mary and sent Clem's club card. I also wrote to Mr. Parton for more beer and to Mrs. Whittaker. Liverpool is seething with riots, plundering and looting of shops. The military have been called out and the Riot Act read. Everywhere is in a most critical state owing to so many being on strike. Miners, policemen, bakers etc. I think they are all gone mad. Mr. Stephenson wrote to Mr. D. Lloyd George about Jack Naylor being recalled off his father's farm back to the Army.

Aug. 6th   Dull. Men in turnips. We did not lead any hay. The strikers are still out especially in West Yorkshire and the Hooligans have done a great deal of damage in Liverpool.

Aug. 7th   Fine. Sun and wind. Our men went in the hay. Got Waterlands. Received a letter from our Mary saying that Clem came home on Saturday but he went to Ripon on Tuesday last and had not come back when she wrote.

Aug. 8th   Very fine. Plenty of sun and wind. Raking up and getting rakings in Waterland and finished Croft Head. There were 7½ loads. Mr. Stephenson entertained a party of boy scouts to tea (in Bland Croft) and their Scout master.

Aug. 9th   Very hot. I believe it to be the hottest day we have had this year. Our men finished the hay tonight. That mown yesterday was ready. 3 loads in little Butts, 11 in Big Butts and one in Pingle. Sam Bramwell, Wm Hallows and Frank Buxton (Harry's lad) have helped us a bit. We sold out of beer and we have no minerals though we have ordered from Whittakers 2 or 3 weeks ago. Began mowing on July 11th, finished getting hay on August 9th:

Hicks top field	2 loads
Hicks next to top field	5
Bole Piece (next Johnson Lane)	13
Seeds on moor	20
Waterlands	8½
Croft Heads	7½
Little Butts	3

Big Butts   II
Pingle   I

Heard from Mary that Clem came home from Ripon on Wednesday night demobilized.

Aug. 10th Very hot. Anthony took me for a drive round Flagg lane and Monyash dale and I sat out and had my dinner when I got back. The bill came for the beer I ordered. A few in tonight (Wm Bramwell, Mr. Simpson and son from Nottingham). (Nothing but port to drink). Mr. Stephenson took the service in Church, collection for choir trip. There was a short service tonight for the children. A many motor cycles went up Sheldon this afternoon (test races). I think it is a shame to have such on a Sunday.

Aug. 12th Very hot. Men on moor. A few men in tonight drinking port as we have nothing else. Poor Jack Naylor had to go to Nottingham (Army). He came on Saturday and went back today.

Aug. 14th Rather cooler and a shower this morning. Anthony and I have been married 33 years. Mr. Burley sent cheque. Mr. Ronston called here and was paid £10.0.0. We did not pay him for the two kils of beer as one of them leaked so much that it has to be sent back so we owe for one. Miss Hawley called and was paid up.

Aug. 15th Very hot. Rain is wanted badly. Our men on moor in swedes. Wm came off after dinner and went to Bakewell station for the Burton beer, 2 barrels and 3 kils. The men were getting the cricket pitch ready for the match with Chatsworth. Mr. Moss called here (excise). Hannah came. Robert Marsden who used to live at Mrs. Gyte's called here. He has been in Canada for years.

Aug. 16th Very close. Chatsworth team of cricketers came, amongst whom was Mr. Hartopp. The match was played and Sheldon won easily. Chatsworth score was 60 and Sheldon 93. Our Tom bowled six and two were caught off his bowling. He got 32 runs. Alf Brockley as usual talked spitefully about Tom, and Wm Gould and he quarrelled. John Naylor and Joe Johnson called here after the cricket match with a horse float. They were asked to take the horse and float away as we considered it had been standing long enough. They were stopped from having any more drink and so they went off quietly before 9 o'clock. I had to go to bed early as I have been very poorly all week with the heat. There was a good tea provided by the Sheldon cricket club for both teams. Mr. Hartopp chatted with me and asked Anthony to spare Tom to play for Chatsworth against Chesterfield next Wednesday. Mr. Hartopp got 32 runs. Tom Frost brought Ormes order and 2 kils of beer. We owe for 3 kils. The one that leaked was sent back by Tom Frost.

Aug. 17th Very hot. Mr. Sherlock took the service in Sheldon Church and Mr. Stephenson had a children's service in Ashford Church. I am not much better, cannot eat. I heard tonight that Joe Johnson had cruelly ill used his father and that a doctor had to be fetched and put some stitches in him, also that two policemen were there.

Aug. 19th Very showery this morning, clears this afternoon. Ethel making cake and boiling a piece of ham for tomorrow's trip. I feel a little better but I was very poorly last week especially Saturday. I sent a paper to Ed's telling them that customers would have to pay for milk when they fetched it after Saturday. Ruth paid 19.6. back money.

Aug. 20th Very wet 1st thing. The choir girls got up to meet the 7.20 train at Bakewell but Mr. Stephenson did not get ready as he thought it was too wet. The girls and he met the 9.10 at Longstone and went straight through to Nottingham for the day. Got back before 10 o'clock. It cleared out in the afternoon. Polly Naylor helped us this morning. The girls bought *Great Heart* and other books for us. Our Tom went to Chatsworth, played with that team against Chesterfield. He got 17 runs but did no bowling. I heard that Joe Johnson had been locked up.

Aug. 21st Finer. The rain will have done good. Our men working in swedes on moor. I made a milk bill out at 1s.6d. per gal and it ought to be 1s. 8d. this month, but I did not send it off. A great do at Bakewell today for soldiers.

Aug. 22nd Dull and colder. All the sheep and lambs in Sheldon were dipped at our place today (251). Our 44 sheep 32 lambs (76). I made milk bill out to Aug. 16th at 1s.8d. per gal which amounted with carriage to £8.6.3. I wrote to our Mary. Heard from Mrs. Hollinshead that Emily could go to Buxton to her house. Joe Johnson was remanded (over his father).

Aug. 23rd Dull. Sheldon cricketers went to play Biggin. Tom took a float load with Young Wager as Fanny is bad with Flu. Biggin won, their score being 37 and Sheldon 31. Our Tom bowled six out and one was caught off his bowling. Billy Naylor played for Sheldon. He got 5 runs and caught two out. Our Tom did not get any runs. Hilda Carson was taken by motor to Derby Infirmary with appendicitis.

Aug. 24th Dull. Mr. Stephenson took the service in Church. Mr. Sherlock went on holidays last Tuesday. Mr. Stephenson had tea here and afterwards went to Bakewell Church with Thos Wm Brocklehurst. Word came that Hilda Carson was operated upon last night. Some say it was peritonitis. Jack Naylor came home this morning (demobilized) from Ripon.

Aug. 25th Drizzling. Anthony, Tom, Vincent, and Wm went to the fair. I had a letter from Clem saying that Mary had had another son and they they were going on well, born yesterday. Aunt H went by conveyance from Bakewell to Grindleford. She rode to Bakewell with Thos Wm Brocklehurst. Word came that Hilda Carson was going on well at Derby Infirmary.

Aug. 26th Very showery. Anthony took Emily and Evelyn and the bath chair to Buxton this afternoon. It was showery on the way but they took the big umbrella. Tom, Wm and Vincent on moor. The milk cheque (to Aug 16) came this morning.

Aug. 29th Wet this morning, clears up this afternoon but no sun. Several nights have been frosty. Anthony and the men have been on moor this afternoon putting stoops and wire netting round rape. Mr. Stephenson went to Derby to see Hilda Carson. Mrs. Hallows is helping us today. I had a letter from Miss Adams and one from our Emily. My rheumatism is very bad and I keep mourning over my poor Tony and the other dear lads.

Aug. 30th Drizzly 1st thing but clears out in the afternoon. Our men finished stooping and wire netting round the rape. Hallows went with a lot from Monyash on a motor drive through the Dukeries.

Aug. 31st Fair but dull at times. Mr. Stephenson took the service in Church. Ethel went to Longstone tonight and called on Maggie Johnson. A good many in house tonight.

Sept. 2nd Heavy showers at times. Our Evelyn came back from Buxton this afternoon and Ethel went to Longstone station to catch 5.15 to Buxton.

Sept. 3rd Wet at intervals. Made out bill to end of August 31 and sent it to Mr. Burley. Tom went to uncle Will's to tea. It was Rose Wilson's 21st birthday. Evelyn did not go as I could not be left alone but some very nice cake was sent up. Received a letter and photo from E. Rawlinson.

Sept. 4th Showery and dull at times. We cannot begin with the binder. Clears out later on. Anthony and Tom went to the sheepdog trials at Longshaw. They put up at Grindleford and Clem went with them. Mary and baby are well. Little Anthony did not want to come unless the others came to Sheldon. Leah, Kate, Ruth and Evelyn carried me down today. Fred Bramwell has come to Sheldon. He has been demobilized. Wrote to E. Rawlinson and Miss Adams.

Sept. 5th Showery at times. Men on moor until dinner. Mrs. Stone brought a telegram for Tom to go to Chatsworth to play with them against Hathersage tomorrow. We sent word he would go as the telegram was prepaid from Mr. Hartopp. Mrs. Hallows helping today.

Sept. 6th Dull this morning. During the night the rain came down in torrents. Tom went on his bike about one o'clock to Chatsworth. Anthony and others went opening out in Bramwell cornfield. Mr. Stephenson brought us some plaice. He does not seem so well. He and Thos. Wm Brockley went to Matlock yesterday. Our Tom bowled 4 out for 8 runs (Hathersage). Chatsworth scored 16 and Hathersage 12 runs. Mr. Hartopp gave Tom his cricket ball[1] which had been sent away for an inscription to be put on.

---

1   Tom had previously received a cricket ball with an inscribed silver disc when, bowling for Sheldon on June 15th 1912, he took all ten Chatsworth wickets for 34 runs.

Sept. 7th Fine at times and a little drizzly at times. Holy Communion (strange vicar) at 9.40. Mr. Stephenson took the service in afternoon. Collection for Church expenses 13s.8d.

Sept. 9th Very fine. Finished cutting Bramwell field with binder. Did not finish setting all the corn up. Anthony took float and fetched Emily and Ethel and bath chair from Buxton getting here between 4 and 5 o'clock. Harold Hawley came round for Barratts.

Sept. 12th Wet and cold. Men could not use binder on moor. Miss Broadhurst's furniture was taken by tractor. She is leaving Sheldon I understand in October.

Sept. 13th Very wet. It had poured with rain during the night and I heard it thunder today. Anthony suddenly made up his mind to go and see Mr. Sneap and he caught the 1.14 train from Longstone. He said he would ask about plums or damsons. D. Goodwin wanted 10d. per lb for damsons. We did not buy any from him. For the last week or two he has charged us 5d. a lb for apples and we bought a stone at a time. In some places they are selling at 3d per lb. Eggs are being sold at fourpence farthing and fourpence halfpenny each.

Sept. 14th Finer than yesterday. A little drizzle of rain 1st thing. My birthday (62) I received cards from Mary, Anthony (little) and Aunt H. Mr. Stephenson took the service in Church and also a children's service at night.

Sept. 15th Finer and brighter but rather dull at times. Anthony did not come back last night from Mr. Sneap's. Mr. Stephenson took a parcel for me to give to the Grindleford conveyance. It was a jacket of Ethel's which she had given Mary to make a coat for Anthony. Evelyn cycled to Bakewell to Mr. Sutton to have her tooth stopped. Mrs. Hallows helped us to wash etc. Mr. Sutton did not stop Evelyn's tooth. Anthony arrived home about tea time. Mr. Stephenson brought me a book called *Jane* by Marie Corelli.

Sept. 17th Dull and drizzly at times. Our men mowing rakes on moor. Mr. Skidmore brought six stones of sugar. This with 2 stones we had last week makes up our allowance for jam. There are about 5 applications for the post of mistress of Sheldon school.

Sept. 18th Fair at first, drizzly afterwards. Frost during the night. Our men brought two loads of hay from rakes on moor. Some people in Sheldon were leading corn (Thos. Wm Brockley and Billy Naylor). Billy Naylor dug a place for Flag Pole in churchyard.

Sept. 19th Rough and stormy, wet. A heavy shower of hail and snow came on tonight. The 1st Partridge shoot. Mr. Wood, Mr. Lowthian and Mr. Sneider had tea here. I charged them 1s. 6d. each, also 1s. 6d. each for 2 men of Mr. Lowthian's (7/6). Mr. Lowthian gave Ethel 2/6 extra. Mr. Wood gave us a hare. They shot five and a half brace of partridges, 4 pheasants and a hare. I had a nice long talk with the gentlemen. Mr. Sherlock arrived from holidays.

Sept. 20th Very frosty. The roofs were covered with snow. Later on it was a bit showery and rough. Walter and Matilda Brown came next door (Ed's). Nothing can be done in corn, either cutting or leading. Our Tom went to a whist drive at Longstone (Wakes).

Sept. 21st Very fine with plenty of sun and wind. Bramwell field is about ready to get. Matilda Brown came in and had a long chat. Mr. Stephenson took the service in Church. Mrs. Carson passed away at about 8 o'clock tonight.

Sept. 22nd A miserable wet day and had been stormy during the night. No corn leading. Anthony took the milk and went to market. Thos. Wm Brockley took two of our cow calves to the auction at Bakewell. One sold for 25 shillings and the other 28. Michael Frost was in our house a good while tonight trying to sell watch chains, watches etc.

Sept. 24th Fine this morning, wind and sun. Tom and Wm went with binder and 3 horses and cut some of Miss Needham's corn (Flagg) but had to leave earlier than they would have done because the rain came on. Mr. Parton came but did not see Anthony as he was on moor fetching some of our sheep out of other people's land. They had jumped out of our rape. Mrs. Carson was interred at half past 2 o'clock. Mr. Sherlock officiated. He called here. Eight of Mrs. Carson's children followed her to the grave. Flavilla was not there. A managers' meeting was held in school to choose a new mistress and to discuss the alterations wanted. The inspector had complained. Evelyn went to Buxton to have a tooth stopped.

Sept. 25th Fine, sun and wind. Anthony and Tom went to Flagg to cut Miss Needham's corn. Received a letter from our Mary saying she would like to come to the Wakes. Finished the corn at Flagg and brought the binder home (charged £3 10s.0d.).

Sept. 27th Fine, plenty of wind and sun. Thos. Wm. went with milk and was met by a porter and told that the gates were locked and there is a strike on with railway men. Thos. Wm brought all the milk back and we set it up for butter.

Sept. 28th Fine. Sun and wind. The service was held to the dedication of Sheldon Church (St. Michael's). Mr. Stephenson had tea here today. We had a cheese today.

Sept. 29th Fine. Wind and sun. Our men and Jack Naylor, Fred Carson got all the corn on our moor today, 8 loads and one load of hay off the grove rakes. We have had another cheese today. Thos. Wm. has made arrangements to send his milk to Nestlés while the strike is on.

Sept. 30th Fine. Anthony went down to Ashford to meet Cauldwells Motor to ask if our milk could be taken by it to Manchester. John Dale sends his by this Motor. We were disappointed as the driver was full up. Another cheese and it is very heavy work every day. A few who have been sending milk to Manchester are sending it to Sheffield while the strike is on. Thos.

Wm sent his to Nestlés today. Our Ethel went to Longstone station to enquire about trains and cans. There are 2 of our cans and 2 of Thos. Wm. Brockley's. We have to give the whey to neighbours as we have no pigs.

Oct. 1st Dull, later on showery. Ethel has been cleaning outside windows and we have had another cheese. We do not receive any news about our milk going and we have no cheque from Mr. Burley. I am writing to Mary to see if she can come to the Wakes. Anthony wrote to Mr. Colin Prince to ask if Nestlés' firm could do with our milk and we received a telegram saying that that firm would have it for a few days.

Oct. 3rd Very fine and sunny. Neither letter nor telegram has come from our Mary so her father has gone to Grindleford. Mr. Edward Fearn brought the new agent in Mr. Hartopp's place but I could not catch his name very well when he was introduced by him to me. Mary and baby, little Anthony and aunt H arrived between 4 and 5 o'clock. Mary had not got my letter and was not expecting her father to come for them.

Oct. 4th Very fine. Nestlés called for the two cans of milk. We heard from Mr. Burley and he wanted us to try and send the milk by motor. Mr. Stephenson and others were decorating the Church for the harvest Thanksgiving tomorrow. The interest on £300 (7s.10d.) came tonight.

Oct. 5th Fine. Wakes Sunday. Holy Communion at 9.30 and our Mary was churched before. There were 22 communicants. Mr. Sherlock officiated. We wanted Mary's baby christening but he objects to Sunday baptism so other arrangements were made. The Harvest Festival was held this afternoon. A good congregation and the collection (for Church expenses) was the best we have had. £4.4.6. in Church. 10s/6d. was given to me by a motor party who came to Alf Brockley's and 10/- was given by Mr. John Frost. Total 5 guineas. We had a many people in our house tonight and we had sold out of beer before 9 o'clock.

Oct. 6th Very fine. Anthony, Tom and Clem went to market. They took a fat cow, a calving cow and some sheep. Calving cow (£47), fat heifer £43.3s.3d, fat sheep £49.2.3. Mary's baby was christened today at 4 o'clock. Clem and Tom were sponsors and Evelyn was godmother. Eben Ollerenshaw called but soon went when we had no beer. There was a whist drive at the school. Mr. Sherlock, and Mr. Stephenson had tea here. Mr. and Mrs. Webb are staying at Sheldon. Mr. Webb would take our milk as well as Thos. Wm.'s if we cared to send to him.

Oct. 7th Very fine. Clem went to Longstone, brought us 4 rabbits etc. Wm and Vincent went for lime ash. We are putting it on Bramwell field. Anthony took milk to station which went off as usual. He telegraphed to Mr. Burley saying he had sent it. The beer has not come and people are drinking port wine and minerals. Our Black and white cow (Holstein) calved a black and white cow calf. There was a dance up at school. Jim Goodwin and Fred played. I have been reading a book which our Tom got at the whist drive called *The Long Arm*.

Oct. 8th Very fine. Anthony and Tom have been dragging on moor. Wm and Vincent fetching lime. No news of the beer so I wrote to Mr. Parton. Eben Ollerenshaw and Fred Brockley (Potteries) came on Monday and are staying at Charles Ollerenshaw's house.

Oct. 9th Fine but very cold wind in N. East. We heard of the beer this morning and Anthony and Tom took Fanny and Wager and dray to Bakewell station and brought 3 barrels of beer. There was a dance at the school. The Goodwins played the music. A good many in house tonight. The beer had no time to settle and was rather thick but that did not matter much. It was beer and they drank it.

Oct. 10th Fine. Clem went to Grindleford. We have been making damson jam yesterday and today. Tom was dragging on moor. Anthony coloured 10 lambs. It is two years today since poor Anthony Brocklehurst was killed.

Oct. 11th Fine but very cold. There was a cricket match between Ashford and Sheldon. Sheldon won. The scores were not high on either side. I went into the parlour tonight. The house place was full of men and a rowdy night they had with singing and drinking. I was fairly sick of hearing the noise and was glad when 10 o'clock came. This was the end of another Wakes, one of the quietest we have ever had. I was very pleased to have it quiet but tonight spoiled it. Eben Ollerenshaw and Fred Brockley went back this morning.

Oct. 12th Drizzling at times and rather cold. Wm Gould took Mary and the two children in float to Grindleford at about 10.30 and got back between 4 and 5 o'clock. Mr. Stephenson took the service in Church this afternoon and a children's service at 6 o'clock. John Gregory and his wife were at Sheldon. She called in the kitchen and Emily gave her one of Tony's memorial cards.

Oct. 13th Frosty and snow showers. Anthony took milk and Tom took some tup lambs to Bakewell fair (four). Two were sold and Anthony bought a shire tup for £10. Our two lambs made £7.0.0. each. Two lambs were brought back.

Oct. 14th Snowstorms, sleet and rain at times. Very cold. Anthony turned out sheep to the ram. Walter Needham came to Sheldon and bought a lamb ram of ours for £9.0.0. Tom and Wm have been ploughing on moor this afternoon. Tom was dragging this morning.

Oct. 15th Cold and very frosty. Tom ploughing. Mrs. Bagnall and Mr. Sherlock had tea with me. There was a managers' meeting at the school (4 o'clock) to appoint a schoolmistress. It was decided to advertise again.

Oct. 16th Frosty first thing but clears out a fine sunshiny day with a cold wind. Our men commenced getting potatoes on moor. Jack Naylor and Freddy Carson were helping us. They got 3 rows. There is a fair crop and no bad ones. Heard that J. Johnson was bound for 12 months at Derby.

Oct. 17th Fine sunshine. Our men and Jack Naylor and Freddy Carson were getting our potatoes on moor. Got 3 more rows. Tom was ploughing. Farmer Tommy and 2 of Lomas's sons (Bakewell) were getting theirs, and Wm Bramwell and his lad got theirs. Mr. Ed was also getting his. These had all set in our field. Alf Brockley went with 4 lambs to Hathersage Fair. He sold two of them. Mr. Lloyd George is speaking at Sheffield. I have not read his speeches as I do not think anything of him.

Oct. 18th Dull. Fine. The men are getting potatoes on moor. Mr. Lowthian, Mr. Drewry (senior) and Mr. Hoyle were partridge shooting. They want tea here. I had a talk with Mr. Drewry. The three gentlemen had tea here and Mr. Lowthian gave Ethel 2s./6d. more than was charged. They only shot 2 pheasants and two hares, no partridges. Sam Rowland seemed to have a deal to say about there being nothing to shoot at Sheldon.

Oct. 19th Fine. Mr. Sherlock took the service in Sheldon Church this afternoon. Mr. Stephenson took duty at Ashford. Miss Thompson (chemist's shop Bakewell) and a tall young man came and had tea here.

Oct. 20th Fine. Anthony went to market. The others including Jack Naylor and Freddy Carson were getting potatoes on moor. Anthony bought a clothes basket which cost 10/6 and a saucepan (2 quarts) for 6s.3d. Mrs. Hallows was helping us to wash. Anthony sent £2.10s.3d. by cheque to Derby Excise for our Licence. A rebate of £5.0.0. had been granted to us.

Oct. 21st Fine. A most lovely day. The same men are getting potatoes today. A letter came from the Wages Board to say that Wm Gould would have a permit from April 10th last to work for us at 10/- per week with board and lodging.

Oct. 22nd Fine. All the men went on moor (same men) getting potatoes and they finished getting them. It has been a grand time for finishing corn and potatoes, so clean and dry. Anthony paid Billy Naylor for his men (Jack and F. Carson) helping us. There came an order from Mr. Challoner of Hyde for 4 cwts, and Mrs. Morton wants her usual supply.

Oct. 24th A most miserable wet day after a very wet night. Our men have been bagging up potatoes. I did not get up until one o'clock. Wm Gould's permit came from Wages Board.

Oct. 25th Dull and cold but fine. George Taylor came and bought a tup lamb from Anthony. He gave £6.0.0. for it and 5 shillings was returned to him for luck. Anthony and Tom went to Lomas's sale at One Ash. They did not buy anything. Mr. Stephenson went to Ashford Vicarage where he had to answer examination papers for Lay Reader. The hunt turned out at Sheldon. We had a few in, made coffee and tea for one or two. Mr. Tinsley gave 3/- to Alf Brockley to spend in our house which he did and gave the men a drink. Charles Gould said he would take £40.0.0. for the old houses across. He and I had a conversation.

Oct. 26th Fine, cold. Received a letter from the *Derbyshire Times* wanting to know if we were inserting a memoriam for Tony. Mr. Stephenson took the service in Church.

Oct. 27th Dull, rough and cold. Anthony took milk and Tom took 14 fat sheep to market. They were graded but Anthony was not satisfied with the weight. He thought they ought to have weighed more. Altogether they made £57.15.5. We sent £1.3.0. to Miss Selina Sheldon (the blind woman) for two shawls which she had knit for Emily and myself, also 8/- to the Editor of the *Derbyshire Times* to insert a memoriam to our Dear Tony (Anniversary of his death Nov. 2nd 1917).

Oct. 28th Very cold and rough. Last night our Ethel, and Evelyn took Mrs. Ed a parcel for her birthday (today). A fowl, cheese (a bit), a pot of jam, and other little items. 4 cwts of potatoes were sent to Mr. Challoner and others.

Nov. 1st Snowstorms - very cold. The wind keeps in North East. Mary sent the Credence Table[1] cloth in memory of our Dear Tony. Mr. Stephenson took it on to the Church. It is two years today by the day of the month since our darling lad wrote his last letter to his father to wish him many happy returns of his birthday. What sadness since then. Mr. Stephenson was chosen to be a school manager.

Nov. 2nd Hail and rain at times. Very cold. Celebration of Holy Communion by Mr. Sherlock who dedicated the credence cloth (linen with crochet). Mr. Stephenson took the service this afternoon and mentioned all the dear lads that had to give up their lives in the awful war. Collection for Church expenses. Ethel and Evelyn went to Ashford Church.

Nov. 3rd A most miserable wet and stormy day. Anthony did not go to the market as he is not well. The men are packing potatoes and Tom has taken some to Mrs. Morton.

Nov. 4th Very cold with snow. Anthony seems a bit better and he was painting cart wheels. Mr. Ed Brockley is repairing our carts.

Nov. 7th Cold and misty. Our Tom and Jack Naylor went by the 9.15 train from Longstone to Lincolnshire. Mrs. Sam Rowland had another son. Mrs. Fanny Thorpe attended her (no doctor). Anthony took her back to Ashford.

Nov. 8th Misty with a little sun at times. Anthony has been painting cart wheels after he had fetched Mrs. Thorpe from the bottom of Ashford Dale. Two P cards came this morning. One from our Tom, the other from Jack Naylor. They had got to Lincoln and were looking out for carriers carts. Mr. Sneap arrived here about tea time.

Nov. 9th Raw and cold. Anthony's birthday (56). He received two cards, one from Mary and Clem and one from little Anthony. Tommy Brockley

---

1 Small table near the altar for the bread, wine and water before consecration in the Eucharist

had tea with us. Mr. Metcalf and Mr. Stephenson had tea with me and a nice chat afterwards. Mr. Sneap and Anthony had their usual walks.

Nov. 11th Very frosty and cold. There was a service in Church (very short) this morning. It is just one year today since the Armistice. It was the King's wish that everyone should devote 2 minutes to the memory of the fallen, wherever they were to cease work for that time. Mr. Sneap went back home. Tom and Jack Naylor arrived home between 3 and 4 o'clock.

Nov. 13th Very frosty and severe with cold. If my dear Tony had lived he would have been 22 years of age today. It is just two years ago today since we heard that our dear lad had died of wounds.

Nov. 15th. Very frosty. Snowstorms at intervals. Anthony went by train this morning to Sheffield to look at an oil engine for chopping etc. He got back between 7 and 8 tonight. There is no work to be done on the land for snow and frost. Kate Brockley went to her post at Derby.

Nov. 16th Frosty and snow at times. Mr. Sherlock took the service in Church this afternoon and Mr. Stephenson went to Ashford school. Mr. Challoner from Hyde came here after dinner. He paid Anthony for the potatoes he had (£2.1.0.). Anthony dated bill Nov. 15th. We have had fires in my bedroom and Emily's for several nights this week.

Nov. 18th Fine. During last night and this morning the rain fell heavily and took most of the snow away. Mr. Joseph Anthony came and all the farmers in Sheldon brought their wool to be weighed (except T.A. Sheldon) at our place. Mr. Anthony made out two cheques: one to our Anthony and the other to T.W. Brocklehurst. We had to pay Billy Naylor and Fred Carson out of our cheque (£66.9.4½). Anthony paid Fred Carson 2 tod[1] 11 lbs at 1.10½ per lb. Billy Naylor's weighed 4 tod 3 lbs and he has to be paid yet. Vincent and Wm were on moor pulling swedes etc. Anthony sent Ethel to fetch Tom to help (from moor).

Nov. 20th Heavy showers of hail and snow. It also lightened and thundered once this morning just before 7 o'clock. No working on the land. We received word that there were £3.0.0. gratuity money for our poor Tony.

Nov. 21st Rain towards night (at times). We heard that Clarice Bramwell had got the scarlet fever. Mr. Stephenson read a letter that had come from Mr. Wm Shimwell saying that the tablet for the fallen boys was ready for the names.

Nov. 22nd Fine. Vincent went to Bakewell to be examined by the Dr. in view of entering Ashford Club. Clarice Bramwell was taken to Darley hospital. Showery tonight.

Nov. 23rd Cold, fine. Mr. Stephenson took the service this afternoon. There was also a service tonight and a collection. All ours went to tea to

1 tod: weight used in wool trade, normally 2 stone

Tommy Brockley's birthday (21) except Anthony. Very rough and windy tonight.

Nov. 24th Cold. Fine. Emily's birthday (29). Anthony took the wool cheque today to the bank and also a paper to change for the £3.0.0. allowed for my Tony's gratuity money. Anthony took the girls' and Tom's bank books to have what Tony had in the savings bank shared amongst them. It reopens the wound caused by our dear lad's death when we are dispersing to others what money belonged to him. There was £6.5.2. each for the five of them. Billy Naylor was paid tonight for his wool £10.14.7¹/₂. A calf of ours (bull) born last Friday made £3.0.0.

Nov. 25th Fine this morning, later on heavy showers. Our men and Jack Naylor and Freddy Carson are cutting and leading swedes home off the moor. I wrote to our Mary and Ernest Rawlinson. I paid Mr. Stephenson 2/6 for diary books and 2/6 to two boys who came collecting (for the Derby Infirmary) sent by Miss Broadhurst.

Nov. 27th Very showery at times. Rain and hail. Mr. Stephenson, Thos Wm B and Anthony went to Youlgreave to look at the *tablet* which they considered was very beautiful. Mr. Sherlock called and had tea. I wrote to Mr. Parton asking about the beer which has not arrived yet.

Nov. 28th Cold. Our men were getting swedes. Evelyn went to Dr. Jackson who drew out a tooth for her. Misty tonight. Anthony took Mr. Sherlock some potatoes. These were paid for yesterday.

Nov. 29th Misty, shower towards night. The men were busy getting the wool out of our chamber. Wm took it to Bakewell station on cart and brought coal back for us. Ted Hooley grumbled about it being taken to station on a Saturday. No swedes cut today.

Nov. 30th Very frosty and rimy with heavy rain tonight. Mr. Stephenson took two services, one in the afternoon and one at night (at Sheldon). He heard yesterday that he had passed a successful examination for lay reader. It is 3 years today since poor Jack Brockley died of wounds.

Dec. 2nd Showery at times. Poor Wm H. Brockley went to Manchester to hospital to see what was the matter with him. It is thought he has a growth in his inside.

Dec. 4th Very wet and stormy especially towards night. Wm took 1 ton potatoes to Shentons and brought coal (11 cwts) for the Church. Nothing has been heard of beer (Burton) which we have been expecting for over a fortnight.

Dec. 5th Very wet and stormy. Wm took potatoes to Mabel Cooper etc. and brought coal back for us. Evelyn paid 5/- to Mr. Stephenson for his layman's licence which he expects to get at Derby tomorrow. Tom Frost brought Orme's things 2 kils ale etc. Mr. Stephenson got a new diary for me at Ashford (cost 3/9).

Dec. 6th Awfully wet, rained in torrents. Mr. Stephenson went to Derby to be *Admitted as Lay Reader*. He got his licence and saw Kate B. at Derby.

Dec. 7th Very wet and stormy. Holy Communion was celebrated this morning (Mr. Sherlock). Word came that W.H. Brocklehurst had gone into hospital at Manchester. Mr. Stephenson took the service in Church this afternoon and night. Received advice note for 3 barrels of beer. Collection in Church 9/4.

Dec. 8th Very frosty and cold. Wm fetched 3 barrels of beer. Anthony took milk and then went to market. Mrs. Fairholm of Churchdale Hall called to see us and brought a receipt for 10/- which Anthony sent her yesterday for poor cripples.

Dec. 9th Very frosty and cold. Alf Barratt brought hat and coat for little Clement Wager. Wm took 1 ton of potatoes to Shentons and went to Hassop for meal.

Dec. 10th Very raw and cold, bitter, snow at intervals. Our Tom, Jack Naylor, Alf Brockley and Sam Rowland went out shooting. Four hares were shot (Tom shot 3 of them). Tom sprained his thigh when shooting. Wm and Vincent have been leading swedes off the moor.

Dec. 11th Dull and cold, slight showers at times. Jack Naylor and Vincent went in swedes. Anthony fetched the oil engine from Bakewell station and Wm fetched 3 barrels of beer (Burton). All the beer we ordered has arrived home.

Dec. 12th Very misty and rather drizzly. Wm and Jack Naylor in swedes. Anthony took milk and then went to Bakewell Station where Vincent met him with Mr. Sneap's young horse which was sent home by the 10.27 train to Belper. A dance was held in the schoolroom in aid of football club. No outsiders attended.

Dec. 13th Raw and cold, showery towards night. Anthony and Tom were fixing up the new oil engine ready for a man coming to show them how to work it. Wm fetched 4 barrels of treacle from Hurdlow.

Dec. 14th Misty and cold. Ethel's birthday (27). She received cards from Mary and Clem also Mr. Stephenson (Mr. Stephenson took service today). A confirmation was held in Bakewell Church. There were the following from Sheldon: Eliza Naylor, Mary Carson, Addie Hallows, Vera Carson, John and Herbert Frost. Ethel and Evelyn and Mr. Stephenson went in Frost's tub and the girls went in Thos Wm B's Float. Ethel is witness for Addie Hallows. Vera Carson and Evelyn for Herbert Frost. The confirmation was at 6.30 tonight.

Dec. 15th Misty and showery at night. Anthony went to Bakewell Farmers meeting which was nearly over when he got there. He could not go earlier because a man came from Sheffield to show how to put out (the engine) and work it. A casting was broken and they could not finish. The milk dealers came from Manchester and Sheffield to see if the farmers would take less than the controlled price but the farmers were unanimous that the price should not be dropped. Mr. Burley met Anthony and J. Dale.

Dec. 16th Milder. Anthony and Tom were cementing the engine bed and some were in swedes. The girls' sporting coats came by post. Kate B had got them and very nice they are.

Dec. 17th A bit frosty. All the men except Anthony are in the swedes. There was a managers meeting at the school. There were present Mr. Sherlock, Mr. Stephenson, Thos Wm B and Anthony. There had been two more applications for the post of schoolmistress at Sheldon and it was arranged that Miss Whitehead (Chapel en le Frith) should be interviewed this week. Rain tonight.

Dec. 20th Very showery all day. Miss Whitehead (and her sister) came from Chapel en le Frith to look at the school and be interviewed by the managers. The managers present in school were Mr. Sherlock, Mr. Stephenson, Mr. John Frost, Mr. T.W. Brocklehurst and Mr. A. Gyte. They offered her the post of schoolmistress and she is to let them know if she accepts it. Mr. Stephenson met them at Longstone station and Anthony drove them back there after having tea here. Mr. Sherlock and Mr. Stephenson also had tea.

Dec. 21st Very showery. Mr. Stephenson took afternoon and evening service. Snow tonight.

Dec. 23rd Very wet. Anthony and Tom are doing something at the oil engine. Anthony wrote to Colin Price to see if he could do with our milk when we had finished with Mr. Burley.

Dec. 25th Xmas Day. Snow storms at intervals. Service in Church taken by Mr. Stephenson. Holy Communion at 9.40. Mr. Sherlock officiated. There were 22 communicants. Several were up from Churchdale Hall. Two women from that place and a sailor came and had tea here. The men sang *Christians Awake* in the house tonight.

Dec. 26th Very wet and stormy. Clem went to Longstone and came back tonight. A man came to look at the oil engine and said Anthony must change the wheels from one place to another. A woman (his aunt) came with him. A good many in tonight. Bakewell and Youlgreave football teams played at Bakewell and Bakewell won 2-1.

Dec. 27th Very stormy at times. The men (Anthony and Tom) were altering the engine and it goes much better. Clem and Tom went after a hare and got it. Mr. Stephenson called in.

Dec. 28th Very wet especially towards night. Mr. Sherlock took the service in Church. Sam Rowland's baby was christened Douglas Frederick. Sam and Tom Critchlow were Godfathers. Mr. Stephenson was doing duty at Ashford this afternoon. Miss Mabel Stephenson called in.

Dec. 29th Wet at times. Clem started for Grindleford before 8 o'clock this morning. Anthony took Mary and the children in trap to Bakewell. She did not go to Grindleford by the usual motor bus as it had broken down. Bennett Needham's car was taking Mrs. Hall (Red Lion) to Grindleford Station and they allowed Mary and children to go in the car (charged Mary 10/-). A Dance was held in Alf Brockley's chamber.

Dec. 30th Wet at times. Tom and his father were altering the wheels of oil engine. It goes better. Jack Naylor and our men (some of them) went in swedes. Fred Brockley had an operation for Poly-pus (sic).

Dec. 31st Very wet and stormy (snow storms). Our Tom, Fred Brockley, Mary Carson and Clarice went to Bakewell whist drive and dance. Mr. and the Misses Stephenson called to see us as the latter are going tomorrow. Leah and Alice Brocklehurst are laid up with measles. Dr. Jackson is attending them.

1920

Jan. 1st Very cold. Frosty at night. Our Tom's birthday (31). A few in tonight. Anthony gave them a drink each. Mr. Ronston came and was paid up. The Misses Stephenson went back to London. They motored from Sheldon to Millers Dale Station to catch the express (11.3) to St. Pancras. I get worse with rheumatism. Emily is very poorly at times.

Jan. 2nd Very frosty and very dull, looks like snow. Anthony and Tom are chopping with new oil engine. We had word from Nestlés that they would accept our milk and send us cans in about a fortnight's time. They sent a contract to sign and send back to Nestlés. I made out bill to Mr. Burley to Dec. 31st 1919. This amounted to £76.9.4¾ and gave him notice (fortnight). Ethel went to Bakewell and paid Mr. J. Thacker all we owe him except this week's end meat which he himself brought to our house.

Jan. 3rd Very raw and cold. Snow storms this afternoon. Orme's man brought things but no bottled stout. The brothers Hodgkinson (Flagg) have been repairing and painting the walls of the school since Monday the 29th of Decr. 1919. Our young stock of sheep were fetched off the moor and the young stock were tied up for the first time. They have never been out so long before.

Jan. 4th. Very frosty. There was a celebration of Holy Communion this morning. Mr. Sherlock came in motor. Mr. Stephenson took the afternoon and evening service. Collection in afternoon 8/-.

Jan. 5th Bitterly cold. There is a bit of snow on the ground on the hills but at Ashford and Bakewell it is quite different and warmer. Anthony did not go with milk or to Bakewell as he has such a severe cold. Gould fetched us a load of coals. The girls are washing. We heard from Mr. Burley this morning that we can stop sending our milk to him at once if we like as he has got another dairy. Wrote and told him we should stop sending on Wednesday. Wrote to Nestlés saying we should start sending to their firm on Thursday next. Eben Ollerenshaw, his wife and son, came to Sheldon.

Jan. 6th Very frosty and bitterly cold. Anthony did not get up to milk as he has such a severe cold. Tom and Wm. went with milk and Tom, Fred Brockley and George and James Frost went to Buxton Town Hall where they began a series of lessons given by different men to farmers. When the horses came into the yard this morning, the grey mare was not with them. Vincent went to look for her and found her in a mine hole. A number of men went with Anthony and they got her out with ropes. They then put her on a sledge and brought her home where they put her in Alf Brockley's shed. She had knocked herself very much especially about the head.

Anthony gave her warmed ale and whiskey and rugged her up but the poor old thing died just after one o'clock. She went with old Naylor yesterday for a load of coals and was as sprightly as ever. We are all very sorry that she came to such an end.

Jan. 7th   Very cold. Dull later on and rough. A party of 3 men and two ladies called here when they had lunch which they brought with them in the motor. They had come to see Sam Rowland. They left 4/6 for using the house place and cups and saucers. They found all their own. Our poor old grey mare was buried today in a pit hole in our own Top Croft. Tom took the milk this morning. Snowing tonight.

Jan. 8th   On getting up this morning there was found to be a deep snow and there were snow storms during the day. We commenced sending milk to Nestlés.

Jan. 9th   Cold. The snow lies about 4 or 5 inches deep. Ten new cans arrived for us from Nestlés. Miss Broadhurst and the remainder of her furniture left Sheldon for Ambergate. Jack Naylor took her furniture to Bakewell station. Mr. Sherlock called here and had tea.

Jan. 10th.   Heavy showers of rain today which is taking away the snow nicely. Sent 3 of Nestlés cans with our milk this morning. A receipt came from Mr. Machin for the oil engine. Had letters from Mary and Hannah. The new schoolmistress (Miss Whitehead) came today. Polly Roberts finished cleaning the school after the painters who finished their work yesterday.

Jan. 11th   Very rough and heavy showers at times. Lightning. Mr. Stephenson took the afternoon and evening services and had tea here. Miss Whitehead called to see me. There are several more cases of measles. Hilda Carson, Ethel Brocklehurst, Arthur Bramwell and some of Frosts at the top are poorly.

Jan. 12th   Showery at times. Anthony and Tom went to market taking two fat cows which were put into 1st grade. One weighed $9\frac{1}{2}$ cwts the other $8\frac{3}{4}$ cwts. They made £77. Mr. Stephenson gave a supper to the choir and churchwardens. There were 16 present. Miss Whitehead was there. She began her duties as Sheldon schoolmistress this morning. Anthony sent potatoes by rail to Challoner etc.

Jan. 13th   A very nice day until night when some snow fell. Tom, Fred and George Brockley and James Frost went to Buxton to resume their lessons on farming. Tom, Fred and George went to the pictures and did not get back until after 10 tonight. I think the work this week was very difficult. The lads dined and had tea with Mr. Hollinshead. Ethel went to Ashford for our trap licence and an exemption form for dogs. This Anthony filled up and sent off. Mr. Burley has not sent cheque yet up to Dec. 31st 1919. Wm. took some potatoes to Shentons and brought us coal back. Mrs. Wright (Dr. Jackson's sister) called.

Jan. 14th   A very nice sunny day, rather frosty. Clarice Bramwell came out of hospital. She went to Alf Brockley's as Arthur had measles.

Jan. 15th   The weather is milder. Tom is ploughing in Bramwell field. Mr. and Mrs. Eben Ollerenshaw are at Sheldon. They came down to our house tonight. A nurse from Derby came to see Hilda Carson and called here.

Jan. 16th   Fine but rather rough winds. Tom has been ploughing in Bramwell field. Miss Whitehead has her eggs and milk from our house. Eggs are 5d each and we sell milk to our customers at 8d per quart. Thos. Wm. Brockley went to Blackpool yesterday. Wm. Henry Brocklehurst has undergone an operation in Manchester Infirmary.

Jan. 17th   Fine but very rough winds. Tom ploughing. I wrote to Anthony Wager and sent him some flannelette. He will be 5 on Monday next. Anthony cut Sam Rowland's pigs.

Jan. 18th   Rough at times and rather showery at night. Mr. Sherlock took the service in Sheldon Church this afternoon. Mr. Stephenson went to Ashford. Eben Ollerenshaw went back this morning.

Jan. 19th   Very rough. Snow and hail storms. Tom and his father went to market. They took a calving cow and sold her for £44.0.0. to C. Gould who made a profit by selling her again. Anthony Wager's birthday (5 years).

Jan. 20th   Rather rough and showery at times. Tom, Fred and George went to Buxton. James Frost did not go as he has measles. They got back about six o'clock. Mr. Barnes (Pilsley) and Robert Holmes came here and had bread and cheese. Sheldon school is closed (by order of Dr. Fentem) for a fortnight owing to measles. I wrote and told Mr. Burley that his milk cheque had not been received.

Jan. 21st   Very rough wind and showery at times. Tom is ploughing in Bramwell field. Wm. is gone for beer to Bakewell station. Miss Whitehead called and paid me for milk 1/-. She is going to Chapel-en-le-Frith this afternoon. We received Nestlés cheque to Jan 13th, £30.5.3. A letter came from J. Gyte thanking us for a donation of 10/- sent night before last to the 'Wm. Goodwin fund'.

Jan. 23rd   Rough winds. Tom ploughing Gt. Stones. Wm. leading manure on seeds (Grindlow Knoll). Two gentlemen (Mr. Haslam and another old gentleman) called and had their luncheon here.

Jan. 24th   Rough and showery at times. Tom ploughing in Great Stones. Wm. and Vincent on moor in swedes. Had price list of potatoes from Tom King. Hannah's (my sister) birthday (70).

Jan. 27th   Very stormy and wet. Tom and Fred Brockley went by milk train to Buxton for lectures. They afterwards went to Cowdale Farm and got wet through. James Frost cycled to Buxton. George Brockley did not go (not very well).

Jan. 28th A very nice day. Tom ploughing in Great Stones. Vincent has gone to Bakewell to see the doctor about his neck. Wm. Shimwell and son and Wm. Brassington (Joe's son) brought the tablet to put up in Sheldon church to the fallen lads. They came here and had tea, brought their own. What work they did had to set before they could go on. Started snowing very heavily and rough winds tonight.

Jan. 29th A very deep snow. Very little traffic. Mr. Ronston came and was paid up (£15.14.0.). He did not go any further than Sheldon and went back through Ashford to Bakewell. The roads were blocked and Nestlés could not fetch the milk. Miss Hawley came and was paid.

Jan. 30th Thawing during the night. Wm. Shimwell and son and Wm. Brassington came and finished fixing the tablet. Mr. Stephenson covered it with a Union Jack until it is unveiled. Anthony gave £5.0.0. towards tablet. Mr. Stephenson had the money. Nestlés came today and fetched the milk.

Jan. 31st Very wet. Mr. Stephenson went to Nottingham to a meeting of lay readers.

Feb. 2nd Very rough wind. Anthony walked to Bakewell and back. Tom was ploughing in Great Stones. Vincent went to Matlock to have his neck looked at. Mr. Stephenson went to ask Mr. Spink, Vicar of Bakewell, to dedicate the Sheldon War Memorial on Feb. 10th at 3 o'clock. Miss Grover has been asked to unveil the tablet. Miss Whitehead reopened the school after measles. W.H. Brockley came from Manchester. Came out of hospital on Saturday. Operation successful.

Feb. 3rd Rough wind but fine. Tom went to Buxton this morning to lecture. James Frost and Fred Brockley went. George did not go as he is only just recovering from measles. Anthony, William and Vincent went on moor and finished pulling swedes and turnips which were sown last year. I filled Vincent's Insurance Card from the age of 16 until Jan. 1920.

Feb. 4th Rough winds. Anthony and William went to Bakewell station for seed oats which had come from Montrose in Scotland. Fred Brockley and Jack Naylor also went for theirs. The Railway carriage is very heavy costing £5.0.0. all but 2 pence. Mr. Sherlock called and had tea and had a long chat.

Feb. 5th Rough but fine. Tom ploughing in Great Stones. Nestlés milk cheque came £80.3.0.

Feb. 6th Very misty, cleared a little in afternoon. Tom finished ploughing Great Stones and all the men went on moor preparing for some more ploughing. A dance was held in the school room tonight. Eben Ollerenshaw is still at Sheldon. Vincent took our licence and 8/6 to Taylor's office, Town Hall, Bakewell.

Feb. 7th   Very misty and raw. Anthony and Tom were chopping and pulping to last several days. The hunters turned out at 12 o'clock. Not many callers at our house. Two men sat a good while and never had a drink.

Feb. 8th   A bit showery at times. Mr. Stephenson took the service in church afternoon and night. Gladys Brockley was asked[1] in church first time.

Feb. 9th   Rough and cold. During the night we had two cows calved, both cow calves; one was a white one off the blue cow and one a roaned one off Mark. Tom and Wm. sat up between Sunday night and Monday. Anthony went to market.

Feb. 10th   An awful wet and windy day. Tom, Fred B and James Frost went to Buxton and afterwards by motor to Hargate Hall Farm with the others who attend the classes. George did not go as it was too rough and wet. Vincent went to Derby Infirmary. His Mother took him. They did not come home tonight.

Feb. 11th   Very rough and very showery; snow, rain and sleet at times. Anthony took the gig and fetched Mr. Spink,[2] Vicar of Bakewell, who had a nice chat with me before going to Church. The Tablet was dedicated and unveiled. After waiting some time for Miss Grover who did not arrive at the time stated, Mr. Stephenson drew the Union Jack aside. Just as this had been done, both Misses Grover drove up. I think the horse and conveyance were a poor lot as they started from Ashford at 2.15. The Service was most impressive. Mr. Spink could feel for our poor lads as he also had lost his only son in the war (Mesopotamia). Vincent came back.

Feb. 12th   Rather better weather, not so rough but a bit showery. Tom ploughing on moor. Tom Clark's men have been a day or two this week trying to do something at the West end of the church but the wind has been so rough that they could not go up the ladders.

Feb. 13th   Rather showery at times. Tom ploughing on moor. Miss Whitehead called and brought me a book. She lodges at Mr. Thos. A. Sheldon's.

Feb. 14th   A nice day. All the men except William were on moor. Tom ploughing. A cricket meeting was held in our parlour tonight. The same men are to continue in office viz Tom Gyte (captain) Sam Bramwell (secretary) Fred Brockley (treasurer).

Feb. 15th   Showery. Mr. Sherlock took the service in Church this afternoon and gave an address on the church's Enabling Act.[3] Papers have been sent out for people who belong to the Church of England to sign so

---

1   Calling of banns of marriage
2   The Rev. Edmund Spink became Vicar of Bakewell in 1919
3   This Act created the Church Assembly (forerunner of the General Synod) and Parochial Church Councils.

that they can have a vote on Church matters. Mr. Stephenson took the Service tonight.

Feb. 16th A lovely sunshiny morning. Anthony took a cow calf to market (Marks). Polly Bramwell (Gregory) rode down with him. Tom took old Mark cow to sell. I reckoned the butcher's tickets up and they came to £6.15.11½ to week Feb. 13th. Evelyn took bills and paid all up. She also had a tooth stump drawn. The cow made £37.10.0. The calf £2.10.0.

Feb. 17th Shrove Tuesday. Fine. Our Tom, Fred and George Brocklehurst went to Buxton. Tom on getting back walked to Monyash to a whist drive and dance which closed at 11.30. Clarice B and Mary Carson, Leah and Alice Brocklehurst went to Longstone to a dance. Eggs are selling at 4d each but corn is no cheaper.

Feb. 18th Very fine. All our men working on moor. Tom ploughing there. Mr. Stephenson brought me a list of the subscribers to the Sheldon War Memorial Fund.

Feb. 19th Fine 1st thing, misty afterwards, rain following and at night snow. Anthony, Alf Brocklehurst and Wm Naylor went by train (after 9) to Mr. Sneap's sale. Things made a lot of money and they got back between 9 and 10 tonight. Tom had just got on moor for ploughing when the rain came on and wet him through.

Feb. 20th A deep snow and continues to snow at intervals. Nestlés' cheque for milk to Feb. 15 came, £81.1.0. The dray did not come to collect the milk, the snow was so deep.

Feb. 21st Fine. The snow is plentiful in the fields. The roads are padded down a bit and Nestlé's dray came twice and brought empty cans. It seems as if it would thaw a bit tonight.

Feb. 22nd Fine. Thawing a little. Mr. Stephenson took afternoon and evening services. Gladys Brockley was asked the 3rd time this afternoon. Our Old Naylor got down in building up back yard. Several men got her up with ropes.

Feb. 24th Very misty raw and cold. Our Tom, Fred and G. Brockley and James Frost went to Buxton; came to Bakewell from there at midday and then went by motor to Castle Farm, Middleton-by-Youlgreave. Mr. J.R. Bond, Mr. George Howe (vet) and Macmillan were with them. Tom had no time to call to see his aunt B and aunt H as he could not leave the company who were having lectures on horses.

Feb. 25th A bit misty and drizzly at times. The snow is melting away nicely. A committee was formed at the school tonight (Liberal Unionist) ready to meet the Marquis of Hartington on Friday next.

Feb. 26th Rather drizzling at times. Mr. Mawer came to Sheldon and had a house to house inspection of water taps. There has not been a good supply for all in Sheldon lately and he came to see if there were any leakages or bursts. Sam Rowland sent his resignation the other night over the water.

Feb. 27th Rather showery, nice sunshine at times. Tom took the young horse and fetched some coal for us from Bakewell station. Little Marjorie Brocklehurst is not so well. They sent for the Dr. and he said she had a feverish cold. Lord Hartington was at Sheldon. Anthony was poorly and did not meet him at school.

Feb. 28th Dull but fine. Gladys Brocklehurst was married today at 2.30 to a man called Ernest Gould from Glamorgan. They had the schoolroom for refreshments etc. Elizabeth Ann Brocklehurst and Hilda Carson were bridesmaids. George Brocklehurst was best man and Tom York gave the bride away.

Feb. 29th Dull but fine. Being Leap Year there are 29 days in this month. Mr. Stephenson took the service both afternoon and evening. Anthony is a bit better. Kate Brocklehurst came last night for weekend.

March 1st Dull. Fine. Anthony walked to Bakewell and rode back in Mr. H. Frost's trap. Hannah rode from Bakewell in a trap which Anthony ordered from C. Critchlow as our horses had gone to Hurdlow for corn. March entered in very mild and still.

March 2nd Dull. Fine. Tom, Fred and G. Brockley and James Frost went to Buxton. Tom and Fred went to the pictures. Anthony and Vin went for artificial manure to Hurdlow. Fred Goodwin brought a hamper for us which Mr. Sneap had sent to Bakewell station.

March 3rd Fine. Mrs. Fairholm called here and had a chat. Emily is very bad at times, so sick etc. Eggs are selling here at 3d each. The corn is no cheaper. I wrote to our Mary and to Mr. Wm. Shimwell thanking him for a bottle of Sloans and chocolate which he sent. Tom ploughing in moor.

March 4th Fine and still, a lovely day. Mrs. Pickard and another lady called and had tea here and afterwards went through Sheldon church. Tom ploughing in moor

March 8th Raw and cold. Frosty. Anthony went to market and to a committee of the Farmers' Club where they voted for a secretary. Their choice fell on Mr. J. Wall of Tinkersley. A calf of ours was sold at auction for £3.18.0. a little over a week old.

March 9th Dull. Fine. Tom and the other lads went to Buxton. Wm. fetched us coal and afterwards went for cake etc. to station. Aunt H is busy making dresses for the fancy dress ball to be held at Easter. James Frost did not go to Buxton as he was not well. Tom, Fred and George had their photos taken with others. They visited a farm of Mr. Lomas at Chapel-en-le-Frith. Brought in the lambing ewes tonight.

March 11th   Fine but dull. Anthony went to Trickett's sale at Rowland and bought a weighing machine etc. Tom was dragging on moor. I was taken bad with influenza. Sam Rowland and Billy Naylor had a row.

March 12th   Very drizzling at times. Anthony fetched the weighing machine and they were weighing a few. Anthony weighed 12 stone 2lbs. Tom 10 stones 13 lbs. Ethel 8 stones. Evelyn 8 stones 12 lbs. Vincent 11 stones 2 lbs. I had a very poor night last night. I could not breathe very well.

March 13th   A nice morning but turns out showery later in the day. Our first lamb for the season was born today. Several farmers in Sheldon have started lambing viz Thos. A. Sheldon, Alf Brockley, Billy Naylor and Thos Wm. Brocklehurst. The hunters turned out at Sheldon. They will not meet any more this season at this village but are having a hunt or two at other places. We had a few callers for tea and bread and cheese. I was so bad with a cold that I had to be taken to bed before opening time. Emily and Anthony also had to go to bed, Anthony with sick headache etc. and Emily with cold. Anthony and Tom had been to J. Wm. Naylor's sale at Flagg. They bought nothing.

March 14th   Fine in morning but at night snow storms came on. Emily and I were so bad that Tom went for Dr. Jackson. We made such a crowing noise when coughing (like croup) that we were frightened. We could not breathe. The doctor brought some medicine with him and took our temperature. Anthony is a little better. Hannah's cold is a little better but she is not well. This is such an awful clinging complaint. Ethel and Evelyn have colds and Wm. coughs incessantly. Miss Whitehead's father and sister came today. Mr. Stephenson took both services.

March 15th   Snowstorms today. Anthony went to Bakewell market and to a farmers' meeting. He was voted for the Committee a week or two since. He got 74 votes. He brought us some more medicine which seems to be doing Emily and I some good. The crowing is not so frequent in my case but we are very stuffed up. The Duke of Rutland's land sales about Youlgreave are today. Many of the tenants have bought their own by private treaty.

March 16th   Dull. Our Tom, James Frost and G. Brockley and Fred went by the after nine train from Longstone station en route for Chesterfield to visit special farms in Nottingham and Derbyshire. They went by motor to some of the farms. Howe the vet was one of the party. They got back to Sheldon between 8 and nine tonight.

March 17th   Dull, rough winds which are drying the roads. The snow is all gone. We have such poor nights. I got up a bit this afternoon and sat in Emily's room. The discharge from my nose and throat is very great at times and we have burnt the rags used as handkerchiefs. We have six lambs up to this time. Anthony is not well. He has such a cold. Ethel and Evelyn have a lot to do and they have colds. Mr. Stephenson came up stairs to see us. Hannah's and Wm's cold are about the same.

March 18th   Dull but fine. Wm leading turnips off moor to home. Arthur Evans of Youlgreave who is in Bakewell union came up to see Mrs. Ed and myself. He did not see either of us as we are in bed. We have had another lamb (7 now). Emily and I are a little better but still stuffed.

March 19th   Fine. The roads are drying up. Tom is dragging on moor. Anthony is gapping. Emily is in bed and I am writing in her room. Ethel has just cycled off to Bakewell for a few things required by invalids; I have not been downstairs since last Saturday. Nestlés milk cheque came £81.7.8. Our licence came.

March 20th   Fine. I got downstairs this afternoon. My cough is rather better but very fast at times. Anthony has a dreadful cold and cough but will go about. Emily is a little better but so weak and full of wind.

March 21st   A lovely day for the commencing of the Spring quarter. Two years ago today the great push back of our troops on the Western front took place. Many a thousand of our poor lads lost their lives on that date and afterwards whilst the great push lasted. Poor Jack Sherwin was one that was reported missing and nothing has ever been heard of him since. Mr. Sherlock took the service in church this afternoon. Anthony is not well at all and Emily and I are only just middling.

March 22nd   A most lovely day. Anthony went to market. Took a calf for ourselves and one for Billy Naylor. He afterwards went to a sale at Wilsons at Hassop Flat. Dr. Jackson came to see Emily. She is so weak. Tom leading turnips.

March 23rd   Another most lovely day. Tom and Fred Brockley cycled to Buxton. Tom took Mrs. Hollinshead a piece of cheese. A cow calved this morning at 5 o'clock (cow calf). Tom and Vincent sat up all night.

March 24th   Fine 1st thing, a bit drizzling with rain towards night. Anthony and Tom went in trap to Bleaklow and bought a young filly for £38. Hallows's sow had a litter of 13 pigs. One born dead.

March 25th   Fine but rough, drizzling towards night. Our dog exemption came. Mr. Stephenson gave a receipt for money he had had to be admitted lay reader. A many people are flitting today. Mr. J. Tricknett is leaving Rowland for Darley Dale. Tom Critchlow leaving Organ Ground for Brushfield. Mr. Mawer went on to moor to see Anthony who was getting hay in. Mr. Ronston was paid up and he promised to rectify a mistake made over Anthony paying too much for a syphon of soda at the shop last Monday. We have had 3 couples of lambs today. We have 19 altogether.

March 26th   Very rough and drizzling. Wm has been to station for bags of feeding stuff. Anthony's cold is still bad. Emily is a shade better and I am improving a little. Hannah is busy making Ethel's and Evelyn's things for dress ball.

March 27th A bit drizzling at times. Mr. Marrison came to a poorly cow and docked our young filly's tail. I have great pain in my bowels today. Anthony's cold is not much better.

March 28th Fine mostly. Mr. Stephenson took both services in church. We have over 20 lambs. Gladys Gould is still lodging with Miss Reece. She has not gone to her husband. Rain tonight.

March 29th A bit drizzly at times. Anthony went to a meeting of the Farmers' Union. A discusssion over the price of milk was on and the payment of farm labourers in Harvest. Alf Brockley's calf broke a leg. Mr. Stephenson took a service in Sheldon Church tonight. The pain in my stomach is still bad.

March 30th Rather misty and drizzling. Our Tom, Fred and George Brockley and James Frost went to Derby to visit different farms. Tom, Fred and George cycled to Bakewell station. Mr. Stephenson called and had tea with me. The above boys went to Melbourne and saw the market gardens. They got back home between 10 and 11 tonight. Mr. Ed. paid rent.

March 31st This month goes out very quietly for wind but a few drizzling showers come on at times. The men have been carting swedes off moor and getting things ready for sowing. I cough very much at night, and Emily is not so well. Three gentlemen and two girls called here, been before.

April 1st Showery. Kate Brocklehurst came for holiday. We have begun collecting for an Easter offering for Mr. Stephenson.

April 2nd Misty and dull, rain at night. Anthony went to Grindleford and brought Mary, Anthony and baby back. Ethel cycled to Bakewell to see the Dr. about Emily. She got wet through coming back. Mr. Stephenson took the service this afternoon. Three ladies called here for tea.

April 3rd Very wet. Mr. Stephenson has gone to decorate the church with white tulips, white carnations and cream lilies and daffodils. Two gentlemen called here. A full house tonight. I sat in parlour. Evelyn has been collecting for an Easter offering to Mr. Stephenson. We have got £12.10.0. up to date. There are some we have not asked.

April 4th Very dull and wet 1st thing. There was a celebration of Holy Communion at 9.40. Mr. Sherlock officiated. Mr. Stephenson took the services this afternoon and evening. Collection (afternoon) £1.18.0. Evening 7/6. which goes to lay reader's stipend. Carsons at the top sent 10/- and George Ward and Becky sent 5/- to Mr. Stephenson's Easter Offering. Anthony Wager gave 1/- which brought the total to £13.10.0.

April 5th Easter. Fair Raw and dull and cold and the roads are dirty. Showery at night. Anthony walked to Bakewell. Vincent and Wm. went to Hurdlow this morning and in the afternoon all the men went to the Fair. Ethel and Evelyn cycled to the Fair. I gave the £13.10.0. to Mr. Stephenson.

He was quite overcome. The £5.0.0. which the Duke of Devonshire has given other years has not been received here.

April 6th Very dull and showery. No sun. The men were fetching hay from the moor. A fancy dress affair was held at the school room which was very successful. Different characters were represented and very good they were. Ethel was dressed as Early Victorian, Evelyn as a Watteau Shepherdess, Tom as a Highland soldier. A sum of over £8.0.0. was cleared with sale of refreshments included. Dancing was kept up until 2 o'clock.

April 8th Very dull and misty. No sun. Nestlés cheque came £92.4.6. We charge 6d. per quart for milk this month. Eggs are 3d. each. Evelyn has made more nests ready to sit more hens. The price of corn keeps up and I am sure the drapery is something scandalous in price. The material for dresses is from 12/6 up to 30/- per yard for anything nice.

April 9th Dull and very misty. The ground is in such a wet state as rain comes on each night. No work to be done on the land. Our Mary cannot take the children out; she has never been even to see her aunts.

April 10th Foggy and wet. A beautiful cup and saucer came for me from Misses Stephenson. Mr. Stephenson went to the Vicarage (Ashford) and Mr. Sherlock gave him £5.0.0. (in notes) which had come from the Duke of Devonshire (yearly subscription for Sunday School and organist). Vincent went to Derby this morning and was operated on for his tonsils. Eggs are $2^3/_4$d each.

April 11th Thick with fog. Very heavy showers of rain at times. Mr. Stephenson took the service in Church this afternoon. Anthony fetched Miss Whitehead from Longstone station tonight. Vincent came home.

April 12th Rough and wet. Mary did not venture to go home as she did not want the children to get wet. Anthony went to market and took a calf of ours to auction. He was going to ask Mr. Daybell to take Mary and children to Grindleford in a covered conveyance. Mr. Stephenson went to Heath for a short holiday. Kate Brockley went back to Derby after having her Easter holiday. At half past three this afternoon we were surprised to see Mr. Hawley with a covered conveyance. Anthony had asked him to fetch Mary so they bundled up and went dry to their home taking about 12 cwt of potatoes with them.

April 13th Very hot. Our Mary has been married 6 years today. Bertha Brocklehurst (Bramwell) was taken ill and Sam fetched the Dr. Vincent Hallows has not returned to work.

April 14th Most miserable and wet. Dr. Fentem came to Bertha Bramwell and he said she had appendicitis and Bennett Needham's motor took her to Derby Infirmary this afternoon. Sam and Sally Brocklehurst went with her. Sally came back but Sam did not. Our Ethel cycled to Bakewell and paid Mr. Thacker up to April 8th for weekend meat by cheque which was made out for £9.8.0.

April 15th Rough and very wet. Mr. Sherlock came in and had tea. He had a stiff neck. Anthony and Tom had to sit up with a sheep. Mr. Stephenson came back tonight. The weather has been awfully wet and rough.

April 16th Very rough and heavy showers at times. Our men went picking stones off the land and got saturated with rain. Mr. Stephenson had tea with me and I wrote to Wm. Shimwell. Three years ago today my dear Tony first put on the hated khaki at Derby. The sheep and lamb died that they had sat up with. A Vestry meeting and a meeting about the Enabling Bill (Church) was held in the school room at 8 o'clock tonight. The old Wardens were put on and Mr. Stephenson and Mr. Thos. Wm. Brocklehurst were voted to see after the Enabling Bill. Miss Whitehead headed the poll. George Brockley, our Tom, Evelyn and Ruth were on committee. Ethel and Emily did not attend. There was over £13 balance in hand for the church.

April 17th Fine and a deal of sunshine. Mr. Steel and his son came here for a few minutes on their road to Bakewell. Three years today by the day of the month my Tony went in khaki to Derby and afterwards to Cleadon camp to receive training and now he lies in a foreign grave.

April 18th Dull and showery at times. Mr. Sherlock took the service in church this afternoon. No evening Service. Received a p. card from our Mary that she had sent us some time by Mr. Johnson (yesterday) and that they were thinking of flitting from Grindleford to Curbar and will live at Curbar in the house where David Peat and son lived as gamekeepers.

April 19th Showery at times. Anthony went to the Guardian and Rural District Council meeting at Bakewell workhouse. A number of farmers signed on at Bakewell with Nestlés for the summer prices of milk. Billy Naylor sold two cows for £84.7.6.

April 20th Very showery and dull. Vincent is not at work. He went to Matlock yesterday and the Dr. told him to lie in bed this week as his temperature was so high. Mr. Stephenson went to see Bertha Bramwell at Derby Infirmary. She had an operation last Thursday for appendicitis. Anthony cut S. Bramwell's young pigs.

April 21st Very wet at times. It is 41 years today since I took up duty as schoolmistress of Sheldon School. What alterations in that time. The salary is above four times as much as I had and where in my time there were 44 children on the books, there are now about 26. Lady Dorothy Cavendish married to Capt. Harold Macmillan (London).

April 22nd Very showery. Miss Hawley (Barrett) called and Mr. Ronston was paid up. He made good about the syphon of soda which Anthony called for. Mrs. Hallows was helping us to clean big room. Eggs are selling at 2³/₄ each wholesale.

April 23rd Misty, sunshine afterwards. Finer. Received a letter from our Mary. They have removed from Grindleford (this week) to Warren Lodge, Curbar. Did not get the furniture wet and she likes the house very much. It has 3 or 4 bedrooms and a bath room and a large garden, stable, cowshed etc. Mr. Stephenson had tea here. Mrs. Hallows helped to clean Wm's room and bathroom.

April 24th Drizzly. Our men are gone on moor, Wm rolling the land and Tom leading turnips. Vincent is away yet. Mr. Sneap came tonight. He is settled in his new house. Youlgreave football team won the Moxon cup (played with Darley at Matlock)

April 26th Showery. Anthony and Tom took our bull to market. It was very rough, led it by a staff, and sold it after grading 1st grade 2 down for £56.5.0. Mr. Sneap took trap down and Ethel. Three years today our poor Tony came back home from Cleadon until the 20th of May.

April 27th Very wet. This afternoon it cleared up a bit and Tom and Wm.went to Hurdlow. Anthony had had a bill for £1.6.0. railway carriage. He sent it some time ago to the station master of Hurdlow by Wm. Gould. This man says he has no entry of it so Anthony will have to pay again as Wm. did not bring a receipt.

April 28th Snowstorms. Mr. Sneap went back. Anthony took him to Bakewell station. He took a hamper of seed potatoes with him. Sam Bramwell's two boys were taken by Mr. Alf Brockley to Chinley to have their tonsils cut. They came back tonight after being operated on.

April 29th Snow storms and hail at intervals. Ethel and Mrs. Hallows are cleaning. My room has been mended (the paper) and they have papered and cleaned the girls' room today. Mr. Sherlock called and had tea.

April 30th Very heavy snowstorms and thunder. Mrs. Hallows is ill and cannot help us today (sickness and purging). Anthony cut Hallows' pigs tonight.

May 1st Very misty and heavy showers of rain. Sam Bramwell has gone to Derby to fetch Bertha. She came back tonight. The children had a May Pole. The Duke and Duchess of Devonshire and suite sailed for Canada

May 3rd Showery and rough at times. Anthony did not go to Bakewell. I heard that our Mary and the children and Maggie Wager were there. She sent three young rabbits. Mr. Stephenson called here and brought us a bit of polony. He has got a severe cold. Mrs. Hallows did not help us today. Our milk cows were turned out 1st time in the day time. Tied up at night.

May 4th Showery a bit; hail and rain. Anthony and Thos. Wm. Brockley went to a sale at Middleton Top. Anthony bought a mare for which he gave 100 guineas. It hurt Anthony's knee when bringing it off the sale ground. Mr. Hewitt armed him to the road and then Graham Kenworthy gave him a ride to Bessies. The mare came all right to Sheldon. Anthony was very lame when he got home. Billy Naylor and Alf Brockley sowed their oats today.

May 5th   Very wet. No work on the farm. The mare was put into the dray; after a bit of trouble fetched a load of hay from moor. It is full of mettle and they can scarcely keep up with it. It is 16 hands 3. Anthony had a very poor night and is not well today. We rubbed his knee with embrocation. Mrs. Hallows helped to clean parlour.

May 6th   A most wet and miserable day. No sowing to be done. Anthony seems better today after a better night. Mrs. Hallows and Ethel have done bar and staircase. I wrote to our Bessie. Hannah is mending Tom's coats. We have had several good hatches of chickens this last day or two but it is difficult where to put them as it is so wet. Mr. Stephenson is ill in bed today.

May 7th   A little finer but shower later in the day. Our Tom fetched a load of coal this morning and three barrels of beer this afternoon from Bakewell station with the new horse. Mrs. Hallows was helping us to clean the house place. Mr. Sherlock came and had tea here. Mr. Stephenson is very poorly. A whist drive at School.

May 8th   Finer. Wm., Tom went on moor. Tom was sowing and Wm. harrowing part of a field - 1st to be sown this year. Anthony is lame and his knee is very painful at times. Dr. Fentem came to Mr. Stephenson who is in bed, neuralgia pains and cold. Thos. Wm. Brockley was sowing today and yesterday. Wm. H. Brocklehurst's mare foaled this morning (filly). Lewis E. Elliot's mare foaled a day or two since. Anthony posted cheque for £1.6.0. for carriage for stuff which came to Hurdlow. Wm. had paid this before but had not been given a receipt so it had to be paid again. This ought to teach folks a lesson to demand a receipt when paying money. The sum of £1.10.0. for bags was also sent the other night. Rain came on tonight. We asked Billy Naylor if he or Jack could help us and he said he would not sow and he should not stop harrowing all day. He came and asked us if we should want him as Vincent came this morning. Tom said we could manage so he went home. He did not want to help us and showed it very plainly.

May 9th   Bright sunshine, but rather frosty this morning. Anthony is a little better. Tom took 11 young stirks to moor to lie out. Mr. Sherlock took the service in Church. Mr. Stephenson is in bed ill. Vincent does not come much. Our Evelyn, Tom and Wm. have to milk all the cows. Evelyn milks 7 or 8. Tom the same.

May 10th   Fine. Tom, Wm and Vincent went on moor and finished sowing the field they started off. Wm harrowed and Vincent served Tom. Anthony could not go to Bakewell. His leg is still very painful and his back is no better. They had the new horse harrowing. It works well but is so mettlesome. Three years today by day of month my poor Tony went back to be trained at Cleadon. What a sorrowful time it has been since then.

May 11th   Very fine 1st thing but rain came on about 3 o'clock. Tom, Wm and Vincent went on moor and sowed another field. Anthony's leg is not so well. I think he walked too much on it. Hannah is not well (cold). Emily is very poorly. Evelyn has got the tic and we are all of us something amiss. Mr. Stephenson got up a bit this afternoon.

May 12th Misty and showery. Tom, Fred and George Brockley went to an examination at Buxton this morning. They biked to station. Ethel has gone to Bakewell for medicine for Emily. Vincent Hallows did not come at all today and Wm has gone on moor. Hannah seems poorly and Evelyn is tired with having so much to do, milking etc. No one seems to think we want a helping hand. Mr. Sherlock called here and had tea.

May 13th Slight showers early but clears out during the day. Our Tom sowed oats in the Great Stones. Wm harrowed it once over. Mr. and Mrs. Fairholm motored to Sheldon to see Mr. Stephenson. Thos. Wm. Brockley's mare foaled (colt) between 8 and 9 tonight.

May 14th Rather frosty, sunshine afterwards. The men went on moor and sowed one field. Anthony went as well. His leg is improving nicely. This morning they finished harrowing Great Stones. We fetched two pigs for our Mary £4.0.0. each.

May 15th Frosty 1st thing but it is the warmest day we have had for weeks, plenty of sunshine. Our men, Anthony, Tom, Vincent and Wm, all went on moor. They finished sowing and brought all things home. They cannot find our cutting knife which was left on moor so I should think someone has walked off with it. Mr. Stephenson came in to see us this morning. He is improving very nicely. Mrs. Hallows cleaned our cellar today. We turned our milk cows to lie out all night, 1st time.

May 17th Very rough and a bit drizzly at times. Anthony went to market and took a calf for us and one for Alf Brockley, Alf Brockley's was 3 weeks old and made £3.1.0. Anthony took the new mare in float to market. He bought a barren cow and lying off calves. He called to see Mr. Hudson about the spirits and beer prices. Hallows paid rent for buildings etc. and for a bale of straw.

May 18th Very rough and very wet. The men, Anthony, Tom and William went in moor to work but came back as it was so wet. Tom took the new mare for a load of coals. He brought 11 cwt which cost £1.4.6. Coal went up in price last Wednesday at the rate of 14s.2d. per ton. Whatever is the country coming to. Mr. Bennett Needham and Mr. Buxton (Burley's) called here today. Mr. Griffiths (Blackpool) called at noon. He and his wife are staying with Miss Reece (Yew Trees). We sell eggs at 3d each. Everything except milk and eggs are dearer than during the war. Murders by Sinn Feiners in Ireland are frequent and nobody brought to justice. We had three young pigs from Hallows £4.10.0. each.

May 21st Very fine. Tom and Wm leading manure. Anthony working on fallow. Vincent took 3 cows to Ashford field but he does not come to work yet. He found a good tup lamb dead. Mr. Stephenson gave a sort of supper to the members of the club and a few others. There was dancing. Mr. Goodwin played.

May 22nd Very fine and sunny. Wm was harrowing and spreading manure. He harrowed in Bramwell field with old Naylor. Anthony was dragging in same field. There was a cricket match between Sheldon and Flagg. Flagg scored 24 and Sheldon scored 8. Mr. Stephenson paid Goodwin 6 shillings for fiddling and they had ½ gallon of beer. They did not pay for it but said Mr. Stephenson told them to get it.

May 23rd Very fine. Some visitors in the village staying at Thos. Wm. Brockleys and Naylors. Holy Communion this morning (Mr. Sherlock). Mr. Stephenson took the service, collection £1.5.6.

May 24th Very fine but rather cold wind. Anthony went to the fair and market. Tom took the young mare (not Fanny) to a horse at Taddington and then went to the fair. Wm, Ethel and Evelyn also went. Mrs. Brown went home today. She came last Saturday.

May 25th Very fine and plenty of sun. Anthony busy in Bramwell field getting ready for swedes etc. Tom on moor getting potato rows ready. I was sat out of doors having tea.

May 26th Very dull and close. Men working on moor and in Bramwell field. There are 40 rows ridged up for swedes. Wm. leading manure with old Naylor into potato rows on moor.

May 27th Dull and close. During last night and this morning rain came down. Tom sowed 26 rows of swedes, then came home and got ready for Chatsworth. He started between 1 and 2. The rain came on soon after two o'clock and it thundered and lightened. No cricket match, too wet. Wm took a load of manure on moor with old Naylor and was manuring potato rows.

May 28th Very dull and close. Tom finished sowing swedes. Wm on moor with old Naylor. Joe Haywood came for seed potatoes. We are having some potatoes on moor and in Bramwell field.

May 29th Thunder and lightning and rain in torrents. Our men were just ready to go on moor setting potatoes when the rain came on. Eggs are selling at 3d each. Sugar 1s.2d. per lb.

June 1st Very dull and wet. Fine and sunny this afternoon. Anthony, Tom, Wm and Vincent went on moor setting potatoes. The interest on £200 War Loan came this morning: £5.

June 2nd Finer but dull. Our men went on moor and finished setting potatoes except 3 rows which were left for Wm Bramwell (Bakewell). Mr. Stephenson took Emily out in bath chair last night and tonight. I wrote to our Mary. Mrs. Hallows helped to clean the kitchen.

June 3rd   Fine, dull and cold. A bit frosty early this morning. Anthony, Tom and Wm have been working in fallow in Bramwell field getting ready for potatoes and cabbages. S. Rowland brought us two rabbits. Mr. and Mrs. Wright (pedlars) have been today.

June 4th   Very cold wind in N and East. Anthony, Tom and Wm in fallow field getting ready for potatoes and cabbage. Esther Naylor went back home after staying at Billy's a week. Mr. Sherlock had tea here. The brawn we bought of Thacker fairly stunk and we had to give it to the dogs. It stank when bought. Ethel paid Mr. Thacker £7.5.0. for meat (not this week's).

June 5th   Very cold and a bit frosty first thing. Wind in East and N. East. Anthony, Tom, Wm and Mr. Ed went into fallow field and were setting potatoes, 15 rows (Bramwell field). Some Sheldon little boys got ready and some went to play Ashford boys but the latter would not play Sheldon. Four years since Lord Kitchener went down in sea and was drowned.

June 6th   Still very cold, wind in East and North. There was a celebration of Holy Communion in Sheldon Church this morning (Mr. Sherlock). Mr. Stephenson took the service this afternoon. Collection for Church expenses 18/4. The black heifer that Anthony bought for Mary calved tonight, a black cow calf. Dr. Fentem came to Bertha Bramwell and Wm. Hy. Brocklehurst who are ill again.

June 7th   Dull and cold. Vincent started work this morning. Anthony and Tom went to Bakewell. Tom took the new mare to a horse at the Rutland. Wm and Vincent carting manure into Bramwell field. Evelyn took some money to savings bank viz: - Tom: £10.0.0. Ethel: £8.0.0. Emily: £7.0.0. and Evelyn: £10.0.0. Paid Mr. H. Bagshaw 4/- for tithe. Evelyn paid Mr. Fred Buxton £2.0.0. for gapping.

June 8th   Sunny but cold. The wind stays in the N and E. The men are working in fallow, Bramwell Field. Anthony's leg is swollen and red with being on it so much. Joe Bolsover and Mary Downs were married at Ashford today.

June 9th   Very cold in wind. The sun is hot. All the sheep in Sheldon were washed today. Tom and Vincent went. Anthony was mostly in the house resting his leg. Mr. Stephenson was planting cabbage plants for us.

June 10th   Dull and colder than ever. The men (except Vincent) are in fallow, leading and spreading manure and covering it. Mr. Stephenson is again helping us to plant cabbage. Anthony is resting his leg again. The black heifer has clammed and we have heard from Mary that Clem is coming tonight and will take her tomorrow early. Clem came tonight. Eliza Naylor and Leah Brockley went to Blackpool.

June 11th   Dull. Clem started very early from Sheldon with his heifer. Anthony took the two pigs and a hen and chickens (16) to Mary's. Emily went with him in gig, starting between 10 and 11 o'clock. About 12 o'clock the rain came down in torrents. Anthony and Emily got a bit wet. Clem and heifer got home about ½ past five this morning. Mr. Stephenson was helping to set cabbage plants which they finished. Tom fetched a load of coals with new mare and was back in two hours from Bakewell.

June 12th Drizzly and dull, clears up this afternoon. Baslow cricketers came and played Sheldon. Sheldon won by two. Mr. Roger Sheldon came with them and I had a nice talk with him. He told me that his son Hubert had married his brother Ben's widow. Eleven of Baslow cricketers had tea here. We charged them 1s.3d. each. Lightning and thunder came on at about 11 tonight and rain fell in torrents. Mr. Sneap came to see us. Fred Bramwell scored 22 for Sheldon. Our men finished setting potatoes - the 3 rows on moor.

June 13th Wet and very close. Mr. Stephenson took the service in church. Collections for Derby Infirmary £2.14 in church and 8 shillings in our house last night. A party of Licensed Victuallers came to Mr. Ollerenshaw's.

June 14th Very misty and the rain came down in torrents. Anthony went to market and bought a cow for us and one for Mr. Ollerenshaw. Hannah was to have met Mary at Bakewell but it was too wet. Our Tom took Fanny to a horse at Taddington. Our blackfaced cat took two of S. Rowland's chickens. Tom drowned her and the kittens were killed as well. Mr. Stephenson and James Frost went into Cambridgeshire. Sent a letter about the interest on our money in War Loan. S. Johnson wrote it for us.

June 15th Fine. Anthony took Mr. Sneap to station and brought some sugar that Mrs. Sneap had got for us which had been left at the King's Arms.

June 16th Thunder and rain at times. Anthony sowed rape in Bramwell field and Tom was rolling corn on moor. The men had just got home when it rained heavily.

June 17th Very fine. Tom finished rolling corn on moor. Michael Frost called here and I was fairly tired out with his company. Ronston called and was paid up; also Miss Hawley for Barratts.

June 18th Very hot. Anthony went to Derby and then on to Mr. Sneaps. Wm drove him to Longstone station. Tom was horse hoeing the potatoes on moor. A telegram brought by the postman came to say that Anthony had bought a bull (Derby) which would be at Bakewell station about 10 o'clock tonight. Tom and Vincent went to fetch it and they arrived all right at ½ past 11. The bull was put inside all night.

June 19th Fine. Tom was horse hoeing the swedes this morning. Sheldon cricketers went to Chelmorton to play a match. Mr. Hawley took them in his motor and fetched them back early tonight. Sheldon won the game, their score being 27 and Chelmorton 7. Martin Oliver played for Sheldon and got 15 runs. Our Tom took six wickets and got one run.

June 20th Showery at times. Tom heard the result of the Farmers exam. Fred Brockley heads the list and gets two prizes. Tom and George have passed for certificates. Mr. Sherlock took the service in church. Wm took Fanny and trap and fetched Anthony from Longstone Station.

June 21st Fine. Anthony went to market. Hannah went with him to meet Mary and go with her to Warren Lodge, Curbar. When they got to Bakewell the motor that Mary and children came in had to be repaired and it was six o'clock before they could start for Curbar. Ethel went down and saw them and bought 3 hats. I wrote to Mr. Stephenson. Fred Brockley's leg is very bad, he having been hit by a cricket ball, the same leg that was hit before. The longest day today. Alf Brockley came back from Nottingham, went on Friday. Our folks milked for him this morning. S. Wilton began working at the Battery.

June 22nd Fine. The men have been gardening. They have gone on moor this afternoon. Some people have started shearing sheep today. Tom fetched our sheep off the moor ready for shearing tomorrow.

June 23rd Drizzly this morning. Tom fetched a bit of coal. This afternoon, Tom and Vincent were shearing. They did 16.

June 24th Dull. Tom and Vincent finished shearing. All the lambs in Sheldon were dipped at our place.

June 25th Dull. Tom took the new mare to Chatsworth to a horse (Commander). He got back and went for beer to Bakewell station this afternoon. Wm also went this morning for some.

June 26th Rather drizzly and dull at times. Our Mary's birthday (33). Chatsworth cricketers came to Sheldon. Some of the old cricketers of Sheldon played. Sheldon won (53). Chatsworth 40. Both teams had tea in schoolroom. Mr. Stephenson and James Frost came back from their holidays. Mr. S brought me some strawberries to eat. We had some papers from the Bank of England about the interest on our War Loan.

June 27th Fine at times and drizzling with rain tonight. Mr. Stephenson took the service in church. A good congregation. Wm Gould fetched Miss Whitehead from station. A full house tonight. My foot is very swollen.

June 28th Fine at times and drizzly at night. Vincent went to Matlock but he is not well and does not come to work. Anthony bought a calving cow off Fred Carson for 48 pounds. He then went to market and bought another for Mr. Ollerenshaw (£38). Anthony brought his new suit from Mr. Hills and paid both for his and our Tom's. Tom had his on yesterday. Mr. Alfred Buxton and Miss Mabel Buxton called here. They had come to see Miss Whitehead about teaching.

June 29th Drizzly and fine at times. The men were in swedes (striking). Vincent is very sick and poorly. Mr. Stephenson had tea with me. The girls have done the washing themselves this last week or two. Mrs. Hallows washed some blankets and Emily's dress last week.

June 30th Fine but rough wind. Our Ethel, Evelyn and Mr. Stephenson took me out in bath chair this afternoon. I went to church and saw the tablet put up for the dear lads who gave up their lives in the war. This is the 1st time I have seen it and I consider it very appropriate. They then took me down Johnson Lane. The growth of all things seems beautiful. Grass, trees, flowers, corn seems grand. The men were in swedes striking them.

July 1st Very wet. Mr. Stephenson's birthday. He came to show us his presents. Evelyn has gone to have tea with him. I wrote to Mary. I am very bad with rheumatics and my foot swells awfully. Three years today my dear Tony came for his last leave before going to France. Oh, the sorrow I have felt since then. Miss M Buxton has been teaching at Sheldon for a day or two.

July 2nd Dull and showery at times. Anthony, Tom and Wm were in swedes this afternoon when the rain came on in torrents. The men had to run and shelter in hen cotes. Vincent is not at work. There was a meeting of the church council at the school. The vicar presided and Tom, Evelyn and Anthony attended from our house. Whilst Mr. Stephenson was away on holidays Mr. Sherlock never came near us only on the Sunday.

July 3rd Very wet. Sheldon cricketers went to play Flagg. Sheldon went in 1st and got 47 runs for 5 wickets and declared for Flagg to go in but Flagg would not play. Alf Brockley's horse and our float took them to Flagg. Henry Frost cut his leg very badly with a scythe. His father and James took him to Dr. Fentem who stitched it. Polly Gregory (formerly Bramwell) is at Sheldon. She is very weak and poor

July 5th Dull and drizzly. Anthony bought a calving cow for £40 off Mr. Herbert Frost and then went to market. Grading is off now. Ethel cycled to Bakewell and paid Dr. Jackson's bill (£3.1.6d.). He had no stamp but settled bill. She brought Emily some more medicine. Three years today by day of month we said our last goodbye to our dear Tony. They have been three years of sorrow to me. I mourn for him as much as ever. I wrote to Ernest Rawlinson.

July 6th Finer and more sun. Tom and Wm went for dried grains to Bakewell station. Drizzling rain at night.

July 7th Showery at times. The men do a bit in swedes but the ground is so wet that the weed is not killed. Vincent went with his mother wood cutting yesterday.

July 8th Showery. The rain came down in torrents during the night. I do not know whenever it will clear up so that people can begin their hay. Anthony and Tom are painting a cart.

July 9th Showery and during the night rain fell in torrents. A bit finer tonight and there was a cricket match between the ladies and gentlemen;

the latter won. Thacker sent us a leg of mutton (English) which was 2s. 3d. per lb.

July 10th Showery. Sheldon cricketers went to Biggin to play. Sheldon went in and got 44 for 5 wickets. Biggin did not play. Mr. Hawley took cricketers in motor. Anthony, Tom and Wm finished striking swedes this morning. Very wet this afternoon. Eggs 4d each.

July 11th Finer and more sun. Dull and a bit showery about 5 o'clock. Three recommends for outdoor patients and one indoor came from the Derby Royal Infirmary. Five pounds were sent on Friday from collection in Sheldon Church (£1.17.0. made up to the £5.0.0. by Mr. Stephenson). Mr. Stephenson took the service this afternoon. Licensed premises are to open from 7 until 10 instead of 6 to nine. A most ridiculous affair altogether as the hours were right as they were. Sid Brocklehurst, his wife and two children came to Alf's yesterday.

July 12th Rough and showery at times. Anthony went to Bakewell Board of Guardians. Billy Naylor bought 4 young calves and a heifer. There is no coal to be had at Bakewell station. Vincent Hallows went to Matlock again to the Dr.

July 13th Showery. Wm went to Bakewell station to try to get a bit of coal. He had to go all through the yard and got 7 cwts ¼ at some one else's (not Lomas). Sam Rowland is mowing the churchyard. Mr. Lowthian sent us £5.0.0. towards cleaning of the church. My foot is very badly swollen.

July 14th Showery. Anthony, Tom and Wm were thinning swedes. Mr. Parton came and was paid up. Mrs. Hall (Red Lion) married again.

July 15th Very showery and dull this morning. St. Swithin's. Breaks out finer this afternoon. Mr. Ronston came and was paid up. Everything is awfully dear. Mrs Hawley came and was paid. Drapery goods are scandalous in price. Tom, Wm and Anthony were thistle mowing on moor.

July 16th Fair but dull. Wm gone on moor. Anthony and Tom thinning swedes. Evelyn went to Bakewell and paid Mr. Thacker for all the meat we owe for including July 16th. Amount £7.13s.5½. Mr. Pearson tuned the organ in Sheldon Church. He charged 15/- which was paid to him at our house out of the church accounts. Anthony took the gig and met Mrs. Goodwin at Bakewell station by the train which arrived at 8.22. Rain fell fast as they were coming to Sheldon but they had our big umbrella. Mr. G. Frost (grocer) gave Mr. Stephenson 5/- towards church repairs and Mr. Broughton opened his heart by giving 1/-.

July 17th Very dull and wet at times. Mr. Stephenson went to Bakewell to meet Mr. Goodwin. They brought a motor to Sheldon. Mr. Frank Lomas came to practise singing with Mr. Goodwin in Sheldon church. Mr. Goodwin is organist at Heath Parish Church. Mr. and Mrs. Goodwin, Mr. Frank Lomas and Mr. Stephenson came here and had tea.

July 18th   Fine at first but just after dinner a heavy shower came on. Evelyn played for the service in Church and afterwards Mr. Goodwin took the organ recital and Mr. Lomas sang. The service was much appreciated by a good congregation. Someone had sent an envelope with £5.0.0., some silver and copper to be put in the collection The collection amounted to £11.6.9. in aid of church repairs. Mr. Lomas had tea with us. A motor fetched Mr. and Mrs. Goodwin to Bakewell station at night. We open at 7 and close at 10 on Sundays. There were 4 men came in, one of them Jesse Nadin of Longstone. Sam Wilton spoke to them but the snobs did not answer him.

July 19th   Fine and sunny but afterwards dull. Anthony went to Bakewell for calf meal and to Robert Smith for wood for Ed Brockley. Vincent came to work this morning and Tom, Wm and he went into the seeds, Grindlow Knoll. Tom started mowing there with the young mare and the new one. Fanny did not mow. She went to Bakewell with float. Anthony got back at dinner time. Mr. Stephenson received £3.0.0. from Lord Hartington. Wm Gregory (Butcher of Youlgreave) dropped down and died in Bradford, Youlgreave. Dr. Jackson came to Emily. She is very dizzy and poorly. Ethel went to Bakewell for medicine. Sam Rowland led another load of hay out of churchyard. He paid Anthony for it; the amount was 5/-. I wrote to our Mary and Mrs. Whittaker.

July 20th   Very dull and like rain. A bit of sunshine now and then and plenty of wind. Tom finished mowing seeds on Grindlow Knoll. Anthony was altering a gap place in Waterlands. Mr. Stephenson fetched a deck chair for Emily from Mrs. Fairholms. Emily has some bad attacks of wind. Our Mary's finished their hay. Rain came on tonight.

July 21st   Very wet. Nothing done in hay. The sum of £5.0.0. came from Mr. Hartopp (for the Duke of Devonshire) towards cleaning of Sheldon church.

July 24th   Fine and plenty of wind. Our men finished thinning swedes this morning and Anthony and Tom horse-hoed potatoes on moor. Wm and Vincent were in seeds which were very wet and there is such a crop spoiling. Mr. Stephenson went to Fairfield to the dedication of the Grovers window.

July 25th   Fine 1st thing. Very wet tonight. Tom went on bike to see our Mary at Warren Lodge. He got wet coming back. Mr. Sherlock took the service in church and Mr. Stephenson went to Ashford.

July 26th   Rough and wet. No hay making. Wm went on moor mowing thistles. Vincent went to Matlock, Anthony to market and Tom stayed about home as we are expecting a cow to calve. Mr. Ollerenshaw sent a calving heifer by Sam Bramwell to market. Mrs. Hallows is washing for us. Mr. Ollerenshaw's cow made £42.10s. and it was bought 4 or 5 weeks ago for £38.0.0.

July 29th   Bright and sunny and plenty of wind. The men were in seeds, hobbing them up etc. Rain came on tonight. Mr. Stephenson went to Ashford to a school treat.

July 30th   Showery 1st thing after a night of heavy rain. Finer this afternoon. Anthony went to the Dr. about his leg. He said it was very likely a plugged vein and he was to rest it as much as possible and bandage it up. Evelyn went to Bakewell and bought a slop pail which cost 10/6.

July 31st   Bright and sunny 1st thing. Dull in afternoon. All hands are busy in Sheldon today trying to get some hay. Our men and Mr. Hallows and Mr. Ed are gone into the seeds on Grindlow Knoll. They are stacking in field as the weather is so uncertain. Ethel and Evelyn are taking their meals. There were 22 loads of seeds got out of the Bottom Grindlow Knoll. Mr. Stephenson was helping John Brockley in hay.

Aug. 1st   Showery at times. Holy Communion early. Mr. Sherlock officiated. Mr. Stephenson took the service in church. Aleck, Ena, her mother and Lily came to Naylors. Ethel and Evelyn cycled to our Mary's. They got back just before 10 and it was a bit showery. A full house tonight. 3 men came seeking lodgings. They stayed all night at Mrs. Sherwin's.

Aug. 2nd   Fine. Anthony took a bull calf to market and was back very quickly. Our men, Mr. Ed and Sam Rowland got all the seeds in Grindlow Knoll, only left one load of rakings. There were 40 loads out of this field which was stacked on the place. Sid Brockley and his friend went back tonight. They came on Saturday.

Aug. 3rd   Showery at noon. Tom went to Sam Rowland's field with machine and finished his part of the field. He then went on moor and moved some of the seeds there but had to leave as the rain came on.

Aug. 4th   Very showery at times. Tom finished seeds (mowing). Miss Grover gave the usual tea party for Sheldon children. They had it in school as it was so wet. Mr. Sherlock, Mr. and Miss Grover and friends called here. Mr. Stephenson received a cheque for 2 guineas from Mr. Brittain.

Aug. 5th   Still wet. Nothing done in hay. Anthony bought a young heifer calf off John Frost (£35).

Aug. 6th   Showery this morning. Finer this afternoon. Ed Brockley and Anthony went to Walter Brown's funeral at Hasland. Anthony took Fanny and trap which were left until night when they came back. Wm was in bed (sick). Tom and Vincent went with two carts for coal.

Aug. 7th   Dull but finer. The men were on moor in hay. The Bakewell Cottage Hospital foundation stones were laid and a great procession marched. The Duke of Rutland and Mr. Hugh Hallet laid them. Mr. Stephenson went to see it.

Aug. 8th Fine in morning but heavy showers came on tonight. Mr. Stephenson took the service in church this afternoon. Emily was very poorly tonight.

Aug. 9th Fine. Anthony and Tom took a cow which we had bought a few weeks ago and sold her for £20. Between £30 and £40 had been given for her but she has never done well. Anthony bought a cow off Harry Ardern for £53. Vincent went to Matlock. Anthony also bought 2 cows for Mr. Ollerenshaw for £39 each.

Aug. 10th Fine. All the men except Anthony went on moor this morning. Tom mowed a few times round another field but they were chiefly in seeds. Anthony went to Bakewell to help get things ready for tomorrow's cattle show and then went on moor in hay. Evelyn took dinner and Ethel took tea to hayfield. Ethel went to Calver to meet Mary who has made butter for the show.

Aug. 11th A fine day. All our men went to the show. Anthony and Tom took one of our ram lambs to the show. Wm and Vincent went next. Ed went on moor in hay. Some people are leading hay today. Mr. and Mrs. Cooper and nephew came to Mrs. Eds. Mrs. and the Misses Lindsay went home after staying 10 or 11 days at Naylors. We have 2 or three cows not very well and think it is owing to the dashing weather. Evelyn went to the show this afternoon. We got no prize but reserve for our lamb. Mary's butter got nothing but some thief stole 1lb as there was only 1lb roll left when Anthony went to fetch it. Several people had their pockets picked at the show. Richard Skidmore had about £5 taken from his pocket.

Aug. 12th Very foggy, afterwards showery. Our men went on moor and were mowing in another field. No hay was got today. Mr. Ronston came and was paid up.

Aug. 13th Fine. Our men, Mr. Ed B and S. Rowland got 16 loads of seeds on moor. Mr. Stephenson got our roses and fixed them in bowls and box covered with moss ready for Ashford show tomorrow.

Aug. 14th Very dull but plenty of wind. The anniversary of Anthony's and my wedding day (34 years). Wm Hallows started with our roses before six o'clock this morning to Ashford show. Our men, Mr. Ed and S. Rowland finished getting seeds on moor (10 more loads). Our roses got 1st and special prize. Sam Rowland got 2nd prize for cabbage and 3rd prize for onions (eschalots) and Alf Brockley 2nd prize for celery. Joseph Hallows got 24 prizes, 14 firsts and 10 seconds. Ethel and Tom went rather late to show.

Aug. 15th Fine. Plenty of sunshine and wind. Anthony took me for a drive with Fanny in float. We went down Flagg Lane and Monyash dale back up the horse lane. I saw the hay stacks (2) and the oats and potatoes and the fields of grass still unmown. Everything looked well but sun is wanted to ripen the corn and potatoes.

Aug. 16th Dull, not much of a hay day. Tom mowed a field which he had begun before but no hay was led today. Anthony did not go to Bakewell. Evelyn went for some flour. There has been none in Sheldon to be got. Tom mowed a bit of Top Hicks field.

Aug. 17th A very good hay day, plenty of sun. Our men, Mr. Ed and Sam Rowland got a field of hay on moor (12 loads). The girls took dinner and tea. Milking was late. I wrote to Mr. Parton and Mrs. Whittaker.

Aug. 18th Very dull and drizzling. Tom and men started this afternoon to mow Hicks field but had to come back as soon as they got there. Evelyn went to Bakewell.

Aug. 19th Very dull, not much of a hay day. Tom finished mowing Hicks field. Ernest Taylor's wife and sister and brother and the sister's three children came to see us. They walked from Tideswell and went back at night. They had a pram for the two youngest children.

Aug. 20th Dull and rather a slow hay day. Tom, Wm and Vincent went to Hurdlow for cake. This afternoon our men and Mr. Ed. got six loads of hay from moor. They put it on stack where the last week's were put. W.H. Bramwell (Insurance), Mr. Simpson of Nottingham and a Mr. Haycroft called here tonight and we had a very interesting conversation over the war and Mr. Haycroft wrote me some lines which were said to be from the Bishop of Birmingham viz: "The Englishman loves his bible and his beer. The Welshman prays on Sundays and upon his neighbours for the rest of the week. The Scotsman keeps the Sabbath and everything else he can lay his hands on. The Irishman doesn't know what he wants and won't be happy when he gets it."

Aug. 21st Rather dull 1st thing, improving later in the day. Our men went in hay, Hicks, this morning and on moor this afternoon. No hay leading as it has not been a good drying day. A scroll came to us this morning in memory of our dear Tony. I believe one is being sent to relatives of every fallen soldier.

Aug. 22nd Dull. Mr. Stephenson took the service in church. Mr. Pearson (dentist) called here with Sam Johnson and Billy Naylor, Mr. Pearson drove them to Monyash and back in car.

Aug. 23rd Bright and sunny in morning. Drizzling at noon which stopped any hay leading. Anthony took two calving cows to market and sold them for £60 each. The heifer that Anthony bought off Mr. Ollerenshaw for £40 calved a bull calf. Mr. Sneap came today. Our Mary and children and aunt H were at fair.

Aug. 24th Dull. No hay day. Anthony bought a bull for £35 off Mr. H. Frost. Lizzie Simpson, Martha Downer and a Mrs. Yates came from Tideswell to see us. Mr. and Mrs. Moore from London called. They came to see Billy Naylor. Mr. and Mrs. S. Smith came to see Mr. Stephenson. No leading hay today. Little Clement Wager's birthday (1 year old).

Aug. 25th Very dull and a very poor hay day. The men went on moor with dray etc. but it is such a poor drying day. Mr. Moore and Billy Naylor called in. Mrs. Kitson died yesterday at Mansfield. Mr. Smith brought a telegram for Mr. Sneap to go home. Mr. Sneap walked to Bakewell to catch the 4.30 train.

Aug. 26th A lovely morning, plenty of sun, dull this afternoon. Our men, Mr. Ed and Sam Rowland went on moor leading hay. They were leading out of field that the last six loads were led. Altogether they got 23 loads out of this field. Mr. Stephenson and Ruth B went to Buxton.

Aug. 27th Dull but fair. Tom went to Bakewell station for ale and wine. There were two bottles of wine broken when examined before he brought them away and Tom signed to that effect. Emily had a post card from Lizzie Simpson saying they missed their train at Longstone and had to walk to Tideswell getting there after eleven at night, the day they were here. We had a letter from Mr. Sneap saying his daughter Mary had had a little boy on Tuesday last (Aug. 24th). I wrote to Mrs. Brown. Mr. and Mrs. S. Smith went back today. Our men, Mr. Ed and Mr. Sam Rowland are leading hay home from Hicks field. I am glad they are nearer home as it has been such a job for the girls carrying dinner and tea on moor. 10 loads out of Top Hicks.

Aug. 28th Fine and sunny. All the sheep and lambs in Sheldon were dipped today: 182 in all. We dipped 32 sheep and 25 lambs of our own and used McDougalls' dip for all. Our men were getting hay out of the other Hicks field, 9 loads, but they did not rake up. Mr. and Mrs. and Miss Hampson came to see Mr. Stephenson. They came in to see us. Wm Hallows, Sam Rowland and Tom Critchlow went from Monyash on a motor trip to Chester, Liverpool and Birkenhead.

Aug. 29th Fine. Mr. Stephenson took the service in church. Mrs. Bagnall came to see me. A good few in tonight. A clerk from Bakewell station and one or two ladies called.

Aug. 30th Fine. Anthony took a calf for us of the cow that we bought off Mr. Ollerenshaw, and one for Alf Brockley, also 10 cockerels, to Bakewell. Tom, Vincent and Wm went with three carts to Bakewell station for dried grain. Ethel cycled down for medicine for Emily and a few other things. The calf of ours (one week old) made £4.6.0. Alf Brockley's calf made £3.0.0. John Brockley made £80.0.0. of a blue cow he took to market. Anthony also took 20 cockerels which made 11/- the couple. Our Tom mowed the greater part of the Bole Piece nearest Johnson Lane.

Aug. 31st Fine but dull. Tom finished mowing Bole Piece and started on Croft Heads. The bottom grass in this field is going rotten and is awkward mowing. Tom finished Croft Heads. Thos. Wm Brockley finished his hay all but the rakings. Mrs. Hampson went back today. Nestlés sent word they could not renew contract for milk.

Sept. 1st   Sunshine 1st thing but the rain came down in torrents before dinner time. Mr. Lowthian, Mr. Wood and Mr. Marriott came partridge shooting and were wet through. They shot 5 partridge and 2 or 3 hares but did not shoot in the afternoon as it was so wet. Mr. Lowthian paid 5/- for the room and fire. Mr. Wood paid 2s.7d. for 4 pints of beer and a cup of tea. Tom and Vincent went to Hassop for cake and got wet through to the skin and had to change all. Anthony went to meet them and he too got wet. Mr. and Miss Hampson went nearly to Lathkill Dale and came back very wet. I wrote to Mr. Burley about the milk.

Sept. 2nd   Very wet. Tom went to Bakewell for coal and had the young horse shod. Anthony was mending hen cotes. Mary Bagnall went back. Her son George is staying for holidays. A fete was held at Ashford in Mr. Flewitt's land.

Sept. 3rd   Very dull, no hay day. Tom was mowing Little Butts, Big Butts (some of it) and Pingle. Received a letter from Mr. Burley saying that when the winter milk prices were fixed, he would come over and try to buy our and Thos. Wm. Brockley's. Mr. and Miss Hampson went home. Mr. Stephenson presented me with an air cushion. I have tried it and found it comfortable. Ethel went to Bakewell and paid Mr. Thacker all we owe him including what he brought today which was a leg of mutton the cost of which was £1.8.6½ The bill Ethel paid amounted to £9.9.7. Anthony made a cheque out for £5.0.0. towards it. Eggs are 4½ each. Everything is most awfully dear.

Sept. 4th   Dull and a bit showery, no hay day. I do not know when the hay will be got. Billy Naylor went with the Bakewell footballers to Hayfield. Mr. and Mrs. Hallows went to Derby. George Goodwin was married to Miss Swindell at Hartington.

Sept. 5th   Dull and showery. Celebration of Holy Communion in Sheldon Church. The Vicar of Buxton officiated in the absence of Mr. Sherlock who has been on holiday for 3 weeks. Mr. Stephenson took the service this afternoon. Collection for church expenses 17.1d.

Sept. 6th   Dull, no hay day, a bit showery. Anthony, Tom and Vincent took 2 fat cows and 2 calving cows to market which were sold for £205. Old Ginger cow made £28. Alf Brockley sold a calving cow for £68. Billy Naylor sold a heifer to Longstone butcher (Wardle) for £44.2.6. tonight. Young Ward (George Ward's son) and Oliver Johnson came with him to try to buy her.

Sept. 11th   Fine but dull and not much sun. We had a lot of helpers in hay this afternoon. Alf. Brockley, Jack Naylor and Mr. Stephenson, Uncle Will Brockley, Hallows, Mr. Ed and our men. They were getting Croft Heads. Alfred Loftus and wife went home today. I bought 1 dozen plates at sixpence each and a white vegetable dish for 3/-. The men got 10 loads of hay out of Croft Heads and 5 out of Little Butts. Sidney Wright and a friend came to stay with Mr. Stephenson. Frosts at the top finished hay.

Sept. 12th Very fine and sunny. Anthony took Emily and I to our Mary's starting just after 11. It was a long drive to Curbar and the rough road jogged me a deal. I kept slipping forward in my chair especially going down hill. We arrived at Mary's somewhere about 1 o'clock. The motor charabank traffic was awful. Everything was smothered in dust. Ethel started after us on her bike and overtook us on the road. Mary's house is a very nice one standing under the Curbar rocks. We found them all pretty well. There were three young men called at our house whilst we were away. One of them (from Harpur Hill) said he saw our Tony wounded (killed). We got back to Sheldon before 8 tonight. Aunt Lizzie Naylor and Jack went to Longstone Wakes. A letter from Annie Haywood came out of Belgium.

Sept. 13th Fine but very dull. Anthony took a cow to market and sold her for £27. This afternoon they were getting hay, 2 loads out of Pingle and 9 loads out of Big Butts. Stephen Rowland was in our house tonight. I did not come down until between 1 and 2 today as I was very tired with my journey yesterday.

Sept. 14th Fine. My birthday 63. A letter from Mr. Stephenson and cards from Mabel and Elsie. Our men are in the hay, Big Butts. The men finished the hay getting six more loads out of Big Butts. The rain came on rather fast.

Sept. 15th Very wet this morning 1st thing after a night of heavy rain. Miss Whitehead and some of the children went to Buxton and Chapel-en-le-Frith. The weather cleared up this afternoon. Sidney Wright and friend went to Manchester. Tideswell sergeant and Taddington policeman called here. Received a card from Annie written from Ypres on Monday saying she had been successful in finding our dear Tony's grave (last Monday). I gave Mr. Stephenson some brandy and port for an old lady in London.

Sept. 16th Fine. Our men are gone on moor to pull and straighten stacks there. Mr. Sherlock called here. Fred Brockley and his sister Harriett came to Sheldon. She called in to see me. Wm Henry Brockley is very ill, much worse. Dr. Fentem is attending him.

Sept. 17th Showery. Tom and Vincent went to Bakewell station with two horses and dray and fetched six barrels of beer, 4 eight penny and 2 seven penny. Poor Wm Hy Brocklehurst passed away at about half past ten tonight.

Sept. 18th Showery, some thunder, frosty night. Tom fetched a load of coal from Bakewell station. John Spencer was in our house tonight talking to the farmers about letting Mr. Burgess have the milk produced in Sheldon.

Sept. 19th Showery. The Dr came to Thos Brocklehurst and said that the poor old man had a cancer. Mr. Sherlock took the Service in Sheldon church this afternoon.

Sept. 20th Very frosty this morning. The sun shone a bit and then it looked gloomy and like rain. We had a post card from Mr. Burley wanting Anthony to meet him at Bakewell to try to arrange over the milk. A good many farmers went to meet Burgess and the Hygienic Co. but no definite understanding was arrived at though prices were offered. Mrs. Hallows was helping us wash but just as the clothes were ready to hang out rain came on. Mr. Burley offered a markets price. The vet came to our cow.

Sept. 21st Very frosty and cold. Wm Henry Brockley was interred today at 3 o'clock. Mr. Sherlock officiated. It was a very large funeral. Mary Ann Brockley called here. Annie Haywood arrived about 3. She gave an interesting account of her stay in Belgium and about finding our poor Tony's grave. She had every help given her and a soldier guide took her to the place. When Annie found Tony's name the soldier stood back and saluted. The Dr. (Fentem) came to Ida Carson who had fractured her arm with falling off a gate.

Sept. 22nd Very cold and very dull. Annie went home at about 11 this morning. Mr. Lowthian and party came shooting and afterwards came here for tea. Most of the farmers in Sheldon have about finished the hay. Our hay record is as follows. Begin hay on July 19th. Finished hay Sept. 14th.

	No of loads
Grindlow Knoll	40
Seeds on moor	26
Another field on moor	12
Another field on moor	23
Top Hicks	10
Other Hicks	9
Bole Piece	23
Croft Heads	10
Little Butts	5
Pingle	2
Big Butts	15
Total	= 175 loads of hay

Sept. 23rd Cold. Dull. Our Tom went to Bakewell with new mare to have her shod and brought back a load of sawdust. A beautiful altar cloth came this morning for Sheldon Church. Mr. Stephenson is presenting it in memory of the fallen. It cost £16.18.0. Mr. Stephenson called here and had tea.

Sept. 24th Very foggy this morning but breaks out into a lovely day. Our Tom fetched some rails to rail out our stacks (from wood). Billy Twelves told Anthony to fetch them. I received a letter written by little Anthony Wager and I wrote back.

Sept. 25th Misty 1st thing but breaks out into a most lovely day, plenty of sun. Our men went on moor and railed out the stacks. Ethel went and had her bike mended this afternoon.

Sept. 26th Fine. Mr. Stephenson took the service in church. There was a very good attendance. A funeral sermon was preached for W.H. Brocklehurst and suitable hymns sung. Jaspar Johnson was in our house tonight.

Sept. 27th Fine. Anthony took a calf to market (bull), then attended a meeting of the Bakewell farmers club. Other farmers went to meet Mr. Burgess and some signed on to send him their milk. Mr. Burley our man was there and we are commencing sending milk to him on Oct. 1st. Mr. Waterhouse proposed the farmers should have 2/9 per gal for 7 winter months and they (the farmers) should pay carriage.

Sept. 28th Misty but clears out later. Our men were on moor gathering hay off the rakes and putting it in the top of stacks. Mr. Stephenson brought some lovely flowers from Ashford .

Sept. 29th Very foggy and does not clear out until about 3 o'clock this afternoon. There were drizzling showers 1st thing this morning. Mr. Stephenson has decorated the church. There is a service tonight as it is the anniversary of the dedication of our church, St. Michael and All Angels. The collection tonight for cleaning church amounted to 2 guineas. Ethel went to Bakewell. Alf Brockley took our dray and fetched cans from Longstone station for those who are sending their milk to Mr. Burgess. Billy Naylor did not sign to sell.

Sept. 30th Drizzling at times. Nestlés firm fetched the Sheldon Farmers' milk for the last time this morning. They also came again for all empty churns. Mr. Stephenson and Thos Wm Brockley went to Heath.

Oct. 1st   Wet at times. Anthony was thinking of moving the corn in Gt. Stones but the rain stopped this. The corn is not ripe and I am afraid that it never will be this year as there is so little sunshine. Eggs are 5 pence each but Mr. Hallwood has only paid us 4½. Mr. Hawley came up at 20 minutes to 8 this morning and took all the Sheldon Farmers' milk to Longstone station. He took it in motor. We began again with Mr. Burley but are not sure of the price yet. He said he would pay as much as anyone else. Billy Naylor received interest on his money in War Loan.

Oct. 2nd   We had a heavy thunder storm and the rain came down in torrents. Anthony took Fanny and float to meet our Mary and children and Aunt H. He had to shelter on the way. Mary etc. had started from her home before rain came on and got as far as Goddards garage. Anthony met them there and brought them to Sheldon, not getting so very wet. Sheldon Wakes Eve. The house place was pretty full but Wakes now are very different to what they used to be before the war. I shall be very glad when this week is over as I cannot do with the noise and singing. Sid Brockley and Tom Ridgeway came; Eben Ollerenshaw, John Gregory and his wife and others.

Oct. 3rd   Sheldon Wakes Sunday. Wet tonight (very). House place full up. The Harvest Thanksgiving. A very full congregation. The Revd. Warden[1] from Monyash preached. Mr. Stephenson was present as well. He came back from Heath yesterday. The collection for cleaning church came to £3.14.0. Four more shillings were added to this tonight. George Carson 2/-, our Mary 1/- and Aunt H. 1/-. Alf Brocklehurst had to have a pig killed today. Holy Communion in Sheldon church early this morning. About 26 present. Mary could not go out tonight as it was so wet.

Oct. 4th   Very wet. The rain came down very heavily during the night and continues all day today. Anthony took Mary and children to Bakewell to meet the bus Curbar way. Alf Brockley drove a cow of ours to market. Nelson's motor fetched his pig. There were a few in at dinner time. Fred Brocklehurst from Potteries came. Poor old Tom Brocklehurst's face seems to get much worse. Our Tom and Vincent went to Hassop for cake. We do not have dancing at our place and I am very glad as since losing Tony and the other poor lads life does not seem the same. The house place was pretty full tonight.

Oct. 5th   Wet at times. Mr. Hawley comes up very early with his motor for the milk. There was a dance at the school which closed before 12. Mr. and Mrs. Eben Brockley and Fred Brockley and his sister Harriet all here from Potteries. Jack Brassington brought a fox which he said he found asleep in Dirtlow plantation and he said he killed it with a coping. A collection was made for him. He got about 5 shillings and sold the fox for 4/- to Alf Brockley for Mr. Stephenson. It came out afterwards that Jack B had not killed the fox at all and it had not a bruise on it. S. Rowland had poisoned a pheasant and he thinks it had got that.

Oct. 6th   Very misty until late. There has been a deal of rain during the nights lately and the ground is very wet. Thos Wm B, Fred and Mr. Stephenson went with Hawley's motor to a sale at Heath. Thos Wm bought a Binder which was brought by the above motor to Sheldon. They had a very difficult job to unload it. A full house tonight singing to violin.

Oct. 7th   Frosty but a lovely day, sunshine. Our men took the binder into Great Stones to commence cutting corn. They had a difficult job with the big new mare. She was very awkward in going through gateways etc. Emily has had such a poor night with toothache. We sent for Dr. Jackson who came and drew her a tooth. Mr. Ronston came and was paid up £24.7.0. Miss Hawley was also paid up.

Oct. 8th   A very fine day. Tom finished cutting corn in Gt. Stones and the men then went on moor and went a few rounds in Alf Brockley's field of corn. Mr. Sherlock called here. He had tea at Mrs Wrapsins. There was a jovial evening in houseplace tonight, singing and violin.

---

1   The Revd. John F Warden went to Monyash from Tideswell in 1914

Oct. 9th   There was no corn cutting today as the fog was thick and did not lift. Fred Brockley and his sister went back (side car) and Eben Ollerenshaw and wife went by train. The Wakes finished up with singing. We do not have dancing at our place now and very pleased I am. There have been two dances this week at the school. Charles Corns came here and stayed all night.

Oct. 10th   Very cold, no sun. Three years today since poor Anthony Brocklehurst was killed. Mr. Stephenson took the service in church this afternoon. Charles Corns had dinner with us. He is staying all night at our house. He had tea at Thos. Wm Brockley. Sid Brockley and his friend went back. They went with Hawley's motor to Grindleford and then by train to Sheffield.

Oct. 11th   Fine. Bakewell Fair. None of our men went. Evelyn cycled down. Anthony and the others went and finished cutting Alf Brockley's field and afterwards took the Binder into one of our fields on moor where they went round 4 or 5 times.

Oct. 12th   Misty 1st thing, clears out after dinner. Emily's foot is gathering. Poor Tom Brockley is not so well. In corn this afternoon on moor.

Oct. 13th   Misty. Fine in afternoon. Finished one corn field and went twice round in the other.

Oct. 14th   Fine. Men in corn on moor, cut about six acres. Came on wet at night. Mr. Stephenson and Mr. Whitehead went through Lathkill Dale and out at Monyash where they had tea at Mr. Prince. Thos Wm Brockley's binder does not work well and they are using the reaper. Sam Rowland's heifer calved a cow calf.

Oct. 15th   Misty and drizzling. We had no cans to put our milk in until Mr. Hawley came and it is often like this. It makes it all hurry and bustle to have to wash them in a morning. We paid Hawley £1.15.8. for taking our milk to station for a fortnight. Tom and Vincent fetched two loads of coal as the miners are expected to be on strike tomorrow.

Oct. 16th   Misty, raw and cold. No corn day. Mr. Hawley comes in good time for milk. Farmers' butter is making 4/-0 per lb. Eggs 5 pence each.

Oct. 17th   Cold and dull. Mr. Stephenson took the service in church this afternoon. The miners are out on strike. People keep getting killed in Ireland shot by Sinn Fein. Tom Brocklehurst is not so well. His face gets more swollen.

Oct. 18th   Very cold and rough wind which will do the corn good. A little sun now and then. Our Tom and Vincent went for stable bricks and cement to Chatsworth. Anthony took a black cow which he bought two or three months ago and which had not done well to Bakewell and sold her for 20 pounds (Anthony lost between £9 and £10 with her). Jim Ogden called here this dinner time. Anthony had a P.C. from Mr. Burley offering 2/4 for

2 months and 2.8d. for 5 months for milk. This price is not as good as Mr. Burgess's and he finds cans. Evelyn cycled to Bakewell. Mr. Hallows went wood cutting this morning. Martha Oldfield, Mary and the baby came here.

Oct. 19th Cold and windy. Tom finished mowing our corn but a great deal has to be set up. I wrote to Mr. Burley over milk. Tom Brockley's birthday (77).

Oct. 20th Very dull and cold. There has been a frost for several mornings. Our men went on moor to set up corn and Anthony went to Miss Needham's sale this afternoon. He rode there with Mr. J. Wallwin and came back with Mr. Flewitt. Ethel went to Bakewell and paid Mr. Thacker all we owe, 8 pounds all but 3$^{1}/_{2}$d.

Oct. 21st A bit misty but a nice day afterwards. Our men went on moor and finished setting up corn. Sent Mary a parcel, nightgowns (2) and 2 petticoats for little Clem. A milk churn of ours got smashed up at Longstone.

Oct. 22nd Misty 1st thing clears out afterwards. Tom went to Bakewell station for beer this morning and to Hassop this afternoon for two of our milk churns which had been put out there instead of Longstone. Anthony etc. were mending stable.

Oct. 23rd Misty. Fine afterwards but no wind. Received a letter from Mary saying she got the parcel all right. Mending stable etc. Mr. Stephenson had tea here. Finish of Taddington Wakes.

Oct. 24th Misty some of the time. Mr. Stephenson took the service in church but it is rather cold without a fire as we have no coal for the church. Sampson Bembridge was in our house tonight. He has not been in for years.

Oct. 25th Misty 1st thing, clears out later and a nice wind is on which will be good for the corn which stands in the fields. Anthony took a cow (old hippy) and sold her by auction at Bakewell for £12.15.0. Mr. Burley came to Bakewell but Anthony did not see him until he met him going to the station. They bargained for the milk, 2/8 for 5 months and 2/7 for this month. Sent 12/- to *Derbyshire Times* Office to insert memoriam for our dear Tony.

Oct. 26th Misty but turns out a good day for fielding the corn. Anthony went to a sale at Meadowplace near Wormhill and bought 4 cans and a sheep trough. The cans were dear, the best cost £4.4.0., next £3.7.6. Two not as much. We had a cheese today as no cans came from station for us. I made out bill to Oct. 16 (inclusive) which came to £5.15.6$^{3}/_{4}$. Sent it and a letter to Mr. Burley. Sent our licence and money to pay £6.12.3. (cheque).

Oct. 27th Misty but turns out a nice day. Emily is very ill today. The men have gone on moor to turn the corn. Ethel has gone to Bakewell for a few things. Mr. John Frost found some more of his cows on moor with their tails cut off. Last week he found 9 or 10 done the same. He went up the village tonight with the Inspector of Police as the matter had been reported. Anthony bought 5 heifers of John Frost last week that had had their tails cut off (for £33 each).

Oct. 28th Very misty. No corn day. Wm and Vincent getting potatoes out of Bramwell field - a very poor crop and small. Tom was thatching on moor. Inspector MacDonald and Ashford policeman called here and asked me if I had heard anything about the cows' tails being cut. I do not think they will be able to trace the culprit. Mrs. Ed's birthday (63). Hannah went to tea. Emily is a little better and came downstairs after tea. Anthony took the can lids he bought at sale to Tom Rowland at Youlgreave to have his name put on. He had them done and bought a frying pan (2.10) and a bucket (4.3).

Oct. 29th Fine. The men have pulled some corn over and are gone on moor to see if there is any dry. Kate B has gone to Crich today. The men got two loads of corn out of Great Stones but it is not very dry.

Oct. 30th Very fine, nice wind and a good corn day. Our men went on moor and got 6 acres. Our Tony's memoriam was in the *Derbyshire Times*. The cost was 12/- this year which we sent. A fire was lit in church with borrowed coal.

Oct. 31st Dull and cold. Rain came on tonight. Mr. Stephenson took the service in church. We opened the house at 6 and kept open until 9 tonight which is much better than 7 until 11. Youlgreave Wakes today. Sam Johnson, Maggie and Eliza came to see us. Emily is a little better.

Nov. 1st Wet and miserable after a night of incessant rain which was very heavy. No corn day. Anthony went to market and afterwards attended the Guardians meeting. Vincent went to Matlock this afternoon. I sent bill to Mr. Burley (to Oct. 31st) with a letter over the cans coming so badly. Tied up our milk beasts tonight.

Nov. 2nd Dull and cold. There was a good wind during last night and this morning. Tom went to Hurdlow. Anthony went to Bakewell station. Three years today since our poor Tony died of wounds. A service tonight in church. Miss Kate Grover and Miss Wardley came to see me.

Nov. 3rd Fine but raw. No wind to do any good. Gt. Stones not ready. Anthony and Tom thatching on moor. Ethel went to Bakewell on cycle. Mr. Parton came. Anthony sent him a cheque tonight for all.

Nov. 4th Fine. Corn not ready. Paid Miss Hawley. Mr. Ronston came and was paid up. A meeting at Ashford over the War Memorial being tampered with.

Nov. 5th Fine a good corn day. Our men and G. Eaton got Gt. Stones. A dance in school tonight, not very well attended. Mr. Hartopp wrote to the farmers in Sheldon saying their rents were being put up from Michaelmas. Ours was put up from £135 to £170. Our licence came back today.

Nov. 6th Frosty. Anthony and Tom are gone on moor thatching corn stacks. Received a letter from our Mary saying she had scalded her hand with hot bacon fat. Ashford War Memorial unveiled.

Nov. 7th Fine. Holy Communion in church. Mr. Sherlock officiated. The service was held in school this afternoon as there is no coal at the church. Messrs. Hodgkinson are going to clean and beautify the church as soon as there is some coal. Mrs. Wright of Longstone sent some clothing to be sold for the good of the church funds (cleaning). Monyash Wakes. Evelyn went and Tom to the service tonight.

Nov. 8th Fine. Anthony and Tom took two fat cows which were sold through the auction. Both together made over £85. Our milk cheque value £50.0.6. came. Anthony went before the Rural Council committee over a pipe being burst belonging to Sheldon water works.

Nov. 9th Fine but does not dry the corn enough for our men to lead it. They turned it all over to dry. Mr. Ed took out the pipe at the water works. Anthony's birthday (57).

Nov. 10th Drizzly. No corn day. Mr. Ed took the pipe to Chapel-en-le-Frith to have one cast like it. Ethel went to Bakewell for some beef. George Bagshaw bought a ram lamb. He made a cheque out for 2 for £10.0.0. Anthony returned him 10/-.

Nov. 11th Dull. The men went on moor and turned the corn but it was not dry enough to lead. Mr. Sherlock and Mr. Stephenson had tea here. There ought to have been a managers' meeting but the men were in corn.

Nov. 12th Fine and plenty of wind. Our men and Alf Brockley and his wife's nephew were helping us to lead corn off moor but they did not finish. Tonight rain came on and the wind was terrific.

Nov. 13th Rain 1st thing but turns out fine later on. Our poor Tony's birthday. He would have been 23 today if he had lived. Tom went to Bakewell station for beer. The hunters turned out at Sheldon. The men were on moor working in corn. Mr. Stephenson had a parcel of clothes etc. sent him last Sunday by Mrs. Wright of Longstone (Dr. Jackson's sister). I bought a little suit for Anthony Wager and a pair of leggings and a sweater. Sally Brocklehurst and Bertha Bramwell bought the others. Mr. Brittain from Longstone Cottage and Mr. Fairholm called to see Sheldon church. Mr. Stephenson saw Mr. Burke about the church.

Nov. 14th Very wet and awfully windy. Mr. Stephenson took the service which was held in School. Tom fetched some coal last Thursday for the church. Thos Wm Brockley took Mr. Stephenson to Parsley Hay Harvest Thanksgiving tonight to take the service there. They were both wet through. It rained all the way there and back. Norman Brassington and Elsie Goodwin asked in school.

Nov. 15th Wet. Bakewell Fair. Anthony and Tom and Mr. Sneap (who came on Saturday) went. Mr. Sneap went back home. Sam Rowland said the shooters had killed a fox in Shacklow (a bitch). Mr. Poë shot it. The pipe at the waterworks has been put in and the water has carried as far as Thos Wm B. Mrs. Brown came to Mrs. Eds. She had tea here, also Mr. Stephenson. Poor Alf Wildgoose died of fever three years ago today.

Nov. 16th Dull. Our men are gone on moor in corn. Mrs. Brown had dinner. Hannah washed the things bought for Anthony Wager. Finished leading corn on moor. The hay and corn harvest have been a tedious and long affair owing to the weather, no wind or sun to dry.

Nov. 17th Fair, raw and cold. Anthony and Tom were thatching on moor. A meeting of the cricket club was held in our house place. Our Tom was made captain, Sam Bramwell secretary, Fred Brockley treasurer, Jim Goodwin and Billy Naylor umpires. A committee was formed and they decided to have a concert at Xmas. A draw was arranged and books were ordered to be printed.

Nov. 18th Cold. Fair. Anthony and Tom thatching on moor. Wm and Vincent getting potatoes in Bramwell field. Matilda had tea with me and we were talking of old times.

Nov. 19th Dull. The men were getting potatoes. Anthony and Tom were thatching on moor. I sent a parcel to Anthony Wager. Mrs. Brown (Matilda) came and spent a bit of time with me. Sam Rowland told some one he should not kill any foxes as Tom Gyte was shooting. Our Tom was trying to shoot crows and he must have heard the shots.

Nov. 20th Fine. A nice day. Anthony and Tom are gone getting thatch pegs. Mrs. Brown went home today.

[In pencil for Nov. 21 and 22]

Nov. 21st Fair. Dull. Mr. Sherlock preached the sermon this afternoon. Mr. Stephenson was also at service which was held in school.

Nov. 22nd Fine. Anthony went to market. The men have to keep drawing thatch and trying to thatch the stacks but it is a slow process. On going to bed tonight we had a nasty experience.[1] Ethel, Evelyn, Tom and his father were carrying me upstairs when the rickshaw handle came into Anthony's hand and let the seat down. I had terrible pain but they got me to the bottom and carried me up in the arm chair. The shock knocked my knees up and the pain is awful.

After this there are no more entries in Maria's handwriting

1   See Introduction p. xxxvi

Index

(*This Index is selective, omitting numerous passing references*)

Index of Agricultural Concerns

Price Index

Bibliography

Before Endeavours Fade - Rose E.B. Coombes
Chronicle of Youth - Vera Brittain's War Diary 1913-1917 - Vera Brittain
The Church of England and the First World War - Alan Wilkinson
The Countryman Winter 1961
Crockford's Clerical Directory
Echoes of the Great War - edited by James Munson
First World War - Martin Gilbert
Flanders Then and Now - John Giles
Great Battles of World War One - Anthony Livesey
Haig's Command - Denis Winter
The History of Magpie Mine, Sheldon Peak District Mines Historical Society
A History of the Reader Movement - W.S. Williams
In Flanders Fields - Leon Wolff
Kelly's Directory
Readers: A Pioneer Ministry - T.G. King
The Road to Passchendaele - John Terraine
Sherston's Progress - Siegfried Sassoon
Testament of Youth - Vera Brittain
They Called it Passchendaele - Lyn Macdonald
Undertones of War - Edmund Blunden
Voices and Images of the Great War - Lyn Macdonald
Ypres 1914-1918 - Les Coate

Acknowledgements

I am grateful for the interest and support of the Duke of Devonshire, and for the assistance of many people, including the late Ethel Gyte who first showed me the Diaries as she sat beneath the portrait of her brother Tony; Margaret Slinn (the daughter of Mary and Clement Wager) who now has possession of the Diaries; and also:

Roger Baker
Adrienne Blackshaw
Derek Buckley
Amy Elliott
Marjorie Fearn
John Gyte
Anthony Gyte
Sarah Herbert
Pamela Hopkinson
Ann Lomas
Deryck Spafford
John Wordingham

Birmingham City Library
Commonwealth War Graves Commission
Derbyshire Record Office
Imperial War Museum
Lambeth Palace Library
Ministry of Defence Army Records Centre
National Army Museum
Readers Board for the Diocese of Derby
Regimental Museum of the 9th/12th Royal Lancers, Derby
Sherwood Foresters Regimental Association

and I am especially grateful to my wife, Annette, for all her involvement throughout the project.

Gerald Phizackerley